For aulXSopdogn

Animals and Ancestors

Animals and Ancestors

An Ethnography

Brian Morris

Oxford • New York

First published in 2000 by
Berg
Editorial offices:
150 Cowley Road, Oxford OX4 1JJ, UK
838 Broadway, Third Floor, New York, NY 10003-4812, USA

Berg is the imprint of Oxford International Publishers Ltd.

Library of Congress Cataloging-in-Publication Data

A catalogue record for this book is available from the Library of Congress.

British Library Cataloguing-in-Publication Data

A catalogue record for this book is available from the British Library.

ISBN 1 85973 486 3 (Cloth)
ISBN 1 85973 491 X (Paper)

Typeset by JS Typesetting, Wellingborough, Northants.
Printed in the United Kingdom by Biddles Ltd, Guildford and King's Lynn.

To the Memory of my Herbalist Friends and
Woodland Companions

Benson Zuwani
Samson Waiti
Ganda Makalani

Contents

Preface

I first came to Malawi in February 1958, sitting with my rucksack on the back of a pick-up truck as it passed through the Fort Manning (Mchinji) customs post. I had spent the previous four months hitch-hiking around south and central Africa, mostly sleeping rough. During that time I encountered no other hitch-hiker, and very few tarred roads, and the only place I met tourists was at the Victoria Falls. I was, however, so attracted to Malawi and its people, that I decided to give up my nomadic existence. I was fortunate to find a job working as a tea planter for Blantyre and East Africa Ltd, an old company founded by Hynde and Stark around the turn of the century. I spent over seven years as a tea planter working in the Thyolo (Zoa) and Mulanje (Limbuli) districts, spending much of my spare time engaged in natural history pursuits – my primary interests being small mammals (especially mice) and epiphytic orchids. The first article I ever published was based on my spare-time activities in Zoa, where I spent many hours with local people digging up mice. It was entitled *Denizen of the Evergreen Forest* (1962), and recorded the ecology and behaviour of the rather rare pouched mouse – *Beamys hindei.*

Since those days I have regularly returned to Malawi to undertake ethnobiological studies. I thus have a life-long interest in Malawi – in its history, in the culture of its people, and in its fauna and flora. Some of my most memorable life experiences have been in Malawi, and many of my closest and cherished friendships have been with Malawians, or with 'expatriates' who have spent their lives in Malawi.

Altogether I have spent over ten years of my life in Malawi, and apart from Chitipa and Karonga, I have visited and spent time in every part of the country, having climbed or explored almost every hill or mountain – usually with a Malawian as a companion, and looking for birds, mammals, medicines, epiphytic orchids or fungi, whichever was my current interest.

The present study, like my earlier study *The Power of Animals*, is specifically based on ethno-zoological researches undertaken in 1990–1, which were supported with a grant from the Nuffield Foundation. For this support I am grateful.

I should also like to thank, with respect to this present study, many friends and colleagues who have given me valuable data, encouragement, support and hospitality over the past thirty years. In particular I should like to sincerely thank: Derrick Arnall, Father Claude Boucher, Wyson Bowa, Carl Bruessow and Gillian Knox, Shaya Busman, Salimu Chinyangala, Dave and Iris Cornelius, Janet and Les Doran, Jafali Dzomba, Efe Ncherawata, Cornell Dudley, the late Cynthia and Eric Emtage, Peter and Suzie Forster, Frank and Iona Kippax, John and Anne Killick, Heronimo Luke, Useni Lifa, Kitty Kunamano and her daughters, John Kajalwiche and his sister Evenesi Muluwa, Catherine Mandelumbe, the late Ganda Makalani, Late Malemia and her family, Bob and Claire Medland, Davison Potani, Kings Phiri, Lackson Ndalama, Hassam Patel and his family, Pritam Rattan, Pat Royle, Lady Margaret Roseveare, Brian and Anne Sherry, Chenita Suleman and her family, Patrick and Poppit Rogers, Francis and Annabel Shaxson, Chijonjazi 'Muzimu' Shumbe, Lance Tickell, Catherine and Stephen Temple, the late Samson Waiti, George and Helen Welsh, Brian and June Walker, John and Fumiyo Wilson, and the late Jessie Williamson.

I should also like to thank those who generously gave me institutional support: The Centre for Social Research, University of Malawi (Wycliffe Chilowa); The National Archives of Malawi (Frances Kachala); Matthew Matemba and many members of the Department of National Parks and Wildlife; and M.G Kumwenda and George Sembereka of The National Museums of Malawi.

Finally, I should like to thank my family and colleagues at Goldsmiths College for their continuing support and particularly to thank Emma Barry who kindly typed my manuscript.

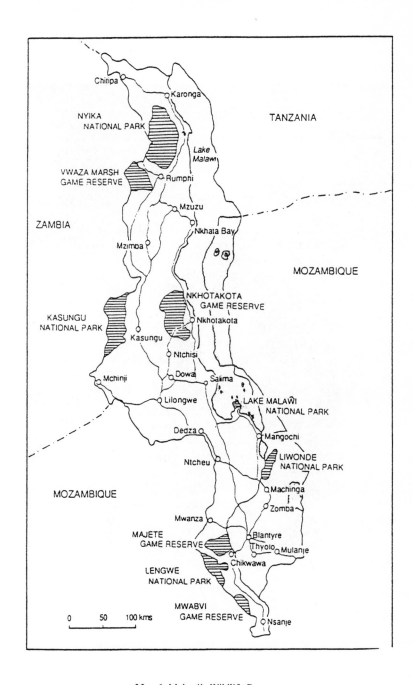

Map 1 Malawi's Wildlife Reserve

Figure 1 The late Samson Waiti, herbalist-diviner, Domasi March 1980

–1–

Introduction

Others have reproached me with my style . . . They fear lest a page that is read without fatigue should not always be the expression of the truth. Were I to take their word for it, we are profound only on condition of being obscure.

Jean-Henri Fabre , *Souvenirs Entomologiques*

Prologue

This book explores the role of animals in the rituals and religious life of the matrilineal people of Malawi. It forms a sequel and a companion volume to my study *The Power of Animals* (1998), which focused on the historical dialectic to be found in Malawi between subsistence agriculture focused around a group of matrilineally related women, and the hunting of animals by men. In that study I describe the hunting traditions to be found in Malawi, the folk classification of animals, and the important part that animals play in oral traditions, and as food (meat) and medicine. I attempted to show the multiple ways in which Malawian people relate to animals – pragmatic, intellectual, realist, aesthetic, social and symbolic. This present study focuses on their sacramental attitude to animals, particularly the role that animals play in life cycle rituals, and the relationship of animals to the divinity and the spirits (*mizimu*) of the ancestors. The two books together aim to affirm the crucial importance of animals in the social and cultural life of Malawian people. It thus counters the mistaken impression that many postmodern anthropologists have, namely that animals are just not worth bothering about as they are a 'topic of marginal interest' (as one scholar put it) to anthropologists.

This introductory chapter aims to provide some of the background material relevant to the study, and discusses the theoretical perspective that informs the study, the social setting, animal/human relationships in an historical context, and my approach to the study, concluding with an outline of its content.

Theoretical Perspectives

Anthropology, despite its diversity, has a certain unity of purpose and vision. It is unique among the human sciences in both putting an emphasis and value on cultural difference, thus offering a cultural critique of Western capitalism and its culture, as well as emphasizing people's shared humanity, thus enlarging our sense of moral community and placing humans squarely 'within nature'. As a discipline anthropology has therefore always placed itself at the 'interface' between the natural sciences and the humanities.

Within anthropology three research traditions have prominence. The first is an *interpretative* tradition which draws on the important writings of the neo-Kantians Dilthey and Boas. It is represented by cultural anthropology, interpretative sociology and postmodernism. This tradition links anthropology to the humanities, puts a focal emphasis on *culture* (defined as local 'structures of meaning') and treats social life as if it were a *text* to be interpreted. A fundamental stress is thus put on hermeneutics. In privileging language and symbolism at extremes this interpretative or literary tradition leads to textualism, and to a form of cultural idealism that not only denies the reality of the material world but advocates an extreme cultural (or linguistic) determinism. Geertz (1973) is often seen as a prototype of this tradition.

The second tradition is a *sociological* tradition which essentially derives from Comte and Durkheim. This tradition models itself on the natural sciences, takes an empiricist perspective, and puts an important emphasis on *society* as an autonomous realm of being. The emphasis therefore is on 'social structure' (as a network of social relations) that is independent of human subjectivity; epistemologically society is conceived as a *thing* (organism). Represented by Durkheimian sociology and social anthropology this tradition, at extremes, leads to a crude positivism, denying the importance of both cultural and subjective meanings. It thus reifies the social, and tends to advocate an extreme sociological determinism, one that repudiates psychology entirely. It therefore, like the interpretative tradition, plays down or denies human agency and the biological dimension to human life. Radcliffe-Brown (1952) with his conception of a 'natural science of society' is often taken as an exemplar of this tradition.

The third tradition in a sense mediates between the interpretative and sociological traditions, and advocates a *historical* or evolutionary approach to social life. It draws its inspiration from Darwin and Morgan and such historical sociologists as Marx and Weber, and puts a focal emphasis on social life as an evolutionary or historical *process*. Although, unlike the other traditions it acknowledges the crucial dialectic between social structures and human agency, at extremes this tradition downplays cultural meanings and the diversity of human cultures, and tends towards advocating a universal teleology, cultural evolution being interpreted in orthogenetic rather than in historical terms. Steward (1977) and Wolf (1982) may be described as following this historical tradition (Morris, 1987, 1991, Burofsky, 1994).

Sadly, in recent years, given the increasingly arrogant and intolerant rhetoric of postmodernist anthropologists (who seem to repudiate empirical science entirely and to equate all knowledge with power) and the equally dismissive attitude some positivist anthropologists have towards hermeneutics (Tyler, 1986; Gellner, 1995) a 'wide chasm' seems to have emerged between these various traditions (Burofsky, 1994: 3). I have elsewhere offered my own reflections on this sad state of affairs. Contrary to the nihilistic ethos of postmodernism I have also affirmed the salience of a realist ontology, and the crucial importance of upholding such conceptions as truth and representation, human agency and empirical knowledge (Morris, 1997). For in an important sense anthropology, as I conceive it, needs to draw on, and to affirm certain crucial insights and perspectives, from all these three traditions. For human life is inherently social and meaningful, as well as being 'enmeshed' or 'rooted' in the material world. An understanding of human social life therefore entails both hermeneutic understanding (humanism) as well as explanations in terms of causal mechanisms and historical understanding (naturalism). Anthropological analysis must therefore combine both hermeneutics and naturalism, and avoid the one-sided emphasis either on hermeneutics – which in its extreme form, 'textualism', denies any empirical science – or on naturalism, which in its extreme form, as crude positivism, oblates or downplays cultural meanings and human values. As Jackson writes: 'people cannot be reduced to texts any more than they can be reduced to objects' (1989: 184). But in acknowledging a naturalistic perspective, and the psychic, moral and epistemological unity of humankind (Brown 1991), this does not imply the 'destruction' of the concrete, the cultural particular, or the historical, nor does it imply that peoples behaviour is the same everywhere – as Hollinger seems to believe (1994: 67). Unity, difference and singularity are all dimensions of the world, and of human life. Cultural and social phenomena thus has to be understood by combining interpretative understanding, causal analysis and historical reason (Collier, 1994: 163–70, Morris, 1997: 335–6). This is the theoretical perspective that informs the present study.

As the present study is largely focused on Malawian ritual practices and cultural representations, and as my own earlier comparative studies have been woefully misunderstood as 'ahistorical', the suggestion being that I conceive of cultures as 'timeless' entities, floating, it seems, completely unattached to their social and ecological moorings (White, 1998) (which is of course nonsense!) some discussion needs to be devoted to the concepts of 'society', 'culture' and 'nature'. For I hold it important to retain these concepts, and the ontological distinctions, they entail.

But I must say that in all my comparative writings (1987, 1991, 1994) I have always taken it for granted that students and colleagues alike were aware that cultural phenomena, like everything else in the universe, including elephants and the ideas of individual scholars, were diverse and continually changing and thus of a historical nature. Having some historical sensibility they therefore did not need some pretentious academic telling them what is patently self-evident. Thus I do not hold, and do not wish to convey in this study, the idea that cultural representations and schemas – at whatever level of analysis – are 'timeless' entities – homogenous, unchanging and rigidly demarcated – or that they are completely detached from people or social moorings, or indeed from the material world.

It is however important to recognize that even to think at all, as John MacMurray reflects, is to discriminate, that is to make some kind of distinction between entities in the world (1957: 92). But making a distinction does not necessarily entail the setting up of a radical dualism, any more than identifying a real unity (elephant, person, society, women, culture, humanity, olive grove) implies an essentialism that ignores the diversity within the category, its 'dividual' character, to employ a current fashionable but rather vacuous term. No two elephants are the same, and as Assiter has written; the use of the general category 'women', for example, does not preclude a recognition of historical and cultural diversity, for diversity within a category, is only recognizable on condition that the concept of 'woman' is identified (1996: 22). And the same goes for all other general categories – reason, history, society, humanity, truth – that post-modernists rubbish as 'monadic entities'. The passion for 'difference', and 'fragmentation' often indicates a complete indifference to unity and dialectics. All concepts are relational; all relations imply things, actual entities that are constituted through relations; all difference entails at the same time a unity, just as all entities (individuals) are at the same time dividual. Whitehead long, long ago (1929) stressed the essential relatedness of all things. Even elephants are not rigidly bounded.

In making certain distinctions in this study, specifically between animals and humans, sex and gender, human agency and social structures, social relations (society) and cultural meaning systems (culture), it must be understood that these paired concepts are not to be interpreted in dualistic fashion, but as dialectically related – i.e. inter-dependent. Thus I advocate, even if only implicitly in this study, neither a radical dualistic ontology, nor do I give epistemological primacy to one side of the dichotomy (relation), even though certain entities, as emergent levels, may not have ontological priority. Thus I reject any form of reductive materialism, such that, for example, gender is reduced to biological sex, or culture is seen as simply a reflection or epiphenomenon or 'derivative' of social practices (cf. Samuel, 1990: 39). Nor do I advocate the opposite strategy and give priority to cultural meanings - reducing human life to an 'effect' of culture, discourses or language, or of social structures. Nor do I imply an 'identity' between these terms, and thus suggest collapsing the distinctions into some wooly abstraction like 'lived experience' or 'mode of being – in-the-world'. Nor, finally, do I see the need to repudiate the concepts of 'humanity', 'society', 'nature' and 'culture' entirely, as suggested by some postmodernist scholars. Even the ubiquitous dichotomy culture/nature is not without its analytical utility. Culture – Popper's (1992) 'world three' – may be defined rather broadly, and relates to the shared meanings, practices and symbols of a human community, and which unlike nature, are not self-subsisting, but are dependent upon human activity. Like Chris Knight I feel that this distinction (not dualism) 'stands for something real, I like this distinction and intend to respect it' (1991: 11). A distinction between nature and culture can thus be acknowledged while at the same time recognizing that 'culture is deeply rooted in biology' (Wilson, 1997: 126), and that these concepts do not have any direct equivalence in the Malawian context.

That Western concepts do not exactly match those of other cultures is only to be expected, for as Michael Lambek writes 'it is only from an objectivist perspective that one would ever have expected them to' (1998: 122). All human cultures it would seem make some distinction between cultural and natural phenomena, between consciousness and the body, and between humans and animals, even if these distinctions do not exactly match (why on earth should they) those of western culture, and are not interpreted in dualistic fashion as in Cartesian metaphysics. Although Signe Howell (1996) critiques Cartesian dualism – a 'familiar western schemata' – as if Western thought and Cartesian metaphysics were synonymous and nothing of any intellectual importance has happened since 1650 – and seems to deny the culture/ nature distinction, she writes that 'the jungle in its totality as a material and spiritual world is . . . cultural space, not natural' (1996: 132). This statement presupposes a distinction between material and spiritual, and between culture and nature. And although she writes that human beings are not set uniquely apart from other beings, and that the Chewong do not distinguish between plants and animals, she continually affirms 'species – bound identities' and writes of transformations between humans, animals and spirits, which would assume that ontological distinctions are in fact being made. Howell's account is typical of many post-modernist scholars who advocate a cultural idealist and cultural determinist perspective, and which in their emphasis on culture and cosmology, oblates nature and biology entirely (see my critique 1997). Although making a great play of being 'anti-dualist' setting up a radical dualism between Western culture (equated with Cartesian metaphysics) and the culture of 'aboriginal' people is equally unhelpful. Needless to say the concept of 'cosmos' is just as much a Western category as that of nature or culture.

The same kind of esotericism is evident in the writings of Philippe Descola (1996) for he sets up a dichotomy between animism – defined as a mode of thought which 'endows natural beings with human dispositions and social attributes' (religion) and totemism (symbolism) – both of which are identified with Amazonian 'tribes', and naturalism which is identified with 'us' – i.e. European ethnographers or culture. Both Cartesian dualistic metaphysics *and* the reductive theories of the sociobiologists are then misleadingly identified with naturalism. But all these three 'modes of identification' (as he describes them) are evident in *all* human communities. Repudiating the concepts of 'culture' and 'nature' because Cartesians have used them in dualistic fashion is as unhelpful and unnecessary as repudiating the concept of 'time' because Newton interpreted it as an 'absolute'.

Humans are intrinsically social and relational beings. They are not disembodied egos nor asocial organisms. Social scientists have recognized and emphasized this for more than a century. It is certainly not the recent discovery of postmodernist scholars. But how one defines the 'mark' of the social is, it appears, a rather contentious issue (Greenwood, 1997). What has to be recognized is that social life exists, as Robert Hinde suggests, on several different levels. At the most basic level it may be defined as social interaction, as a behavioural regularity among two or more organisms (Wallace, 1997). Thus sociality is a matter of degree, and found throughout the animal kingdom, humans, as evolved apes, being perhaps among the more sociable of animals. Social interaction can therefore take place between humans and other social mammals. At this level, as Lloyd Sandelands has perceptively written, society is something that is felt, and manifested through bodily gestures. Society, he writes, is known to us through the body as feeling, and everywhere affirmed through gesture and ritual.

> We feel society in a thousand quotidian acts - of handshake, hug, kiss, embrace, dance, wave, a returned smile or gaze. (Sandelands 1997: 142)

Thus we can interact socially not only with dogs, but with people whose culture and language is completely alien to us.

At another level, and with regard to another definition of the social, it may be described as *interpersonal* behaviour. This is how social life tends to be interpreted by methodological individualists (Hayek, Homans, Ayn Rand), who deny the reality of social structures or social collectives. For such scholars social life consists of patterns of aggregate behaviour that are stable over time. As Collins put it:

> Social patterns, institutions and organisations are only abstractions from the behaviour of individuals. (1981: 989)

Although interpersonal relationships are important, this approach denies the objective existence of such entities as states, ethnic groups, social classes and other social forms, and reduces social structures (and cultural schemas) to the social interactions and dispositions of individual humans. Although this approach is salutary in emphasizing human agency, its limitations have been stressed by numerous scholars (Porpora, 1989; Archer, 1995: 34–46).

Methodological individualism in fact now has recently been given a new lease of life among anthropologists. Cognisant of the fact that societies are not homogenous or rigidly bounded (Marx and an earlier generation of anthropologists never assumed that they were) and that social action is embedded in an ecological context (again Marx et al. never thought otherwise), such anthropologists, as noted earlier, have repudiated the concept of 'society' entirely (cf Barth, 1992). They thus join forces with Ayn Rand (and her devotee Margaret Thatcher) in declaring that there is no such entity as 'society'.

A third level of social existence is that of social structures, defined as patterns of enduring relationships between people. As Marx wrote:

> Society does not consist of individuals, but expresses the sum of the relations within which individuals stand ... to be a slave, to be a citizen are social

characteristics , relations between human beings. A human being as such is not a slave. He is a slave in and through society. (1973: 265)

But there has been a theoretical tendency within the social sciences, usually described as collectivism or holism, which has been prone to treat social structure as law like regularities among social facts, and to regard such facts as a domain that is completely autonomous of people (the psychological level). It thus treats social structures or society as the fundamental reality, and treats human agency and consciousness as epiphenomenal. This 'top-down' approach is characteristic not only of much Durkheimian sociology but of mechanistic versions of Marxism and of structuralism. It has also been given a new lease of life by postmodernists, who, in a critique of the transcendental subject of Cartesian metaphysics, have gone to extremes in eradicating human agency from the analysis. Thus the human person has either been erased entirely, or is seen as simply an 'effect' of ideological discourses or language, or of social structures. With the further eradication or 'decon-struction' of 'society' and 'social structures' such as classes, by trendy postmodernist and literary anthropologists, we are left, it seems, only with a 'subjectivism without a subject' (Anderson, 1983: 54), or frag-mented, incoherent, inter-personal relations or a 'montage of polyphony' (Marcus, 1994: 48).

The problem with the holistic approach is that it tends to reify social structures, and ignores the fact that connections between social facts are always mediated by intervening processes involving humans. Thus, although it is necessary to acknowledge the reality of social structures (and cultural representations) and their constraining influence, via social praxis, on human life, it is equally important to affirm the salience of human identity and agency (Morris, 1985). But the human person must be conceptualized not as a transcendental epistemic subject, nor as an asocial organism, but as an embodied being, embedded both in an ecological and a social context (Benton, 1993: 103; Morris, 1994: 10–15). Humans (people) are thus both intrinsically social, *and* ontologically distinct from society (enduring social relations).

There have been many recent attempts to transcend the 'duality' of structure and agency, namely Giddens (1984) structuration theory and his 'ontology of praxis', Foucault's (1980) genealogical approach and his emphasis on 'power-knowledge", Elias's (1978) theorising around the concept of 'figuration' and Jackson's (1989) radical empiricism may be taken as examples. But what these approaches tend to entail is a *conflation* of the central dialectic between human agency and social structure, a dialectic which is oblated through an undue emphasis on, respectively, social practices, discourses of power, social configurations, or lived experience (see Manicas, 1987; Layder, 1994: 94–149; Archer, 1995).

What many writers have thus suggested is the need for a critical realism that acknowledges both human agency and social structure (or cultural representations) as distinct levels of reality, each having emergent properties that are irreducible to one another (Bhaskar, 1979; Archer, 1995). Both the classical approaches to social theory are thus inadequate. An emphasis on methodological individualism reduces social life to human dispositions and social interactions – and humans are invariably depicted as possessive individuals. This implies a form of *voluntarism*. On the other hand, treating collective phenomena – social structures, society, cultural representations, discourses or language – as *sui generis*, as the fundamental reality, with regard to which humans are simply an effect, entails a *reification* of social phenomena and is equally untenable. A human being, as Erich Fromm long ago put it, is not 'a blank sheet of paper on which culture can write its text' (1949: 23) – for humans are beings with natural capacities, charged with energy and structured in specific ways, as well as being intrinsically social. The asocial organism is an abstraction, as Marx long ago emphasized (Brown, 1991: 130–41; Morris, 1997: 324–30).

This brings me to a consideration of a further 'level' of the social – that usually referred to as 'culture'. Just as a distinction can be made between inter-personal relations, the informal and local practices of everyday life, and social structures – what de Certeau (1984) refers to as 'objective structures' or the 'grid of socio-economic constraints' – so a distinction can also be made between social structures and what Hinde (1987) describes as the symbolic or sociocultural practices. A distinction (not dualism) can thus be made between society, defined not as some rigidly bounded social entity, but as Marx defined it, as a network of social relations, intrinsically embedded in a material world, and cultural schemas, categories and representations – Durkheim's 'collective consciousness' – which forms a structural ideal and system of symbols and meanings (Holy, 1996: 6).

Although some scholars repudiate the dichotomy between culture and society, it is in fact articulated, even if only implicitly, by a wide range of scholars. For example: the functionalist sociologist Robert Merton makes a distinction between cultural structure – defined as an organised set of 'normative *values*' and social structure, as an organised set of 'social *relationships*' (1957: 162); the interpretative anthropologist Clifford

Geertz likewise distinguishes between cultural symbols as 'vehicles for thought' and social structures as forms of 'human association' (1973: 89); the cultural materialist Marvin Harris (1980) stresses the important distinction between behavioural (action) and mental (thought) events; while finally, Robert Murphy (1990), who proposes a dialectical approach to social life, makes a distinction between social action (deed) and symbolic forms (word). These four important scholars represent very different schools of thought. Yet they all articulate a widely recognized and useful *distinction* between social structures and institutions (enduring social relations) and cultural forms (embodying normative values, beliefs and patterns of meaning). But the important point to recognize is that these distinctions do *not* imply a dualistic metaphysic, and that the various forms of sociality are rooted in the behavioural propensities of humans, though not directly determined by them. Moreover, the various 'levels' of social life – social interactions, informal networks of interpersonal relations, social structures, or institutions, and cultural forms are not to be conceived as entities, but, as Hinde writes, as 'complexes of inter-related processes in continuous creation thorough the dialectical relations between levels' (1987: 26).

But the ontological reality of social structure as a form of organisation has to be acknowledged; and it is distinct from the human person. Humans (people) and social structures (society) are dialectically related. For as Bhaskar writes, social structures or forms 'are a necessary *condition* for any intentional act, that their *pre-existence* establishes their *autonomy* as possible objects for scientific investigation, and that their *causal power* establishes their *reality*' (1979: 31). But the causal power of social structures is only mediated through human agency, for social collectivities do not exist apart from human activity. Moreover, individual humans do not 'create' society, but rather, as we noted, either sustain or transform social (or cultural) structures through the medium of social activity (Archer, 1995: 71).

Culture has been defined as shared *understandings*. These must be acknowledged for any communication to be possible. It has also been described as 'systems of *knowledge*' that are more or less shared by members of a society. Kroeber and Kluckhohn long ago defined culture as consisting of patterns of and for behaviour, acquired and transmitted largely through *symbols*. Understandings, knowledge, meanings; this is what 'culture' entails. It is however quite misleading to see cultural representations as completely separate from lived experience, for they are embedded in the practical constitution of everyday life, both social and material. Such structures of significance (configurations, cosmologies, paradigms, normative values, epistemes) are both the products of human action and are 'conditioning elements' of further social action (1963: 357). As critical realists have also emphasized, cultural systems have exactly the same temporal priority, relative autonomy and causal efficacy, vis á vis human activity, as do social structures (Archer, 1988).

As I have already broached, in recent decades the concept of 'culture', like that of 'society' has become the subject of contentious debate. Postmodernist anthropologists, suffering somewhat from historical amnesia, have offered harsh critiques of an earlier generation of anthropologists. Such anthropologists it is alleged, thought of the world as consisting of a mosaic of discrete, isolated cultures. Each culture, in turn, was treated, so it is argued, as a 'physical substance' (Appadurai, 1996: 12) (sic) or organism or as a 'cultural totality' – homogenous, unchanging, coherent, clearly bounded, and as existing independently of people, who were it seems, seen simply as a microcosm of culture. Moreover, the concept of 'culture' was used as a 'distancing device', setting up a radical disjunction between ourselves (the European ethnographer) and other people. Other cultures were thus exoticized and devalued, for 'culture' operates to affirm hierarchy and a 'radical alterity' (Fabian, 1983; Abu-Lughod, 1991; Ingold, 1993: 212).

I have myself been critical of Durkhemian functionalism, which tended to conceptualize 'society', as a totality of bounded social relationships rather than as a nexus of economic, political and ideological relationships that not only connect with other nexuses (and thus are not bounded) but relate to different levels of social reality (1987: 139). But the above portrait of an earlier generation of anthropologists (Boas, Radin, Kroeber, Firth, Steward, Mead, Gluckman et al.) is not only unfair but constitutes a complete 'misrepresentation' of anthropology. For these 'old-time' anthropologists, as Herb Lewis writes, *did* believe in the importance and validity of treating all people equally and with respect and dignity, and many, like Boas were radical scholars; they did not ignore history nor did they treat cultures as isolated and unchanging; many strove to avoid the reification of cultures and recognized the diversity of ideas, beliefs and practices within any social community; they also emphasized the individuality of the human person, many translating local autobiographies, as well as fervently believing in a common humanity. It is indeed highly ironic that postmodernist anthropologists like Fabian treat their scholarly forebears in ways that exactly match their own critique: for their treatment of past anthropology is ahistoric, homogenizing and a clear expression of the 'radical alterity' they profess to disdain (Lewis, 1998; for a defence of the concept of culture see Brumann, 1998).

It is equally ironic, as we have hinted above, that in critiquing Western culture (always equated with Cartesian dualism and bourgeois ideology) and in setting up a radical antithesis (dualism) between this 'culture' and that of hunter-gatherers or the forest people of Amazonia or Melanesia, contemporary and post-modern anthropologists (Strathern, Descola, Ingold, Howell) seem to suggest a more pervasive esotericism (the 'radical alterity' of other cultures) than did an earlier generation of anthropologists?

In this study therefore I critically affirm the concepts of 'society' and 'culture' as well as that of generic 'humanity' and 'nature'. Thus although 'cultures' are not rigidly demarcated, timeless systems of meanings – nor must they be interpreted as consisting of 'one single, symbolically consistent universe' (Douglas, 1966: 85) – nevertheless it is still important to recognize the 'force of culture'. As Strauss and Quinn write, some understandings are widely shared among members of a social group 'surprisingly resistant to change in the thinking of individuals, broadly applicable across different contexts of their lives, powerfully motivating sources of their action, and remarkably stable over succeeding generations' (1997: 3). It always came as a surprise to me, when talking with Malawians, that they often expressed cultural ideas in words that almost replicate what I had read in accounts by ethnographers such as Stannus (1922), written over half a century before.

But culture must not be understood in monolithic fashion, nor equated with 'ethnicity', for cultural representations are expressed, as it were, at many different levels – in relation to a unique individual (cultural schemas), to a specific locale or kinship group, to such ideational constructs as gender and ethnicity, to regional or even global terrains, as well as to cultural universals. Moreover, at both the individual and societal level, culture is always plural, for within any individual or society there always exists a 'repertoire' of cultural ideas or problems, or what Samuel (1990) describes as 'multi-modal states'.

This, of course, has long been recognized. Aristotle outlined several different ways of knowing (1925: 137–48) and Epictetus describes, the many diverse beliefs relating to the deity among the ancient Greeks (1995: 32–3). Scholars of the renaissance period in Europe, apart from Foucault, have described the co-existence of many different religious beliefs and ontologies, ranging from gnosticism and Christian neoplatonism to hermetic (occult) philosophy and pantheism. My own study of the anthropology of religion (1987) outlined that within the social science tradition (which is a culture) there were 'multiple' theoretical perspectives or approaches to this phenomenon. In all human societies therefore one finds a multiplicity of co-existing, and often contradictory, cultural forms. Malawi is no exception. This diversity of cultural forms is not some recent phenomenon, associated with late or global capitalism, but has existed throughout human history. This implies, of course, that throughout history, people's self-identity has never been 'unitary' but always complex, shifting, relational and multiplex, as anthropologists have long recognized. But to say this is not to deny the tremendous impact of global communications and the commodification of culture that has occurred in recent decades.

Moreover, like social phenomena, cultural forms, though actual entities, must not be conceived as 'thing like' – although I doubt whether any anthropologist has ever thought of 'culture' as if it were a physical substance. But rather it must be viewed as a process. Cultural representations thus come into being; they are relatively enduring (have duration), they have a certain coherence (unity); they have causal efficacy; they are open systems with conditions of existence (human social life); and they perish – just like people and elephants and everything else in the world.

When in this study I write about Malawi 'culture' I am not then referring to some homogenous and clearly demarcated entity that matches the boundaries of the present Malawi state, but rather as a rubric to cover the many diverse cultural representations, that are expressed within the Malawian context, at many different levels. Dan Sperber's suggestion (1996) of explaining 'culture' with reference to an 'epidemiology' of representations seems to me therefore a fruitful one. I thus try to indicate throughout the text, even if I do not highlight, both the degree of specificity and the historicity of Malawian cultural ideas.

Malawi: The Social Setting

When David Livingstone travelled through southern and central Malawi, in the 1860s on his way to the lake he did not find, as some colonial historians have suggested, 'a comparatively empty land' (Debenham, 1955: 24). European missionaries and planters would never have settled there had it been – but rather it consisted of a fairly well wooded region with numerous scattered villages. Shifting cultivation was the dominant mode of production. The main crops cultivated were maize, millet and sorghum, with such legumes as beans and pigeon peas, as well as sweet potato, pumpkins, cassava, sesame, and various gourds. Agriculture however, was complex, with rice, tomatoes, groundnuts, sugar cane and coco – yams grown in *dimba* gardens near water. But Livingstone found that a crafts industry was also well developed, with the production of iron, salt, pottery and cotton goods, and he was evidently much impressed by the quality of the iron produced by local iron smelters (Livingstone, 1887: 79–82).

Evidence suggests that throughout the colonial and pre-colonial periods social life in Malawi was structured around an explicit gender division, with women being mainly engaged in agricultural work, in the processing and cooking of food and in basic childcare, while the men were away for long periods, especially in the dry season, actively employed in fishing, in long-distance trade, or in what was a critical activity for men of all ethnic communities, namely the hunting of the larger mammals. In the pre-colonial period there were, in fact, extensive trade networks, both local and long-distance. Later, towards the end of the colonial period, many young men spent time abroad as migrant labour.

The gender division was thus an important organizing principle, as it still is, although at the present time hunting is a peripheral activity, even in rural areas. But the trapping and hunting of mammals is still important, usually as a part-time activity, and communal hunts are still held in certain forest areas.

Since the nineteenth century the economy has diversified, with the introduction of cash crops – tea, bananas, tobacco, coffee – and the estate (plantation) sector has continually expanded. In recent years this has involved the alienation of customary land for private (tobacco) farming, the withdrawal of labour from the subsistence sector, and the undermining of matrilineal kinship and the power and autonomy of women within the household. There has indeed, as Vail (1983) suggests, been a 'structural continuity' between the colonial and post-colonial periods. It is, of course, worth emphasizing that so-called 'modernity' (capitalism and the market economy) is not some recent introduction of the post-colonial period but has been implicated in the social life of what is now Malawi for several centuries.

Despite the profound changes that have taken place in Malawi over the past century, the majority of the population – now around nine million – are still largely subsistence hoe cultivators. The basic crops are still very much what they were in the nineteenth century. Some 85 per cent of people in Malawi are thus rural dwellers, living in village communities and largely dependent for their basic livelihood on land, although most people seek to augment their income through paid labour, the selling of cash crops, and the informal economy.

Although Malawi has a high population density (87 persons per sq. km) – one of the highest in Africa – it is still a fairly wooded country, some 33 per cent of the land area still being under 'natural vegetation', with wildlife conservation areas and forest reserves constituting some 20 per cent of the total area. The Brachystegia woodland is of vital importance for rural Malawians – as a source of firewood, building materials and thatching grass, of medicines, wild food plants and fungi, as well as being the key habitat of wild animals, many of the larger mammals still being fairly common. As we shall explore in this study, animals and Malawian people have long co-existed in close proximity, and animals are not only a source of food and medicine but a constant threat to people's well being during the agricultural season, when they cause widespread crop depredation. Given the fact that the GDP per capita income for Malawi is extremely low (US $160); that 80 per cent of rural households are now unable to meet their basic food requirements; that there are growing economic inequalities as an 'elite' class 'captures' vital resources; and that there has been a rapid increase in human population – so inevitably there has been increasing pressure on the natural environment, particularly with regard to the surviving forests and woodlands.

What is significant in Malawi, where social life is still largely focused around the village community (*mudzi*) and where subsistence agriculture is the basic form of livelihood for the majority of people is that for many of its people matrilineal kinship still has salience. Matriliny has proved to be remarkably resilient despite tremendous change that has taken place over the past century – and which I have described elsewhere (1998: 40-46). For despite the intrusions of patrilineal people into Malawi at the end of the nineteenth century (Swahili traders and Ngoni, who both set up petty states or chieftains); the emphasis on the patriarchal family by Christian missions and Islamic culture; and the attack on matriliny and the privileging of men by many development (i.e. capitalist) projects and agencies – despite all of these challenges matriliny still has a living presence in Malawi, both as a form of social organization and as an ideology. As Father Chakanza recently put it: 'the abiding influence of the lineage mentality is still with us' (Chakanza 1998: 28). (For useful discussions of matriliny in Malawi see Rogers, 1980; K.M. Phiri, 1983; Peters, 1997; Morris, 1998: 17–60).

During the colonial period there was a tendency, understandable at the time as the colonial government sought to control and administer the country, and sought political intermediaries, to conceive of Malawi (then Nyasaland) as consisting of a mosaic of different ethnic communities or 'tribes', each with their own territory and self-contained culture. This, however, is a somewhat misleading portrait. Unfortunately, discussions of ethnicity – or what in the past was described as 'tribal affiliation' – tend to oscillate between two extremes. On the one hand some scholars seem to imply that ethnicity – derived from the Greek ethos, which simply means custom, or way of life – has some 'primordial' quality about it, that 'tribes' or ethnic communities have existed since time immemorial, as a 'natural' form of human sociality. As cultural units based on proto-kinship links, they had a primordial salience prior to the formation of state structures. On the other hand, there are those who see ethnicity in 'instrumental' terms, as the artificial creation of the colonial state, ethnicity, or the notion of 'tribe', being used to further the collective interests of political elites, or social classes in their struggles for power or to achieve political hegemony. Both these polar extremes seem untenable as interpretations of ethnic identity, though it must be recognized, as Anthony Smith suggests, that ethnic identity has a certain continuity over time, with specific historical and symbolic attributes. As with other forms of collective identity – gender, class, religion, territory – ethnicity exhibits both constancy and flux, and has a cultural durability that sets limits to re-definitions. He thus defines the main attributes of an ethnic community in terms of the following: a collective name, a myth of common ancestry, shared historical memories; one or more differentiating elements of a common culture, a sense of solidarity, and as association with a particular 'homeland' (1991: 21, cf. Eriksen, 1993: 11). With regard to ethnicity in Malawi, or at least with regard to the Northern Zambezia region, three points may be made.

The first is that many historians of Malawi have tended to used the term *Maravi* (from which the name of the present state is derived) rather indiscriminately, and thus to conflate the political, cultural, ethnic and linguistic levels of social analysis. This tends to simplify what has historically been a rather complex situation (Pachai, 1973).

In political terms, Maravi has been seen as a seventeenth-century 'empire' under the Kalonga chief, which later splintered into a number of chiefdoms. Thus the nineteenth century is described as being decentralized, or politically fragmented. This is a misleading scenario, in that the three main Maravi Kingdoms of the seventeenth and eighteenth centuries – Kalonga, Undi, Lundu – were essentially independent, and, as political structures, similar to the many chiefdoms that emerged in the nineteenth century. Maravi, then, essentially referred to *territories* under the suzerainty of the three main Maravi chiefdoms, namely the south western lakeshore, the Kapoche region and the Lower Shire Valley. It is therefore somewhat misleading to describe Maravi as a single ethnic community or 'nation' that subsequently – like the kingdom itself – fragmented, the 'mother tribe' splintering into various sections, the Nyanja, Mang'anja, Chipeta, Nsenga, Sena, Nyungwe and Chewa, as denoted by Bruwer (1950: 33).

Rather the people who came to be described as Maravi were essentially those who came under the political dominance of the various Maravi chiefs – and besides those noted above, included also the Mbo, Ntumba, Yao, Lolo and Makua. Interestingly, Gamitto, in describing the boundaries of the Undi (Maravi) chiefdom, does not include the Chewa, Lolo and Mang'anja within its domain. It is important then to recognize that Maravi is essentially a political concept or grouping, and that culturally all the ethnic communities of the Northern Zambezi region share a common heritage – even if they may have had distinctive historical trajectories and traditions.

Secondly, from the histography of Northern Zambezia there is evidence of the existence, from the very earliest period with regard to which we have historical records, of distinct ethnic communities in the region. Early Portuguese travellers write of such people as the Chewa, Nsenga, Lolo, Mang'anja and Makua. These ethnic communities were clearly distinct from the political structures or chiefdoms that were collectively described as Maravi - Lundu, Kalonga, Undi – and they were evidently associated with particular localities. Indeed their names usually referred to landscape features – Chipeta (a place with high grass), Nyanja (of the lake), Mbo (of the termite hills), Mang'anja (association with iron smelting), Nsenga (of the sand country – the Luangwa Valley), Makua (likuwa, valley or grassland) and Kokhola (woodland) or the specific community derives its name from its hill of origin – such as Yao or Lomwe (Nguru) (*nlomwe* – the black soil on Namuli hill). (Morris, 1998: 6).

The final point is that although these ethnic communities spoke a Bantu language (or dialect) that was distinctive, though often mutually intelligible, they did in fact share a common cultural heritage. This has been commented upon by Malawians and Europeans alike. Antonio Gamitto while describing the various ethnic communities of the North Zambezia region – Chewa (Cheva), Lolo (Bororo), Mang'anja (Maganja), Makua (Makwa), Nsenga (Senga), and Yao (or Nguru) – all of which he saw as belonging to the 'Maravi Race' – nevertheless recognized their cultural affinities in terms of 'habits, customs, languages, etc.' (1960: 63). Cullen Young, Levi Mumba, and more recently, Edward Alpers all affirm that the people of east central Africa share a common culture. Thus Cullen Young suggests that Chewa, Nsenga, Mbo, Makua, Nyanja and Mang'anja, are for practical purposes – in discussing their religious culture – 'one people', which were, he writes – and this is a contentious issue, sharers of a common name, Maravi (Cullen Young, 1950: 37). Alpers, in similar fashion, writes of the 'cultural unity' of all the three major peoples – Makua-Lomwe, Yao and Maravi – of east central Africa (1975: 7), a sentiment that had earlier been expressed by Clyde Mitchell when he wrote that the 'tribes' of the southern region – Yao, Nguru and Nyanja – were culturally 'all very similar' (1956: 14).

As someone who has travelled widely throughout Malawi and undertaken ethnobiological research in all parts of the country (apart from Chitipa and Karonga) it has been my impression that many cultural ideas and beliefs – with respect to the divinity, medicine, witchcraft, ideas about bodily humours and the dangers of 'heat', disease concepts, human/animal relationships, and beliefs relating to the spirit's of the dead (*mizimu*) – are widely shared and common throughout the country. For example: throughout Malawi commemorative rites are held during the dry season, sometimes almost a year after the death of a person. These are communal rites, food and drink is shared, and the main function of the rite is to settle (*kukhazikitsi*) the spirit. This rite is known by different names throughout the country *chikumbutso* (Nyanja), *bona* (Mang'anja), *mphalo* (Chewa), *nsembe* (Lomwe), *sadaka* (Yao). Now there are wide variations in the nature and scope of this ritual: some of these differences are ethnic (the appearance, sometimes, of nyau dancers in some Chewa villages); some relate to the status of the person or to the locality; some differences are linked to the degree of influence that Christianity or Islamic culture has had on a particular community or kin group. But nevertheless, there is evidence of a shared culture. The important point, however, is that in Malawi 'culture' cannot be equated with 'ethnicity', and that cultural representations, as earlier noted, are diverse and exist on many different levels, one of which reflects a common cultural heritage shared by all the matrilineal people of Malawi. Given the fact that all these matrilineal people have common origins and historical traditions, and that there have been complex and long-standing cultural, economic and linguistic inter-relationships between all the matrilineal people of Malawi, it is hardly surprising that common social institutions and cultural representations are evident. Indeed many of these cultural ideas are evident throughout the Northern Zambezia region (among also the Bisa, Bemba, Mbo, Kunda and Nsenga, for example).

Many contemporary scholars, however, still write of the Chewa or Tumbuka as if they constituted ethnic enclaves with their own specific bounded culture or cosmology. Yet to stress this intermingling and common cultural heritage is not to deny that ethnic affiliation and ethnic identity are not important in Malawi. But it is probable that ethnic consciousness itself came to be fully articulated only during the colonial period, partly through the system of indirect rule and the ethnic stereotyping of the European colonialists, and partly through the struggles of local people themselves, for political autonomy, for economic and educational advance, and as a form of resistance against the missionaries and the colonial state. In doing so they affirmed the validity of African culture and traditions. In an illuminating essay, Vail and White (1989) have described – with respect to the Tumbuka, Ngoni, Yao, Lomwe and Chewa – how, out of an 'ethnographic melange', these communities forged a sense of ethnic consciousness. Although this has to be set against the economic and political realities of the colonial period – indirect rule, the Thangata system, labour migration, the growth of the tobacco industry – they indicate the important role that local intellectuals played in this process – people like Saulos Nyirenda, Yesaya Chibambo, Levi Mumba, Yohanna Abdallah and Lewis Bandawe and the ubiquitous stereotyping of the 'tribes' by the European administrators. Given the complex multi-ethnic composition of Malawian social life, it is not surprising that ethnic identity was shifting and situational, and that many prominent Malawians were of mixed ethnic ancestry – even those who played a prominent role in affirming a particular ethnic consciousness – like Levi Mumba and Lewis Bandawe.

When in this study, as I earlier denoted, I use the term 'Malawi culture' I am simply using it as a rubric to cover all the diverse cultural representations and practices that are evident among the matrilineal peoples of Malawi – the so-called Maravi cluster (Chewa, Chipeta, Nyanja, Mang'anja) as well as the Yao, Lomwe and Tumbuka. Although the Tumbuka are nominally patrilineal and virilocal, they have a decided matrifocal emphasis, and were historically a matrilineal people with a dual economy combining hoe cultivation focused around women, and the hunting of the larger mammals. A description of these ethnic communities, on which the present study is focused, is given in my companion volume (1998: 7–11).

I use Chewa (*Nyanja*) in this study for reference, simply because this language has long been the national language, a lingua franca that is widely spoken throughout Malawi, and because this is the language that I used in conversing with Malawian friends and informants throughout the country.

Animals and People: the Historical Context

Throughout human history, ever since the emergence of modern humans and human culture around 100 thousand years ago, humans and animals have co-existed in close proximity. Indeed humans and animals have long shared the same life world, and the relationship between humans and animals has always been one that is complex, intimate, reciprocal, personal and crucially ambivalent. For humans have always recognized both their continuity (kinship) with animals and their fundamental differences, in that animals have often been a threat to their own well being. But importantly, ever since humans first appeared on the African landscape, animals have, as Andrew Rowan writes, 'been an essential part of our history, culture and existence' (1988: 9). It is hardly surprising then that animals evoke strong emotions in humans, both positive and negative. Given our long and close involvement with the biotic world – particularly animals – Edward Wilson has suggested that we have an inherent tendency which he calls biophilia – 'the innately emotional affiliation of human beings to other living organisms' (1997: 165).

Among earlier human communities, and most contemporary hunter-gatherers, a pervasive egalitarian ethos is evident and there is no pronounced gender hierarchy, nor an attitude of dominance towards nature, or towards animals. Hunting is not undertaken in an aggressive spirit at all, and is certainly not a 'blood sport' or motivated by sadomasochistic tendencies as some eco-feminists have argued (Collard, 1988; Adams, 1990). As Frank Speck long ago remarked (1938: 77) hunting among hunter-gatherers is not a war upon animals, but rather almost a sacred occupation.

Hunter-gatherer social attitudes towards nature, though complex and diverse – it cannot be reduced to a single metaphor (Bird-David, 1990) – expressed neither an attitude of 'dominance' towards the natural world, nor of passivity or abject submission toward over-powering natural forces, but rather stressed the need to maintain a sense of harmony with the world. Hunting therefore invariably involves a sense of kinship between the hunter and the animals he – and sometimes she – hunts. As Matthias Guenther writes with reference to the 'Bushmen' of the Kalahari, each hunt is a renewed encounter with a fellow creature. He writes:

> Activated in each hunt is a feeling of sympathy and implicit recognition that the animal is a moral and sentient kindred being. (1988: 198)

Among hunter-gatherers, therefore, an attitude of respect towards animals is pervasive. Ritual power is seen as manifested in the game animals that they hunt, and typically hunter-gatherers view animals as spiritual equals who, in an important sense, allow themselves to be killed if the hunter is in the right mental and spiritual condition. There is always a close and intimate relationship between animals and the spirits, and the animals themselves, in certain contexts, are believed to embody divinities or spiritual beings. Among many native American Indian communities animals are ultimately seen as under the control of spiritual guardians – often described as the 'masters' of the animals. Given this sense of kinship and empathy between themselves, and the animals they hunt, hunting is invariably hedged with religious ritual and approached in a manner of regret. This empathy and identification is built into the act of hunting itself, which requires that a hunter to be successful must ask himself what he would do if he were an animal. And, as Louis Liebenberg writes 'In the process of projecting himself into the position of the animal he actually feels like an animal' (1990: ix). Thus although anthropomorphism may have been important among early hunter-gatherers its 'utilitarian benefits' (Mithen, 1996: 192) were probably limited. Much more important and pervasive was theriomorphic thinking. Thus the subsistence hunter invariably develops a sympathetic relationship with the hunted animal.

Many years ago James Frazer noted the 'apparent contradiction' in the lives of many hunter-gatherers who venerate and almost deify the animals that they habitually hunt, kill and eat. He noted also that such people regarded all living creatures as practically on an equal footing to themselves (1922: 678–80), and that with regard to many of the larger mammals, rituals of atonement are conducted to show respect to the animal that is killed for food and clothing (ibid. 698). Indeed the powers of the larger animals were felt to exceed those of humans – both empirically and spiritually. Given the sense of kinship that exists between humans and the animals they hunt, it is not surprising that among hunter-gatherers, some kind of atonement for killing the animal is enacted. Serpell (1986: 145) has written perceptively of the 'undercurrent of guilt' that is found among many hunter-gatherers, and has discussed its cross-cultural variability. Importantly, however, among hunter-gatherers it is usually only certain species of the larger mammals that are the focus of rites of atonement; those noted in the literature include: caribou, eland, buffalo, elk, kudu, bear, elephant, gemsbok.

Although hunting has fundamentally a religious dimension, this is not to deny that it is also an important empirical and pragmatic activity, for the data suggests that hunting was an important source of meat (and clothing and utensils) among hunter-gatherers. Up to 20 per cent of the daily intake of calories may come from animals (Hill, 1982; for sympathetic accounts of hunter-gatherers see Nelson, 1983; Brown, 1992).

The importance of animals among early hunter-gatherers is illustrated by their rock-art, which invariably depict animals or human/animal relationships. It seems generally agreed that this rock art – in both Europe and Africa – had a religious significance. Many of the figures – such as the famous 'sorcerer' of Trois-Freres, Ariege in France – though usually interpreted as therianthropes, could equally well be seen to represent spirit-mediums who as masked dancers embody spiritual beings in the form of the animal. Many of the animals depicted in the rock art of Europe (which were not those regularly hunted as food) – particularly wild horse, bison, auroch, ibex and rhinoceros – were probably representations of spiritual beings in animal form, as was the eland, kudu, giraffe and elephant in African rock art. Although the evidence suggests that hunter-gatherers make clear ontological distinctions between humans, animals, and spiritual agencies, there is no radical dichotomy between these different forms of being: thus transformations (metamorphosis, rather than incarnation) may occur in specific contexts, spirits in particular becoming embodied in animals, either living animals, or their representations in rock art (Morris, 1996b; Lonsdale, 1981; Boudet, 1964; for useful discussions of rock art see Leroi – Gourhan, 1982; Lewis-Williams, 1983; Anati, 1994).

The advent of farming undoubtedly had a profound effect on the way that humans related to the natural world, especially towards animal life. Felitas Goodman (1992:19) speaks of the cultural changes ushered in by the advent of horticulture as being profound, the working of the soil representing a 'fundamental break' with hunter-gatherer attitudes though she has little to say on peoples attitude to animal life per se. In his lucid study of human-animal relationships Serpell (1986: 174–6) is equally explicit in contrasting hunter-gatherer attitudes towards animals – predominately one of respect and egalitarianism – with those of farming communities. The Neolithic revolution is seen as a 'journey of no return' and a 'fall from grace', for farmers' have no choice but to set themselves up 'in opposition to nature', in keeping the fields clear of weeds, protecting themselves and their crops from wild animals, and in controlling and confining domestic livestock. The entire system, Serpell writes, 'depends on the subjection of nature' and of the 'domination and manipulation of living creatures' (1986: 175, cf. also Kent (1989). But is important, I think, to maintain a distinction between the 'control' and manipulation of the natural world as exhibited by agriculturists – indeed by all human communities in their subsistence activities (use-value), and the 'domina-tion' of nature as expressed in seventeenth-century mechanistic science and in capitalist ideology, in which nature is seen simply as an inert resource to be exploited for its exchange value (O'Neill, 1993: 154–5; Morris, 1998: 170).

The important point to recognize, as I have explored in my companion volume, is that the advent of agriculture does not entail a fundamental break with regard to the close and intimate relationship that humans have with animals. For hunting still retains its sacramental dimension; indeed hunting in Malawi – as among the Ndembu, Lele and Bisa – is in many ways more highly ritualized than among hunter-gathering societies, and has a social and cultural significance that goes well beyond its economic role in subsistence. Equally important, among farming communities not only does hunting continue to be of cultural salience, but a close and intimate association between animals and spirits continues to be reflected in their ritual practices and religious beliefs. This is nowhere better illustrated than in Egyptian religion prior to the advent of Christianity and Islam. For ancient Egyptians – as in many communities throughout Africa – had an 'immanent' conception of divinity, and all their major deities were thought to be embodied in animal forms. Thus the lives of humans and animals were not only linked at the empirical level, but closely interwoven spiritually. Thus their various deities were either symbolically associated with specific animals, or manifested themselves, in animal form – becoming embodied in animals, or their iconic representations. Some of these associations may be noted:

Deity	Animal
Ptah	Bull
Thoth	Ibis/Baboon
Amon	Ram
Horus/Ra	Falcon
Anubis	Jackal/Dog
Sobk	Crocodile
Hathor	Cow
Sekhmet	Lion
Ejo	Vulture
Khepri	Scarab Beetle
Geb	Egyptian Goose

(Armour, 1986)

The Egyptians, however, did not equate the deity with the animal: so it is quite misleading to think that they 'worshipped' animals. The hermetic philosopher and pantheist Giordano Bruno was quite emphatic that the Egyptians were not 'idolaters' and his book *The Expulsion of the Triumphant Beast* (1964) is a veritable glorification and advocacy of the 'natural religion' of the Egyptians. In it, Bruno insists that living things (animals) were not worshipped in themselves as if they were divinity, but rather the divinity was 'immanent' in diverse, living beings – the baboon, ibis, cobra and lion, for example were all theophanies of the divinities.

It is thus evident among agricultural peoples throughout the world that a close and intimate relationship exists between animals and spiritual beings, particularly the spirits of the ancestors. In his important compara- tive study Steven Lonsdale (1981) gives numerous examples of dance rituals where human beings as masked dancers or through theiromorphic behaviour, become spiritual beings in the form of animals. Much of his material, in fact, is drawn from the African context. Numerous ethno- graphic texts, far too numerous to mention, emphasize the important role that animals – particularly mammals, and such reptiles as the crocodile, tortoise and python – play in the religious imagination of African people. Given that the focus of these studies is usually on hermeneutics and on the sociology of the various ritual practices and religious beliefs – it is understandable that little focus is put on the animal per se. But nevertheless animals have an essential presence in such ethnographic texts – as medicine, as divining instruments, as key figures in folk tales that evoke a moral imagination, as ritual symbols in initiation and spiritual rituals, and as the manifestation or embodiment of witches, spirits of the ancestors or of divinities (for example, Krige, 1943; Swantz, 1970; Turner, 1975; Bourdillon, 1976; Beidelman, 1986).

Shifting the emphasis away from the rituals and the cultural representa- tions themselves, and on to the animals the present study (as with my companion volume) aims to explore and demonstrate the crucial role that animals play in the ritual life and the religious imagination of one African people, the matrilineal people of Malawi.

What is also evident from recent ethnographic studies both in Malawi and throughout much of sub-Saharan Africa, is that, with the spread of Christianity and Islamic culture, animals have tended to become less and less salient in the cult rituals and symbolic life of African people. This is not simply an urban phenomenon. Thus while accounts of initiation rites and the various rituals associated with the ancestral spirits or with cults of affiliction often depict the important role that animals play in these various rituals – particularly as cultural symbols (Turner, 1967, 1968; Fernandez, 1982; Devisch, 1993; Beidelman, 1997), this is not the case with other forms of contemporary religion in Africa. 'Syncretic' and revitalization movements like Bwiti (in Gabon), independent churches throughout Africa, Christian-inspired witch-finding movements, charis- matic and Pentecostalist churches and even contemporary spirit-possession cults in what is now described as the 'universe of post-modernity' – accounts of all these diverse forms of religion in Africa are significant in that they hardly ever mention animals. That is, apart from the role that domestic animals may play in sacrificial rites, and the association of animals with witches (Sundkler, 1948; Martin, 1975; Blakely et al., 1994; Corin, 1998). In 'coping with evil', or in 'weaving the threads of life', the religious dialectic is largely focused around humans and the spirits (or the divinity), animal life being by-passed. Even a study of 'Kongo spirituality' by a Zairean scholar and 'itinerant preacher' is significant in that, apart from mentioning the sacrifice of a goat to the ancestral spirits, it makes no mention at all of wild animals – even though animals still continue to be an intrinsic part of the human life-world in Africa (Bockie, 1993).

In Malawi many of the 'new' religious movements and independent churches make little reference to animal life, and may be opposed not only to local herbalism – which they identify with witchcraft - but also to many important aspects of the local culture, such as beer drinking. Pentecostal-type sects and such independent churches as the Zion Christian Church and the Independent Assemblies of God, stress healing through prayer and faith and the importance of baptism and purification, and prohibit tobacco, alcohol and folk medicine. Animals seem to have no religious significance at all in such churches (Schoffeleers, 1985; Peltzer, 1987).

Swantz wrote perceptively of the close connection – the biophilia – that African people, specifically the Zaramo of coastal Tanzania, have with organic life:

> There is an obvious sense of the biological unity with nature. It becomes mystic, as the correlation of the human organism with other forms of life does not derive from a thought-out process but is an intuitive and existential expression. (1970: 233)

This organic unity was expressed in people's religious imagination, in the use of animals as medicine, or as cultural symbols, and in the fact that the spirits of dead kin become embodied – 'immanent' – in animals and other forms of organic life. This organic unity has, it seems, been severed in the kind of spirituality emphasized in many contemporary religious movements in Malawi given the important influence of the transcendental theism of Christianity and Islam. It is noteworthy that zealots of both these religions were responsible for destroying or defacing the religious icons of the early Egyptians, which depicted their divinities in animal form. A similar ethos is now prevalent in the Christian-based churches in Malawi. In the 'Born-Again' Puritan preachers, as graphically described by Van Rijk (1992), there seems in fact to be a wholesale rejection of all that symbolizes village life and the rural community. Animals have no place in the religious imagination of these Christian fundamentalists, who, inspired by God, feel able to dictate to the anthropologist what he should write about them. But although an 'immanent' conception of divinity and 'pagan' (rural) beliefs are in the process of being marginalized in these Christian-inspired religious movements, as well as in radical forms of Islam, animals still continue to play an important role in the religious imagination of the most rural people in Malawi, as we shall explore in this study.

Approach to the Study

This book is essentially an ethnographic study and is primarily based on two years anthropological fieldwork, undertaken in the years 1979–1980 and 1990–1991, although I have lived and worked in Malawi for more than a decade. It differs from other ethnographic texts in a number of ways.

Firstly, it covers a very broad canvas: the ritual practices and religious culture of the matrilineal people of Malawi, as these relate to animals. It is therefore neither rooted in one particular locality, nor is it focused on a specific ethnic community. Its focus is rather on Malawi as a whole, as both a geographical and as a social location. My fieldwork studies have taken me all over Malawi and, with a particular research focus on ethnobiology, I have lived and researched in every region of the country. I have visited at various times all the forest reserves (except Tuma) and all the wildlife sanctuaries, camping for several days in each. I have had numerous discussions and chats with people throughout the country, though my understanding of Malawian social life has largely been gained from discussions with informants who are close friends of mine, some of whom I have known for over two decades. I have especially drawn on their knowledge as herbalists, local hunters, spirit mediums or as ritual participants. I have also actively participated in many social activities and rituals. Although my interests have been specifically ethnobiological, and I have thus not studied any particular religious complex or ritual in depth, I was initiated into the Yao Jando in 1980 (fortunately I was already circumcized and only had to expose myself to the *ngaliba*) and have attended several spirit rituals, as well as visiting the rain shrines at Thyolo, Mabuka, Soche and Nsanje.

Secondly, given my focus I have incorporated into my study not only data derived from my own fieldwork experiences – which I have described elsewhere (1998: 12–13) – but historical and ethnographic data from a wide range of sources. These include archival material, school essays, newspaper reports, unpublished articles, and earlier ethnographic studies. The pioneering studies of such anthropologists as Stannus, Hodgson, Sanderson, Rangeley and Schoffeleers have a presence throughout the text. I have also drawn on the seminal writings of many Malawian scholars – Ntara, Soka, Gwengwe, Makumbi and Chafulamira – much of which is in the vernacular and generally bypassed by visiting academics. I have taken pains to cite my sources, so that the ethnographic data may be contextualized with regard to both time and place. But because I range widely over time and space, drawing on cultural data from a wide range of ethnographic contexts in relation to the matrilineal peoples of Malawi, this does not mean that the study is 'ahistorical', an account of 'timeless' cultural entities. The ritual practices and cultural representations I describe are enduring, but certainly not 'timeless', everlasting or unchanging. Has any anthropologist ever thought otherwise? Dismissing a past generation of anthropologists as 'essentialists' or as 'ahistoric' may be fashionable scholarship, but it is just another example of the 'radical alterity' that anthropologists are supposed to have outgrown.

Something must be said about my style of writing. This book has no controlling thesis or argument. As far as I am aware, none of my books do. It consists rather of a kind of ramble across an ethnographic terrain, in which I try to present to the reader a descriptive analysis – an interpretation – of Malawian ritual practices and cultural beliefs. Although my approach is critical, as I engage in various theoretical debates relevant to my themes, I try to avoid the kind of 'slash and burn' scholarship that seems to be prevalent in academia, as well as the tendency of many academics to offer monolithic explanations of social and cultural phenomena. Even more do I try to resist the kind of 'stereotypical originality' of which Frederick Barth writes (1994: 350).

Because my study does not have a thesis or 'central argument' many academics may find my style somewhat disconcerting. One colleague has written that my writings, though interesting and insightful, consist of 'bits, pieces, glimmers, glimpses, asides, clashes, refutations, challenges and associations'. This is exactly what my ramble is meant to convey, although I trust my presentation of Malawi culture is an ordered exposition. I have, of course, been selective in my theoretical 'asides' for the anthropological literature on such topics as gender and sexuality, animal/human relationships, the body, self and personhood, ritual and religion – which are my main themes – is, putting it mildly, 'vast'. I only dip into this extensive literature.

Equally important, I try to write in a style that is readable, lucid and accessible to a wide range of people, not only to academics but also to lay persons who may be interested in the subject-matter, especially Malawians. I try to write, as the pioneer entomologist S.H. Skaife put it in 'plain, everyday language'. I have been continually criticized for this tendency, colleagues suggesting that I should write specifically for – and thus try to impress – other academics! This I adamantly refuse to do, either by advocating monolithic or reductive interpretations, or by writing in an obscurantist or pretentious style that suggests erudition and originality. You will thus not find in this study such statements as: rituals

> are a rhetoric of transformation which evoke embodied sacramentality, involving an interplay of multiple senses and verbal modalities, a dialectic of embodiment and objectification that elaborates previously unacknowledged and unrecognised forms of learning.

This may sound profound, but it is in fact rather vacuous. If journalists described a football match – a ritual – in these terms they would be laughed at. Still less will you find me spluttering Heideggerian jargon in the fashion of Derrida and Tyler, inventing words and phrases that sound profound but are often either blather or convey sociological truisms. I also do not engage in what is described as 'thick description' or ethnographic 'poetics'.

I am acutely aware, of course, that Hegelian metaphysics and Husserl's phenomenology (see Morris, 1991) are complex, abtruse and multitextured, as are Malawian rituals and cultural practices. But my aim is not to replicate their complexity and obscurity (for an outsider) but rather to elucidate their meaning in ways that are understandable to an ordinary person

I also try to avoid labouring the obvious. In Malawi there are endless debates about the uses of plants and animals, about the meaning and interpretation of cultural phenomena, and both the historicity and the idiosyncratic nature of cultural beliefs and rituals are recognized. Thus newspapers and journals are full of discussions and arguments about whether or not the *fisi* rite should be proscribed (see Chapter 3), and about exactly what constitutes a proper funeral. That social practices and cultural representations are historical in their very nature; that all social phenomenon – hunting, witchcraft, funerals, medicines - have diverse forms; that culture is a 'terrain' where interests are 'contested'; that Malawians like everybody else are unique individuals who may hold very idiosyncratic notions; that there are diverse opinions and interpretations evident in Malawi – all these I take to be so self evident that I never bother to emphasize and elaborate upon them.

As the book is focused on human/animal relations, as reflected in Malawian ritual practices and cultural representations, it does not of course attempt to deal with such practices and representations in their totality or full complexity. Nor does it link Malawians religious culture to the wider socio-historical context and to the 'world system'. This is quite beyond the present study, and would constitute a very different project. But I have discussed more fully elsewhere human/animal relations in their wider historical context.

Finally, it must be noted that when speaking of Malawians – as with Malawi culture – I am essentially referring to the matrilineal people of Malawi who form the majority of the population – not to Malawians who may be Ngoni, Sena, Lambya or Ngonda, or of European or Asian descent.

This study consists of five chapters.

Chapter 2 outlines human/animal relations in Malawi from a historical perspective, emphasizing that these relationships have always been complex, diverse and multi-faceted. I argue that although Malawians make a clear ontological distinction between humans and animals, this does not constitute a radical dichotomy, for animals are thought to share many attributes with humans in having sociality, consciousness and subjective agency. I then go on to discuss the concept of the person, stressing that a distinction must be made between the human person as a generic being, and the person as a cultural or normative category. In section three I outline the Malawian conception of the human person, as an embodied being, and then, in the following section, discuss the person as a social being. Although, as a cultural ideal, Malawians put a fundamental stress on the sociality of the person this does not oblate, I suggest, an equal emphasis on a person's uniqueness and individuality.

In Chapter 3 I outline those rituals focused around childbirth, and the initiation of women. After some initial reflection on the importance of sexuality and the hot/cold symbolism that is implicit in Malawi culture, I focus on the three main rituals that together constitute the initiation of a girl into motherhood, the menstrual (*ndakula*), maturity (*chiputu*) and first pregnancy (*chisamba*) rites. I make some initial reflections on the role of mammals in these rituals.

In Chapter 4 I outline the initiation of boys in Malawi, focusing on the *Jando* rituals of the Yao and the Nyau rituals of the Mang'anja, Chipeta and Chewa. I stress the crucial importance of mammals in the ceremonial masked dances that are associated with the life-cycle rituals, and critically discuss the various theories that have been suggested to explicate these rites. I conclude the chapter by examining the nature of the funerary rites. I emphasize that for Malawians, life and death, living people and the ancestral spirits, the village and the woodland environs, are conceptualized as but aspects of an ongoing cyclic process that sustains human life.

In Chapter 5 I focus on Malawian conceptions of divinity, and on the ecological cycle that is implicit in their creation myths, a cyclic process that is centred around a symbolic polarity, a complementary opposition between the wet and dry seasons, fire and water, and hunting and agriculture. I explore the role that animals play in these myths. I then, after discussing the different conceptions of divinity, examine the significance of the various rain shrines, and associated deities that are to be found on the forested hills throughout Malawi, and the important role that the python plays in its manifestations as the rain spirit.

In the final chapter, I discuss the role of the ancestral spirits in Malawian social life, how they manifest themselves as wild animals, and the nature of the various spirit rituals that are to be found in diverse forms throughout Malawi. I emphasize that Malawians have an immanent conception of both the divinity and the spirits, a conception that is essentially pantheistic, for both the divinity and the spirits manifest themselves, or become embodied, as natural phenomena. This conception, I suggest is neither mystical nor animistic. Throughout the chapter I explore the role that wild animals play in Malawi religious life.

At extremes social scientists are of two types: those like Habermas and Giddens who focus on theory, offering high-level generalizations about social life, sometimes unsupported by empirical data; and those like Fernandez and Devisch who write excellent ethnographies but often of such depth and sophistication that one sometimes gets lost in the detail. Both these approaches to social life are important and necessary. But theory and comparative studies - if I may parody Kant – without ethnography and empirical data are empty whereas ethnography without a comparative perspective is blind. This book lies midway between these two extreme approaches: it is an ethnography but is informed by theoretical asides and a comparative perspective. And it is essentially concerned with exploring conceptions of personhood and gender in Malawi, as these are mediated through two realms of being, the organic (animals) and the spiritual. One final point may be made to conclude this introduction. Although I am aware that much has been written on the supposed 'religiosity' of African people, I may note that many Malawians are extremely sceptical about various aspects of their own culture, and some may describe themselves as outside (*wakunja*) the main religious traditions.

–2–

Animals, Humans and Personhood

Human/Animal Relationships

For many centuries the people of Malawi have lived 'cheek-by-jowl' with wild animals, particularly the larger mammals, and the relationship between humans and animals has always been close and intimate. The early hunter gatherers, known as Akafula (the diggers) or Batwa in oral traditions, were reported to be hunters, and hunting was a crucial occupation of the early iron-age – probably Bantu – people who moved into the region around the second century AD, judging from the archaeo-logical evidence (Crader, 1984; Morris, 1998: 74–6). The social and political history of Malawi, in fact, makes little sense if we do not take into account the importance of the hunting of the larger mammals, particularly elephants, but also serval, rhinoceros, lion, hippopotamus, leopard – whose skins, horns and ivory were important trade goods. Unfortunately the history of Malawi has tended to be interpreted in terms of a series of 'invasions'. First we have the Abatwa hunter-gatherers; then the invasion of agriculturists during the iron-age, and later, Bantu-speakers who are identified with the 'proto-Chewa' and the Banta clan, as if Chewa was some timeless and hegemonic social unit and a 'clan' constituted a viable social entity. Around the sixteenth century came the Phiri clan who by conquest set up the Maravi state under the Kalonga, based at Mankhamba on the southern lake shore. Later rival Maravi states were established such as Undi in Northern Zambezia and Lundu in Lower Shire. The power and influence of these chiefdoms have been somewhat exaggerated – but the scenario is that through dynastic rivalry the power of these states collapsed in the seventeenth century, and Malawi was then largely a politically decentralized region until the advent of colonial rule at the end of the nineteenth century (Pachai 1973).

What this historical account tends to ignore – which I have explored in my other writings – is the crucial importance of the ivory trade – the hunting of elephants especially – in the rise and consolidation of the Maravi chiefdoms, and the fact that during the nineteenth-century Malawi

(North Zambezia) was *more* not less, centralized than in earlier centuries. For the nineteenth century saw the rise of many polities based on long-distance trade, the chiefdoms having a symbiotic relationship to various groups of intinerant hunter/traders (Chikunda, Bisa, Yao, Azimba) who organized the hunting of the elephant and/or the transportation of the ivory to the coast. In the nineteenth century a tusk of African ivory was extremely valuable – worth more than a chattel slave – and it was through this trade that the various chiefdoms acquired muzzle-loading guns, brass or copper wire, cotton goods, glass beads, and various other trade items. These were utilized both in the internal economy and as a means of control. Throughout the nineteenth century there was a complex and intricate relationship between this hunting economy, guns, and the power of various chiefdoms. Thus during this century what is now Malawi was not 'decentralised', but consisted of numerous petty states or chiefdoms (Kalinga, 1984; Phiri, 1988; Shepperson, 1966; Alpers, 1975; MacMillan, 1975) Much of the conflict in the early colonial period was in fact over the control of trade, ivory in particular.

Thus we may conclude that the political history of the North Zambezia region can only be understood if we take in to account the importance of the ivory trade, which involved the hunting of elephants. During the period 1891 to 1904 it is estimated that Malawi (then British Central Africa) exported 80 tons of ivory (Baker, 1971: 91). This only implied legal trade – but it amounts to the killing of more than three thousand elephants.

Mammals were not only important in the political economy of the region, they were, throughout the history of Malawi, closely implicated in the social life of the people. They were an important source of food – through subsistence hunting and the trapping of small mammals – activating medicines (*chizimba*) and clothing (skins). They were the primary subjects of oral traditions – and the hare, lion, elephant, hyena, leopard, tortoise and other animals, are all key figures in Malawian folk tales (*Nthano*) and proverbs (*Chisimo*) (Morris, 1998: 173–82, 237–41). Animals, as we shall explore in this study, play an important part in Malawian rituals and religious life – as divining instruments, as medicine, and as the embodiment of spirits of the dead (*mizimu*) and witches (*afiti*). Even the hunting of mammals in Malawi, as we have explored (1996b, 1998: 61–119), is ill understood as a form of 'predation' for it has an important ritual dimension, the killing of the larger, more 'potent' animals (eland, kudu, bushbuck, elephant, buffalo, sable, roan) being akin to homicide. Its is thus hedged with ritual, as well as being seen as symbolically analogous to iron smelting and human reproduction. Finally, throughout the history of the region, Malawian people, as subsistence hoe cultivators, have expressed an essentially ambivalent attitude towards wild animals. On the one hand, animals are the source of meat (*nyama*), of activating medicines, and, in being closely identified with the spirits of the dead, as essentially the source of fertility, and thus the continuity of the kin group. Wild animals, as we explore below, thus form a crucial point in the on-going cyclical processes of life and social regeneration. But on the other hand, animals are also seen as fundamentally hostile and antagonistic to human endeavour.

It is, I think, difficult for people living in urban contexts to realize how precarious life is for subsistence agriculturists. And it has to be remembered that historically the matrilineal peoples of Malawi were fundamentally subsistence hoe cultivators, and in rural areas the majority of the population are still dependent on this form of economy. Not only is such agriculture highly dependent on rain, but the depredations of wild animals are a constant source of concern and anxiety. The depredations of wild animals in Malawi focus around two distinct groups of animals – leaving aside the birds, snakes and insects. The first are the larger carnivores – lion, leopard and hyena. Throughout Malawian history these predators have taken a toll of livestock, and of human life, particularly young children. At various times there have been 'outbreaks' of 'man-eating' lions and hyenas, which have spread terror in particular localities. Around 1930, for example, a lion in the Fort Manning (Mchinji) district caused at least thirty-six deaths during a five-month period. The second group of animals responsible for depredations are those that raid village gardens for crops, and the most important of these are the elephant, baboon, monkey, hippopotamus, porcupine, bushpig, and in certain circumstances, such antelopes as the kudu. Essentially monkeys and baboons raid the garden by day, bushpig and porcupine by night, all four species still being widespread and common in Malawi. But during the colonial period the animal that caused most problems for humans was the elephant, and prior to muzzle-loading guns it has to recognized that humans and elephants almost vied with each other for living space. Ecologically and in terms of their social life humans and elephants are very similar (Graham, 1973: 97–8) But during the colonial period the elephant often had the upper hand, wreaking havoc in gardens, reducing local people to famine and 'terrorizing' villagers, even raiding the maize granaries after the harvest. People were trampled to death while trying to defend their gardens and granaries with lighted torches.

In Malawi during the past decades there has been a tremendous increase in the human population, Less than two million in 1930, it now stands at around nine million. As an inevitable consequence there has been a great reduction in the number of larger mammals over the past fifty years of so. Zebra, oribi and blue wildebeest, for example, are no longer to be found on the Phalombe plain (Dudley, 1979). Nevertheless wild animals are still fairly plentiful. Thus leopards and hyenas still roam at night in the Zomba and Blantyre townships and in rural areas throughout Malawi, local people are still engaged during the agricultural season, particularly at harvest time (*masika*), in a constant battle with hippos, monkeys, porcupines, baboons and wildpigs – not to mention the smaller rodents – in an effort to defend their crops. We therefore still find, as in the past, much time and energy being devoted during the planting season to warding off crop predators. Where gardens border woodland area special shelters (*chirindo*, *msasa*) are built, often on raised platforms, and people may eat and sleep in these shelters for several weeks – especially to guard against baboons. The importance and severity of what is now described as 'wildlife pest impacts' has been of special concern to the department of National Parks and Wildlife, especially in relation to those village communities at Vwaza Marsh, Kasungu and Liwonde, which are immediately outside wildlife conservation areas (Morris, 1995).

Thus humans and wild animals in Malawi have always co-existed and the relationship between humans and animals has always been one that is complex, intimate and multi-faceted.

Until the recent decades few anthropologists, philosophers and historians expressed much interest in the natural world, or in animals. Nature was simply the existential background that could safely be ignored, and mammals hardly existed apart from the role that they played in religious symbolism. Since then a wealth of interest has been generated in the 'animal estate' and some important texts have been published (Nelson, 1983; Serpell, 1986; Rivto, 1987; Ingold, 1988; Robinson and Tiger, 1991). The tendency has been to set up a radical dualism between the Western conceptions of animals (identified with Cartesian dualism, mechanistic philosophy and the Baconian ethic of domination) and the conceptions of other cultures, which are likewise interpreted in a rather monolithic fashion as involving trust, giving, reciprocity, sacramentality, or a 'benign' attitude towards animals. But it has, I think, to be recognized, as I have argued elsewhere (1998: 2) that human social attitudes and relationships to animals are never monolithic and that all human societies have diverse, multifaceted, and often contradictory attitudes towards the natural world, especially towards animals (Benton, 1993: 62–9). In my companion volume *The Power of Animals* (1998) I have explored at some length the relationship of the matrilineal people of Malawi towards the animal world, with a specific focus on mammals. Some of the basic themes expressed in this study, may be briefly summarized here.

Firstly, Malawian people have a *phenomenological* attitude towards animals, expressed in the intuitive – imaginative and psychological – recognition of the discontinuities of nature. Like human beings everywhere Malawians acknowledge that the world of Nature consists of particular 'things' ranging from inanimate objects like stones and artefacts, to various forms of organic beings – 'kinds' (*mitundu*) of insects, frogs, trees, fungi, birds, and mammals, all reflecting the manifold diversity of nature. Every kind of organism, as a 'species-being' (to use Marx's term) is in a sense unique, and has some defining characteristics by which it can be identified as an entity different from all others. Humans are thus a distinct form of being, and although Malawians have no terms that are equivalent to the English terms 'animal', 'plant', 'mammal' or 'insect' they do recognize ontological distinctions between these various forms of being – all of which they see as having been created (*kulenga*) by the supreme spirit (*Mulungu*). Thus Malawians make a distinction between those aspects of the natural world that have 'life' (*moyo*) and those things which do not (*zinthu zopanda moyo*). Those beings or entities that are generally regarded to have life, and which are ontologically distinguished include: *munthu* (human), *njoka* (snake), spirit entities like *Napolo* (spirit serpent associated with mountains) and *mizimu* (spirits of the dead), *bowa* (edible fungi), and *mbalame* (birds). There is some ambiguity as to whether soil or rain have 'life' but what is clearly evident is that in the Malawian context people clearly recognize a category of living things (*zamoyo*, that have life). Malawian people therefore do not see the whole world as animate, and I very much doubt if anybody does – for the concepts of both animism and anthropomorphism presuppose ontological distinctions, as does the notion that there can be transformations (*ku-sanduka*) between various forms of being. Malawians thus recognize ontological distinctions between the main life-form categories – animals (*nyama/chirombo*), humans (*anthu*), plants (*mitengo*) and fungi (*bowa*). I have elsewhere given a full discussion of the life-form categories to be found in Malawi, as well as of their folk classification of mammals, of which more than 100 species are described (1998; 140–67). In recognizing nature as a phenomenon, Malawians put a special emphasis on the particularity of 'things'; they thus tend to relate to animals and plants as organic species beings, rather than relating to the world through the kind of high-level abstractions that so fascinate anthropologists – nature, space, landscape, cosmos, environment, the life world.

A constant plea of phenomenologists like Husserl and Heidegger was that Western philosophy should abandon metaphysics and 'return' to Being (existence), to the 'things themselves'. This call could not have been addressed to Malawians because they already have, like the pre Socratics, a 'primordial sense of nature' (Foltz, 1995). In putting an emphasis an existential things, rural Malawians thus express ideas that are akin to those of Aristotle. But it is highly misleading to set up a dualism, as many anthropologists are prone to do, between a 'thing' as an individual entity and a 'person' (as a relational being), or between 'things' and 'processes'. As Whitehead noted with regard to this second dichotomy 'process and individuality require each other' (1938: 132–3). To adopt some of the basic ideas of Whitehead – whose metaphysics emphasized that the world was a process and that events were its basic constituents – we may perhaps suggest that for Malawians every organic being (but especially the larger mammals) is an actual entity or thing. It comes into being and perishes (it has duration); it is fundamentally a process constituted through relations, while at the same time having subjective agency and a unique unitary identity (individuality). Thus, as we shall explore in this study, Malawians put an emphasis both on the individuality of species-beings, as well as on transformational processes, particularly in relation to social activities (hunting, iron-smelting, sexual reproduction) and the sociality and gender identity of humans.

Secondly, and again this is akin (though not of course identical) to the organic philosophies of Aristotle and Whitehead, Malawians do not conceive of nature as inert matter. They have rather a dynamic conception of being, as Father Tempels (1959) long ago suggested with regard to African culture more generally. They thus express a *realist* attitude, and acknowledge that the natural world, mammals especially, have intrinsic value and inherent powers, properties and potentialities that are independent of humans. This is similar to the Greek notion of nature as *physis*. This acknowledgement of a 'real' world independent of human cognition, and with inherent powers is not 'positivist notion', and the conflation of realism with positivism by interpretative anthropologists and post-modern philosophy is obfuscating (Morris, 1997). This perspective is particularly reflected in the use of animals as medicine (*chizimba*), though the 'powers' of nature may, of course, be harnessed for diverse purposes, for strengthening the blood, curing a disease, protecting a person form evil influences, as well as for malevolent purposes. It corresponds to what Roy Ellen describes as nature as 'inner essence', the notion that the natural world has an essence, or 'vital energy or force' (1996:111–12). I have described the use of animals as medicine more fully in my other writings (1998: 209–34).

The notion that the world consists ontologically of different forms of being (mountains, stones, fungi, grass, woody plants, snakes, birds, animals, humans), and that each mode has its own unique properties, capacities and inherent powers – something stressed by ethnobiologists and critical realists – is probably universal. It is certainly not unique to Malawi, or to Mongolian shamanism as perceptively recorded by Humphrey (1996: 84–105, Morris, 1998: 213–14).

Thirdly, Malawians do not make a *radical* distinction between humans and animals, but rather conceive of humans and animals as sharing many attributes. In this sense Malawian cultural ideas are closer to those of Aristotle and Whitehead than to Heidegger, the guru of the deep ecologists. In fact, although Heidegger is commonly heralded as an ecological thinker, with his emphasis on 'dwelling', this is a misconception for he always made a radical dichotomy between humans and animals. Only humans had 'EK-sistence' as the 'shepherd of Being' and there is an 'abyss' separating humans and animals. The animal, he writes, 'has no world nor any environment' (Krell, 1978: 230–4, Heidegger, 1959: 45).

Although Malawians do make a clear distinction between humans – as generic beings – and animals, they do not conceive of this distinction as constituting a radical dualism, or as an 'abyss'. Their *socially engaged* attitudes to animals are, in fact, complex, reflected in both friendships (*chibwenzi*) which is expressed towards domestic animals – especially cats and dogs – and the strong empathy that is experienced between humans (the male affine) and the hunted mammal, and that I have described fully in my earlier studies. This socially engaged attitude recognizes the fundamental affinities between humans and mammals as living beings who share a common world and are often in competition. Animals, as we have noted, are the primary subjects of folk tales, in which the dichotomy between animals and humans breaks down, and the animals are humanized – and humans become animal like – in order to express and affirm what are considered to be important social values. These are: to share and not to be greedy or selfish, to respect elders, to persevere in a task despite difficulties, to listen to others and be attentive to their well being, to be patient and show discretion, and, above all, to use one's common sense (Morris, 1998: 184).

Malawian attitudes towards animals – if I may be allowed yet another comparison – are very similar to those of the artist naturalist, Ernest Thompson Seton. Around a hundred years ago Seton wrote:

we and the beasts are kin. Man has nothing that the animals have not at least a vestige of, and animals have nothing that man does not in some degree share (1898: 12)

What Seton tried to emphasize in his writings was that animals have complex and intricate forms of communication and sign language, an aesthetic sense, a social system, that much of their behaviour is learned not instinctual, and that animals express emotions, have a moral sense, subjective agency and unique personalities, and often form close relationships with humans. Deriving his ideas from Darwin's evolutionary biology, from his deep empathy with Native American Indian culture, and from a close and intimate relationship with animals in the wild, Seton long ago initiated a critique of anthropocentrism and the development of an ecological world view.

In a recent important text on human–animal relations Barbara Noske (1997) reaffirmed Seton's essential ideas, drawing on recent ethological studies of primates, whales, dolphins, wolves, and elephants. Thus, although like people everywhere, Malawians often indulge in anthropomorphic thinking – the attribution of human dispositions and characteristics to animals (or to plants, artefacts, things or events) much of this thinking – like that of Seton – is based on a real knowledge and understanding of the behavioural characteristics of animals in the wild (woodland, *thengo*).

In the recent decade there has been much debate about anthropomorphism, and in a scholarly and provocative book *Faces in the Clouds* (1993) Stewart Guthrie has offered a new theory of religion, suggesting that religion *is* anthropomorphism. Religion, defined as a belief in 'human-like beings', Guthrie suggests derives from anthropomorphic cognition – 'attributing humanity to the world'. He further argues that these postulated anthropomorphic beings (deities, spirits) help humans to understand the world about them and to explicate events – or at least disturbing events and uncertainty. Anthropormophism, he concludes, is 'the core of religious experience' (1993: 7). This 'intellectualist' theory of religion is hardly 'new' – as Guthrie himself admits (1993: 178), for it was proposed by Tylor and Muller in the nineteenth century, and was later developed by Boas, Horton and Levi-Strauss. Indeed Levi-Strauss defined religion as the 'anthropomorphism of nature' (1966: 21) – but refused to make a study of this phenomenon. What is important about Guthrie's study is that he emphasizes that anthropomorphic thinking, along with animism – seeing non-living things or events as alive – is widespread in all human communities. He thus details that in European culture anthropomorphism is pervasive in philosophy, science and the arts, as well as being evident – indeed synonymous – with religion.

What is of interest in the Malawian context is that not only is anthropomorphic thinking persuasive – evident in many ritual and social activities – but so is its opposite, theriomorphic thinking. In his study of the prehistory of the mind Steven Mithen suggests that anthropomorphic thinking – 'attributing animals with human like minds' (1996: 49) – is not so much a reflection of the detailed empirical and intuitive knowledge that hunter-gatherers possess with respect to the capacities and behaviour of the larger mammals but rather of the 'cognitive fluidity' that is unique to modern humans. This 'integrative' consciousness, which developed between 100,000 and 30,000 years ago, is according to Mithen, reflected in totemic and metaphorical thought (symbolism) and in anthropomorphism. Mithen seems to suggest, contrary to the knowledge of animal behaviour that is now emerging (Noske, 1997), that animals and proto-humans have no 'cognitive fluidity'. He also seems to suggest that such anthropomorphism had a 'practical value' and 'utilitarian benefits' for hunter-gatherers of the upper Palaeolithic. He writes: 'Anthropomorphizing animals by attributing to them human personalities and characters provides as effective a prediction for their behaviour as viewing them with all the understanding of ecological knowledge possessed by Western Scientists' (1996: 192). In fact, many Malawians – like hunter gatherers – often have a much more detailed empirical knowledge of animal life than do Western scientists – apart from the likes of Seton, Goodall and Moss. But treating animals as if they were humans while out hunting (which nobody does) would hardly bring practical success.

Attributing personhood to animals, usually the sense of seeing them as the embodiment of spiritual agencies, only takes place in specific contexts. In fact, as I have described elsewhere (1998: 87–8) Malawian hunters when out hunting engage more often in theriomorphic thinking, trying to imagine themselves as the hunted animal – to anticipate its movements and actions. Such theriomorphism, as we shall explore in this study (Chapter 4) is also reflected in the Inyago and Nyau rituals where the dancers not only take the form of an animal (elephant, eland, hare, baboon) but in stylized and often exaggerated fashion mimic the behaviour of the animal. What was important in the evolution of humans was not only anthropomorphic (and totemic) thinking but also the close relations that humans developed with animals, particularly the dog. The dog was in essence a 'tool' that augmented not the human hand but the senses, greatly improving the success of the hunt. Even today in Malawi, as we have discussed elsewhere (1998: 85–7) the dog is an important hunting aide.

Such theriomorphic thinking is important in Malawi. 'Thinking like a Mountain' is a title of a biography of the well-known ecologist Aldo Leopold. Advocating an ecological attitude to nature, Leopold's basic ideas were derived from Seton – though Seton is never mentioned by the deep ecologists (Flader, 1974). Malawians do not advocate thinking like a mountain – for mountains do not 'think', but while out hunting or in their rituals, or even digging up mice, they do try to think like animals, for animals have subjective agency, consciousness and knowledge (*nzeru*) and can often outwit humans. Malawians do not see animals and humans as 'ontologically equivalent' (Ingold 1988: xxiv) – the alternative to dualism is not identity theory and the dissolution of boundaries, but dialectics – for they recognize and emphasize the distinctiveness and uniqueness of humans: but they also recognize, as Seton put it, that humans and animals are 'kin'. We thus need to recognize as Noske (1997) writes – and this Malawians seem to implicitly affirm – the essential continuity between humans and animals, while acknowledging also, and respecting the differences and integrity of the many forms of animal life.

Fourthly, Malawians express a highly *pragmatic* attitude towards the natural world, which suggests an anthropocentric world view. Indeed Mbiti (1969) long ago implied that the ontology underlying African religious philosophy is 'firmly anthropocentric' in the sense that humans are placed at the centre of their ontology, the natural world, the means of constituting their environment and means of existence. Even African religion, he suggests – as distinct from ontology – is 'pragmatic and utilitarian rather than spiritual and mystical' (1969: 5). In my discussion on Malawian folk classifications – of fungi, plants and animals – I have emphasized that many of the life forms and intermediate categories are prototypically functional categories, and their folk classifications cannot be understood without acknowledging this pragmatic bias (Morris 1984, 1991b). This utilitarian attitude is particularly evident in the use of animals as food – *nyama* is a term that means both meat and animal – and as medicine. When Graham wrote that many Africans consider wild animals 'either meat or trouble' (1973: 117), though somewhat stark and simplistic, he was nevertheless conveying an essential truth. Thus the Malawian attitude to animals has a strong pragmatic emphasis. The fundamental concern of this practical or utilitarian attitude is both the control of nature, and the practical and material use-value of the surrounding world, animals in particular. As an attitude it is somewhat similar to the Greek concept of *teche*, and what Heidegger refers to as *Zuhandenheit*, things 'ready-to-hand' (1962: 102–5). Unfortunately, Heidegger, in the most obscurantist fashion, tends to conflate this attitude, or relation to the world, not only with *theoria* (the rational contemplation of nature) but with the techno-logical mastery of nature (capitalist ideology). But importantly, and crucially, this pragmatic attitude must be distinguished from that of 'dominion' which is particularly reflected in instrumental reason and the technological form of power. This attitude was evident perhaps with the commercial hunting of elephants – mimed in certain Nyau rituals by the Ajere hunter – but generally speaking an attitude of conquest or dominion over nature is not emphasized in Malawi culture. Even in the past, the hunting of elephants was a highly ritualized affair, as Fraser (1923) indicated. Hunting in Malawi, as I have discussed elsewhere, as well as meat eating, cannot therefore be simply read as a symbolic expression of human control and mastery of nature. Indeed the conflation of 'control' over nature, expressed in subsistence hunting and in the pragmatic attitude towards nature – animals (so evident in Malawi) with 'dominion' over nature by Heidegger, critical theorists, deep ecologists and eco-feminists is highly misleading (CJ Adams, 1990, Fiddes, 1991, and for critiques O'Neil, 1993: 154–5, Morris, 1994b).

The Concept of a Person

In the 1990's there was a resurgence of interest in cultural conceptions of the person. In a wide variety of academic disciplines theories of the person or of the human subject are now commonplace. The 'self' and 'identity' have both become fashionable concepts in social theory and some general texts in philosophy take the issue of 'self' as their main organizing principle (for example, Barrett, 1986; Solomon, 1988). Indeed Madan Sarup (1996: 28) has suggested that the current pervasive fascina-tion, even obsession, with self and identity is but a symptom of post-modernity, i.e. contemporary capitalism. But it is of interest that while Howell and Melhuus (1993: 47) draw attention to the lack of dialogue between those engaged in comparative studies of the person (Heelas and Lock, 1981; Shweder and Levine, 1984) and those concerned with issues of gender, there has been even less engagement between the former and ethnobiologists – although Ingold (1986, 1991) has long tried to bridge the gap between evolutionary biology and cultural anthropology. The studies of Berlin (1992), Atran (1990) and Ellen (1993) have little to say on the category of 'human', while much psychological anthropology has focused on the dialectic between 'culture' and the 'psyche', and seen the body largely as a site of metaphors. It is now engaged in an internal critique, of 'putting people in biology', namely, a belated recognition that humans are biological, as well as social and cultural beings (Schwartz et al., 1992). More significantly 'person-centred' anthropology has tended to by-pass animals completely, and one gets the decided impression that in this tradition personhood is largely defined and expressed only in the ritual context, particularly in spirit rituals. (Lambek and A. Strathern, 1998). But both humanity and personhood can only be understood in terms of a dialectical relationship with animals, and, of course, rituals constitute only a small part – even if an important part – of people's lifeworld and social activities.

Whether or not humans can be considered a 'natural kind' has been the subject of some debate by philosophers. As the biological concept of species has been defined, ever since Darwin, in terms of a reproductive population rather than in terms of types or essences (Mayr, 1982: 273), some have suggested that as biological species are not natural kinds, then humans do not constitute a universal category – except in some Platonic sense – and therefore the notion of 'humanity' cannot validate either moral humanism or anthropological theory (Clark, 1998; but see the critical humanism of Fromm, 1984; Bookchin, 1990, 1995). Others have acknowledged that humans are a natural kind – but interpreted this as applying only to humans as natural 'organisms' not as social persons (Scruton, 1986; 57–9). As I have written a good deal on the anthropology of the person, both in terms of conceptions of the person in the Western intellectual tradition and cross culturally (1985, 1991, 1994), I do not wish, as it were, to get side-tracked here – particularly as the subject of the self is now a culture industry. But two points need to be made; the need to distinguish between social praxis and cultural representations and to distinguish between three distinct concepts of the person – as a social being, as a cultural category, and as a psychological self, as a locus of identity and experience.

There has been a long-standing distinction made in the social sciences as discussed in Chapter 1 between society and culture, between social praxis, the social processes and relations that people are engaged in – which intrinsically incorporates a relationship with the material world – and the collective representations and cultural notions of members of a community. They form, in both an epistemological and ontological sense, two distinct realms or levels of social reality. Through their social actions and activities people – as *human* social agents – make a direct impact upon the world, whereas cultural conceptions, as both Holy and Ingold suggest, in a sense do not do anything, they simply provide 'models' for social action, and are a part of the shared knowledge of a community (Holy, 1986: 4–5; Ingold, 1991: 374).

The conceptual distinction between social praxis and cultural representations as an 'ideational' system, has often lead scholars to overstress one or other of the domains. Either culture is seen as simply a reflection or effect of social practice – which is how anthropologists rather misleadingly interpret Marx – or culture is conceptualized as a unified system of symbols and meanings, as in the 'savoir African' tradition of writers like Marcel Griaule, endowed with its own logic, which then has a determining effect on social processes, people's behaviour simply following the cultural logic. As Holy writes, people are social agents, and their actions and choices are not directly determined by their cultural notions, but rather they are 'made in the context of these notions' (1986: 9).

The relationship between social praxis and cultural representations is therefore a dialectical one. It is misleading however to interpret this distinction in dualistic fashion, as if cultural paradigms were completely separate from lived experience, for as I stressed earlier, cultural representations are embedded in the practical constitution of everyday life, both social and material.

This distinction between society as patterned and co-ordinated social interaction, and culture as shared knowledge, is a key distinction made by Fitz J P Poole in his important essay on the development of personal identity. For Poole makes a crucial distinction between socialization, which has to do with 'the set of species – wide requirements and exactions made on human beings by human societies', and enculturation 'the process of learning a culture in all its uniqueness and particularity' (1994: 831). Thus socialization implicates interactive processes – how one learns to become a social agent, enact roles and forge social relationships within a community, and Poole stresses that children are actively and creatively engaged in such social processes. In contrast, enculturation is seen as those processes by which one acquires understanding and competence in the 'ideational realm' that constitutes culture, seen in terms of schemata, scripts, models, codes and classifications, though these should not be conceived in monolithic fashion. Poole goes on to discuss three intertwined 'senses of identity', relating, respectively to personhood – the person as a social being – selfhood – the person as the locus of experience with a sense of an enduring, stable identity – and in terms of individuality (1994: 942–5).

Consonant with these distinctions are the three quite distinct conceptions of the person that I have discussed elsewhere (1994: 10–14).

The first conception of the person identifies the individual as natural *human being*, which is recognized in all cultures. The person as a human being represents a realist perspective on the world, shared by all humans, it is part of the basic or 'first-order' cognitive dispositions which conceives of living beings in the world as material 'essences' with underlying natures. Thus people in Malawi, as elsewhere, conceive of the human person *munthu*, (plural *anthu*), as a living being intrinsically related to the material world, depending for their very sustenance on the earth, nourishing themselves by drinking water, and by absorbing substances as food (*chakuda*), or in certain circumstances, as medicine (*mankwala*). As a generic being the person is conceptualized as embodied, with consciousness, and as intrinsically social, with language and moral agency. The human person is also seen, even more so than animals, as quintessentially an individual. People in Malawi thus do not conceive of the human person as a disembodied conscious ego (subject) – as in Cartesian metaphysic; or as simply a reactive organism as in behaviourist psychology; or as a possessive individual detached from the social context as in neo-liberal economic theory; or as an ek-sistent, a subjective self-reflective agent who is completely divorced from mammalian life (for Malawians there is no 'abyss' between humans and animals) and certainly Malawians do not view the person as a 'commodity', as in bourgeois capitalist ideology; nor, finally, do they conceive of the generic person as fragmented, incoherent, or decentred as in post-modernist theory. It is extremely doubtful if ordinary people in Western cultures, in their social praxis, ever conceive of the person in the above terms, although this is not to deny the pervasive influence of Cartesian dualism, nihilism, and neo-liberal individualism on Western cultures, functional as these are to the maintenance of capitalist hegemony (Gare, 1993). It seems to be an occupational hazard among anthropologists, especially the post modernists, to portray Western conceptions of the person in the most monolithic stereotypical fashion (Shweder and Bourne, 1984; Strathern, 1988). In theorizing on the person as a human being, some scholars have drawn a distinction between human agency, personal identity and the person as a social actor – although it seems to me quite misleading to equate agency with the possessive individual of neo-liberalism and rational choice theory (see Archer, 1995: 254-88; Hollis, 1994: 115–41).

In a useful discussion of humans as generic beings – 'universal people' – Brown emphasizes the social nature of the human person, and that in a psychological sense

> they distinguish self from others, and they can see the self as both subject and object. They do not see the person as a wholly passive recipient of external action, nor do they see the self as wholly autonomous. (1991: 135)

It has to be recognized, of course, that psychologically humans are both generic and personal beings, with a sense of humanity and of their own unique selfhood.

Although Brown notes the importance of culture, language, consciousness and subjective agency, for Malawians these are not unique to humans. Malawians recognize that humans like kudus and elephants are unique beings, but they also recognize – as we earlier discussed – that humans and animals share many of these attributes.

The second conception of the person is as a *cultural category*, the conception articulated specifically in the cultural representations of a specific community or religious or philosophical tradition. Such cultural conceptions, as I have indicated in my earlier studies (1991, 1994) are extremely diverse, and by no means coterminous with the notion of the person as a human subject.

Finally, there is a conception of the person that focuses on the human person as an individual, as a unique *self*. As a psychological concept, self is a process that lends structure and continuity to experience, it involves being embodied, self-aware and reflective, with some sense of personal identity (Marsella, 1985). A critique of the Cartesian epistemological subject and bourgeois egoism, the emphasis that humans are intrinsically social beings, embedded in a web of social relations – which implies that human social identity is complex and 'multiple' – does not imply in the least that at a psychological level the human personality is fragmented or lacks coherence and unity. Laing hinted that behaviourist psychology and Cartesian philosophy with their 'schizoid theory', were mystifying, pathological discourses (1967: 44), and the same could be said of some post-modernist theory! But self conceptions, and a person's social identity, as I discussed in an earlier study, are by no means isomorphic with cultural conceptions of the person, for social identity, in the Malawian context specifically, relates to other social experiences – in respect to a person's age, gender, ethnic and religious affiliation, occupational and recreational interests, kinship roles and relations, as well as to their inherent character – *makhalidwe* – and general life experiences. As I put it, personal being (self) involves a social identity that is wider in scope than cultural definitions of the person (1994: 14).

One academic, with some pomposity, suggested to me that the distinction I make between humanity and conceptions of the person is 'embarrassingly stupid' and stridently proclaimed that 'all social beings are persons'. The distinction between the person as a generic being (ontology), and cultural conceptions of the 'person' (as a normative or ideological category) is, of course, one of long-standing, and has been affirmed by moral philosophers (like Singer) and by generations of anthropologists, particularly those pioneers of psychological anthropology (Rivers, Mauss, Hallowell, Fortes) whose work I have discussed at length elsewhere (1985, 1994). In a decade of 'post-modern' scholarship when various meanings of the person are collapsed under the concept of the 'subject', and the subject in turn is conceptualized in the most isomorphic and reductive fashion as simply an 'effect' or a 'product' of such abstractions as language, discourses or power, the distinctions made by an earlier generation of anthropologists, outlined above, seem to me important. Needless to say, as we shall explore in this study, social beings (ants, termites, banded mongooses, some humans) are not necessarily considered 'persons' in the Malawian context whereas some non-social beings and entitites (puff adder, python, winds, divining instruments) may be conceived as 'persons' or social agents. At least to the degree that they are envisaged as embodying or manifesting spiritual beings.

It has long been recognized, of course, by social scientists that humans in all cultures are intrinsically social beings, and that self-identity – personhood – is complex, shifting, composite, relational and involves multiple identities. Such identities may often be fragmentary, conflicting, ambiguous, or even alienating. In different contexts certain identities may be given primacy – socialists emphasize class identity, religious fundamentalists their Christian or Islamic identity, feminists gender identity, and white supremacists or black nationalists racial identity, whereas anthropologists tend to put an inordinate amount of emphasis on ethnic identity. But it has always been recognized that self-identity is composed of multiple identities or relations – relating to family, kinship, locality, gender, class, occupation, religion, race, politics and ethnicity – although some scholars write as if this was some recent discovery of post-modern anthropologists (Moore, 1994b: 55; England, 1996: 275). Long ago Radcliffe-Brown described the person as a relational being. He wrote:

> The human being as a person is a complex of social relationships. He is a citizen of England, a husband and a father, a bricklayer, a member of a particular Methodist congregation, a voter in a certain constituency, a member of his trade union, an adherent of the labour party, and so on. Note that each of these descriptions refers to a social relationship. (1952: 194)

Thus working-class men in England – who are thought to typify 'modernity' – are, like Malawians and people everywhere, social beings with multiple identities. Of course, in a psychological sense, they have a unity, a self, reflected in their individuality, and in their sense of subjective agency. This is quite distinct from the 'unitary subject' that is reflected in cultural (ideological) conceptions of the person derived from Cartesian meta-physics and bourgeois (capitalist) political theory, which depicts the human person as an isolated, asocial, bounded and homogenous entity. Even Descartes himself, in his letters, recognized that in ordinary everyday life the mind/body split was untenable, and that people were social (i.e. relational) beings (Leclerc, 1958: 58; Descartes, 1970: 172; Clark, 1993: 55).

It has long been known, of course, ever since the days of Burckhardt, that so-called 'Western' culture presents the self (body) as deeply 'individualized' or 'bounded', sharply demarcated from its natural and social environments. But to set up an exotic dualism between 'us' (the so-called 'Western person') and 'them' (Malawian or other cultures) in the fashion of Shweder and Strathern is unhelpful and obfuscating, and verily *equates* the self-conceptions of ordinary 'Western' people (which are just as relational (i.e. social) as that of other people) with bourgeois ideology, which depicts the human person either as a disembodied ego (read: capital) or as an asocial organism bounded by the skin, which can be utilized as a commodity (read: labour). The idea, for example, that Europeans eat simply for bodily nourishment while Melanesians eat to express and monitor 'relationships' (Strathern, 1988: 302), hardly accords with the literature on food habits among European people. While recognizing differences we need to get away from such exoticism. Thus to set up the individual (Western) and dividual (Melanesian) conceptions of the person as a dualistic opposition, as if they were antithetical concepts, is obfuscating (Lipuma, 1998).

All people are not only social beings (*dividuals*) but unique individuals, actual entities, and must be so logically and dialectically in order to be dividual. Indeed individuality is a defining feature of personhood, and ought not to be equated with bourgeois individualism.

Thus to re-affirm, people in Malawi like humans everywhere see the human person as constituted of multiple identities, and as being a participant in a wide range of social relationships and groups, based on locality, kinship, ethnicity, occupation, religious and political affiliations and gender, as well as being intrinsically related to the natural world in varied ways – phenomenologically ('things') and ecologically. Spirit rituals in fact are largely devoted to establishing a relationship between a person, often a woman, and a particular spirit, who provides support and protection. This relationship becomes part of a persons social identity, but it does not displace other social relationships. The same may be said with regard to a person's affiliation to fundamentalist 'born-again' Christian groups in Malawi (Van Dijk 1992).

The notion that a person has a 'multiple identity' or self (personhood) is not some modern phenomenon, even less a characteristic of the post-modern condition (as many scholars seem to imply – as if we all had unitary Cartesian identities until Lyotard got disillusioned with Marxism!). It is evident throughout human history, and was clearly evident in Northern Zambesia during the pre-colonial period. As Ranger has perceptively written:

> Almost all recent studies of nineteenth century pre-colonial Africa have emphasised that far from there being a single tribal identity, most Africans moved in and out of multiple identities, defining themselves at one moment as subject to this chief, at another moment as a member of that cult, at another moment as part of this clan, and at yet another moment as an initiate in that professional guild. These overlapping networks of association and exchange extended over wide areas. (1983: 248)

This state of affairs has continued through the colonial and post-colonial period, even though colonial authorities, in order to establish their power through indirect rule, tended to reify 'tribal' – ethnic – divisions. Even chattel slaves, though defined as commodities 'things', and whose lives are naturally circumscribed by coercive power, do not cease to be human – to be social beings with personhood.

Concepts of the person have always been an important topic in African anthropology, as well as among African scholars, who since the time of Leopold Senghor and his theory of negritude, have offered discourses on the 'African personality'. This was particularly aimed at countering the racist stereotyping and negative portraits of African people that were conveyed in much colonial writing. It is beyond the scope of the present study to go into this vast literature here, particularly relating to the second topic (but see Abraham, 1962; Tembo, 1985; Mudimbe, 1988). I shall, instead, simply offer a summary of some of the key themes that have emerged from discussions on African conceptions of the person.

Firstly, African cultural conceptions of the person are complex and variable, implying what can almost be described as a 'faculty' theory of the human person. Thus many African cultures recognise that the person has many distinctive 'attributes' or 'principles', what Abraham calls 'factors and influences' (1962: 61). These relate to conceptions of a vital force ('breath' or life energy (*nyama*)), to a 'soul' independent of the body, to psychic concepts that refer to an individual's personality, to body constituents or substances, as well as to social 'aspects' which are often expressed in spiritual terms linking a person to a collectively of ancestors.

Such conceptions fit uneasily into Western dualistic philosophy – whether the body-soul of Plato, or body-mind of Cartesian metaphysics. Although such conceptions of the person reflect a spiritual ontology in many ways, the essential unity and substance of the person is often expressed in a concrete metaphysic and in concrete metaphors. There is thus no radical dualism between the material and spiritual (unseen) 'realms' of existence.

Secondly, African cultural conceptions of the person do not suggest an 'individuated' self-structure, but rather a sense in which the person is seen as intrinsically linked to the world, to his or her kin groups and to the ancestral spirits. As a Twi proverb puts it 'Man (i.e. a human person – the translation was probably faulty) is no palm nut, self-contained' (Taylor, 1963: 43). This did not imply the kind of holism, or mystical participation in which individuals did not conceive of themselves as separate from nature, or from other humans in his or her social community (Senghor, 1965: 26; Riesman, 1986: 74), such that they had no sense of their own individuality. It is important to recognize, as we shall later explore in relation to the strong communitarian ethos in Malawi, that persons 'exist in relation to others', and that in African societies the person 'can be understood in large part as constituted by those relations to which his position in the system is connected' – to quote from Riesman's perceptive essay (1986: 100). But we should recognize that the notion that the human person is fundamentally a social – i.e. a relational-being – is not unique to African (or Melanesian) societies, but is characteristic of human societies everywhere in their social praxis. We should recognize, too, that a socio-centric emphasis does not preclude an equal emphasis on individuality in African communities, although there is some variability in the degree to which a collectivist orientation may be expressed in a particular culture (Horton, 1983; Gyeke, 1987: 161–2; Kaphagawani, 1998: 173). As earlier structural Marxists seemed to confuse empirical knowledge and empiricism, so post-modernist anthropologists seem to conflate individuality and individualism (see Poole, 1994: 844–5 and Morris, 1994: 138–9), and thus came to suggest that we should exorcise the concept of the 'individual' (along with 'society' – misleadingly interpreted as a 'bounded entity') from theoretical discourse.

Riesman's plea for a 'person-centred' anthropology and for a 'phenomenological' approach that puts a focal emphasis on individual consciousness and subjective experience, though seen as countering the cultural determination of the idealist 'savoir African' tradition, is, however, equally limiting. For it is still caught up in the culture/psyche (experience) dialectic, for phenomenology as a many since Hiedegger have stressed – is thoroughly Cartesian in its emphasis on individual experience and consciousness. Human persons are more than creators of meaning – 'being a person is essentially a process of making meaning' (1986: 112) – they are also engaged in actively changing the world through social praxis, for as Hegel and Marx implied life is prior to thought. (For useful discussions of African conceptions of the person, besides those noted above see Beattie, 1980; Levine, 1982; Fortes, 1987: 247–86; and Jackson and Karp, 1990, and my own study, Morris, 1994: 118–47).

The Person as a Human Being

The Chewa term for a human person is *munthu* (plural *anthu*, Yao *mundu*). It is used in a rather restrictive sense to refer to human beings. It is not used with reference to God (*mulungu*), even though divinity is addressed frequently as ambuye (grandparent or male mother (MB) though rarely it seems as father (*bambo, tate*) at least outside the Christian context. People deny that the creator spirit is a person: it is rather the creator of persons. Nor is *munthu* used in reference to spirits (*mizimu*) of the dead, or animals, even though humans by the use of medicines may take animal form. The spirits of the ancestors and witch-spirits may also take animal form. The character of the animal is related to the spirits whose form it is: if a witch takes the shape of a lion it is dangerous and destructive of humans and livestock; while if it embodies the spirit of a dead chief, the lion will be protective and harmless. The divinity may also take animal form – as a python (*nsato, thunga*). And spirits often possess humans. Despite these transformations there is a pervasive sense in Malawian culture that the divinity, spirits of the dead, humans and animals are different kinds of beings. The distinctions are not radical, but they are ontologically important, and all transformations recognize the differences and are expressed by such terms as – *sanduka* to change shape or form, *ku-lowa* to enter, *ku-gwira* to take hold.

Although for Malawian people there is no radical dualism between people and animals, an ontological distinction is nonetheless maintained. Tim Ingold has suggested that non-Western people see both animals and humans as 'persons'. This does not accord with the Malawian ethnography. Malawians recognize, that mammals, like humans, have agency, awareness and intentionally – as well as having knowledge (*nzeru*) and share similar 'sentiments' like shame or compassion, but this does not indicate that they are people even though in folk tales humans may be described as 'animals (meat) without hair' (*nyama opanda ubweya*). In critiquing the radical dualism between animals and humans – the nature/ culture dualism – Tim Ingold seems to collapse into an undifferiated

– 50 –

identity 'a night in which . . . all cows are black' in Hegel's famous phrase (1807: 9) – suggesting that animals *are* persons and that they are 'ontologically equivalent' with humans, humans and animals constituting 'real relational unities' (Ingold, 1988: xxiv). Malawians affirm that humans are 'animals', but animals are not necessarily 'persons', either in an ontological sense, or normatively, even though in specific contexts spirits may take animal form (lion, puff adder, python) and thus the animals may be conceptualized as 'persons' (as chief, or a grandparent). But importantly, as with the *Ojibwa*, only spirits (or humans with special powers – medicines) *not* animals, have the ability to transform themselves into other forms of being. It is important to note, of course, that for the *Ojibwa* (as interpreted by Hallowell) 'non-human persons' refers not to animals per se but to the spiritual 'masters' of the animals, as well as to other 'spiritual' beings like the thunder bird, who are described by the *Ojibwa* themselves as 'our grandfathers'.

In this context it is worth noting Hallowell's reflections on the fact that while the *Ojibwa* often speak of bear and stones as if they were 'persons' this did not imply an ontological unity or conflation (1958: 65).

Prototypically, *munthu* means Bantu-speakers (Malawians), and people describe Europeans (*mzungu*) and Asians (*mwenye*) in a cultural sense as different, outsiders, *mlendo* (visitors). But both Europeans and Asians are recognized socially as people and Malawians refer to themselves as *anthu wakuda* (-da, black, dark, *kwada*, darkness). But Europeans are not white people, but *anthu wofira,* red people (-fira, red, fiery). (Yao *juamcejeu* redman, Sanderson, 1954: 31). One of my Yao friends said to me that Europeans are often described as *matamati* (tomatoes) which I took to refer, not to myself personally, but to the red-faced, bombastic, whisky-drinking colonial! In 1915 Rev Harry Kambwiri reported to a meeting of the Blantyre mission that local people considered Europeans to be *zirombo* (wild animals) that came from the water (Linden, 1974: 93). The term *zirombo* seems to have been widely used during the colonial period, by the Watchtower preachers especially, to describe the Catholic missionaries, as well as Europeans more generally. A clear ontological and moral distinction, however, is always between humans (*munthu*) and animals/witches (*nyama/chirombo, mfiti*).

The distinction Malawians make between *munthu* (the human person) and *mzungu* (European) is quite misleading interpreted by Deborah Kaspin. Rather than interpreting this distinction prototypically, as in terms of their mode of classification, or cosmologically, in terms of the cultural categories – which in fact she emphasizes – she imposes a Western dualistic metaphysic on to the Malawian ethnography, suggesting that

Europeans are not 'people' (i.e. *anthu*) (1993: 47). But, as she notes, Europeans are quintessentially 'outsiders' (*mlendo*) (who are people!) – that is like hunters, the Nyau, male affines and spirits, which are all associated with the woodland and with wild animals (*zirombo*). But 'outsiders' are an integral part of the Malawian conception of the world. If Malawians did conceive of Europeans as non-people sexual relations and marriage with them, on the part of Malawians, would be inconceivable! Needless to say, all my friends when asked if Europeans were people (*kodi mzungu a munthu?*) replied affirmatively, though not a person truly (yeni-yeni)! (ie in a normative sense). (For reflections on the person as a prototype category, and criticisms of a similar standpoint by Benedict and Leach see Morris 1991b: 175.)

My own interpretation has been confirmed by the Malawian scholar, Didier Kaphagawani, who suggests that when Chewa people say that 'whites are not human' (*Azungu siwanthu*) they are not indicating that Europeans are non-human but rather that they are not 'persons' in terms of Chewa understanding of personhood (1998: 171).

Although Malawians clearly recognize that people are conscious beings, and think (*ganiza*) they do not have a concept of 'mind', and thus do not articulate a body/mind dualism. Karl Peltzer's use of the term *mtima* (heart) as a synonym for 'mind' is misleading, as is his use of *asewera* (to dance, play, amuse oneself) for 'group' and *khalidwe* – which essentially refers to the nature or inherit disposition of an animal or person – for 'personhood'. And following Riesman, Peltzer's suggestion that a Malawian person's 'basic value' resides in his 'fusion with the group' and that his or her behaviour is a 'manifestation of the collective virtues of the family and the group' is equally misleading, denying, as it does, the important emphasis that is also placed in Malawi, on individual autonomy and moral responsibility (Peltzer, 1987: 11–19, see my study *Chewa Medical Botany* (1996a: 109) for further reflections on Peltzer's dualistic paradigm).

As people elsewhere, Malawians recognize that a person is an embodied being, and as such is the locus of experience and moral agency. They recognize that their body (*thupi*) is both an intrinsic part of themselves, and people identify with the body, as well as looking upon the body as a possession. Thus they will use phrases like *zidza pa thupi pache*, 'they came upon him (his body)', or *osamwenya ine* 'do not hit me', identifying a person with his or her body. There are many context where the term *thupi* (body) is used by Malawians to refer to 'one's self' or to a person. In protecting a person from witches and harmful influences by the use of protective medicines, people will always refer to the body, *ku-tsirika thupi*.

On the other hand it is common to use the expression *thupi wanga,* my body, and the term *mwini* which means 'owner', 'guardian' – and is used with respect to the country *(dziko),* village *(mudzi),* household *(nyumba)* and the communal hunt *(uzimba),* as well as more generally – is also used to refer to personhood. *Mwini* thus means 'self', *mwiniache* 'he himself', *inendeka* 'me myself alone', *eniache* 'they themselves'. Like people everywhere Malawians thus recognize the duality of human existence, that we *are* active agents intrinsically connected in a practical way with the world – both material *(poietikos)* and human *(praxis)* – as well as being through our consciousness, contemplative beings, separate from the world, and able to look at ourselves self-reflectively *(theoria).* This duality is expressed through the personal pronoun 'I' *(ndi)* which expresses agency, *ndifuna* 'I want', *ndipita* 'I go', and the objective pronoun 'me' *(ine).* Thus 'I myself' *ndemwe,* 'I am' *ndine.*

In the most general terms Malawinans conceive of the human body (person) as consisting of four vital parts, the skin, bones *(pfupa),* the flesh *(mnofu)* and blood. As we have discussed in an earlier study, the skin of a human person and of animals generally, is symbolically thought of in terms of the essential form of the animal. The skin – *khungu, chikopa* (as hide) – is thus in a sense disposable like clothing, and may be adorned by another animal, who then takes the form of that particular species being. In Malawian folk tales the motif of a detachable skin plays a significant role, and, as we shall explore later in the study, both diviners and spirit mediums and the dancers in the Nyau and Chinambanda rituals often don the skins, masks or animal structures that are seen as embodying the spirits of the dead in animal form.

As we shall also discuss later, a child, is formed through a productive process, analogous to cooking, in which the blood of the woman and the semen of the man combine in the womb, and as flesh and bone assume the form of the infant. Blood *(magazi)* in its potent form *(chirope)* is for Malawians the essence of 'life' and is associated both with 'life' in terms of a living entity and vitality, and with the health and general wellbeing of persons: 'are you well (alive)?' *(muli ndi moyo?)* is a common greeting (Morris, 1996: 109). But blood is also associated with women and the matrilineal kin group, and with 'life force' and vitality in the most general sense. For Malawians (not just the Chewa) bodily humours are basic to human life, and as Kaspin perceptively affirms 'Moyo is concentrated in the blood, to a lesser degree in semen, and to a still lesser degree in saliva, milk, urine and phlegm. All bodily humours contain the life-force, which ebbs and flows through the course of life . . . Bodily fluids thus generate, sustain and invigorate life, while their diminishment leads to infertility and death' (1996: 568–9). As I have discussed in an earlier study with respect to Malawian hunting traditions (1998: 102–8), blood is also closely associated symbolically with 'heat' (*otentha*), and with fire and sexual activity. Heat, like blood, fire and sex, is essential to human life and is implicated in many important productive transformations (sexual and social reproduction (initiations), hunting, cooking, pot making, beer brewing, iron smelting) – but in excess can lead to destruction, sterility and famine. Thus the ideal bodily and social/ecological condition is not to be hot (or cold) but to be warm (-*fundu*).

As there is a close symbolic association between blood, women and matriliny, so there is also a close association between semen, men, bones and affinity, and in the boys initiation rites, particularly of the Yao (*jando*), medicines used for vitality and potency always emphasise hardness (-*limba*). Hunting implements and the horns of animals (*nyanga*) are also symbolically associated with the male sexual organs.

Two points may be made. Firstly, I think it is quite misleading, and oversystematizes the cultural reality, to conceive of the body as a 'microcosm' of the world in a 'unified theory' (Kaspin, 1996: 573). Although the body is conceived by Malawians as analogous to the earth, to be fertilized by the rains (symbolically linked to semen) it is only a woman's body that is so conceived, and her body represents not the cosmos but only the earth (*dziko la pansi*) and the village (*mudzi*), which is contrasted symbolically with the heavens (*kumwamba*) and the woodland. As in many other cultures, the woman's body in Malawi is symbolically linked to the garden, hearth and house.

Secondly, although Malawians conceive of the human infant as constituted of both male (semen) and female (blood) components, and closely identity blood, women and matriliny – sexual imagery like anthropomorphism is pervasive in Malawi culture – I would be extremely hesitant to make too many inferences from this in terms of the 'partible person' (Strathern, 1988; Busby, 1997). As far as I am aware Malawians do not conceive of the human infant – or the individual person – as an androgynous being. Neither does semen, as an 'objectified' substance which is part of a person, cease to be masculine. Because women are constituted as a human person through semen, this, equally, does not make semen 'feminine' or 'female' nor women androgynous. Finally, because a man is an intrinsic part of the matrilineal kin group through his mother (blood) and blood is symbolically associated with women and matriliny, this does not make a man, as far as I am aware, either androgynous or a female in relation to this kin group. I have, however, discussed elsewhere (1998: 72) the fact that the mother's brother/brother as 'guardian' (*mwini*) of his sister (*mbumba*) is expected to reflect 'maternal' qualities, and thus to be protective and supportive in relation to his sisters, and to exemplify the peace and harmony necessary for the village community – in contrast to the man's role as a male affine. As an affine the emphasis is put on the man being a hunter and outsider, assertive, aggressive, strong, sexually potent – like a hyena or baboon. Equally, though, grandparents (*ambuye, agogo*) and the ancestors (*makolo*) are thought to be both female and male, I would be reluctant to describe them as therefore androgynous or as 'cross-sexed' – they are rather ungendered categories. As far as I am aware, all humans, as natural beings, have 'permeable' and 'partible' bodies and all human societies make analogical associations between sexual life and other social domains. Sexual imagery is thus pervasive and widespread in all cultures: Malawi is no exception.

Malawians also conceive of the human body as consisting of a number of parts and organs, all of which they share with the animal world, specifically mammals. All mammals possess a body (*thupi*) although the term will be figuratively used to describe types of grain. It is not however used to describe plants. All mammals are thus described as having certain body parts, those having particular salience being, head (*mutu*), chest (*chifuwa*), neck (*knosi*), throat (*mmero*), back (*msana*), heart (*mtima*), lungs (*mapupu*), liver (*mphafa*), stomach/belly (*mimba*), arms (*mikono*), legs (*miwendo*), the gall bladder (*ndulu*), the loins (*chuno*), genitals (*mapheto*), skin (*khungu* or *chikopa*) and intestines (*mathumbo*). The body will be described as having strength (*nyonga*) or power (*mphamwu*), as being hot (*otentha*) or cold (*ozizira*), and with humans it will be protected by medicines, through incisions made in the skin, into which the medicines are rubbed, by washing with medicines, or by the wearing of amulets (*mphinjiri*) or a medicine bag, (*chitumwa*) either around the neck or loins. The body is also described as having an inside (*m'kati*).

Although Malawians recognize the biological affinities between humans and mammals, recognizing that they both have life (*moyo*), blood (*magazi*), breath (*mphumo*) and reproduce their kind (*ku-bala*) they also stress the distinctiveness of humans. This is reflected in language use. Although humans, like animals, die (*-fa*), the passing of humans is described normally by the verb *ku-mwalira*. Both humans and mammals are sexual beings, but people in many contexts use the term *mphongo* and *thadzi* to refer respectively to male and female mammals. All creatures have existence and being (*ku-li, alipo* – s/he is well) but only humans are described normally as living or dwelling (*ku-khala*). The verb *ku-khala* has a wide range of meanings – to sit, to wait, to reside, to have (*ku-khala ndi mimba* – to be with child), to happen, to be at home-all with a sense of continuity. Makhalidwe thus essentially means a person's nature, character, disposition or customary behaviour – often with the sense that it is inherent (*chibadwa*, as born).

The three body parts that have particular salience with respect to the human personality are the belly (*mimba*), the head (*mutu*) and the heart (*mtima*), which, in a broad sense, refer to a person's physical, mental and emotional state. The term mimba in Chewa refers both to the stomach and to the womb. Digestive disorders are usually referred to by such expressions as *mukundipwteka m'mimba* (I have a sore/painful stomach), or *m'mimba kupotokola* (the stomach turns). On the other hand, the expressions *ku-tenga mimba* (to bring stomach) and *ali ndi mimba* (she is with stomach) are used to express conception or that a woman is with child. As I have discussed elsewhere (1991a) there are many physical ailments focused around the stomach, which seems to be the focus of physical wellbeing.

The head (*mutu*) on the other hand, is the locus of consciousness and thought. Although Malawians have a concept of brain (*ubongo*), and often use the term in the sense of mind – *ubongo wanu ndiwo uku-kuchititsani za matha*, 'it is your brain (mind) that makes you afraid' (Scott, 1929: 587) – all afflictions of a mental nature are discussed in terms of the head (*mutu*). These not only include the severe head complaints that are associated with sorcery (*matsenga*) and spirit illness such as *vimbuza* and *nantongwe (nyundo, mutu waukulu)* but also madness (*misala*). Spirit possession rites and the ailments identified with them (*majini, matzoka, nantongwe*), are normally associated with the head. One person said to me: *nthenda ya majini ndi mutu basi* – spirit illness is only a head ailment. The spirit may be seen as entering the head (*imalowa m'mutu*) and the initial stages of the possession syndrome are associated with fainting or collapsing (*kukomoka*) and trembling (*njenjemera*). Likewise, madness is seen in terms of a 'spinning' head (*mutu umazungulira*) and although it may be seen as an organic disorder and often treated through herbal medicines, it is essentially associated with the head *(mutu)*. Madness is seen as expressing itself in non-rational ways, that is, the kind of behaviour that is not associated with humans as moral agents. Such socially disrupting symptoms include: burning down huts, walking around naked, not washing, wandering aimlessly about, eating faeces, destroying crops and assaulting people and being without knowledge (*opanda nzeru*) (see Marwick, 1965: 225; Peltzer, 1987: 200–1; Morris, 1996a: 118–24).

With regard to consciousness, which is associated with the head, Malawians make a distinction between thinking (*-ganiza*) and knowledge (*nzeru*), the latter being something one has (*ali ndi nzeru*). Although

Malawians do not usually think of mammals as 'thinking', they frequently refer to them as having knowledge – even creatures like mice who have elaborate escape holes to make good their escape. Baboons and monkeys, especially, are seen as having *nzeru* (knowledge), but the process of knowing is *ku-dziwa,* which is a general term for knowing about something or someone. To know in terms of recognition however is *ku-zindikira* and a sign is *chizindikiro.* Given this distinction between 'knowing' *(kudziwa)* and knowledge *(nzeru)* some Malawian scholars have suggested that *nzeru* essentially means 'wisdom' and is associated with the cumulative experiential knowledge that older members of the community acquire (Kaphagawani and Chidammodzi, 1983). Stevenson Kumakanga's little booklet (1975) on Chewa proverbs is entitled *Nzeru za kale,* which could well be translated as *Wisdom of the Olden Time.* Mdziwa can mean 'one who knows' or an acquaintance. But wisdom and experience in Malawi is normally referred to as *luso* and this became the title of the University of Malawi literary journal. However a skilled person, like a blacksmith or builder, is called *mmisiri,* while astuteness, cleverness or cunning is *chenjera,* of which, in folk tales, the hare is the epitome. 'Beware of the dog' notices are always written in terms of being clever – *chenjera ndi garu.*

Although the heart is only infrequently mentioned with reference to afflictions – it may be described as 'beating' or 'hurting' *(mtima kugunda . . . kupweteka)* – the heart is seen, either figuratively or literally, as the locus of personal disposition, emotion, desire and character. To give strength is *ku wawa ntima (ku-wawa* – bitter, sour); to be gentle *ku-fatsa mtima (ku-fatsa* to be gentle or quiet); to be easily provoked *ku-psya ntima (ku-tembenuka,* to turn round); to be greedy, *ku kulidwa mtima, mtima wakulu (-kula,* large). If a person is kind, considerate, sensible, helpful he or she is 'with heart' *(ali ndi ntima),* if they are unkind, unhelpful and lacking in consideration for others, they are 'without heart' *(alibe mtima).* The 'heart' is thus the essence and focus of a person as a moral being. But it is always the body as a whole *(thupionse)* which is protected by medicines against witchcraft and sorcery. Kaphagawani has stressed that, as far as Chewa culture is concerned, by 'heart' *(ntima)* is meant 'the personality of an individual human being' (1998: 174).

In Malawi culture five senses are recognized – taste *(kulawa),* smell *(ku-nunkha),* sight *(ku-ona),* touch *(ku-khundza)* and hearing *(ku-mva).* Each is associated with a body part, respectively, the tongue *(lilime),* nose *(mfuno),* eye *(diso),* hand *(manja)* – with extensions and ear *(khutu).* In recognizing five senses, Malawians thus indicate their affinities to European cultures, to Aristotle and the classical Greek tradition, to

Buddhist psychology, to the Samkhya tradition of Indian philosophy, as well as to cultures throughout the world. These distinctions clearly have their basis in human biology. Because the Hausa recognize only two senses, with one term for sight and another for the other senses and the Hindu tradition considered the mind as a kind of sense and thus distinct from the soul (*atman*) and because contemporary scientists have broken down 'touch' into a multitude of specialized senses, Constance Classen has argued that the senses are a 'cultural construction', simply expressions of 'particular cultural codes of perception' (1993). If by 'construction' Classen means that culture creates the senses like a carpenter makes a table, then this is a highly misleading metaphor, for people see or hear independently of culture. If, on the other hand, she means by 'construction' the fact that cultural meanings influence the way we understand the world – including the senses – this is to suggest something has been common knowledge since Hegel.

Even the simple recognition of a bushpig or elephant involves the intentional act of meaning – giving, for we have no access to the world unmediated by language or cultural representations – as anthropologists have long emphasized, or sometimes overemphasized to the neglect of social praxis and human subjectivity. But of course an elephant, like the senses, has a reality, even though contemporary scientists might see them quite differently in terms of chemical and atomic substances. While emphasizing that the senses are purely cultural constructs, however, Classen assumes their reality in discussing the various 'sensory models' of different cultures, of which she gives a good account and the sensory shift in Western culture 'from olfaction to vision'. She even writes of the repression of sight among the Suya of Brazil and the repression of smell in Western culture as examples of 'culture subverting biology'(!) (1993: 8–9). So it would seem that smell and sight are not simply cultural constructs? There must be 'sight' for culture to suppress it?

Being closely associated with the natural world – men as hunters, women as gatherers of wild foods, especially fungi – rural Malawians tend to place an emphasis on all the senses. Women gathering mushrooms, as I have recorded elsewhere, will tear up the mushrooms and use taste and smell in identifying the species, as well as feeling the texture (Morris, 1987: 5). Men, while hunting, employ all the senses, especially hearing and smell – but this in no way implies a devaluing or suppression of vision. As we shall note, Chisiza argues that 'observation' is a distinctive characteristic of the African 'out-look' – in contrast with the Asian emphasis on inner 'meditation' and the Western emphasis on material acquisition and in actively transforming the environment. Although there have been important changes in Western culture, with its growing emphasis on vision and the suppression of the 'olfactory consciousness' it is much too simplistic to link this 'visualism' simply to the Enlightenment tradition or to see such 'visualism' as a uniquely Western phenomena. For the importance of vision was not only emphasized by the Romantics – who were against Enlightenment thought, but by many religious traditions – for salvation often tends to be described in terms of illumination, insight, enlightenment and spiritual adepts have been noted as seers or visionaries – all utilising sight as a metaphor. As Iris Murdoch rightly suggests 'The activity and imagery of vision is at the centre of human existence' (1992: 461). Vision in Malawi has similar connotations, for it is the essence of the diviner to make visible what is hidden (-*bisala*). Spirits of the dead also have a reality only when they are seen, either in dreams or in human or animal form, or their presence is observed – by mice or black ants taking away the food that has been placed as offerings. *Ku-ona* means both to see and to be true. The exclamation for 'truth' or 'truly' is *zoona, or zoonadi.* There is a proverb *kantu ndi aka kawa mu maso* (that which is the eyes is a (real) thing) (Young, 1931: 270). Although my interpretation has been questioned by one colleague, the Malawian philosopher, Kaphagawani affirms that

> the word which stands out as the Chewa equivalent of truth is *zoona*. This word literally means "the seen", because it is derivative of the verb, *kuona*, meaning "to see" (1998: 240)

Equally important, when hunters mimic animals, its purpose is to make them visible, to bring them into the open, so that they may be shot at. The importance that Malawians give to smell does not, then, imply that vision is repressed. Even cultures like the Suya of Amazonia who are reported to 'denigrate' and 'repress' vision, clearly use their sight in their subsistence activities, especially in their hunting? As Malawians, like most people everywhere, see themselves as diurnal mammals – the night is associated with witches, who are prototypically non-persons – the importance to them of touch, smell and hearing, does not entail either a denigration or a suppression of vision – quite the contrary. Openness, transparency are what is valued – particularly in their social relations.

A distinction also has to be made between 'visualism' – reflected in the so-called objective 'gaze', detached observation or 'looking', and 'seeing', as in Malawi, which implies meaningful participation in the world and accurate observation based on experiential knowledge. That early colonial anthropologists like Richards and Turner, were guilty of the former is debatable (see Fabian, 1983). As the mechanistic materialists of the pre-Enlightenment period were primarily interested in astronomy and you can neither hear, taste, touch nor smell the planets, it is not surprising that their emphasis was on 'sight' and 'visualism'! To accuse these mechanistic philosophers of 'visualism' is to completely misunderstand their rationalist project, which was to discover a 'hidden order' through 'intellectual intuition' (as Descartes called it), and to deny the validity of the senses, including sight. As de Fontenelle (1686) put it: 'Your true philosopher will not believe what he doth see' (See Hollis, 1994: 23–9).

It has to be recognised, of course, that Malawians, like all other humans are highly audio-visual beings and have little developed sense of smell. This is why they have hardly any vocabulary to describe smells, and rely on dogs as important aids in hunting. There is a sense in which animal species have different 'images' or 'world' views – that of humans being audio-visual, in contrast to the acoustic, tactile and olfactory images of other mammals (Turner, 1997: 110; Wilson, 1997: 110; Noske, 1997: 158).

The term for 'smell' in Malawi, like the English term, has essentially a double meaning, for -*nunkha* means both smells in general, as well as smells or aromas that are considered bad – *woipa*. A good smell is described by using the applied form of the verb -*ku-nunkhira*. Thus if you suggest simply that a person has a smell *nunkha*, as in English, this has negative connotations. *Pfungo* is also a general term for smell, and is a correlate of the term for nose (*mfuno, mphuno*). Significantly, the civet cat, which carries a strong scent – it is a member of the family Viverridae – has the common term *fungo*. Smells are generally categorized into those that are good, well, satisfying and those that are bad *pfungo loipa*, bad smells usually being associated with rotting vegetation, decaying matter, and the faeces of animals and humans. To defecate is *ku-nya* or *ku-nyera* and the faeces of humans and mammals is usually described as *manyera*, or *tudzi* (pl. *matudzi*). To express disgust is *iku-nyansa*. Given the close association of mammals with defecation it is noteworthy that this is sometimes reflected in language: *nyama* (wild animals/meat) and *nyani* (baboon). The dung of domestic animals is usually described as *ndowe*. All these are described as being a 'bad' (-*ipa*) smell. Malawian hunters recognize the importance of smell – of both themselves and the mammals that are hunted, which have distinctive smells. The droppings or contents of mice burrows will be smelled for indications of the mammals' presence, the smell of mammals is described as *chifwenthe*, and it particularly alludes to those mammals that have strong aromas – especially the mongooses (*nyenga*), zorilla (*kanyimbi*) and the civet cat (*chombwe, fungo*). Chiswiri also denotes the smell of mammals, and the common shrew, which carries a strong musky smell, is called *swiswiri*. Mammals are reputed to be able to smell the semen of a hunter who has recently engaged in sexual intercourse. It is said that Europeans have a very different smell to that of Malawians, and women have a stronger smell than that of men.

Hearing in Malawi is closely identified with feeling and understanding. Aching limbs due to malaria are described as *kumva malungo* and the verb -*mva* will be used not only with respect to hearing, but also with regard to experiences, such as the feeling of hunger (*kumva njala*), or the wind (*kumva mphepo*). But it is also with respect to understanding – and the admonitions *kumva!* or *kumvera!* which mean 'listen' or 'do you understand?' A response is expressed as *kumveka*. Listening to and hearing one another – *kumuvana* – is a clearly expressed ideal, particularly with regard to court cases (*mlandu*), whose function, as Marwick wrote, is essentially the removal of hatred and malice from human hearts by listening (*ku-mva*) and by 'patient examination and persuasion in terms of commonly accepted code' (1965: 226).

Taste (-*lawa*) in Malawi is linguistically related to testing, to trying out something, as well as setting-off early in the morning. With regard to food and medicines taste is described in terms of sweetness (*tsekemera*), bitter (*wawa*), sour – or rotten (*sasa*) and salty (*lungudza*). The verb *kukoma* is used to mean 'having a good or pleasant taste' and thus has a wide range of referents – to be good, kind, well, agreeable; and to be of pleasing or gentle disposition as in *kukoma mtima* – 'gentle heart'. This brings us to an important aspect of the Malawian conception of the person as a cultural ideal, and that is the fundamental emphasis that is placed on sociability. As elsewhere, a person is essentially defined in terms of moral agency, and moral status.

The Person as a Social Being

It is clear that Malawians very much agree with the Greeks that the human person is *zoon logon echon*, an animal with language and reason – or in Latin *animal rationale*, a rational animal (Krell 1978: 226). For the Malawians, however, the person is not only a being with a body and consciousness, but also a social being, and the veritable embodiment of the spirits of the dead. People in Malawi do not speak of a person as having a spirit or soul. They have no concept of an indwelling soul, and to ask as person if they have a spirit, *uli ndi mzimu*, is likely to be greeted with a quizzical look, for *mzimu* is what one becomes after *death*. But there is a sense in which living people are thought to be the embodiment of ancestral spirits, usually a grandparent of the same sex, whose name they often inherit. There is a sense, then, in which a person is an intrinsic part of a matrilineal group that includes both living and dead members. It is hardly to be wondered, then, that rural Malawians put an important emphasis on the person as a social being. In their social practices and in their rituals and oral traditions (folk tales, proverbs) they clearly express, as a 'cultural ideal', what a person should be. This ideal was lucidly expressed by Dunduza Chisiza in his essay 'The Outlook for Contemporary Africa' (1964).

What is of relevance in the present context is Chisiza's reflections on the African 'outlook', which essentially derive from his own rural background in Malawi. Comparing Africans with Easterners who are given to 'meditation' and to Westerners who have an 'inquisitive turn of mind' Chisiza suggests that Africans – Malawians – 'are fundamentally observers, penetrating observers, relying more on intuition than on the process of reasoning. We excel in neither mysticism nor in science or technology but in the field of human relations. This is where we can set an example for the rest of the world.' And he goes on:

> With us, life has meant the pursuit of happiness rather than the pursuit of beauty or truth. We pursue happiness by rejecting isolationism, individualism, negative emotions and tensions, on the one hand; and by laying emphasis on a communal way of life, by encouraging positive emotions and habitual relaxation, and by restraining our desires on the other. We live our lives in the present (1964: 46–7).

Chisiza emphasizes the crucial importance of kin relations and communal activities. Thus, dances and rituals are communal; hunting game animals is communal; fishing with hooks is always done in groups; agricultural tasks, he writes, are all done in parties of men or women. Individualism is foreign to us; we are by nature extroverts, he concludes – and so delight in humour, generosity, rhythm, sociability, kindness and hospitality. 'Our society' abhors melancholy, malice and revenge (1964: 49–53).

Such generalizations, are, of course, always problematic, but the emphasis on a communitarian ethos was expressed by all the early missionaries to Malawi and it still – as an ideal – has resonance in the contemporary rural context. The courtesy, the friendliness, the hospitality, the emphasis on peace (*ntendere*) and good neighbourliness – which often led to protracted court cases (*mlandu*) as parties sought to reach an amicable settlement agreeable to both parties in the dispute – all these were commented upon by early travellers and missionaries in Malawi (Mills, 1911: 227; Fraser, 1915: 51).

Duff McDonald records that anyone living a 'hermit's life' or living a solitary existence – which some men he knew did – were considered by relatives to be 'mad' (1882: 144). The social ideal strongly emphasized that a person should be intrinsically involved with his local kin group and in the early period the term for a free person – as opposed to a slave *kapolo* – was *mlukosyo*, which, in Yao literally means belonging to a kin group (*-kosya* – to care for; *lukosyo* – clan or kind). In rural areas at the present time there is still a strong emphasis that a good person (*munthu wabwino*) is generous, sociable, hospitable and actively engaged in the wellbeing of his or her neighbours, kin and dependants. Marwick (1965) writes of the 'intensely social orientation' of the Chewa of Zambia, and this applies equally to the rural Malawians. A recluse – someone who avoids the company of others – is the subject of derision, disapproval and is often feared as a potential witch. One man I knew well in the Domasi Valley, who had served in the Kings African Rifles during the Second World War, lived entirely on his own, visited only occasionally by his daughters. He was well versed in herbal knowledge, but I was strongly advised by my friends not to fraternize with him, as he was considered a witch (*mfiti*). A person who lives alone was clearly not felt to be real human person. Conviviality, warm-heartedness (*ali ndi mtima*), cheerfulness, someone who enjoys the company of others and who likes to visit and chat – *ku-cheza* is the widely used verb that expresses the combined virtues of visiting neighbours and conversing – these are cherished virtues. Chisimo is a special medicine that is commonly used to make a person agreeable and affable towards others – described as *ku-koma mtima*, to be good-hearted (*kukoma*, to be good, kind, agreeable). Conversely, of course, verbal abuse (*-tukwana*), aggressive behaviour (*-kalipa*), the open expression of anger (*-kwiya*) and malice and envy (*njiru*) towards other people are all strongly condemned. Malawians would probably have agreed with Schopenhauer that malice and compassion are fundamental human motivations, but for Malawians malice has no part in the makeup of the ideal person and certainly, as Chisiza empha-sized, melancholy and pessimism are not sentiments usually expressed by Malawians (see my discussion of Schopenhauer 1991b, 60–6).

Equally important is the very strong emphasis on sharing (*ku-gawa*). As noted elsewhere (1996b) the proceeds of a communal hunt, or even of an individual's hunting expedition, are always shared among partici-pants, kin and neighbours and the emphasis on sharing permeates all aspects of Malawi culture, with respect to beer brewing by women, income from wage labour or petty trade, or subsistence cultivation. This emphasis on sharing and on sociability – and a derogation of individualism – creates dilemmas and anxieties at all levels of social life. Such dilemmas and anxieties are even experienced by the ethnographer.

This emphasis in Malawian culture on generosity (*ufulu*, which also means freedom), on sharing, on amiability (*chisomo*) and on friendship (*chibwenzi*), does not imply – as Stephanie Netall suggests (1995) – that Malawians therefore put a premium on being meek, submissive, timid and 'innocent'. On the contrary, the Malawian conception of the person, emphasizes not only sociability but also that a person should be actively engaged in world. Those who are incompetent – especially regarding those life tasks that are linked to gender roles – who are lazy, leaving work to others, who do not actively and conscientiously fulfil their social obligations, who show impudence (*chipongwe*) towards other persons – such individuals are pitied or derided. Neither sociability, nor the emphasis on friendliness and being polite – lacking *chipongwe* – implies meekness or a denial of people's individuality. In fact the individuality of the person is strongly emphasized in Malawi. Should one meet a group of people on the path formal greetings are extended to *each* person. The inquiry *muli bwanji*? ('how are you?') is met with *ndili bwino, kaya inu?* ('I am well, how are you?'), to which the response is *ndili bwino* or *choncho* (the same). A person extends this greeting to every member of the group individually. People are often given nicknames that express their unique personality. One of my close friends was called *Nganga*. As he was an experienced and well-known herbalist I thought the name was derived from his interest (*sing'anga* – herbalist). However, he told me one day that he got the nickname because as a young lad he tripped over a stone – much to the amusement of everyone present. So they called him 'stone', the name being derived from the Yao *liganga*. When I worked at Zoa I was given the nickname *Mjambula* – because I was always making sketches on bits of paper. Jessie Williamson, who pioneered ethno-botanical researches in Malawi, was known by people in the Dowa hills as *Mdyachiani* 'what do you eat?' – as she was always asking people this question. Malawians thus put a focal emphasis on the individuality of the human person, as well as on the person as a moral agent with respect to the 'cultural ideal' of the person outlined earlier.

In contrasting the 'autonomous individualism' of Western culture with that of 'folk' cultures, Shweder and Bourne's suggestion that the 'socio-centric conception' of the person involves the notion that 'the individual per se is neither an object of importance nor inherently worthy of respect' and that the individual as a 'moral agent' ought 'not to be distinguished from the social status she or he occupies' (1984: 158) is not borne out of the Malawian ethnography. A human person in Malawi is thought worthy of respect, and as a moral agent is not identified with his or her social role, and social autonomy is acknowledged. A lack of individualism does not imply a lack of individuality (see Poole, 1994: 844–5; Morris, 1994: 138–9).

This cultural ideal of the person is expressed in terms of a number of moral sentiments that are strongly emphasized in Malawi culture, and I will briefly discuss some of these.

The first is that of shame (*manyazi*). Early writers, in discussing the emotions, suggested that Malawians – specifically the Nyanja – had no sense of shame (Stannus 1910: 287). Malawians do have a sense of shame, but it is not viewed in a negative sense – as a feeling of distress or humiliation at having committed some wrong – but rather as a positive attribute of a person. A person who does not have a sense of shame – expressed as *ku chita manyazi*, to 'make/do' shame – is not a good person. It is closely linked with another moral sentiment, that of respect (*ulemu*). People will say that shame is respect – *manyazi ndi ulemu* – for having a sense of shame is showing respect to people, particularly towards elders. Equally, a person with shame – it is something one has or does, *amakhale ndi manyazi* – is someone who has a good heart (*mtima wabwino*), shows compassion, and has thoughts of friendship (*chikondi*). The opposite of shame is *chipongwe*, cheek, insolence, showing no respect towards other people. A person who thus does not have shame (*opanda kuchita manyazi*), is not a good person (*munthu wabwino*).

Respect (*ulemu*) is also an important moral sentiment. This entails respect towards oneself, towards other people, particularly towards elders (*mkulu*), the local chief (*mfumu*) and the ancestral spirits (*mizimu ya makulo*) as well as respect towards the customs (*mwambo pl. miyambo*). This sentiment is instilled into people during their early life, particularly during initiation rites (*chinamwali*).

Another important moral sentiment is compassion or pity (*chisoni*). Compassion is a feeling people have (*kumva chisoni*) or should express (*kuchita chisoni*), when they encounter someone who is poor (*wosauka*), or ill, or recently bereaved. Compassion reflects appropriate feelings, and good thoughts (*maganizo wabwino*) that are the essential attributes of a person of good character. Compassion is love (*ndi chikondi*) and the 'heart of a person who has respect' – as one person expressed it to me.

Chikondi is thus another important moral sentiment, and one also sustained and promoted by the use of medicines (*mankwala*). Coudenhove wrote (1925: 100) that as Malawians lacked the kind of imagination that Europeans, had, they had no 'faculty to feel love'. Such a conception is quite misleading for the expression of love (*ku-konda*, to love, *chikondi*) and of friendship (*chibwenzi*) is highly valued in Malawi and deemed crucial to human relationships. What qualities people value most in the opposite sex is never expressed in gender roles – which seem to be taken for granted – but in terms of love (*chikondi*) and character (*makhalidwe*).

It is significant that although fear (*mantha*) is viewed in European cultures as a rather negative emotion or sentiment, Malawians often describe it as necessary attribute of the human personality – particularly as an attitude towards the spirits of the ancestors. Although fear is a necessary emotion when a person is confronted with something frightening (*-opsya*) or fierce (*-ukali*) – such as elephant or buffalo – with respect to the spirits it also has a moral quality for Malawians. One person said to me 'fear is good thoughts' (*mantha ndi kuganizo bwino*).

A very different and contrary moral sentiment, and one widely expressed in social discourse is that of jealousy (*nsanje*). Envy and jealousy are not considered to be good emotions, for they reflect a bad heart (*ndi kuipa mtima*). Jealousy is an emotion that destroys (*ku ononga*) close kin and neighbours (*anzake*, his own). It is seen as being provoked by other people's possessiveness, that they do not share but take everything to be their own (*choti zonse zikhale zache*). To envy or covet (*ku-dukidwa*) something or someone, is seen as an emotion that has dire social consequences, for it is linked with sorcery and witchcraft. Its salience as a moral sentiment is reflected in the fact that one herbalist I knew well, who spoke and knew very little English, frequently used the term 'jealously' in his divinatory rites.

It can be seen that the conceptions of the person in Malawi are intrinsically linked with moral concepts, and that although the person as a generic human being and the person as a cultural category or ideal are intrinsically linked, they are not coterminous. For in a sense a human being who is isolated from others, who is ungenerous, unhelpful, melancholy, individualistic and with a 'bad heart' (*mtima woipa*) is not a real person. Both these conceptions of course, are distinct from the notion of the person as a unique, individual self. A witch (*mfiti*) is a human being, and often a close kin, who is not because of his or her malevolent and selfish proclivities – considered a real person.

Indeed a witch can be defined as a generic human being who is not a real person – defined as a social and moral being – but who rather, motivated by greed, malice, anti-social tendencies, and using medicines, wreaks harm or even kills, his or her kin or neighbours. Witches (afiti) are associated with animals in four ways: an animal may be a sign (*chizindikiro*) of the presence of a witch; it may be used as an instrument or familiar by the witch; the witch or a person of evil intent may employ medicines to transform (*ku-sanduka*) themselves into animals that cause harm to other humans; and finally, after death, the spirit of the witch may take the form of an animal (*chiwanda*), which is conceived as intrinsically malevolent (*mzimu woipa*). It may thus be noted that in Malawian moral discourse a clear distinction is made between the good (*-bwino*) and the bad (*-ipa*) and thus that all the basic ontological categories have a moral import. Thus

Good	*Bad*
Munthu	Mfiti
(Person)	(Witch)
Nyama	Chirombo
(Game animal)	(Wild animal)
Mzimu	Chiwanda
(Ancestral spirit)	(Spirit of a bad person)

(For further discussion of divination and witchcraft in Malawi see Morris 1986, 1996: 143–66).

Although there is this crucial emphasis on the person as a social and moral being no radical divide – Heidegger's 'abyss' – is seen to exist between humans and mammals. Thus mammals are often discussed in terms of the above moral sentiments. Animals that are thought to express a sense of shame are domestic sheep (*nkhosa*), pangolin (*ngaka*), tortoise (*kamba*) and hedgehog (*chisoni*). All these in their behavioural attributes are seen as expressing shame. It will be noted that the name of the hedgehog is 'compassion', and, along with the domestic pigeon, sheep, baboon and the tortoise is also thought as emplifying this moral attribute. The baboon is said to have compassion, because it is seen as caring for its young, as using medicines, and as mourning its dead kin (*mzache akafa amalira kwambiri* – (when) its "kin" die, they cry a lot'). Elephants, too, are felt to express compassion in this way. Similarly, animals are seen by Malawians as expressing jealousy (*nsanje*) like humans, and in this regard the baboon, the domestic fowl (*nkhuku*), goat (*mbuzi*) are often mentioned. Fear (*mantha*) is also a sentiment that animals share with humans, and the prototypes in this regard are the grey duiker (*gwape*) and hyena (*fisi*).

Animals are also described as being gentle (*kufatsa*) (sheep, tortoise), as being fierce (elephant, lion, dog and leopard) and as having intelligence. This is expressed by the words *ili ndi nzeru* (it is with knowledge) or the animal is described as with cunning (*yochenjera*). Most mammals are described, in certain circumstances as having intelligence, but those particularly so regarded are the giant rat (which stores its food), hare, baboon and many field mice. Mammals that cause depredations to humans – leopard, monkey, baboon, hyena and bushpig – are often described as *nyama ya chipongwe* (insolent animals). Finally, it is worth noting that people sometimes use the term *unyama* (animality) to describe someone, especially a child, whose character, behaviour or appearance (*maonekedwe*) is felt not to match that expected of a human person – not relating to others *(sagwirizana)*, not washing or bathing regularly, doing things without sufficient thought, sleeping all the time, not heeding what they are told to do. Thus Malawians do not make a radical distinction between humans and other animals, but nevertheless the human person (*munthu*) is seen as ontologically distinct from both wild and domestic mammals (*nyama/chiweto/chirombo*).

Finally, it is worth noting that for many rural Malawians human life is seen as essentially fragile and precarious and as beset with difficulties. They thus acknowledge the importance of luck (*mwayi*) in human life.

–3–

Rituals of Childbirth and Womanhood

Sex and Sexuality

'Everybody knows that men and women are different.' With these words Ann Oakley began her seminal introductory text *Sex, Gender and Society* (1972). But the thrust of Oakley's book was to disentangle 'sex' as a biological category from 'gender' as a psychological and cultural one, gender being expressed in terms of social roles and gender identity. Oakley emphasized that although every society uses biological sex as a criterion for the ascription of gender, this is simply a 'starting point' or 'basis' and that there is no simple or reflective relationship between biological sex and gender. Recent studies have emphasized what has long been recognized, namely that sex itself is culturally 'constituted', and therefore, it is argued, the distinction between sex and gender is 'misleading' or 'redundant'. The term 'constituted' is derived from Husserlian phenomenology, and these suggestions imply a form of cultural idealism that oblates biology. Not only sex but everything in the world is culturally constituted, but to say this is not to deny the reality of sexual differences and elephants (see Assiter 1996: 112–36, for an important discussion, which upholds the sex/gender division, criticising both the biological determinists who reduce gender to sex, and the social constructionists – the feminists and post-modernist anthropologists who, following Foucault, completely efface biology and sexual difference). It is much more sensible to make a distinction between sex, sexuality and gender, or to view sex and gender as two distinct but overlapping domains of social practice, as two long-standing feminist anthropologists have suggested (Rubin, 1984; Caplan, 1987). Sexuality is then the socio-cultural construction of sex, as shaped and defined in specific human communities, and as earlier studies have shown, it is variable within the African context, although there are evidently common themes, particularly with regard to the association between heat and sexual relations (see the classical accounts by Kenyatta, 1938: 155–62; Schapera, 1940: 161–96).

Sex, as many people recognize, is one of the most basic of human activities, and it is the one activity, along with eating, that brings us closest to our mammalian kin, with whom – apparently – we share some 95 per cent of our genes. In Malawi sexual difference is taken for granted, as something that is 'natural', in the sense that this is how we are born (*chibadwa*). For Malawians we are born sexual beings, but neither our humanity, nor our gender identity, nor our sexuality is given at birth; they are something that is acquired in the course of one's life, and this is what this and the following chapter is all about – personhood and gender identity.

Malawians attitude to sex – by both men and women – is an extremely positive one. Sexual relations with a member of the opposite sex is seen as a wholesome, enjoyable, and necessary activity, and essential for general wellbeing. All people are seen as intrinsically sexual, and most Malawians I knew well refused to believe that there was any normal person who did not want to engage in and enjoy sex. They thus refused to believe that any Catholic priest or nun could possibly remain celibate, and usually pointed to plenty of evidence that indicated that priests and nuns, like everyone else, engaged in sexual activity. To participate in a sexual relationship was deemed to be important for one's general health and wellbeing, and the Malawian ethnography accords with how Jamaican men and women view sex: 'to have sexual intercourse is to avoid the danger of blocking up natural vitality and therefore it promotes health' (MacCormack and Draper, 1987: 155). Thus, for Malawians, to repress sex, or to be celibate, is not held to be conducive to a healthy life – and this is quite separate from the equal emphasis on the bearing of children. A desire for sex is seen as instinctive, and as akin to thirst – to want sex is expressed in terms of being thirsty (*ku-ludzu*), and powerful sexual passions, which are also associated with animals like the dog, baboon and the hyena, are described as *chilakolako*. Significantly, such desires are also linked with meat and food. Foucault's (1979) contention that sexual desires and instinct is purely a cultural artifact hardly does justice to how Malawians view sex. One Malawian described the sexual prohibitions relating to pregnancy, which both a man and a woman have to undergo, as a kind of 'punishment' (Lumeta, 1975: 24).

Even spirit mediums associated with the various rain shrines, who are 'wives' of the spirit (*mkazi achisumphi*) who should remain celibate, have sexual relations, for they are visited at night by a shrine official (*kamundi*) who represents the spirit in the form of a python (*thunga*). The relationship between the spirit mediums and spirits throughout Malawi is often of a sexual nature, except when it involves matrilineal kin.

But importantly although there is an important emphasis put on sexual expression – openly depicted, as we shall see in the initiation rites (much to the horror of the Christian missionaries), Malawian culture advocates neither promiscuity nor does it see sex as unproblematic. For sexual intercourse is symbolically associated with blood and fire, and also with the generation of heat (*otentha*). We discuss this symbolism below.

There is no Malawian term for 'sex'. This does not imply that they have no conception of it, for they describe sexual intercourse by the use of such terms as *kukwatana* (implying marriage, *kukwata*, to marry – for men, *kwatiwa* – for women) and *kugonana* (to lie together), and there is often the association of sharing a mat (*mphasa*, made of bamboo reed *Phragmites*). Sometimes the term *kugundana*, may be used, meaning to knock against each other. Sexual desire and activity of humans is distinguished from animals, for sexual activity among animals is referred to as *kukwerana*, to climb on each other. Adultery (*chigololo*) is considered a separate category, and although the ideal is a close conjugal bond that constitutes a household (*banja*), people freely engage in extra-marital sexual relationships. But while in a partnership both men and women put an emphasis on love, sharing resources, and being 'faithful' (expressed as *sayendayenda*, not to wander about). People's motivations for sex are complex and varied, but include: to satisfy sexual desires and for pleasure, to express love and affirmation of a relationship, to have children, and to obtain the services and resources of a partner. Some people have conjugal relationships that are longstanding or lifelong, but most people in rural areas that I knew well had formed a series of marriages during their lifetime, and women had had children by two or three men – all within established relationships. As around a third of all rural households are matricentric and the women is without a permanent male partner, women often have transient relationships with men, essentially exchanging sex for money (to buy clothes, food for their children and so forth) in ways reminiscent of the exchange of sex for meat noted by Ntara.

Because sex is viewed positively by Malawians, sexual relations begin early in life, and extra-marital relationships are common, the latter are usually referred to as friendships (*chibwenzi*), and are sometimes long-standing. Often men have polygamous relationships visiting and staying with women – who are viewed as spouses *akazi anga* – in different villages. A girl's first sexual experience is between eight and twelve years, while that of a boy between fifteen and sixteen (McAuliffe, 1994). Sexual relations thus begin at an early age, and such experiences, though criticized by some men and Christians, is seen by many Malawians as an important preparation for married life. Girls first menstruate between thirteen and fourteen years on average, and around 60 per cent of young women interviewed by Helitzer-Allen (1993) reported as having had sex before either menstruation and/or initiation, usually with an older boy. Many girls thus became pregnant at a very early age – and this has long been the case, Williamson noting, more than 50 years ago, that many girls had their first child when they were fifteen to sixteen years of age. This is still common (Williamson, 1940: 6).

There is strong emphasis on heterosexuality in Malawi, and on being sexual. A man who is impotent is derided, and is seen as lacking strength (*opanda mphamvu*), and there are inumerable medicines that are taken by men as potency medicine. Equally, there is a strong emphasis on sexuality and child rearing among women, and there is stress on having firm breasts and on elongating the labia, and medicines are used to enhance sexual receptivity. The stretching of the labia, as we shall note, plays an important part in the girls' initiation, and this is done to produce maximum sexual pleasure for both partners, as well as to ensure pregnancy. The wearing of beads around the waist by a woman is viewed as sexually enhancing, and one person remarked that when they hear the sound of beads, boys and young men become sexually excited, their penises becoming erect (*mbolo kudzuka*). Normally sexual matters are not discussed in public, but both songs and dances in the rituals are explicit about sex, and often sexually provocative, and women (who are not prostitutes) may be quite explicit in making sexual proposals to a man. I was once surrounded by a group of women whom I knew, who were on the way to collect water to brew beer for a *litiwo* ceremony. They teased and ridiculed me regarding my sexual inadequacies, one elderly woman – old enough to be my mother – moving her hips provocatively in a sexual manner, inviting me to share her mat with her that night – all the other women ululating (*ntungululu*) in merriment.

Sexual relations with close matrikin (*incest*), with animals (*bestiality*) and with a person of the same sex (*homosexuality*), though they evidently occur, do not meet with approval by most Malawians. The first is seen as destroying the kin group (*mbumba*), and the second is associated with *mfiti* (witchcraft). Young girls often form close relationships, and stimulate each other's genitals, but two women cohabiting is not common, and it is of interest that some African feminists see the emphasis on lesbianism as being a Western phenomenon (McFadden, 1992: 169). When I discussed sexual relations between women with one of my friends, she burst out laughing, and exclaimed *bwanji* ('how?'). The central focus is thus on heterosexuality, on enjoying sex, and having children.

In rituals, and more generally in social life, there are symbolic associations between certain objects and attributes and the gender division. Thus softness (*-fewa*) is associated with women, along with such items as the winnowing basket (*lichero*), clay pot (*mbiya*) and the grass head ring (*nkhata*), while men are associated with hardness (*-limba*), and with such things as hardwood trees – *mphingo* (*Dalbergia melanoxylon*), *mwanga* (*Pericopsis angolensis*) and *mlombwa* (*Pterocarpus angolensis*) – and metal tools (axe, hunting arrows, spears).

Malawians tend to see life and death not in radical dualistic terms, but as polar aspects of an ongoing cyclic process, with life associated with the village, with living matrikin and the present, while death is associated with the woodland, the spirits of the dead ancestors and the past (*kale*). The two aspects of this ecological cycle, if one may call it that, life and death, are interdependent, for living people (*anthu*) must continually make offerings to their dead ancestors, and, in the past, when a village community was abandoned, the area and the gardens reverted back to woodland. In the past, when shifting cultivation was still practised, there were elaborate rituals centred around the establishment of a new village community, with the ceremonial making of fire by means of fire sticks, and other rituals to symbolically 'warm' (*kufunda*) the place. Likewise, it is from the woodland, and from the spirits of the ancestors that essential activating agencies – *chizimba* medicines and rain – and fertility comes to sustain living people. The human lifecycle is but a part – the living part – of this ongoing ecological process. In a sense, throughout life a person is animated by the spirits of the ancestors – one's *ambuye*, grandparents, and on death a person will become transformed (*kusanduka*) into a spirit (*mzimu*). During this life a person passes through several clearly defined stages, and this is particularly elaborated in the rituals that focus around women, and I shall, in this chapter, discuss various rituals, indicating, where appropriate, the role that animals play in them.

Rituals of Childbirth

According to older women, a human child is formed on conception from the blood of the woman combined with the semen of the man, the semen serving as a kind of activating agent, that is analogous to *chizimba* medicines, and to *ndiwo* relish in the ingestion of medicinal and food substances. It is deemed important, after the woman becomes pregnant – *akupatsa mimba*, to give a stomach, or *mimba woima*, the stomach stands, i.e. the menstrual blood has stopped flowing – for the couple to continue to have sexual intercourse in the early months, as the semen is believed to strengthen the blood of the child.

As throughout Malawi symbolic equations are made between semen and rainfall (water, cool, white) and the blood of the woman and the land (garden, pot, hot, red) analogical correspondences are often made between agricultural production and human procreation. As maize needs water, so the formation of the child needs a continuous supply of semen. As Kaspin writes – rather misleadingly, implying that such knowledge is of an esoteric kind limited to *anamkhungwi* – it is suggested that:

> just as garden crops require a lengthy rainy season, gestation requires a lengthy period of sexual activity during pregnancy. For this reason they urge expecting couples to engage in sex nearly every day. (1996: 572)

After four months the woman is described as *mpakati* (in the middle) or as *ali ndi mimba*, she is with stomach, and from then on there must be no sexual contact between the woman and her husband. Nor must the man have sexual relations with any other woman, for this is held to 'cut' his spouse, and to have serious consequences both for her and their child. A woman must be kept in a 'cool' (*ozizira*) condition, and must not therefore come into direct contact with any sexually active person who is deemed to be 'hot' (*otentha*). Around the eighth month a woman is described as *wakutha* (satisfied) or *watopa* (tired), and the womb is described as turning *ku-tembenuza*.

The birth of the child is in a secluded place or house. In the past Yao women had their babies delivered in the woodland. Many women I knew affirmed that the reason for this is that the midwife could be sure that the woman and child remained cool, for unlike the village environs, the woodland was considered a cool place. In rural areas the woman is assisted in giving birth by a local midwife, *namkhungwi* or *nkhalira*, helped by the woman's close relatives, often affines (*alamu*) – never, it seems, her own mother. Various lubricating medicines are used to assist the birth, of which the *mphosa* (*Annona senegalensis*) is the most common. For about a week the woman is confined to her house or special hut, the period of confinement being known as *chikuta*. The umbilical cord and the afterbirth (*katumba*) is thrown on to the ash heap or in the refuge pit (*dzenje*). Initially the young child is described as *chinthu* (thing) and is not considered a person, and should he or she die in the early months, or if there is a miscarriage, older women relatives of the woman will take the body and dispose of it without ceremony in the woodland. During the first three or four days of the child's life, the baby is looked after by one of the elderly grandmothers, who is considered 'cool'. She washes the baby. The mother is not allowed to cook food, nor is anyone allowed to touch the baby, especially a woman who has recently menstruated or a person who has recently had sex. Towards the end of the week there is a special washing with medicines, a time called *chilowera*, to enter (the world), the medicines being described as *mpungabwe*, the aromatic *Ocimum canum* mixed with msatsi castor oil (*Ricinus communis*), which is believed to have strengthening properties. The oil is prepared only by women past child bearing. This is done to protect the child from the disease *tsempho*, discussed below. Around the child's waist or neck is placed a piece of string on which is threaded small pieces of wood (*mphinjiri*), which serve as protective amulets. The head of the child is also shaved at the end of the *chikuta* period. The birth of a child is a time of great rejoicing, and the women of the village ululate (*ntungululu*), a high pitched yodelling; once for a boy, twice for a girl. This is because girls are more highly valued in a matrilineal culture. After about a week the baby is taken out of the house (*kuturuka chikuta*), and is now described as *mwana wa khanda*. But the child is still considered to be in a vulnerable condition, and must be kept 'cool' and protected by medicines — specifically against witches (*afiti*) and the disease *tsempho*. Until around five or six months, when the *ku-tenga mwana* ceremony is held, the woman and her husband must continue to refrain from sexual activity — to do otherwise would be to destroy (*-ononga*) or cut (*-dula*) the child. Nor must the child be allowed to come into contact with anyone in a 'hot' condition — a sexually active person.

Around six months after the birth of the child a *kutenga mwana* ritual (*ku-tenga*, to bring) is enacted. With respect to this ritual the child becomes a person. If the child should die before the ceremony, he or she is hurriedly buried, as said, in the woodland, in a shallow grave. Only women are said to attend the burial, and Stannus records that the body of such a child is called *litunu*, hyena. It thus still belongs to the woodland (1922: 239). Although it is difficult to assess just how widespread this ritual is at the present time, many women herbalists I knew well in the Shire Highlands often talked about the *ku-tenga mwana* rite, in relation to medicines used for young children. The crux of the ceremony was this. A woman and her husband must have sexual intercourse, with the woman keeping her legs closed, and the young child held between them. The man must not fail to achieve an erection otherwise he is deemed to have missed (*ku-tsempha*) the child, and he will be blamed for any subsequent illness of the child. The semen and vaginal secretions are rubbed on the child, and s/he is also passed over the fire. Father Malipa (1971) suggests that anointing the child with semen was seen as the link between the ancestral spirits and the new child. They thus make the child a person. The essence of the ceremony is to warm the child (*kufunda*), to bring to an end the 'cool' period. The child is now brought into the world to be more freely handed by people, is given a name, and the couple can now resume normal sexual relations. If the husband is away, it is important that either another couple perform the ritual for the benefit of the child, or relatives of the woman will arrange, with the woman's consent, for a *fisi* (hyena), a surrogate male to perform the sexual intercourse with the woman. The hyena is viewed by Malawians not only to be associated with witches (*afiti*), but also to be a highly sexual creature. Stannus notes that, among the Yaos, to end the woman's confinement a piece of burning wood was placed between her legs and allowed to smoulder for several hours – its function is to 'warm' the woman symbolically, but Stannus refers to this as a 'means of purification', assuming that the pregnant woman is ritually in a 'unclean' condition (Stannus, 1910: 311). It is, I think, misleading and unhelpful to impose on the Malawian ethnography notions such as ritual 'uncleanliness' or 'purity', when the key theme is the dangerous implications of 'hotness' (*otentha*) which stems from blood (as in the hunting of large mammals like the kudu, elephant and eland, and when a woman menstruates), as well as from sexual intercourse. A woman while menstruating, a man hunting large mammals, and a person who has had sex are not 'unclean', but as they generate and transmit 'heat' they are ritually dangerous to others – particularly people involved in other transformatory activities – childbirth, initiations, hunting, pot making, beer brewing. Similarly, when Margaret Read writes that 'During and after the confinement the woman is in a state of "uncleanness" and is not allowed to cook food for other people', this is a misleading inference. As a pregnant woman (and the child) must remain 'cool' during the *chikuta* period, she cannot cook as this will make her 'hot', for the same reason a menstruating woman, who is a cold condition, cannot cook for her husband or attend to the fire in the house. She is not 'untouchable' because 'unclean', but, like a child and a pregnant woman, is in a vulnerable condition, and must be kept 'cool'. But because a menstruating woman sheds blood – which is 'hot' – she is dangerous to others, especially to men (Berry and Petty, 1992: 52; Young, 1931: 40).

The first-born child among people in Malawi is called *mwana wa chisamba*, on account of being associated with the first pregnancy ceremony *chisamba*, (*Yao litiwo*), which is described below. Any child born after is said to tread on the child's head, (*woponda mnzache pamutu*), and an importance is always stressed on spacing the births of children.

Until the child has been virtually incorporated into the matrilineage, at the *kutenga mwana* ceremony, it has to be protected, and kept in a 'cool' condition – as do hunters, iron-smelters and initiates. Bruwer suggests (1948: 186) that such a child is a source of 'menace' to others, and thus subject to taboos. But in reality it is the child – like a menstruating woman and a hunter – who is ritually vulnerable and susceptible to the influences of others, especially those in a 'hot' condition, namely those who have recently had sexual relations. It is these people who might seriously impair the health and wellbeing of the child – especially an adulterous father. To describe the child as a 'menace' is completely contrary to how Malawians view a young child – as in need of care and protection, practical, medicinal and ritual.

As with women everywhere, pregnant women in Malawi during pregnancy often develop cravings for certain foods, described as *chilakolako*, desire. Common among such cravings is the soil from termite hills (*chulu*), which are probably rich in minerals. (For early discussions of the *kutenga mwana* rite see Williamson, 1940: 2; Rangeley, 1948: 37–8; Bruwer, 1949: 196; Van Breugel, 1976: 234–9).

Bruwer concludes that up to the time of the *kutenga mwana* ritual, the child was *mwana wa khanda*, a baby, and thus not looked upon as a full member of the community, a person for whom funerary rites would be conducted. Although people recognize and describe children as male (*wamwamuna*) and female (*wamkazi*), in the early formative years there is not a strong emphasis on gender. But children tend to be recognized as full human personalities when they begin to speak. Weaning often extends two or three years, but children are quickly introduced to solid foods in the form of *phala*, a thin porridge made of maize flour. The child also begins to learn in social practice what is later emphasized in the ritual context during the initiations, namely the basic norms of social life, some of which are moral edicts relating to the person, others being specific to gender. In the early years children spend a lot of time with their grandmothers, from whom they receive a great deal of care, fostering and education. But as time goes by, young girls increasingly spend time with their mothers, helping in the household tasks, fetching water, pounding grain, collecting vegetables and firewood, usually accompanying her mother. Out of school, boys tend to go around in groups hunting grasshoppers and mice. In the past dormitories for young men (*gowero*) was an important institution.

Blood, Sex and Fire

In an earlier study, particularly in relation to hunting rituals, we have discussed the hot/cold ritual symbolism that pervades Malawian culture. This symbolism is closely linked, though not coterminous, with *mdulo* or *tsempho*, which, as a disease category, is a central concept in Malawian culture, particularly among Chewa, Nyanja and Mang'anja people. Ndaka is the Yao equivalent. It has been discussed at length by various writers. In this section I want to focus on this category, and on the hot/cold symbolism that underlies it. But first I want to briefly outline, for comparative purposes, the ritual symbolism relating to hot/cold in two African people – the Southern Bantu and the Ju/'hoan hunter-gatherers, although such symbolism, of course, is widespread throughout the world, though culturally variable.

In his discussion of the Southern Bantu – Venda, Tsonga, Sotho, Tswana and Nguni peoples – Adam Kuper (1982) emphasized that their culture focused on a dialectic between pastoralism, focused around men, and agriculture, which was largely the domain of women. Hunting was not an important subsistence activity, although it had a ritual function. The key institution was bridewealth, centred on the idea that 'cattle beget children', involving an exchange between the two socio-economic domains. In contrast, he noted, the traditional division of labour among the central Bantu, was concerned mainly with horticulture and hunting, and bridewealth was evident only among people like the Ila-Tonga of Zambia, who kept cattle. But although Kuper's study focuses on the set of exchanges between the male domain of pastoral production and the female domain of agriculture, he also notes another dimension to the thought of the Southern Bantu, namely the opposition between 'hot' and 'cool'.

Certain things and conditions are considered to be 'cool' and 'white', such as water, rain, and semen, which are fertilizing agents. Semen is directly associated with water and rain, and the fertilization of woman is seen as analogous to the fertilization of the fields by rain water.

On the other hand there are things which are 'hot' and 'red', such as lightning, fire and blood. These are considered dangerous, and may cause sterility or death. There is a tendency for women and female sexuality to be regarded as hot and potentially dangerous – especially to men and cattle. Cattle are always thought to be 'cool', and cattle dung is used as a cooling and healing agent.

Witches are the prototype of 'danger'. They are generally represented as women and are seen as being preoccupied with destroying the fertility of humans, cattle and the fields (Berglund, 1975: 268). Witches are viewed as having insatiable sexual appetites. Female night witches are associated with heat, and the 'fires of the night'. They are directly contrasted with the ancestors who are thought to be white and cool.

Menstrual blood and semen are also contrasted: the blood of menstruating women is 'hot' and 'red', and dangerous to men, and to the fertility of the crops and cattle; semen, on the other hand, is like water – 'white', 'cool' and fertilizing. The child is a combination of maternal blood, which provides its 'red' flesh and blood, and the paternal 'blood' (semen) which provides its 'white' bones and hair.

There is no identification of gender with the 'hot'/'cool' symbolic opposition, for any man or woman many become 'hot' – through anger or jealousy, or through sexual relations. Men who have recently had sexual relations are also 'hot' while women, Kuper writes, may be 'cool' before and after their phase of sexual maturity (1982: 19). A young pre-pubescent girl is often favoured for conducting rain-making rituals, and, as a mothers milk is considered 'white' and 'cool', a nursing mother is thought to have a positive influence on crops (Berglund, 1975: 340). But significantly a nursing mother must avoid sexual relations.

The 'hot'/'cool' symbolism as outlined by Kuper, constitutes a dualistic rather than a binary opposition, for health and wellbeing is not conceived as a 'balance' between the two symbolic domains but rather the hegemony of the positive pole – 'coolness'. Thus the opposition is between healing and fertilizing agents, and dangerous and sterilizing forces. As Kuper writes: 'The "cool" things heal or fertilize the "hot", while the "hot" endanger the "cool"' (1982: 20). He points out some linguistic connections in Zulu and Tswana between 'to heal' and 'to cool', and between 'hot' and unhealthy and fever.

The symbolic oppositions he summarizes in the following table:

Hot	*Cool*
(causing sickness and sterility)	(causing health and fertility)
red	white
menstrual blood	semen
lightning	rain
witches	ancestors
witches' familiar	snakes, crocodiles

(Kuper, 1982: 20)

I want to turn now to a society where the hot/cold symbolism expresses not a dualistic schema, but rather a more balanced polarity, focused on reciprocal gender relations, not those of inequality, as among the southern Bantu pastoralists, which of course are represented in Malawi by the Ngoni – the Ju/'hoan (!Kung) of the Kalahari.

Megan Biesele's perceptive study of the folklore and foraging ideology of the Ju/'hoan suggest that these hunter-gatherers have 'one basic symbolic scheme' which is based upon the two main social categories that constitute Ju/'hoan social life – the polarity between men and women (1993: 195). Hunting is typically a male activity and though it is more highly valued and ritually elaborated than fishing or the gathering of wild vegetables, which are the domain of women, there is little emphasis on hierarchy, and the economic roles of men and women are seen as reciprocal and complimentary. Hunting is thus symbolically opposed not to gathering but rather to the women's reproductive capacity. The two important initiation rites among the Ju/'han, the 'first kill' ceremony of boys, and the rites of menarche for girls are thus seen as balanced and equivalent.

But whereas the Southern Bantu associate 'heat' with sickness and sterility, the Ju/'hoan view heat positively. The essence of the trance-dance (*!kia*), performed mainly by men, is to activate a special kind of energy or spiritual power, *n/om*, which inheres in the body of the person. The dance takes place around a central fire, which is considered to be one source of the heat required to heat up the *n/om*, the power in the bellies of the trance dancers. The metaphor of 'boiling' is used to describe this process of activating the *n/om*, and Richard Katz's study of community healing among the !Kung is appropriately entitled *Boiling Energy* (1982). The *n/om* energy, it is worth noting, is also found in certain animals and plant substances. There is a symbolic association between boiling water, activating medicines, cooking meat, sexual motivation, the ripening of fruit – and the healing of the *n/om* energy in the trance dance. The *n/om* energy released in the dance is believed to have healing properties. But the essence of Ju/'hoan symbolism is the emphasis on reciprocity, mediation and balance. Thus the energy – heat – generated by the men's 'hot' role as curers, must be complemented by the 'coolness' of the women. As one person expressed it 'Fire is good if it cooks, bad if it burns you' (Biesele, 1993: 80).

The Ju/'hoan take joy and pleasure in the 'heat' of the trance dance, and significantly the verb 'to burn' is the same as that 'to cure' (*ku'u*). But Biesele stresses that the desired state of being is one of balance, 'neither hot nor cold' (1993: 80), and if the men get too 'hot' during the dance the women offer them water to 'cool' them. Arrow poison and a man's sexual potency are considered hot, and the arrow poison's and men's hunting equipment become 'cool' and ineffective if they come into contact with a menstrual woman or the moon – both of which are considered 'cool'. When shooting game the hunter must not, therefore, look at the moon.

A basic symbolic polarity of hot and cold thus provides a comprehensive 'framework' or a schema of 'structural oppositions' that permeates all aspects of Ju/'hoan social life. It can be understood, Biesele suggests, only in terms of the 'mediation', 'balance' and 'complementarity' of the basic social division between men and women, and between the domains of hunting and gathering/childbirth. Hunting and childbirth are described as the great 'procreative' powers associated with men and women. Menstruation is not a 'condition' of 'uncleanliness'; it is one of power, and the blood of menstruation is seen as combining with the semen to form a baby, but such procreative power associated with a menstrual woman should be kept separate from the hunting realm, and a man whose wife is menstruating should not go hunting – for game will either disperse or he will suffer an accident.

The symbolic opposition focused around hot and cold symbolism, and the gender division, is as follows:

Hot (da'a)	*Cold (a'v)*
men	women
sun	moon
fire	water/rain
day	night
hunting of animals	plant gathering
trance-dance	childbearing
kori-bustard	python
dry	wet
semen	menstrual blood

But central to Ju/'oan culture is the notion of complementarity, and the 'uniting' of the oppositions, thus generally they 'combine wet and dry, cold and hot, female and male elements to promote good weather and fertility' (1993: 108). Mediation between the two symbolic domains, Biesele suggest, largely focuses around eating and intercourse, and thus the Ju/'hoan make a number of important symbolic equations. Eating meat is symbolically associated with sex; thus to 'eat meat' is a common metaphor for sexual intercourse (1993: 152). Men are sympathetically associated with game animals, such that Biesele speaks of a 'peculiarly intimate identification between hunter and prey' (1993: 199) and women are seen as having a particularly fondness for meat (men?) – and they 'demand meat as a social right' (1993: 187). 'Women like meat' is a common phrase, and any man who did not bring meat back to the camp would find difficulty in obtaining a wife. There is thus a 'sex for meat' exchange of which Chris Knight (1991) has written at length. Yet at the same time there is a metaphorical equation of women with prey animals, and men as their hunters, so that women are likened to meat among the Ju'hoan. The essential point, however, is that these symbolic equations are shifting and reciprocal, as are the exchanges. The opposition between hot and cold, men and women, is a balanced one (for a similar analysis of the hot/cold symbolism as a balanced polarity see Signe Howell's (1984) perceptive study of the Chewong of Malaysia).

What is important about Malawian culture, as we discussed earlier in the chapter on their hunting traditions (1998: 97–113), is that they in essence combine, or perhaps reaffirm, cultural motifs characteristic of hunter gatherers, with those of agricultural communities. For in essence their culture combined, in the pre-colonial context, subsistence agriculture focused around a group of matrilineally related women, and hunting (or fishing) focused around men – as affines and outsiders with respect to the kin group. For the Southern Bantu pastoralism is focused around men and 'cattle' are cool; for Malawians hunting was the compliment to agriculture, and it was the woodland (with its wild game, and the spirits of the dead) that was cool. But essentially, like the Ju/'hoan hunter-gatherers, the pervasive hot and cold symbolism found in Malawi represents, like the polarity between the woodland and the village, and between kin (women) and affines (men), a balanced opposition. Unlike the Ju/hoan, the hot/cold symbolism in Malawi is not a 'totalizing' phenomenon, but is restricted to specific contexts. Unlike the Southern Bantu, although heat has its 'dangers', it is not looked upon negatively – as destructive and antithetical to human wellbeing, but as something essential to it. The idea therefore, like the Ju/'hoan, is a 'balance' between hot and cold – referred to as 'warm' (-*funda*). Heat is associated in Malawi with three elements that are absolutely essential to human life – blood, sex and fire. Blood is essential to human life, life indeed almost being identified with it. It forms the substance of a human person, and is closely associated with matrilineal kinship, even though matriliny is described in terms of the breast. Among the Yao an unrelated man or woman could establish an *ulongo* relationship (brother-sister link) by drinking each other's blood (Malcolm 1936: 153). Blood, and plenty of it, is essential for a healthy life, and there are many medicines whose purpose is to 'increase' the blood (*kuonjeza magazi*). As we shall discuss in the chapter six, the ingestion of meat and blood (*chirope*, a form which expresses the mystical power of blood) is an important part of many curing rituals, such as vimbuza and *namtongwe*. But blood is 'red' and 'powerful' and 'hot' and in excess it can be dangerous, upsetting the ritual balance ('warmth' is the normal living state) in others. This is why the blood of the menstrual woman is dangerous to men, although the woman herself is 'cold' (*ozizira*) in having lost vital blood, and of course in this state she herself is vulnerable, and must be kept 'cool' – as initiates, metal-workers, hunters, pregnant women must also be kept cool. (For an interesting discussion of the cultural significance of blood see Hauser-Schaublin, 1993.)

Sex, too, is vital for human wellbeing, and is positively affirmed, as we have noted, by Malawians – which creates problems in an era of sexually transmitted 'diseases' like Aids. It also gives moralists and Christian fundamentalists scope to denounce the 'promiscuity' and 'adultery' of Malawian people, even though malnutrition is an equally serious problem in rural areas, a large proportion of rural households being unable to meet their basic subsistence needs. Sex is also important in the ritual context, as well as an important source of pleasure and of children. For the sexual act is seen as generating 'heat', and this is an important transformative agent, enabling initiates, a young child, a widow, to move from a state of 'coolness' to one of warmth in normal life. The *kutenga mwana* rite, the *fisi* complex, as well as the ritual intercourse of the chief and his or her spouse on important ritual occasions – such as the creation of a new village, or to signify the close of an initiation – all these function as providing 'warmth' – to the people or the land. A baby can only become a person if they are heated, warmed, cooked – to become a warm human. Land can only become a viable place for hunting, or for human habitation, if it too is 'warmed' (*ku-funda*). But as with blood, sex in certain contexts – especially contexts which already entail the generation of 'heat' (like hunting, iron-smelting, pottery-making) or which need to be kept 'cool' (childbirth, menstruation, initiation, rain rituals, offerings to the ancestral spirits) – is positively dangerous, and thus heat from sexually active people must be kept away from these contexts and domains.

So it is with fire, which is the heat-generating agent *par excellence*. Fire is absolutely essential to human wellbeing, and is positively used in cooking, hunting, pottery making, iron smelting and metalwork, and in ritual contexts, where fire is used to 'warm' the child, the pregnant woman or the initiates. But again, in excess, it is dangerous. This is why heat-generating activities such as sex, cooking and hunting are so antithetical to each other. It is not simply gender linked. Nor is it related to a person.

Heat like coldness (and the ideal balance 'warmth') is a ritual condition, not the attribute of a person. When Peter Probst writes (1995: 9–10) that 'men are hotter than women, but not as hot as a woman when she is menstruating', and that at the end of the girls initiation the ritual intercourse involves 'adjusting' the cold condition of the girl to the 'hot forces' of the man, this is somewhat misleading. Although, of course, young sexually active men may be seen as in a general 'hot' condition, hotness is not an attribute of maleness, and elderly men, like elderly women, are looked upon as generally 'cool'. Generally speaking, most people are considered to be neither hot nor cold, but warm, only becoming 'hot' on engaging in sex. In the initiation rite it is the sexual act itself that warms the girl, not the man. Nor is a menstruating woman 'hot'; on the contrary, she is 'cold', as all women affirm, for she is losing blood. As in the Jamaican context, 'menstrual loss puts women in a "cold" and vulnerable situation, but it also cleanses them, therefore having a health-promoting and strengthening effect' (MacCormack and Draper, 1987: 155). It is even more problematic to conflate this hot/cold symbolism with the Judeo-Christian ritual dualisms between unclean and pure, and thus conceive of the menstruating woman as 'unclean', and the fisi rite as a form of 'purification' (Tembo and Phiri, 1993: 47–8). A menstrual woman is not unclean – but her blood is dangerous to others, as also is sex – but this does not make sex an unclean activity, any more than it makes it a rite of 'purification' when it is used positively to 'warm' a person – whether a child initiate or a widow – or the land.

Given that blood (and 'heat') is intrinsically linked, indeed equated with life energy and good health, too much blood (or heat) can neverthe-less be destructive, and, paradoxically, lead to a state of 'coolness' (*ozizira*). Thus too much sex or drinking beer or eating meat to excess can, like the loss of blood by a menstruating woman, lead to 'coolness' and thus debilitation or illness. In a sense, too much heat leaves you cold. A man, therefore, suffering from the ailment *kanyera*, as I discuss below though caused by menstrual blood entering his body, is often described as being in a 'cold condition'.

I want now to describe the Mdulo or Tsempho concept, drawing on my earlier studies (1985), as well as saying a little more later about menstruation, which, given the strong Christian influence in Malawi, tends to be viewed in the ethnography in very negative terms. Tsempho or Mdulo is considered to be a particular kind of wasting disease which may have fatal consequences if countermeasures are not taken in the form of medicines. The disease is related to promiscuous sexual relationships, or to the indulging of sexual intercourse by spouses during ritually prohibited periods. The disease affects men, women and young children, and is caused by another's social transgression.

This affliction may be caused in many ways, or as one herbalist described it: *mtsempho uli njira zambiri* – 'tsempho has many paths'. A husband guilty of sexual misconduct who comes home and nurses his children without taking special medicines will cause them to die of tsempho. I spent almost an hour with one market herbalist while a young man expressed concern over his children at length. Confessing to having had sexual relations with a number of women in Blantyre, he was now about to return home to his wife and children, and was fearful less they should contract the disease. He himself was perfectly healthy, but he thought it necessary to buy medicines to protect his children. Interestingly he was given as medicines some roots of *Heteromorpha trifoliata*, which is often called *nsemphana* or *mpambano*, both terms meaning 'to cross each other' – reflecting its association with the disease.

A man should be particularly concerned during his wife's pregnancy, and refrain from committing adultery during this period. Failure to do so may affect both the mother and child. For as Marwick has written, during the period of pregnancy the woman and the unborn child are considered 'cold'. But the 'heat' (*wotentha*) generated by the illicit sexual intercourse, is transmitted to the child and may even 'kill the foetus'. As a strange mystical tie is assumed to exist between the father and child, special ceremonies and medicines as we have described, are necessary to 'take the child' (*kutenga mwana*) or to strengthen her or his heart (*kulimbika mtima*) (1965: 66–7).

Conversely, if a woman commits adultery and then puts salt in her husband's relish, this is believed to lead to illness. She will 'cut' him, the name of the disease being derived from the verb *ku-dula* (to cut or break).

Sexual abstinence is also required during the mourning period, at the time of the initiations, as well as during such activities as hunting and metal-working. Thus if a man goes hunting or to smelt iron in the woodland, and one of the party has recently engaged in sexual intercourse, or the wife of the man is having an adulterous affair, they are described as 'cutting' (*-dula*) or 'missing' (*-tsempha*) the man. The consequences of this is, of course, variable, for, like *matsenga*, *mdulo* is not so much a 'disease' as an etiological rubric. Thus the man may kill no game, develop a cough (*ku-kosomola*), the smelted iron may be useless, he may develop chest problems (*chifuwa*), or the body of his young child may become swollen (*amatupa*).

Intrinsic to the *mdulo* complex are its hot/cold symbolism, the notion that salt is a medium of disease transmission, and that the affliction has a social control function.

As the cause of the disease *tsempho* is always a contravention of the moral code (though the sufferer of the disease may be the innocent party, or even a small child), we have here a causal link between a moral transgression and misfortune that does not involve a spirit entity or a praetor-natural agency like a witch. Yet such beliefs bolster secular authority and serve, as Marwick writes (1965: 68) to preserve those 'social relationships conducive to effective human reproduction'. But he notes that their ultimate reference, through symbolism and mystical belief, 'is to the fertility of the soil and to the fecundity of animals and men'.

The illness *mdulo* or *tsempho* can thus be said, as Hodgson (1913: 130) long ago noted, to have no 'specific form'. It refers to two syndromes that are similar in many respects. One is pulmonary tuberculosis – the symptoms of which include loss of body weight, fever, the coughing up of blood. One herbalist described *tsempho* as 'TB waukulu'. The other is kwashiorkor, a severe form of malnutrition due to protein deficiency, in which the affected child has swollen hands and feet, sores and peeling skin and a pale colouration. All herbalists stress that a child suffering from *kutupirana* (*ku tupa* – to swell) is miserable, and cries all the time (*akulira nthawi onse*). One early Malawian writer James Mikochi (1938) suggested that mdulo causes 'dysentery'. But, as indicated, *tsempho* is an aetiological category, and is not specifically related to any specific disease, or bodily malfunction, but like *matsenga* may relate to any misfortune that may be experienced – a lack of game animals on a hunt being only one. The wasting disease marasmus is usually described as *kankozi* or *utumbidwa*, and is linked to the notion that one child is born too soon after another. (For early accounts of the *mdulo* complex see Hodgson, 1913: 129–31; Rangeley, 1948: 34–44; Marwick, 1965: 66–8; Van Breugel, 1976: 260–7).

I turn now to discussing initiation (*chinamwali*) and funeral (*maliro*) rituals in Malawi, both of which are complex and variable in the degree of their ritual elaboration. After some preliminary remarks on animals and initiations, I will discuss, in this chapter, the initiation of girls, focusing on the Yao context. In the next chapter I will discuss the *jando* (boys) initiation among the Yao; the *nyau* rituals of the Chewa, Mang'anja and Chipeta; and finally funerary rites. With regard to the Nyau I will focus particularly on the theriomorphic structures, and on the interpretation of these rituals.

Preamble: Animals and Initiations

That wild animals play a significant role in religious rituals has long been attested. It certainly goes way back into antiquity. Evidence from rock paintings from both Europe and north Africa suggest that masked dancers in the form of animals – the dancer dressed in skins and wearing masks – was an important aspect of the rituals of palaeolithic peoples. The most famous of these are to be found in the caves of Trois Freres in Southern France and Tassili in Algeria and have been variously described as the 'sorcerer' or 'buffalo dancer'. Such paintings have been seen as intrinsically connected with shamanistic rites and the 'mythology of the hunt' (Kuhn, 1956: 6–8; Campbell, 1959: 286–312; Laude, 1971: 26–8).

Equally evident, with respect to Eurasian shamanism, is the close relationship that seems to be widely found in many cultures between animals and spirits of the dead. In his recent study of the witches' sabbath in Europe, Carlo Ginzburg stresses that within the folk culture masked dancers' involving animal 'disguises' were important and that there was a 'profound identification of animals with the dead' (1991: 262). He sees the roots of such beliefs in a remote Eurasian past. Earlier, Margaret Murray (1931: 23–30) had written of the importance of the 'horned god' in Eurasian and Egyptian rituals. But the significance of masked dancers involving animals and spirits was by no means restricted to the Eurasian context; it was also widespread among Amerindian communities (Hultkrantz, 1979: 100–1).

In the contemporary African context, masked dance involving animals structure which temporarily represent the spirits of the dead have been reported widely, both among Khoisan and Bantu-speaking people – especially in association with initiation rites. Among the Nharo of Botswana for example, Alan Barnard records that at the time of the girls' initiation, an 'eland bull dance' is held – the eland representing the sexuality of an affinal category (1992: 154–5). Although focused largely on west and central African studies, Jean Laude (1971) suggests that masked dancers representing animals or spirits were largely found among the agricultural peoples of Africa, and thus absent among pastoralists. This seems in fact generally to be the case; for classical studies of communities having a developed pastoral economy do not appear to have such rituals. The Nuer, for example, have little interest in wild animals; they rarely hunt them and much of their religious life is focused around cattle. Animal sacrifice is the principle ritual and there is a close spiritual identity indicated between sacrificed cattle and the lineage. Although spirits (*kwoth*) are associated with animal species, many having totemic affiliation, the dead are more identified with the homestead than with the bush or wild (Evans-Pritchard, 1956). Similarly, among the Zulu, communion with the ancestral spirits is largely maintained through animal sacrifices – usually cattle – and it is the cattle kraal, not the bush, that is associated with these spirits (Berglund, 1976: 11). In the thought patterns of both the Nuer and the Zulu there is a clear association between cattle and humans, (both living and dead) and these relationships are all focussed within the homestead. This contrasts markedly with the matrilineal peoples of central Africa, where the spirits of the dead are associated with the woodland, and wild animals play an important role in their ritual life.

On the subject of initiation rites, there has been a plethora of important studies, both ethnographic and theoretical. In an anthropological context, much of this has focussed on Melanesia and on Africa (Richards, 1956; Allen, 1967; Turner, 1967: 151–279; 1968: 198–268; Droogers, 1980; Barth, 1975; Herdt, 1982). In a lucid and interesting survey of the literature on initiation rites, Jean La Fontaine (1985) pleads for an understanding of these rites in terms of their total social context. She deplores the tendency of anthropologists of a symbolic and structuralist persuasion to isolate ritual symbols not only from the ritual sequence itself, but also from the social context. She is insistent, too, that the psychological aspects of initiation rites must not be ignored, nor must the participants' statements regarding the social purposes of the rituals be bypassed or dismissed. Initiation rites, she concludes, have a 'many-textured quality' that must always be recognized, but her overall analysis suggests a functional interpretation of initiations that is the antithesis of Turner's (1974) theory of communitas, namely, that initiation not only serves to transform individuals but also has an effect, which is 'to demonstrate the power of traditional knowledge and (to) legitimatise a continuing social order' (1985: 179). Her analysis, therefore, essentially has similarities to that of Maurice Bloch (1974, 1986).

Animals do not feature prominently in La Fontaine's account of initiation, although the wearing of a Colobus monkey skin is important in Gisu male initiations (1985: 12) and masked figures impersonating the spirits who are associated with the forest or bush play a crucial role in Mende initiations (1985: 93–100). But what emerges from La Fontaine's account of initiation is the important role that gender and affinal ties play in maturity rites, and the emphasis that is often placed on sexual symbolism. Whether expressed in terms of male potency or the power of menstrual blood, sexual expressions connote 'hidden powers of genera-tion'. Ritual actions thus becomes infused with potency and generative force. Thus she writes, 'sexual symbolism is not so much a reference to human sexuality as an attempt to harness immaterial powers to social purposes' (1985: 115–16).

Such immaterial powers in the Malawian context are, as we have explored in an earlier studies (1998), inherent in the natural world and wild animals are seen intrinsically as the means whereby generative power is transmitted to humans, both as individuals and in terms of the social groups.

The importance of initiation rites in the cultural life of Malawian people has been attested by numerous observers. The influence of the Christian missions and Islam along with the intrusions of the market economy, has had a fundamental impact on Malawian culture; yet initiation ceremonies still continue to flourish. Throughout most of the country during the dry season – but specifically in August and September – evidence of initiation ceremonies will confront the visitor. A fleeting glimpse of a masked dancer, perhaps, or a group of young girl initiates being escorted along a roadside by their guardians may be observed. In rural areas, many people will still insist that these initiation ceremonies have a social and moral equivalence to the school system. Without prompting, they will be described as 'our schools'.

These initiation rites, like initiation rites generally, have a many-textured quality and serve many social functions. With respect to the present study however, there are important aspects of these rites that need to be highlighted. Firstly, they are fundamentally concerned with sexuality and the construction of gender identity; secondly, at a local level they implicitly articulate the 'moiety' system, which is intrinsic to the kinship patterns of the matrilineal peoples of Malawi; and finally, it is through the initiation rites, specifically, that the powers of nature are ritually harnessed for social reproduction. And with respect to the latter aspect the role of animals are fundamental, both as medicine and as the forms or representations of the ancestral spirits or powers who are identified with the woodland.

Like rituals everywhere else in the world – even bonfire night ceremonies in my home town of Lewes – initiation rites in Malawi, in their public aspects, are utilized for a wide variety of purposes, and to express many local concerns and grievances – personal, social, moral and political.

The general term for initiation rites in both Nyanja and Chewa, is *chinamwali*. It is derived from the term for a young initiated girl, *namwali*, who has passed through the Chiputu initiation but who has not yet become a mother (*chembere* – or *mai* – the term here referring to the breast, while the verb *ku-bereka* means to bring forth fruit). *Mwali* is the general Yao term for an initiate, boy or girl, whereas *wamwali* and *phale* are its Tumbuka and Lomwe equivalents.

In normal conversation however, *chinamwali* tends to refer specifically to the girls' initiation ceremonies. The initiation process itself is seen in terms of movement or dancing, the verb *ku-bvina* (Yao – *ina*) means 'to dance' and its passive form *ku-bvindwa* essentially means 'to be initiated'. Dancing, singing and drumming form an essential ingredient of every initiation rite. Significantly, *ku-mwalira* means 'to die' (from the verb *ku-mwala* 'to be lost' or 'scattered'), thus reflecting the fact that initiations and funerals are for Malawians but two aspects of one cyclic process.

In a sense, initiations in Malawi can be viewed as a process whereby humans are gendered for the purpose of social reproduction, the gender divisions only being recognized essentially at two generational levels. The ancestors *makolo*, do not take a gendered form, although *kholo*, (singular) certainly has a matrilineal bias, with connotations of 'mother of the village, ancestress, one who has borne many children' (Scott 1929: 193).

Initiations in Malawi are complex and are variable in both form and in their degree of elaboration. All initiations, however, are gender specific with respect to the initiates, although many people may be involved in the initiations. Indeed, as Jean La Fontaine has stressed, initiation rites are in many ways like theatrical performances and thus involve many people and many concerns beyond that of the initiates. But in Malawi, the maturity rites – as distinct from the puberty rituals focussed on a girl's first menstruation – are crucially linked to gender identity. As she clearly noted, maturity rituals are essentially concerned with 'affirming adult status in terms of opposed categories of gender' (1985: 118). Nevertheless, male and female ritual are closely interlinked, complementary and essentially form a part of the complex whole – *chinamwali*. (For a useful general account of the relationship between dance rituals and theriomorphic structures and masks mainly focussed around men see Lonsdale 1981).

The Initiation of Girls

The initiation of girls is a complex process that takes several years to complete.

In essence, it consists of three stages: maturity rituals undertaken when the girls are between seven and eleven years old – although in some areas this is held after the first menstruation; a puberty ritual that is undergone when the girl has her first menses; and, finally, a ritual that celebrates a woman's first pregnancy.

Among the Tumbuka, there are no communal maturity rites. At her first menses the girl undertakes a complex ritual involving a period of seclusion, special rituals and instruction undertaken in the woodland (under the authority not of her mother but of the muzamba – who is also a midwife) and a 'bringing out ceremony'. The latter involves ritual washing, shaving and anointing with oil, beer drinking and the uzamba dance. In the past, betrothal proceedings took place before the ritual, and the key feature of these proceedings was the presentation to the prospective mother-in-law of a specially prepared meal with cooked and spiced chicken (*nkhuku*) (Young, 1931: 50–3). It was the uzamba dance that seemed to arouse such indignation and ire among the Scottish missionaries like Elmslie and Fraser who were shocked at the 'obscenity' and 'moral degeneracy' of the 'awful customs' of the Tumbuka (Elmslie, 1901: 50–6). It is worth noting that the ritual preparation and eating of medicated chicken is an important part of all initiation rites.

Although the Mang'anja, Chewa, Lomwe and Yao would seem to have pre-puberty maturity rites, the Chewa *mkangali* ceremony often took place some months after the first menstruation, usually in August or September. It is sometimes referred to as *chinamwali chachikulu* (the large initiation) in contrast with the puberty rite, which is described as *chinamwali chaching'ono* (the small initiation). However, most writers (for example Williamson, 1940: 6; Marwick, 1968: 8) have used the former concept to describe the first pregnancy ritual, *chisamba*, and it is the *mkangali* ceremony that is *chinamwali chaching'ono*. There is also sometimes a ritual for the woman after she has given birth to her first born child: the ceremony is described in Nyanja as *chitulutsa mwana* (from the verb *kuturuka*, to 'come out' or 'leave'.

I shall describe each of the main stages of the girls' initiation rites in turn, focusing specifically on Yao rituals. In this section I will discuss the maturity rites; in the next section the rites associated with menstruation and first pregnancy.

Chiputu: Maturity Rites

Among the Yao the chiputu ceremony for girls – which is sometimes described by the Swahili term *msondo* – is a pre-puberty maturity rite that usually takes place in August or September. This is a time when crops have been harvested and there is plenty of food available. The term *chiputu* is derived probably from *buthu*, which in Nyanja describes a young girl who has not yet reached puberty. The general organization of the ceremony is the responsibility of the village headman (*mfumu*), and the first part of the ritual consists of a beer brewing ceremony and offerings of millet flour (*ufa*) to the ancestral spirits (*mizimu*). Flour is initially smeared on the forehead for each initiate as a blessing. The beer-brewing aspect of the ceremony usually involves much singing and play acting, especially when the women and young girls go, collectively, to draw water and to have the millet pounded or ground at a local maize mill (*chigaya*). The women will often attire themselves with pieces of red cloth, worn especially around the head. One typical song went as follows:

> Kuli nyerere
> Ine Osagona
> There are black ants
> I do not sleep

It is sung to the accompaniment of hand clapping and with the women forming a circle, several of the younger girls lying on the ground, gesticulating and moving as if being attacked by ants. The movement of their hips make it evident that the play act is a euphemism for sex.

The right of the village headman to hold initiations is symbolized by the possession of a shallow basket (*nsengwa*) from which flour offerings (*nsembe*) are taken.

The age at which the girls are initiated is between nine and fourteen years and from two to fourteen girls may be initiated at any one time. Among the Yao, the communal initiation given at the chiputu is supplemented by individual instruction when the young girl first menstruates. In the past, according to Stannus (1922: 271), the initiates (*wali*) would be under instruction for about a month, but nowadays the initiation, expressed as 'to dance' (*ku-bvinidwe*), often last only five to six days, beginning or ending at weekends when people have more free time. In some areas some initiates may remain in the lodge for up to two weeks.

Although the village headman, as head of the kin-group, is ultimately responsible for initiations, the activities themselves and the instructions are always organised by a group of three or four senior women (*anamkungwi*). They are under the leadership of the 'mistress of ceremonies'. She may also be described as *mteresi* (from the verb *ku-teleka*, 'to put on the fire', or 'brew beer' suggesting the transformatory nature of the ritual) or *m'michila* (the one with the tail). The possession of a medicine tail, made from the tail of an animal, is always an insignia of office for the *namkhungwi*, as it is for other ritual specialists. The term *m'michila* is, however, more commonly used to refer to the circumcizer in the boys' jando ritual.

Throughout the ritual each girl (*mwali*) is under the care and guidance of the 'counsellor' (*phungu* or *mkamusi* – from the verb *kamusya*, 'to help'). The counsellor is usually a young initiated woman or elder sister, or an affine.

The separation of the girls begins early one morning in an area of fallow land within the village environs, unlike the boys' initiation, which takes place in woodland often some distance from the village. The place chosen to build the girls' initiation hut – usually referred to as *ndagala* or *simba* – is often close to the house of the village headman. A group of girls initiated the previous year hoe the site. Then a pit (*dzenje*) is dug in the middle of the area and the senior *namkungwi* comes forward and, hidden by a cloth, takes flour and certain medicines from a basket and places them in a hole. One by one the senior women also come forward, and, on their knees and covered by the cloth, look into the hole and make further offerings of flour (*nsembe* or *mbepesi*). Such offerings are made to obtain the support of the ancestral spirits. All the women present come forward in turn to inspect the medicine, and although a public ceremony, men have to keep their distance. A number of drums are brought to the site, and the women begin to dance in a circle, singing. About forty women were present at the ceremony I witnessed.

When the dancing was well under way, another group of women arrived from a neighbouring village, singing and dancing and carrying two poles (*phanda*). The two trees used as poles, which make the main posts of the simba hut, are always *mlombwa* (Pterocarpus angolensis) and *mtombozi* (Diplorhynchus condylocarpon). These are trees that, incidentally, have a important symbolic role in Ndembu rituals (cf. Turner, 1967). Containing red sap and white latex respectively, they represent in Malawian context the two genders, red (blood) being associated with women (kin) and white (semen) with men (as affines), or, in an alternative interpretation, the hard *mlombwa* trees being associated with males (affines) whereas the *mtombozi* tree is linked with the breast (women, kin group). The two poles were held high and carried around by all the women. Then, at a given signal, with the women's drums beating furiously, they were placed together in the pit. Several women then sat on their buttocks with open legs and with their skirts lifted high pushed the soil into the hole with their feet. Their movements had sexual innuendoes. When this was done, all the women stamped around near the post and there was ecstatic dancing and yodelling (*ku-luluta*).

All the women then left the site together, singing and dancing. When they had departed, young boys and men, kin of the novitiates, came forward and constructed a long grass shelter. This constitutes the initiation lodge (*simba* or *msakasa*).

In the evening, the initiates enter the lodge, but only after its surroundings have been protected (*ku-sirika*) with special medicines against witches (*afiti*). The *namkungwi* always sleeps at the foot of the two trees (*mitengo iwiri*) poles that form the main posts of the lodge. In the evening of the first night in the lodge, all the women gather at the *simba* and there is much singing and dancing, which goes on through the night. One of the songs that is sung points to the need for the young girl to set up her own house (*nyumba*) as she is now coming of age (*kuti wakula*). Another song expresses the young girl's sexual maturity:

> Kwacha kale eh eh
> Sititope eh eh
> Yayaya mapeto kucha eh eh
>
> Dawn is long ago
> We are not tired
> The genitals are mature

During the week or so that the novitiates (*wali*) are undergoing the initiation, a complex series of different rites and activities are performed, the girls often leaving the initiation lodge (always with head covered so that no man can see them) in order to receive instruction at a nearby stream, or in some place in the woodland. Some of these activities have been recorded in early ethnographies (Stannus, 1922: 269–73; Mair, 1951).

Although, as a man, I was unable to fully observe these rites, discussion I have had with various women friends in the Zomba district, suggest the following are important aspects of the chiputu rites.

Sexual Instruction.   An important emphasis is placed during the period of seclusion of the sexual education of young girls. They are given sexual instruction by means of symbols, riddles and obscene songs, as well as by simulated action, and are taught basic sexual knowledge. They are taught the use of medicinal herbs and the normative rules that are associated with sexual conduct, particularly as these relate to the disease-complex *mdulo* or *tsempho*. As far as I could ascertain, no clitoridectomy is practised in Malawi, but the stretching of the lips of the vagina is widely taught and practised. The vulva is pulled (*akamakoka nyini*), so that the lips will be long, soft and supple (*zimafewetsa*). The verb *kuphwadza* specifically refers to the lengthening of the lips of the vulva. This is believed to heighten sexual satisfaction, particularly for the male. 'A vagina without lips cannot hold the penis. Let us therefore *pull*' are the words of one song. The vagina of the young girl is widened and an egg inserted – to be later taken out and mixed with other medicines. The massaging of the vulva is often done with charcoal and castor oil (*nsatsi*), the making of which is the monopoly of older women. The oil is widely used to soften the skin especially of babies (cf. Turner, 1968: 248 for similar rites). It is during these rites that the girl is instructed not to have sexual intercourse during her menstrual period, and to observe the special rules associated with it. If she has sex with a man during this period, he is believed to contract the wasting disease *kanyera*. While menstruating, the woman must avoid 'hot' things – she must not even touch the fire. Under no circumstance must she come in to contact with activities that are associated with heat (*wotentha*) such as sexual intercourse, or with hunting or iron-smelting. The overt sexuality expressed in many of the women's songs and the lengthening of the lips of the vulva seem to be highly disapproved of by many Christian and Islamic women – although they are still widely practised.

Matrilineal Solidarity.   Associated with this stress on sexuality there is an equal emphasis on the solidarity of woman, specifically of the matrilineal kin group. There is in Malawi, a close identification between women and kinship, such that mothers' brothers and brothers are seen almost as belonging to the female gender – with respect to their kin. Many of the songs learnt and sung during the initiation period reflect this kin solidarity, essentially deriding the male affine – residence normally being uxorilocal. The implication is that the male affine functions specifically to provide sex and to give the kin group children.

It is worth noting the important symbolism that centres on the male chicken (*tambala*). Not only is it associated with dawn, and it thus became a symbol of the independence movement, but its red fleshy crest and strutting actions makes it an appropriate sexual symbol of the male affine. The term 'cock' in English carries the same connotations.

The Giving of Custom.   During the seclusion period, one rite involves the *namkhungwi* or an older women feigning death. She is covered with a black cloth and the young girls are told it is their mother. In this episode the initiates are taught to control their emotions and to play the role of mourners. Other informants suggest that the girls themselves have to undergo a period of 'death', which has clear affinities to that described by Turner in the Nkanga's girls' puberty rite among the Ndembu (1967: 23). During the initiation the young girls are also given moral instruction. It is described as being given the custom (*kupereka mwambo*). The girls are taught that they must show respect to their elders, and develop a good character (*makhalidwe abwino*). The latter implies not being lazy, and caring for one's husband, which is particularly expressed in bringing him hot water to bathe in at the end of the day. The provision of firewood and water for the household is one of the central tasks allotted to women. The girls are warned of the dangers of illicit sex – men are often described as like animals – and in the past any girl who became pregnant before the *chiputu* ceremony was severely reprimanded by the village headman and the mothers of the kin group. She was described as a vervet monkey (*chitumbiri*). Monkeys, like other animals such as hyenas or baboons are seen as inherently sexual but in an uncontrolled way. Sanderson (1954: 91) records that a child born to an uninitiated girl in the past was discarded from the house and left to die.

As initiates must be kept in a 'cold' condition, all persons associated with the *wali*, which includes the village headman and his wife, the *anamkungwi* and the *aphungu* as well as the close kin of the girl must abstain from sexual intercourse during the *chinamwali* period. Thus there is taboo on sex by her close associates from the time the sorghum or millet is put to soak to make the beer until the concluding ceremony. Any transgression of these rules is seen to destroy or to cut (*kudula*) the young girl, and this gives rise to illness or possible sterility.

Mwambo has been defined loosely as 'secret knowledge' (Kaspin, 1993: 40), with the implication that the term centres mainly on ritual matters. But the concept *mwambo* is fairly broad and general, and refers specially to cultural traditions or folk wisdom. Some of the instructions given during the initiations are gender specific relating to the basic subsistence tasks of men and women – women being associated with cooking, and men with hunting and *chizimba* medicines. Some of the traditions relate to specific cult activities like the Nyau, or specific activities like hunting. But much of what is learned during the initiations – by both sexes – are of a general nature, and relate to moral edicts that all Malawians should heed; showing respect for elders (*ulemu*) and parents in law; never entering the parents bedroom; observing the sexual prohibitions associated with the mdulo complex; and not being unkind, slanderous, or greedy. 'Tradition' reflects, above all, a concern for moral norms and values, as Probst suggests (1995) – and such values focus on the cultural ideas of the person. Thus mwambo, secret or otherwise, is concerned fundamentally with gender identity and personhood.

In an important article on the Chewa cosmology of the body, Deborah Kaspin (1996) tends to equate *mwambo*, and symbolic thought more generally with the esoteric knowledge conveyed by chiefs and rainmakers, and by the *anamkhungwi* who are responsible for the initiation of girls. It may be useful, at this junction, to offer some critical reflections on this article, not on its data (much of which is common knowledge to anyone who has read Malawian ethnography) but rather on her mode of analysis. Offering a cosmological interpretation of Chewa cultural life she essentially replicates the 'symbolic schema' that Father Schoffeleers long ago proposed in his structuralist analysis of Mang'anja religious culture. It is a style of interpretative anthropology that has a long pedigree, found among Boasian cultural anthropologists, Oxford cultural idealists, Durkheimian symbolists and French school of anthropology associated with Griaule and Dieterlen (Reichard, 1950; Hicks, 1976; Douglas, 1966; Griaule, 1965). The limitations of this mode of analysis has long been the subject of critical debate. I offer the following reflections on this article.

Firstly, most of the cultural ideas, ordering principles and symbolic analogies that Kaspin views as constituting Chewa cosmology – interpreted as a single unified cultural 'order', a totalizing 'system of correspondences' – are not, of course, specifically Chewa, but are shared by matrilineal peoples (Mang'anja, Chipeta, Yao, Njanja, Lomwe) throughout Malawi. Indeed, they are evident throughout much of North Zambezia.

The cosmological schema she thus evokes as a 'totality' or as a 'symbolic order' is not ethnic but regional. She likens the Chewa 'ideational system' to Catholicism, without also recognizing that Catholicism – like the spatial cosmologies of the native American Indians – are regional not ethnic cosmologies. It is misleading to equate culture with either language or ethnicity; it is independent of both, and particular cosmological schemas often extend beyond a particular locality or ethnic enclave.

Secondly, the distinction she makes between common sense and symbolic (esoteric) knowledge is also misleading, for cultural ideas are complex and multiple, and never simply replicate cognitive modes. Geoffrey Samuel (1990: 30–43) has offered some cogent criticisms of this kind of 'bi-modal' theorizing, in relation to the work of Bloch and Sperber, who likewise make similar radical distinctions between common sense and ideological cognition (Bloch, 1977) and rational and symbolic mechanisms (Sperber, 1975). The fact is that all societies, and the Chewa and the Catholic Church are no exceptions, have diverse forms of knowledge (cognition, culture) – a 'multi-modal' framework, as Samuel describes it. Thus, many of the cultural notions and symbolic analogies –

which express an organic rather than simply an 'agricultural' sensibility (Morris, 1998b) – that Kaspin describes with respect to the Chewa, are neither esoteric nor do they express common sense intuitions. Kaspin over-systematizes and thus reifies the cosmological (symbolic) representations that are found in Malawi, in suggesting that among the Chewa these representations constitute a single totalizing schema, that is both 'self-contained' and internally 'coherent'. But culture, as she implies, is 'very layered' and relates to many distinct 'modalities of experience': it is ill understood by reference to a single 'symbolic order' or logic, that 'formalizes' or 'routinizes' common sense. The whole analysis has a very Platonic ring. Both Bloch (1989) and Bourdieu (1990: 11) have rightly cautioned us regarding the limitations of such logical models, which although aesthetically pleasing may be too procrustean to capture the fluidity and flexibility of social life. Some writers have even suggested that such symbolic schemas are largely a function of the ethnographers own imagination and search for order. But as my own studies have indicated (1989, 1994) there are – in all cultures and not just the Chewa – cultural schemas and symbolic homologies that unite in a meaningful way various dimensions of social experience. But whether such schemas, which clearly have a mnemonic function, indicate a single cultural logic is debatable (Morris, 1987: 295–6).

Finally, it is I think misleading to equate 'symbolic' knowledge – the cultural schemas that unify the various modalities of social experience – with esoteric (secret) knowledge, and thus see them as essentially the preserve of ritual 'experts' like the chief, rainmaker and *anamkhungwi* – as if these 'experts' are the sole repositories of cultural knowledge. Although much esoteric knowledge is indeed conveyed through the initiations – esoteric (secret) meanings of proverbs, songs, and the plants and animals used in the rites are indeed complex and abstruse – most cultural knowledge that is expressed in Malawi is neither that of the common sense variety – shared by all humans – nor esoteric: it is rather manifested and imbibed in many everyday social contexts – gardening, herbalism, sex, cooking, hunting, collecting mushrooms, eating – many of which Kaspin alludes to in her article.

For example the hidden meanings of proverbs and riddles – which play an important part in initiation rites – are by no means esoteric. Thus the riddle: *amnzake ayenda usiku, iye ayenda masana* ('his relatives move at night, he at midday') has the answer *zolo*, the elephant shrew, which is diurnal unlike other *mbewa*. The proverb: *wakwatira mende waleka chitute* – 'he married the creek rat and left the pouched mouse' – only makes sense if one realizes that the creek rat has an iridescent fur and is easily caught in a bamboo trap, while the pouched mouse lives in a deep burrow and stores much food, bringing it back to its burrow in its cheek pouches (Morris, 1998: 183). These meanings may be obscure to an outsider, but they are by no means esoteric, but based on close observations of mammalian life. But their main function in the initiations is to impart moral edicts.

It seems somewhat ironic that in an era of postmodernist theory, which has emphasized almost to the point of *reductio ad absurdum* the incoherence and fragmentary nature of cultural discourses, as a 'montage of polyphony', even questioning whether the very concept of 'culture' has any meaningful place in anthropological theory that Kaspin should reaffirm the utility of a 'totalizing' theory that interprets all social life as structured by a single cultural logic. The truth I feel, and this is what I try to express in these pages, lies somewhere between these two extremes – for cultural schemas are neither monolithic nor are they fragmentary. I shall return to Kaspin's cosmological approach in the next chapter, in discussing the *nyau* rituals.

The Hyena Ritual. In the past, marriage clearly followed on from the initiation ceremony. The young man, who may himself have been undergoing the *lupanda* (*jando*) ceremony, was actively involved as a young man in the *chiputu* ceremonies. One ceremony was known as *kulukwi*, and the man had to prove his 'manhood' by cutting a piece of firewood (*lukwi*) with an axe (Stannus, 1922: 272–3). Also important with respect to the *chiputu* ritual is the ritual intercourse that is said to take place towards the end of the seclusion. Ideally, it should be performed by the husband-to-be. One person suggested to me that while the *anamkungwi* insisted that the girls should be virgins when they enter the initiation, they make sure that on leaving the *simba* they shouldn't be. The man – always an affinal relative or an outsider – designated to perform ritual intercourse and initiate the young girl's first sexual experience, is known as the hyena (*litunu*).

The hyena is the prototypical chirombo or wild animal. It is associated with the woodland, and is recognized as an animal that has great strength and courage. The hyena is viewed as a relentless and tenacious hunter that wanders over great distances, and is seen as embodying sexual vitality. Parts of the animal, but especially its tail, brain and sexual organs are in great demand as medicine, particularly for strength and male potency. In essence, the hyena symbolizes the affinal male. It is difficult to ascertain how prevalent is this custom of ritual intercourse, but several Christian women I know speak in very disapproving terms of the *chiputu* ceremony and what it involves. Early writers describe a similar Yao custom in which a man called *litunu* came incognito to have sexual intercourse with a widow, in order to remove her from a state of ritual incapacity (*muchi*).

In a recent paper, Tembo and Phiri suggest that hyena has 'filthy habits', and that the ritual intercourse 'cleanses a woman of her sexual potency and stigma as being a danger to people's health' (1993: 46). This gives a rather Judeao-Christian interpretation of this ritual, for both the Yao and the Chewa, sexual intercourse is viewed in affirmative terms. It is not seen as something 'polluting' or 'filthy', and the hyena symbolizes the sexual potency of the male affine who in essence 'warms' the young woman. The young girl is considered 'cool' (*wozizira*) and must be kept so throughout the initiation period and neither she nor the sexual act itself is seen as 'filthy' or 'unclean'. As both Williamson (1940: 4) and Rangeley (1948: 40–1) long ago suggested, the essence of the *fisi* (hyena) ritual is to remove this coolness (*wozizira*), and thus warm (*wofunda*) and strengthen the young girls. The ritual intercourse after the birth of a child, *kutenga mwana*, has the same function. The ritual coitus is thus believed to bring an end to the girl's dangerous 'cold' condition, and among the Chewa, the unidentified man who performs this task is described as having 'eaten her maidenhood' (*kudyachinanmwali*) (cf. Hodgson, 1933: 125; Marwick, 1965: 237).

Animals and Liminality.   Many of the rituals undertaken during the chiputu express the fact that the young girl in a 'liminal' state. As part of the rite, she is shaved, and while undergoing the ritual the girls are given 'bush names' (*maina akutengo*). They are called such names as *chatengo iwe* ('you of the bush') or *chigombantiko* ('beat the porridge stick'), or they may be given the names of small mammals – *litawala, naliyeye* (both species of elephant shrew) or *chingaluwe* (musk shrew) (Stannus, 1922: 271).

When they return to the village they will be given more respectable names (*maina aulema*). Whilst undergoing the rite they are therefore seen as being associated with the woodland and many ritual activities described above take place specifically in this environment. Some of the rituals involve dancing naked.

An important aspect of all *chiputu* ceremonies is not only the partaking of the medicated chicken but also the ritual consumption of bat (*mleme*), which is put into the millet malt (*chimera*) used to make sweet beer (*tobwa*). The bat, associated with caves and crevices, with fruit trees, with the night and the woodlands, is believed, like other animal medicines, to give strength and potency to the young girls. When Duff Macdonald long ago described the *namkungwi* as the 'cook' of the initiation 'mysteries' (1882: 125), he was stating an important truth, for in 'being danced', the young girls are also symbolically being 'cooked' or 'warmed' (*wofunda*) via contact with the generative spirits of the woodlands, the abode of both spirits and animals. The incorporation of the *chinyago* animal structures into the girls' initiation expresses this contact with the 'wild' even more fundamentally.

Affinity. What is significant about initiation rites is that they are often occasions which bring together, and entail cooperation between two kin communities (or villages) that are linked by marriage. The initiates have a ranked order. The first girl is called *nachinlongola*, which means the 'one who started it' (*ku-longola*, to be first). The second girl is called *nachilundamisi*. According the Anjamila Mtila, the meaning of this term suggests 'the one who joins villages', and thus signifies that through the ritual there is a close association between village communities. This is clearly expressed in many *chiputu* songs.

Chinyago. During the period of seclusion, and particularly on the final night, there are several rites that involve other members of the community, particularly young initiated men. Representations of animals are made of grass, bamboo and hessian bags, animal figures which are similar to the *nyau* masked dancers among the Chewa and Mang'anja, which I shall discuss in the next chapter. These animal figures are often referred to as *nyau*; but more commonly the Yao people call them *chinyago* or *chinambande*. Among these people, however, there are no organized cult fraternities such as we find among the Mang'anja and Chewa; instead the masked dancers organize themselves, even if secretly, on a more ad hoc basis. The masked dancers are mainly young initiated men in their early twenties, although they work in close cooperation with the village headman and the senior women of the *chiputu*, the *anamkungwi*. I will discuss these *inyago* figures more fully in the section on the Yao boys' initiation (*jando*).

With regard to the girls' *chiputu* ritual among the Yao, the masked dancers make their appearance in three different contexts.

The first context is when several men and boys approach the girls' initiation lodge at night. It is usually on the second or third day of the girls' seclusion. Using a large clay pot and various other devices, the men make sounds like that of the jackal (*nkhandwe*) calling, an animal of evil omen to the Yao, or the roar of a lion. The sounds are highly realistic, and their aim is to scare, even terrify, the young girls. The men may not only initiate the sound of a lion, but will simulate a lion springing on the girls in the dark, armed with thorns rather than claws. On the intimation of the *namkungwi*, they will specifically attack any girl who has been ill-behaved, or who has not shown proper respect towards her elders. It is not that the young men are seen as carnivores and the young girl initiates as 'meat', but the aim is to scare the girl, according to everyone. I found little evidence that the aim of the female initiation was to 'turn girls into succulent meat', other than the fact that a symbiotic analogy is sometimes expressed between hunting and marriage (sex). Nor were the men involved in the *unyago* depicted as specifically carnivores – and the women as game animals (nyama) – but rather men are associated with *all* animals, *herbivores* being the most crucial (cf. Kaspin, 1993: 43 on the Chewa).

The second context is the daytime appearance of the masked dancers at rituals which are described as *chinambande*. Meredith Sanderson's intimation that *chimbande* refers specifically to the first pregnancy ceremony (*litiwo*) (1954: 44) was not borne out by my own researches. The term is mainly used as a synonym for the *chinyago* figures, and for their appearance as a dance ritual.

The essence of the day *chinambande* ritual is the meeting, or rather the confrontation, between the animals of the woodland and the masked dancers, as well as the various *chinyago* – both described as *chirombo*, and the group of women associated with the initiates. The latter grouping includes members of the initiates' own kin group and women who are affinally related to her (*alamu*). There may be around 100 women present on these occasions, but very few men. The women, singing and dancing collectively near the initiation lodge, call on the wild animals (*zirombo*) to make their appearance. Prominent among these inyago that 'dance' at this time are *kasinja*, and the sable antelope *mbalapi* although depending on the village, many other *chinyago* may make their appearance. The *kasinja* are associated less with the woodland, than with abandoned cultivations. They represent 'spirits' or rather 'sprites' of the wild, sexual and untamed. The masked dancers are sparsely dressed, almost naked and completely covered with old rags, grass, or banana fronds. Their heads are covered too and they wear a red headband and pieces of red cloth on their arms and legs. Approached by the women, the *kasinja* dance close to them, rhythmically and erotically thrusting their loins towards them. Until they are given a coin, they sexually entice the women, whose gestures are not less suggestive towards the *mbalapi*. To the other *chinyago*, the women's attitude are much less friendly. The antelope is usually accompanied by three to four young initiated boys holding sticks.

Figure 3.1 Inyago figure, Chiputu ritual, Likonde village, Domasi August 1990

They guard, protect and guide the animals towards the initiation lodge. By its actions, the *mbalapi* expressed fierceness (*ukali*) and frequently charges not only its minders but also the women, who scatter in all directions. The women usually express both fear and merriment. A series of *chinyago* may make their appearance, always accompanied by songs, drumming and dancing, in the area of the initiation lodge. The *kasinja* and the antelope essentially symbolize the affinal male, especially the former, for there is much sexual banter expressed by the group of women towards the wild creature. (cf. Yoshida, 1992: 220–3 on the role of *kasinja* as an affine among the Chewa of eastern Zambia).

Figure 3.2 Kasinja dancers during Chiputu ritual, Ngobola village, Domasi September 1990

The final context is where the *chinyago* make their appearance is on the final night before the girls (*anamwali*) leave the initiation hut. A complex, public ritual takes place after dark, usually at the *bwalo* close to the headman's house. Although the head and senior men may be present, the ritual is largely attended by the women, and such younger men who are involved in the organization and presentation of the *chinyago*, the animal structures. In essence, the ritual consists of the appearance within the village environs, of various masked figures and animal structures, who are described as coming from the woodland (*ntchire*) or from the marsh lands or water (*dambo, doko*).

The ritual begins with the gathering of the women and the setting up of the drummers, usually three or four men. The initiates sit in a row with their heads covered, the women in a group behind them. Opposite them, at a distance of about 15 or 20 yards, stand the rest of the villagers, mostly men. They are greatly outnumbered by the women. The ritual begins with the singing of various *chiputu* songs, to the accompaniment of hand clapping and drumming.

The content of some of these songs I have indicated earlier in the discussion. Then the women begin collectively to sing refrains calling on the *chinyago* to come. A man, or two young boys will join in the songs as a lead singer, the songs usually being sung in two or three parts. Typical examples are as follows:

1. Eha balapala
Eha kudamboko
Nyama yi yandani eh
Kopa! (women respond)

Hi! Sable antelope
From the marsh
What kind of animal
Entice me!

2. Eha bwititi
Ndani adziwa kanyama
Kamagona Ntchire
Eha bwititi
Tidziwa bwititi (women respond)

Hi! Bwititi
Who knows the small
Animal who sleeps in the bush
Hi Bwititi
We know the Bwititi

The songs are an invitation for the various *chinyago* (masked dancers and animal structures) to appear and this they do in turn, much to the amusement and excitement of those present – but especially the women. The *inyago* are called from the bush, they arrive spectacularly, dance around or chase the women and then they disappear back into the darkness. Described as either wild beasts (*chirombo*) or an animal (*nyama*), the relationship expressed between these *chiyago* and the collectivity of the women is of dialectical opposition, but a relationship that, judging from the gestures of both the *chinyago* and the women, is highly eroticized.

On the final day of the *chiputu* ceremony, the girls are taken to the river to bathe and are given medicines to wash themselves, especially the genitals. This is to make them fertile. Their bodies are rubbed with groundnuts or castor oil (*kudzola mafuta*) and often at this time they eat a chicken cooked with special medicines. This is believed to give them strength. As they leave the lodge for the last time, dressed in new clothes, the *namkungwi* stays behind to set fire to the initiation hut. Once it is alight, no one looks back. The young girls and all the women then go to pay their respects to the village headman (*mfumu*). Many of the senior women are dressed in men's clothes and their behaviour and antics cause much merriment among the women as they present themselves before the headman. He sits alone on a chair. The *namkungwi* sprinkles him with medicine infusion made from the pounded leaves of *nchenga* (Jubernardia globiflora). This is intended to bring good fortune to the headman, and to all the young girls who have been initiated. The *namkungwi* sprinkles some of the medicated water over her associates as well as over any bystanders. The girls then stand in line facing the headman and, dancing and singing, the women surround him. Many of them are dressed as men. One of the songs the girls sing suggest that they should keep 'an open hand' and give food freely; this way they would become a large village (*mzinda*). After the headman has given each of the girls a small gift of money, they leave for their own homesteads accompanied by their women kin. They then are fed, bringing an end to the *chiputu* rites, the *chinamwali chaching'ono*.

Schoffeleers records the *chibutu* as a pre-puberty ceremony among the Mang'anja. Williamson, however, noted that among the Chewa of the Dowa area it was necessary for the girl to have first menstruated before she underwent the *mkangali* ceremony. Between her first menses and the initiation ritual, she was not allowed to have sexual intercourse, even if married. The *chinmwali chaching'ono* initiation (*chibutu, mkangali*) among both the Mang'anja and the Chewa followed the same pattern as that described above among the Yao. The girl spent several days in the company of the other young girls in the initiation lodge, and she was given instruction relating to her duties within the household by the *namkungwi* and her associates; she was ritually shaved; she was con-sidered to be in a 'cool' (*ozizira*) state and this implied sexual abstinence by her instructors (the *anamkungwi* and *aphungu*) as well as by her close kin; there was massaging of the genitals and the lengthening of the vulva; and at the conclusion of the ceremony, there was an act of ritual intercourse by the husband or a close cousin, or by the surrogate 'hyena' (*fisi*) on three successive nights. The latter rite was specifically designed to 'warm' (*wofunda*) the young girl before she left the initiation hut.

Before the initiation, it was strictly forbidden for the girl to bear a child, as this would expose the village headman and her close kin to *mdulo*. A special ceremony was held for such an eventuality, *chimbinda* (*chimbwiira* – an impotent person; *kuwinda* – to protect with medicine). A girl was much despised for having 'cut' (*kudula*) her kin, and the child was known as *mwana wa kuthengo* (child of the woodland). Oral traditions suggest that she was made to undertake rather degrading tasks such as carrying on her head a broken pot containing dog excrement (Williamson, 1940: 3–6; Schoffeleers, 1966: 115–30).

The *chinamwali* ceremony for girls among Lomwe as recorded by LD Soka (1953: 45–7) seems to follow the basic pattern described above, although Soka puts a strong emphasis on the fact that the ritual (*kubvinidwa* to be danced) is centrally concerned with imparting *miyambo*, the custom relating to sexual and social morality.

Yoshinda (1992; 245–52) provides an interesting account of the girls' initiation ceremony (*chinamwali*) among the Chewa of Eastern Zambia, which is undertaken after menstruation, and appears not to be communal. Nor do the Nyau dancers participate in the girls' initiation, being focused on funerary rites only, and in the initiation of boys. In the past clay figures (*vilengo*) were made in the woodland – similar to the *zinyago* figures of the Yao. Around these the *namwali* danced. Decorated with white flour (*ufa*), soot (*mwaye*) and red clay (*katondo*), these figures depicted the python (*nsato*), a snake called *thunga*, a crocodile (*ng'ona*), tortoise (*fulu*), and hare (*kalulu*). Among the Chewa of central Malawi clay models are still made, but these are in the shape of small figurines, (*chingondo*), which are placed on the heads of the girl initiates. They represent the more important *nyau* figures – hare, elephant, snake, and especially the *kasiya maliro*, the eland (antelope) (Gwengwe, 1965: 71–3, Kaspin, 1993: 44). These figures are seen as representing images (*chithunzi*) of the animals of the woodland (*m'tchire*). It is worth noting the root of the word *chingondo* (*chi* – large, important; *ngondo* – blue wildebeest, which was an important game animal, like the eland, in the past). It may be noted, in response to the suggestion by post-modernist anthropologists, that gender has no 'basis' in human biology, that although Malawians emphasize the social construction of gender (the woman as mother (*mai*)), they only attempt to put little girls through the *chiputu* ceremony! Of course, sexual difference is also socially recognized, but then we have no way of describing the world adequately except through language. Baboons in Malawi have no problems at all in distinguishing between male and female humans!

Ndakula and Chisamba: Menstrual and First Pregnancy Rites

Whether or not menstruation takes place before or after the maturity rites, it always constitutes an important ritual occasion among all matrilineal peoples of Malawi. It is a clear signal that the girl has reached maturity (*ku-kula*). Menstrual rites, are, therefore, often described as *ndakula*.

Jessie Williamson recorded (1940) that the majority of girls in the Dowa district first menstruated between the ages of twelve and fourteen years. In the years proceeding this when they were nine or ten, or during their maturity rites, they were told by their mother or kin to report it at once to the grandmother (*agogo*) when they first menstruated. Otherwise they might die. Thus, when the first signs occur, the young girl goes immediately to her grandmother's hut or to a senior relative. After a ritual washing at daybreak with medicinal herbs, the young girl is then excluded from the normal social life, under the guardianship of an older women who acts as her *phungu*, and who is often a cross cousin (*msuwani*). The young girl, as with the initiates, must be kept in a cold (*ozizira*) condition, as they are susceptible to *mdulo*. She must, therefore, refrain from sexual intercourse which generates heat (*otentha*) and not come into contact with any 'hot', (sexually active) person. She is only allowed to leave the hut before dawn or after dusk, and no one, particularly her mother, must visit her. Whilst menstruating she may come into contact with infants (who are also considered 'cold') but she is instructed that while menstruating she must not put salt in relish, touch the fire or put a pot on the fire, roast maize, nor even take salt in her own relish. The village head, to whose kin group she may belong, must refrain from sexual intercourse during the girl's first confinement, otherwise *mdulo* may result and the girl becomes ill.

Menstruation is described normally as *kusamba* (*ku-samba* – to wash the body) or as *kumwezi* (*mwezi* – month); but the first menstruation is termed *wakula msinku*, to reach maturity or *kuthyola bano* (to break the arrow shaft). A woman in her menses may also be described as *mkazi wa dothe* – woman of the earth – although this expression does not have the negative connotations or imply that a menstruating woman is 'unclean' or 'polluting' in the Judeao-Christian sense. Body dirt is referred to as *litsilo*, and this does have a connotation of dirt or a lack of cleanliness. But a menstruation women, although in a vulnerable 'cold' condition, nonetheless is a source of danger to men and sexual intercourse with a woman in her menses is believed to give rise to serious physical ailments.

It is worth emphasizing that Malawian women do not look upon menstruation in a negative sense, or as being 'polluting' and 'unclean', and in need of 'purification'. The imposition of Judeao-Christian conceptions on the Malawian data, which is common among ethnographers and many Malawian Christians, is misleading, as I suggested earlier. Women have a positive attitude to the menstrual flow, and the first menstruation is the cause of much rejoicing. It is not considered a disease (*nthenda*), but the woman menstruating may be described as cold (*ozizira*), and as noted, must herself be kept in a cool state to avoid serious complications. But her blood is 'hot' and contact with this can seriously endanger others, particularly men. This does not imply she is 'impure' or 'unclean', any more than sexual activity that also generates 'heat' and can cause disease, is seen as 'unclean' or 'polluting' in the Malawian context. Nevertheless, contact with a menstruating woman, as noted, leads to a serious disease among men, which is known as *kanyera*. Chitayo is a related ailment, but it is not, as suggested by Helitzer-Allen (1993), normally linked with sleeping with a menstrual woman, but rather with a woman who has recently suffered a miscarriage or abortion (*ku-taya*, to lose, throw away), and is seen, by men, as a much more serious ailment.

Sleeping with a woman too quickly after childbirth is also seen as leading to *kanyera*, which, in a sense, is a physical manifestation of *mdulo*. A man with *kanyera* is always described as being very 'cold' (*ozizira kwambiri*), as being very weak and without energy, as becoming thin, eventually dying of the ailment if it is not treated. A man with *kanyera* likes to stand by the fire, and has a craving for salt, chillies and meat – all of which are 'heat' generating substances. But treatment of *kanyera* is essentially by medicines, to wash (*ku-chapa*) the body, and to get rid (*kuchosa*) of the bad blood (*magazi woipa*) that has come from the woman. AIDS, because of its association with sex and contagion, has been described as *kanyera* (*chinyera*) *waukulu* (*chi* – large; *ukulu* – senior, important). As such, *kanyera* now tends to be seen as affecting both men and women, and to have a multiplicity of symptoms, especially relating to coughing, chest infections, fever and dysentery.

The crucial importance of 'heat' at the end of a ritual, whether in relation to the *kutenga mwana* ceremony, the *fisi* rite, or as we shall see in the next chapter, the boys crossing the fire at the end of the *jando* initiation, is to 'warm' (*ku-funda*) the child or initiate. It is not a rite of 'purification' (cf. Tembo and Phiri, 1993). Equally the important colour symbolism of many of Malawian rituals, which, as Schoffeleers long ago perceptively outlined (1968: 346), often entail a sequence from red to white via black (as a transition colour), must not be interpreted specifically in terms of ritual purification. Grey ashes and white flour, used frequently in rituals, do not so much signify that the initiate or menstrual woman is now 'pure' or 'clean' (cf. Fraser, 1922: 148), but rather that they are 'cool', for ashes and whiteness (*-yera* – white, *-tuwa* – ash-coloured), are prototypically associated with the coolness of the ancestral spirits. (For a useful text on the anthropology of menstruation which counters some stereotypes see Buckley and Gottlieb, 1988.)

There are no particular dietary prohibitions associated with menstruation but, at the first menses, the young girl is given special medicines called *mkundabwi* which consist of a medicated chicken. As during the initiation rite, this medicine both protects the girls from possible ill effects of *mdulo* and strengthens her body. The chicken used for this purpose is called *nkhuku ya kundabwi*; an alternative term is *pfundabwi*, relating to its warming attributes. Scott described it as 'medicine given in food, probably for its tonic effects' (1929: 209), the chicken constituting the *chizimba* or active principle of the medicine.

It is worth emphasizing that the partaking of the medicated chicken, including its blood, does not signify 'bloodthirst' on the part of the initiates, nor does it suggest that the initiate or menstrual woman has become a 'predator' – as Kaspin interprets a similar rite in the Chewa boys' initiation (1993: 43) – but rather, as in the *chirope* (blood) ceremony of the Nantongwe rituals, the chicken as a *chizimba* medicine gives strength (*mphamvu*) and warms (*kufunda*) the menstrual woman.

At the conclusion of the menstrual rite, the head and the pubic (*chinena*) hairs are shaved (*kumeta*), and the girl is anointed with oil and decked in beads (*mikanda*). It is of interest that a menstruating woman should not wear beads around her waist as beads are widely believed to be a sexual stimulant.

After the first initiation the girl ceases to be a young girl (*buthu*) and is described as a maiden (*namwali*). This she remains until she bears her first child, irrespective of whether or not she is married, for the namwali is not seen as having yet arrived at womanhood (*sanafika kwa chikazi*). This brings us to the final phase of the girls' initiation.

The *chinamwali chachikulu*, the large or senior rite, is held at the first pregnancy when a woman is in her third or fourth month. In Chewa, it is described a *chisamba* (*ku-samba* – to wash the body), in Yao as *litiwo* or *unyago wakumalisya*, the initiation to complete the ceremonies (*ku-malisya* – to finish, accomplish). I will briefly outline the *litiwo* ceremony among the Yao; the Lomwe, Chewa and Man'anja have rites that are very similar. The ritual derives its name from the plaited cord (*ku-tiwa* – to plait), which is put around the woman's neck during the ceremony. As with the *chiputu* ceremony, after initial contacts have been made with the namkungwi or nakanga, who is often a midwife and a close relative of the village head, the women associated with the pregnant girl begin preparations for the brewing of the sweet beer (*thobwa*) which is done with singing and much excitement, the women collecting the water from the stream in a procession. The *namkungwi* carries a red flag, and the faces of the women are smeared with white flour (*ufa*) as a blessing from the ancestral spirits. As in all *chinamwali* rites, the hair of the pregnant woman is shaved off, and this happens during the pounding of the maize, which is done collectively. An important part of this rite was the tying of the *litiwo*, or the sango beads, around the young woman's neck. Made of special sisal, the ring-like structure carried red, black and white beads. Mussa Lumeta described their meaning as follows: red beads meant danger, the black beads meant darkness or seclusion; and the white beads meant re-integration into the society or showing good luck (1975: 11).

About a week later, when all the food and beer has been collectively prepared, the women hold an all-night dance, *chindimba*, a ritual that is performed on other important occasions such as at funeral feasts. Only married women are allowed at these festivities, the women often dancing naked. Throughout the night there is much beer drinking – essential, one woman said to me, to avoid getting tired. Throughout the night a pot filled with beans, *nzama* (Voandzeia subterranea) and *ngunde* (Vigna unguiculata) is kept boiling. In the morning, the pregnant woman is taken for a bath and after this she is seated on a mat with her husband who is accompanied by a sponsor (a woman relative). The women sit around in a circle and all those present partake of a communal meal. The young couple are given instruction by the *nakanga* on the obligations of marriage, and especially on the sexual taboos associated with pregnancy and childbirth. The husband is cautioned not to have extra-marital sexual relations, as this could result in a miscarriage or death of the pregnant woman. Christian women usually avoid the all-night dance, and attend only the communal feast the following morning.

After they have eaten, the women spend the rest of the day dancing and singing the well-known *litiwo* songs, which, as Stannus remarked (1922: 275), are full of poetic license, though it is often difficult to give an exact translation of them, as many of the words and phrases used are euphemisms that only women understand. They usually relate to sexual matters or to childbirth. At a ceremony I was allowed to attend near Domasi, about seventy women were present singing and dancing, and there was not a single man to be seen in the vicinity of the homesteads.

A typical litiwo song recorded by Stannus went as follows:

> Mlasi ugwile mbungo tetemera
> Chikata ngolekwe, wajoje
> Ngolengolekwe wajoje!

> The bamboo has fallen with the wind
> Trembling, patch of mud
> Suspended, well dressed . . .

When it is noted that *chikata* is a euphemism for a woman's genitals (a wet, soft place), and *wajoje* is a slang expression meaning 'everything, everything is out', the erotic meaning of the song is better understood. Stannus suggests that it refers to parturition; but its sexual connotations are unmistakable. Songs I recorded were invariably suggestive, either of sex or childbirth.

As with the *chiputu* rites, the *litiwo* rituals not only express the solidarity of the matrilineal kin group, but also the importance of affinal ties within the rural setting. The mother of the pregnant woman who plays a central role in the *chisamba* rituals, initiates the ceremony by offering a chicken to the village headman, who may well be a brother, or the guardian of her own sorority group (*mbumba*). She also offers gifts to the mother of her daughter's husband. This is expressed with the words, *wathu walasidwa*, meaning that your kin have 'speared' (*kulasa*, to shoot game) my daughter, suggesting a close analogy between marriage and hunting. In return, the husband's mother gives her chicken, which is later eaten with medicines by the pregnant women (Lumeta, 1975: 10).

But what is significant about the *chisamba* ceremony, the final phase of the girl's initiation (*chinamwali*), is that there is no appearance of the *nyau/unyago* masked dancers. Neither men – apart from the husband of the pregnant women – nor animals play a significant role in the rituals which is very much focused around women and the birth of the child.

When Kenji Yoshida wrote, with respect to the Chewa of Eastern Zambia, 'Men in charge of death, women in charge of birth' (1993: 42), although he did not elaborate on this, he was expressing an essential truth about the culture of the Northern Zambezia. For the *chinamwali* ceremonies relating to women, which with respect to the matrilineal cultures, are far more elaborate and important than those of the boys – though, because of their exotic quality, scholars have tended to exaggerate the importance of the *nyau* dancers (although they are important). These *chinamwali* rituals, focussed around women, fundamentally emphasize the positive nature of sexuality and the role of the male affine, symbolized – as *mkamwini* – as a cock or hyena; the importance and fragility of human reproduction which is hedged with rituals, and the social construction of gender. With regard to the latter, the young girl, from the maturity rites at sometimes a very early age, through the *ndakula* ceremony to the first pregnancy, is instilled in both the obligations and the virtues of being a 'mother' (*mai*), a mature female. And this social role is positively affirmed in Malawian culture, and, as in one of the Yao chiputu songs, the suggestion is made that the young girl has the potential of becoming the focus of a large village (*mzinda*).

—4—

Boys' Initiation and the
Nyau Fraternities

Jando: Boys' Initiation Among the Yao

In November 1990, a letter appeared in the *Malawi Times*, suggesting that due to Christian influence, the initiation of girls in Malawi is 'now history in most places' (cf. Banda, 1975: 10). This has not been the case in my experience.

Efforts have been made by both the Catholic and Presbyterian churches to take over the initiation ceremonies – after a long period of denigration and hostility towards *chinamwali* ceremonies by the colonial missionaries. (On this hostility see *Life and Work*, October 1894; Schoffeleers and Linden, 1972: 260.) Apart from the Tumbuka, the initiation of girls, via maturity rites (*chiputu*), was widely practised among matrilineal peoples in Malawi, and still is. The initiation of boys seems to have been more variable, oral traditions suggesting that in many areas of southern Malawi boys were not initiated. (cf. Department of Antiquities, 1971: MNZ 2/1; Werner, 1906: 127).

However, the initiation of boys has a cultural salience and is an important aspect of the social life of all main communities in Malawi, Lomwe, Yao, Mang'anja and Chewa. Indeed, one early writer described the *unyago* ceremonies of the Yao as the most important part of their culture, their celebration representing a 'real fountain of life' (Heckel, 1935: 19). Hence there is no doubt that the initiations have, in the past, been the focus of ethnic identity.

I shall here focus specifically on the *jando/lupanda* rites among the Yao, and the *nyau* rites among the Mang'anja and Chewa for it is evident from my own observations in the Phalombe district and from written accounts (Soka, 1953: 41–5; Boeder, 1984: 51–2) that boys' initiation rites among the Lomwe, termed either *dzoma* or *chidototo*, followed a similar pattern to those of the Yao. Oral traditions, indeed, emphasize that the customs (*miyambo*) of the Yao, Lomwe and Mang'anja are very similar, sharply contrasting with those of the Ngoni who did not hold maturity rites for girls. (Phiri et al., 1977: 256).

Although Yao-speakers use the term *chinamwali* to refer to initiation rites, mwali being Yao for a novitiate, the more usual term is *unyago*. This is a collective concept, and refers to all the three main initiation ceremonies, *chiputu*, *litiwo* and *jando* (*lupanda*). The word is clearly a cognate of *nyau*, which is a secret male society among the Mang'anja, Chipeta, and Chewa (which is discussed below), and it is found widely throughout south east Africa, *isinyago* referring to animal structures – the 'mysterious animals' – among the Mkua of Tanzania (Wembah-Rashid, 1975: 124).

As with the girls' initiation, the *jando* ceremony is sponsored by the village headman, the right to hold and to organize the rite giving public recognition to his authority as headman (*mfumu*), although village heads may often be women. The ceremonies are held annually. The opening of the rite, expressed as to put (*ku ika*) or to make dance (*ku-bvinidwa*), is usually at the end of July, or in early August. In the Zomba district, the *jando* ceremony is always opened before that of the girl's initiation (*chiputu*) and lasts much longer, usually one or two months, depending on the food resources of the village community. Jando is not a Yao term, as it essentially refers to the Islamic circumcision rite: its use indicates the degree to which a community is associated with Islam. The Yao term is lupanda, which concretely refers to the conical mound where medicines are placed. But *jando* and *lupanda* are used almost interchangeably, and the rites now referred to as *jando* are long and complex and follow the essential pattern of the *lupanda* rites as described by earlier ethnographers (Stannus and Davey, 1913; Stannus, 1922: 246–69). It is, as Monica Kishindo remarked, mainly a change in name only (1970: 2). (For an important discussion of the spread of Islam in Malawi and its impact on initiation rites see A.W.C. Msiska, 1995.)

Whether described as *jando* or *lupanda*, the Yao boys' initiation rite follows a similar pattern throughout a wide area, stretching from Makanjira to Zomba. Local people, however, stress that the true *jando* ceremony, unlike the *lupanda*, entails two distinguishing, and, as it were, additional features; there is always full circumcision involving the removal of the foreskin, and a Moslem teacher (*mwalimu*) officiates at the closing of the ceremony when the boys are baptized (The *msondo* ceremony for Yao girls also involves baptism by the *mwalimu*.) Apart from these two features, Islamic influence on these rites is minimal. It has been suggested that the *jando* ceremony lasts only one week, but it has been my experience that the boys usually spend at least three or four weeks in the initiation lodge (Wembah-Rashid, 1975: 124).

Figure 4.1 Young Ngaliba, Likonde Village, near Songani, September 1991

When a number of uninitiated boys (*msongolo*) are present in the
village, the local headman together with the parents and kin of the boy,
liaise with a recognized circumciser (*ngaliba*) who lives in the neighbourhood. Like village herbalists (*asing'anga*) this is a part time activity, and
other than performing this function, the circumciser tends to be an
ordinary villager. I once asked a friend what occupation one *ngaliba*
followed, and he answered with the expression *kulima basi*, he 'only hoes',
insinuating that he has no important standing in the community. The two
circumcisers I knew well were both non-literate and spoke little English.
Earlier studies by Stannus suggests that the *ngaliba* played an important
role throughout the initiation rite. This is no longer the case, the function
of the circumciser primarily being to open the ritual and to circumcise

Figure 4.2 Village headman, Circumcisers (Ngaliba) and young initiates. Ndumu Village, Domasi, Jando ritual, August 1984

the boys. What is important then about the *ngaliba*, is not only their knowledge of medicines, for they have to protect the initiation against harmful influences, but their surgical skills. A *ngaliba*, indeed, builds up his reputation by having no serious mishaps with regards to the circumcision. The *ngaliba* may act as a circumciser for several different villages at the same time. Thus in a single day, he may hurriedly travel around the district with all his paraphernalia, circumcising different groups of boys and opening different initiation 'schools'.

Besides the *ngaliba*, two other people have important roles to play in the initiation. The first is the *nakanga* or *namkungwi*. Usually a senior man, he is responsible for looking after the well-being of the boys (*kuyang'anira ana*) and for organizing the various activities within the lodge during the period of seclusion. It is he, not the circumciser *ngaliba*, who is the 'Master of Ceremonies'. Both *nakanga* and *namkungwi* are terms that also apply to the women ritual leaders in the initiation of girls. The former term is derived from the verb *ku-kanga*, to draw the picture models (*inyago*) at the lupanda ceremonies. Namkungwi is of Mang'anja derivation. It is probably derived from *ku-kungira*, to put a pot on the fire, and is thus a cognate of the Yao term *ku-teleka (mteresi)*, which, as we have seen, is the term used to describe the leader of the *chiputu* rite. The initiation of boys is, therefore, like that of girls, seen as analogous to cooking or to the brewing of beer. It transmutes the young boy, who is held to be 'cool', into a sexual ('warm') male person.

The other person who plays a key role in the ritual is the boy's sponsor, *mlombwe* or *mkamusi*. Each boy has an individual sponsor or helper, usually an elder brother or perhaps a cousin (*msuwani*), who is directly responsible for his welfare during his initiation, and who, under the *nakanga*, also helps in giving instruction and in organizing various ritual activities during the seclusion period. Particularly important among such activities is the construction – and display during the various ceremonies – of the *chinyago*, the masked dancers and animal structures. Among the *alombwe*, various tasks are allotted and one of the sponsors acts as the senior boy (*chitonombe* or *nachilongola, ku-longola*, to go before, be first). Much secrecy surrounds the activities of the *alombwe* or guardians who tend to be young initiated men in their early twenties, although among the Yao, their activities do not constitute any cult fraternity, such as one seems to find among the Chewa, Chipeta and Mang'anja.

Prior to the initiation, groups of young men, usually *alombwe* with associates, go through the villages with drums, singing, collecting foodstuffs and money, and mustering up support for the *chinamwali*. When the day of the circumcision has been decided, usually at the weekend, a group of men under the guidance of *nakanga* or *ngaliba* construct a long grass shelter (*msasa* or *lisakasa*) that constitutes the circumcision lodge. The initiation site itself is described as *ndagala* or *tsimba*, or occasionally, as *dambwe*. It is situated in an area of Brachystegia woodland or scrub vegetation and is always near a stream, and hidden from general view.

The firing of the woodland does not take place until after the initiations have been held. The initiation lodge is approached by a narrow path about 50 yards long, at the beginning of which, near the public path, is an especially constructed gateway (*dimba*). Both the circumcision lodge and the gateway are temporary constructions made of grass and poles tied together with string, made from *chilambe* (*Cissampelos mucronata*). The clearing of the site and the building of the lodge usually takes place in the early morning. When this is done, and prior to its use, the *ngaliba* alone takes some specially prepared medicine and smears the oily substance on the post and some of the trees near the lodge. This is to protect (*ku-tsirika*) both the site and the participants of the ritual from witchcraft (*usawi* or *ufiti*). As with the medicines rubbed into bodily incisions by *asing'anga* (the diviner-herbalist) the protective medicine consists of the charred ashes and bark of various trees mixed with oil. Those invariably used include: *mdima* (*Psorospermum febrifugum*), *njombo* (*Brachystegia longifolia*), *muwanga* (*Pericopsis angolensis*) and *msongole* (*Strychnos spinosa*). All are hard woods that are associated with male potency and strength.

I will describe the jando ritual in three stages.

The Circumcision Rite

In the afternoon, a large number of people gather at the *bwalo* (courtyard or meeting place of the village), often outside the house of the headman. A group of four or five drummers beat out a rhythm and there is much dancing and singing, the gist of the songs being to call the *ngaliba*. The young initiates – who may have spent the night in the headman's compound – are lined up, dressed only in a loincloth and bead necklaces. As in the girls' initiation, they are known as *anamwali*. The village headman or the close female kin of the boys usually smear their foreheads with flour (*ufa*). It is always made from millet pounded in a mortar (*wotibula mum'tondo*), never ground at a maize mill. The flour is an offering (*nsembe* or *mbepesi*) to the ancestral spirits (*mizimu*) and an appeal is made to them to protect the boys during their ordeal. Behind each boy stands his guardian, holding a long stick of sugar cane. A common expression given to the boys who are about to undergo the ceremonial is that they will taste sweet honey (*msoma*). In many villages, the night prior to the circumcision is taken up not only with further offerings to the spirits, but with an all-night dance, maganje. A plea is made by the headman or *nakanga*, to the effect that the dancing should be done without any expression of *conflict* (*osati kufikira ndeu*).

At a given moment, during the afternoon, the *ngaliba* arrives suddenly on the scene, amid much excitement with the women yodelling (*ku-luluta*). The circumciser is always dressed in various mammal skins – genet, bushbaby, leopard, serval. The latter species seems to be the most popular, as it is both a carnivore and is still available for it is a fairly common species. Ideally, I was told, the skins of a leopard (*chisuwi*) or lion (*lisimba*) should be worn. In the past, such skins were the prerogative of important chiefs and senior men (Abdallah, 1973: 13). Additionally, the face of the ngaliba was smeared with red powder, he had several bells tied to his feet and around both his legs and arms he wore strips of red cloth. Strips of bark cloth (*liwondo*) made from the *njombo* tree hung from his waist. Asked why he wore such attire, everyone with whom I discussed the matter suggested that the *ngaliba* represented a wild animal (*chirombo*) and it was to express his fierceness and to scare the initiates and the participants of the ceremony. In a sense, the *ngaliba* embodies the spirit of ancestors in animal form.

The *ngaliba* always carried his important items of equipment, one is his medicinal tail (*mchila*). This is symbolic of his 'office' and as with the *asing'anga* (diviners), it consists of the tail of an antelope or some other mammal. In the past the tail was ideally from a blue wildebeest (*sindi*) or zebra (*mbunda*) but both of these two ungulates have disappeared from southern Malawi during the past century. The base of the tail forms a handle filled with medicine, the charred ashes of various plants mixed with oil (*sile*). The tail plays a crucial role in many ceremonies, and the circumciser is often referred to as *m'michira* (the person of the tail). The other item of importance is the small axe (*nkwangwa*) made from ebony wood (*mpingo*) (*Dalbergia melanoxylon*) carried by the *ngaliba* in his left hand. The ebony wood is black in colour and extremely hard. Together the medicine tail and the ebony axe represent the power, strength, courage, endurance and potency that the initiates are expected to imbibe during their weeks of seclusion.

At the *bwalo*, the *ngaliba* strutted and leaped about shouting aggressively at the audience, his threatening behaviour meant to frighten the boys (*ku-opsya*) and seemed, indeed, to do so. He examined the boys attentively, their ages being between six and ten years, which indicates, like the *chiputu* rite, that this is a maturity and not a puberty ritual. After more flour had been poured out to please the spirits, usually by women related to the initiates, the *ngaliba* left the village followed by all the men and young boys.

On the arrival at the circumcision lodge, there were shouts of 'gate' and men with sticks stopped any individual entering the lodge who has not been circumcised. Any Christians who have not been through the initiation ceremony are not allowed beyond the *dimba*, nor are young boys or women. These rules are taken seriously, and I was not allowed to enter the lodge until I had been examined by the *ngaliba*. At the lodge, the men accompanied by drummers chant songs as the young boys are brought in one by one. The essence of one of these songs is expressed in the following rhythmic phrase:

> Oh oh namabvuto kulira mai
> Mwana wanu akupita ulendo
> There is suffering and tears
> Mother your child is going on a journey

The boys are held to the ground while the *ngaliba* using a sharp knife and a piece of bamboo quickly and deftly cuts the foreskin away. Stannus (1922: 256) was probably correct in suggesting that the complete circumcision, now commonly practised, was a result of Swahili influence. After the circumcision, the penis is bathed in medicines; one circumciser used an iodine swab. In the past, the latex of various trees were used as an astringent, particularly those of the Apocynaceae family. While the operation is being done, the young boy, assisted by his *mlombwe* or an elder male relative, must show fortitude. He must not flinch or cry. The foreskins of the first two boys to be initiated are kept for later ritual burial, those of the others are discarded.

In most of the jando initiations that I attended, the boys went immediately to the *ndagala* from the village *bwalo*. In some areas, however, and certainly in the past in the Zomba district, several days were taken up in a complex series of rituals at the lupanda, prior to entering the initiation lodge itself (*ndagala*). The lupanda was a cleared area of bush between the village *bwalo* and the initiation lodge (*ndagala*), and it is here, at the conclusion of the initiation, that the chinyago figures are drawn.

The Seclusion Period

The boys stay secluded in the initiation lodge for between four and six weeks. During that period they are put through various ordeals and treated with strict discipline. As punishment for misdemeanours, they may be rubbed with itch bean *chitedze*, Mucuna pruriens. As local people describe it, they are instructed – not simply taught – the traditions or customs of the ancestors (*ku-langa miyambo ya makolo*). This is done by means of learning songs, riddles and drumming chants, the latter with the aid of a large piece of bamboo (*nsunguni*). It is beaten rhythmically in unison by all the boys with a stick as they respond to a question or a riddle put to them. They are also given, like the girls, instruction about sexual matters, particularly about the times when it is necessary to refrain from sexual intercourse. They are particularly instructed to show respect (*ulemu*) to senior people and under no circumstances to enter the bedroom of their parents.

The *ngaliba*, however, seems to be little involved in this instruction. What Hugh Stannus wrote more than half a century ago is still relevant today:

> the wale are occupied in receiving instruction given by the *akamusi* on the discipline of manhood, they are taught custom as applied to their relationship with their fellows, and exacting code of etiquette to be observed to their elders, and the observances of married life. They learn to become proficient in the arts associated with their sex – the making of baskets, mats, traps, etc. the method of agriculture, drumming and dancing' (1922: 258).

Gerhard Kubik graphically described the lodge as an 'informal workshop and meeting place for the men' (1978: 12).

During their period of seclusion it is important that initiates should remain 'cool' (*wozizira*); to become 'heated' is seen as having detrimental consequences to their health and wellbeing, particularly the healing of their genital wounds. The village headman, the *nakanga*, the *ngaliba*, the *akamusi* and all close kin of the initiates must therefore refrain from sexual intercourse during this period of seclusion. To do otherwise is to potentially destroy (*ku-ononga*), or cut (*ku-dula*) the young boys. Menstrual women, too, are seen as a source of danger. No women and no person in a 'hot' (*otentha*) condition must enter the initiation lodge or come into contact with the initiates.

Each day women bring food to the *ndagala* but they must stay outside the lodge and it is placed a the gateway (*dimba*). Here there ensues a ritual calling of the sponsors to collect it. The head coils of grass (*singwa* or *nkhata*) that the women use to carry the plates of food are always left at the gate, being placed on a long pole. These are ritually burned at the close of the *jando* ceremony. Ideally, the person bringing the food to the lodge should be a young girl or a woman past child-bearing. During their stay in the lodge, the initiates should eat porridge (*nsima*) and relish (*ndiwo*) that is unsalted. Also, when sitting around the fire, the initiates must be careful not to expose their genitals to the fire, as this would be detrimental to the healing process. Care must be taken, too, not to handle metal instruments such as knives or axes. All these restrictions are related to the attempt to keep the initiates 'cool'. This is taken very seriously by the sponsors. They examine the food brought to the initiates. If the porridge is too dry and cracked, this is taken as a sign that someone close to the initiates has engaged in sexual intercourse – expressed as adultery (*ku-chita chigololo*) even though it may be the parents of a boy involved. The *alombwe* throw away the porridge, rather than endanger the boys under their care.

Many people speak of the initiation lodge as a 'school', and the boys are always initiated collectively. Usually there are between ten and thirty boys in the lodge.

An important symbol of the initiation lodge is the tree or 'root' (*msisi*), a wooden stand holding a flat basket containing flour used as an offering. Each morning and evening the boys are smeared with this flour in seeking the help of the ancestral spirits (*mizimu kuthandiza*) so that their wounds will heal quickly. At the base of the tree is a pot containing medicines. This shrine has affinities to that found in many villages where offerings (*nsembe*) are made at the foot of a custard apple tree *mposa* (Annona senegalensis). The msisi tree is constructed immediately after the circumcision. The *alombwe* digs a hole (*dzenje*) and in this they place two or three saplings, those of *njombo* (*Brachystegia longifolia*) and *chikolola* (*Heteromorpha trifoliata*) are frequently used. But before doing so, medicines are placed into the hole by *ngaliba*, together with and egg and the foreskins of the two leading initiates. Sometimes a chicken is sacrificed – usually a cock (*tambala*), its head being placed in the pit, the rest ritually consumed with medicines.

Throughout the initiation rites, medicines are used – both to protect and to strengthen the initiates. Of the latter, the most important is *mtibulo*, which consists of various herbs all regarded as potency medicines. *Chikolola* is one of these; others included *msuwi* (*Apodytes dimidiata*), *mtesa* (*Grewia micrantha*), *gondlosi*, (*Mondia whytei*), *mkuta* (*Adenia gummifera*) and *nakaundi* (*Steganotaenia araliacea*). The roots or bark of all these trees are important general medicines but they are specifically noted for their strengthening powers and as a potency medicine for men. In Lomwe, the term *mtibulo* is often used to describe semen. Stannus records that one of the songs associated with this medicine specifically relates to the bonds of affines (*tawaga mlamu*) (1922: 250).

Also important are the protective medicines in the form of an anklet provided for each initiate by the *ngaliba*. This consists of a string necklace made from *njombo* bark and a small bag (*chitumwa* or *mnasa*) containing various medicinal tools and *chizimba* (animal) medicines. It forms a protection against witchcraft for each boy.

An important rite (dance) is undertaken during the seclusion period and is associated with the blue-headed agama lizard, *nampopo* (*Agama mossambica*) which is found in the Shire Highlands. One night a person, usually one of the *alombwe*, is decorated with flour in the form of stripes and comes to the initiation lodge. There he dances, pretending to be the lizard, simulating its actions, specifically the bobbing up and down of its head.

Meredith Sanderson noted the phallic meaning of the nampopo lizard in the lupanda rites (1954: 194). What is expressed is that the initiation rites is a symbolic death, the initiate being reborn as a sexual being. Animals have a significant role in this respect, being perceived as sexual and as outsiders (as affines).

Throughout the period of seclusion, there is thus a close identification expressed between participants – whether initiates or their sponsors – and the animal world. While undergoing initiation, the boys are given names, and often these are the names of animals, although usually the names are more personal. The names given to the initiates are commonly carnivores such as *chisuwi* (leopard) or *likule* (jackal) but names such as *sungula* (hare), *chipembere* (rhinoceros), *ngolombe* (duiker) and *njobvu* (elephant) are also noted (Nkondiwa, et al., 1977).

Even more important are the *chinambande* ceremonies, which take place on several days during the *jando* initiation, and, more significantly, form an essential part as we have noted, of the *chiputu* rites. With regard to the latter, these are organized by the *namkungwi* of the *chiputu*. It is she who largely liaises with the *alombwe* arranging for the appearance of the *nambande* or *chinyago* at specific times. The *anamkungwi* are the only women that are allowed into the ndagala as they are usually elderly women, past child-bearing, and may be a grand parent (*agogo* or *nganga*) of the initiate. They are in a sense close to the spirits of the dead (*mizimu ya makolo*) and beyond gender categories.

Importantly, although there is a strong emphasis on gender instructed and imbibed throughout both maturity rites through the female *anamkungwi* and the *alombwe*, there is a close inter-relationship between the two rituals (*chiputu* and *jando*). They could therefore be seen as aspects of a single ritual complex, *chinamwali*. The distinction being that whereas in the jando rites, a strong identification – kinship almost – is emphasized between men and animals, in the *chiputu* rites the animals (men) appear in opposition to the women – as affines.

Nambande or chinambande (*chi*, large, *chinyago* is a synonym) is a representation of an animal consisting of a framework made of bamboo tied with *chilambe* vine, that is covered with grass, bark, hessian or a blanket, daubed with mud and painted with flour in characteristic patterns depending on the mammal or species involved. Stannus (1922: 252) wrote of a sable (*mbalapi*) with a spiral markings, suggesting that the name itself is derived from *mbande*, the spiral shells from the east coast. In the past, these shells were worn only by the chiefs as ornaments, but are now found among the accoutrements of many herbalists. But a sable I observed in the Domasi district had a chequered pattern and other mammal representations may have no distinct pattern at all. The head of the animal often consists of a wooden shape or mask and where appropriate, the *chinambande* have horns or shaggy hair as well as tails. There is a young man – usually one of the *alombwe* – hidden inside the animal structure and they are adept at moving around at remarkable speed. The *nambande* make their appearance at public rituals and they are called by the women as a collectivity, whose songs enquire as to the identity of the animals:

Kodi nyama imeneyi ndi yandani
What is this animal?
To which the alombwe respond.

The animals move about, dance within the *bwalo* space, before returning to the woodland. The *nambande* are spoken of as coming from the woodland (*tchire*, *thengo*), marshy valleys (*dambo*) or the water (*madzi*). They are described as either a wild animal (*nyama*) or as a harmful beast (*chirombo*). There are sexual innuendoes in the movements of many of the animals, and they may dance in unison with the women, although a distance is always maintained. The role of the *nambande* is always seen as being fierce (*ukali*), aiming to scare or frighten (*opsya*) the women, or the initiates. In this way, good character (*amakhalindwe abwino*) and respect for the traditions, it is said, are impressed upon the participants. The animals thus represent the spirits, especially at the night dances.

During the day ceremony, the *nambande* usually keep their distance as with real wild animals, but at the night ritual they come amongst the women. I have records of the following animals represented at the nambande ceremonies:

mbawala	bushbuck
mphalapala/mbalapi	sable antelope
mkango	lion
bwititi	unidentified (note: *lititi* is the ground hornbill, whose nest is a source of medicine)
mvuu	hippopotomus
njobvu	elephant
litunu	hyena
nyamandondo	said to be an antelope (*Dondo* wilderness, thick bush)
mbunju	eland
chisuwi	leopard
liguluwe	bush pig
chipembere	rhinoceros
mbunda	zebra

All these animals are rather large species, most rather uncommon and rarely, if ever, seen by people in the Mangochi or Zomba districts.

Besides these animal structures there are also *inyago* that are not specifically animals but rather represent human or quasi-human figures, although during the ceremony they are usually described as *nyama* (wild animals); examples include *kasinja* (covered in banana leaves, and equivalent to the Chewa figure *kapoli*); *chigalimoto* (car), *ndege* (aeroplane), *lololo*, *haji* and *kimu*. The Swahili influence is apparent with

Boys' Initiation and the Nyau Fraternities

Figure 4.3 The Chinyago Mphalapala, chasing boys, Domasi, September 1990

some of these characters, although there is no reason to suspect that the *nambande* or *inyago* animal structures are merely derived from the Chewa, for such masked *chinyago* dancers are found over a wide area of Tanzania and Mozambique. They are a good deal less elaborate than in the *nyau* ceremonies. In most of the *nambande* rituals I attended only two or three animals structures appeared, one of which was invariable the sable antelope (*mphalapala* or *mbalapi*).

During the seclusion period the *alombwe* and the initiates spend a lot of time constructing one animal structure that makes its appearance at the closing ceremony of the jando initiation. This is *mwanambera* ('child of the breast', *liwele* or *bere*, the breast or matrilineal kinship group, *kubereka*, to bear a child). Surprisingly, this structure is not mentioned by earlier ethnographers.

The Closing Ceremony

On the final night of the *jando* ritual, the *alombwe* and all the senior men gather at the *ndagala* and final instructions and preparations are made with regard to the final ceremony. This includes the ceremonial bathing of the boys. At the same time, people of the village community sponsoring the *jando*, mainly women, gather at the *bwalo*, usually a meeting space close to the headman's house. Here there is much singing, to the accompaniment of drums and whistles. Singing, dancing and general merriment (*wosangala*) may be enacted at the *bwalo* for several hours. During this time the *alombwe* prepare the animal structures (*inyago*), moving them secretly to near the *bwalo*. The initiates are instructed to remain within the *ndagala*. Then about three to four hours after dark, at a time deemed appropriate by the *nakanga*, the initiation hut is fired. The initiates are inside the grass shed when this is done. They do not know what is happening – so are quite taken by surprise. They have to quickly break through the sides of the ndagala. This procedure has its dangers. In August 1990, three young boys were burned to death at a *chinamwali* ceremony at Chiradzulu (*Malawi News*, 8 August, 1990), an event that invoked much discussion. The initiates then have to leap over a fire – made on the path at the dimba. It is made with the grass coils (*nkhata*) that have been gathered during the period of seclusion. These, as said, have been placed each day on the long pole at the gateway and, as Sanderson noted, the *singwa* symbolize the women's genitals (1954: 196) and by extension childhood. Leaping over the fire therefore does two things; it symbolizes the end of the childhood and the partial breaking of the ties with their mother and their kin group. It also plays a role in 'warming' (*wofunda*) the initiate, putting him in an appropriate condition for the wider adult world.

The fire is described as *chilangali*, derived from the verb *ku-langa*, to bid farewell. *Mlangali* is the names of the red calico used in the past and Sanderson (1954: 65) suggested that leaping over the fire was designed to confer fertility on the boys. The warming of the fire marks them as sexual beings, and ends the seclusion when they were 'cool'.

The initiates then, together, enter the *mwanambera*. These take various forms but their general appearance is of an enormous water monster, some eight to ten metres long, made like other *inyago* from a bamboo whicker construction covered in painted hessian. A dozen or more initiates may enter the 'animal'. Even though in modern idiom these structures may sometimes take the form of an aeroplane and be described as a 'super jet' they are invariably referred to as a wild animal (*nyama*) from the water. The meaning of this *chinyago* was described to me as follows: the white lines made of flour signify a person who gives birth to children (*obereka*); the dark background signifies and impotent person; the bamboo framework are the ribs (*nthiti*) of the animal, the cord (*luzi*) the intestines and the boys inside who move it are the heart of the animals (*mtima wa chinyama*).

Responding to the singing and calls of the women this animal (*nyama*) enters the *bwalo* and dances around, often charging the crowd much to the merriment of those present, the women yodelling loudly. Led by the senior sponsor, *chitonombe*, the initiates hidden inside the *mwanambera* sing various songs which they have learnt during the initiation. These are known as *kungwe* songs, the term derived from the Swahili. The songs take the form of a two-part refrain. The *alombwe* leading, the initiates respond in unison. The following is a typical song chanted at the bwalo.

> Mwaitane makolo
> Akhale m'mbali imodzi
> You called the ancestors
> They stay at one side (place)

The songs allude to the fact the *mwanambera* is seen as coming from the water, that marriage is uxorilocal, the young boys (initiates) going away to live (possibly) in another village far away, where they will be expected to build a house for their spouse in the latter village.

Then comes an important song in which the boys inside the *mwanambera* call out, in turn, their name or at least the name of their father. The refrain goes as follows:

> Munene dzina amai amve

Initiates response:

> ine ndine mwana
> Obadwira kwa bambo –

> You speak your name (so that) your mother will hear
> Me, I am the child born to father (name of father).

At the response of each initiate, his mother and female kin respond with cheers and yodelling and the mother gives the boy's sponsor a gift of money. The response of the boys signifies to their kin that they are alive and well – they have not been seen by their female kin for well over a month. It also signifies a change in the boys' status; they are given new names with the prefix *che* added to it. This is a prefix of politeness used when addressing a person. The boys' old names must not be mentioned again. The boys' place is now with the men. Other *inyago* may make their appearance and many other songs are sung, and the festivities and dancing go on through the night and with drums beating, and whistles blowing, testing the stamina of the ethnographer. The *manganje* is one of the more important and stylized of these dances, and there is often transvestite masquerading by the *ngaliba* and various men, including the village headman, much to everyone's enjoyment. The *manganje* dance is performed in a circle with the male drummers seated in the centre, the circle expressing the unity of the kin group. Throughout the celebrations harmony is emphasized, and the close inter-relationships between the group sponsoring the *jando* ritual and the neighbouring villages who attend, is stressed. It is these other groups who will take the initiated boys – now 'sexualized' and potent, as *akamwini*, in-marrying male affines.

The celebrations continue the following morning. A feast is held (*phwando*), there is much drinking of sweet beer (*ntobwa*) and gifts are given by the kin of the initiated boys to the *nakanga* and the *alombwe*. There is much rejoicing, singing, dancing and merriment.

In the past, on the last day of the initiation ceremony the boys are taken to the *lupanda* site to view the *inyago*. This is still practised in some areas. This was a cleared area between the village and the ndagala. Here representations or model pictures were made by the *nakanga* and *alombwe* of animals and other things, using mounds of earth and line drawings of flour (*ufa*). As with the animal structures (*nambande*), these are collectively known as *chinyago* (pl. *inyago*). Both Stannus (1922: 265–9) and Sanderson (1955) give excellent detailed accounts of the *inyago* picture models and I draw freely from their accounts here.

The number of picture models drawn (*ku-kanga*) was variable but three were rarely omitted; *namungumi*, a large water creature usually referred to as a 'whale'; the moon (*mwezi*) which included the *ngwena*, the crocodile in the relief and the *ching'undan'unda*, a model of Yao Hill, the place of origin of the Yao people. The chinyago figures were normally approached in a long line, with the 'hill' at the eastern end near the lupanda tree, the *namugumi* at the western end.

Inyago picture-models included many figures of symbolic significance to the initiates – such as *chomboko* (the place of crossing over from childhood to adulthood), the person *mundu* (said to be a man suffering from a disease due to neglect of taboos), and *chiuta* ('place of the spirits') – it is of interest that the majority of the picture-models are of animals, many of which are also represented as animal structures in the nambande ceremonies. Those recorded include:

lisimba	lion
chisuwi	leopard
ngaka	pangolin
ndomondo	hippopotomus

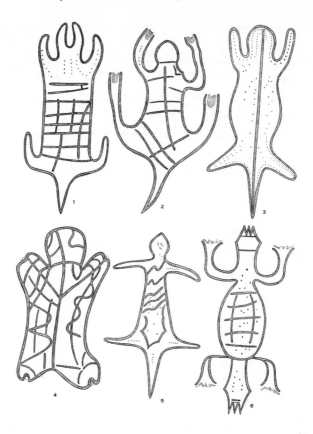

1. Ngwenu (Crocodile)
2. Ngaka (Pangolin)
3. Chisuwi (Leopard)

4. Ndomondo (Hippopotamus)
5. Sakata (Monitor Lizard)
6. Likoloto (Scorpion)

Figure 4.4 Inyago models (after Stannus 1922)

njobvu	elephant
ngwena	crocodile
litunu	hyena
mbunda	zebra
mbalapi	sable antelope
likoloto	scorpion
ngasi	turtle
sakata	monitor lizard
ndandala	kudu

Figure 4.5 Inyago Model (after Sanderson 1955) Sato (Python)

liguluwe	bush pig
sungula	hare
nbunja	eland
sato	python
ndope	reed buck
songo	mythical snake
lijoka	snake
acinauko	mound of mole rat

There is a suggestion by early writers that these picture-models may have totemic significance, but there is no evidence that this is so.

The initiates are taken by the *nakanga* and their guardians to these picture-models and there they are instructed as to their meanings. The *anmwali* are told of the animals' habits, whether or not they are edible and various stories and riddles relating to them. What is emphasized is Yao custom and moral edicts, the *miyambo*, in which they have been instructed over the past several weeks. In the interpretations, particular emphasis is placed on virility and the procreation of children and again there appears to be a strong identification between the boys, animals and sexuality. Sanderson (1955: 38) notes that the time spent on the brief ceremonial perambulations of the inyago picture models, seems highly disproportionate to the amount of time and energy spent on their construction. But the depiction of the *inyago* picture-models is more that merely of an 'object lesson in natural history' (Stannus and Davey, 1913: 122); it offers a deeper instruction in Yao custom and ontology.

What is also of interest is a strong association of some of the inyago figures with the water and with pools, and of the ancestors with both. The water creature, *namungumi*, seems to have affinities not only with the contemporary *mwanambera* but with the Nyanja *napolo*. Sanderson

(1954: 195) noted that *namungumi* was sometimes described as *napolo*, which is a large mythical water serpent associated with flooding, and he himself suggest that it may have been a 'primeval water-mother'. Referring to the animal as *nalumgumi*, Stannus (1922: 267), although accepting that it is a water creature, questions whether it is a 'whale' as the picture-models always depict it as having four limbs. Gerhard Kubik (1987) notes the *namungumi* as a nyau figure in ceremonies in the Blantyre district, and in his earlier seminal paper on African graphic systems, he notes that Lupanda ceremonies away from Islamic influence in the Blantyre district, still depicted a 'picture gallery' of inyago figures. Seven ideo-graphs were drawn, including *namungumi*, which was associated with incest, the *amichila* conducting the initiates around the site on a moonlight night at the conclusion of the ceremony. No animal *inyago* are mentioned (1985: 83–9).

While the antelopes and the carnivorous animals seem to be associated with the woodland, the water creature, *namungumi*, like *mwanambera* is associated with the water and with kinship.

After their examination of the inyago picture-models and the accom-panying instructions, the initiates are returned to the *ndagala* circumcision lodge to begin preparation for the closing ceremonies described above.

I turn now to the *nyau* rituals of the Chewa, Chipeta and Mang'anja.

Nyau Rituals

Cullen Young and Banda long ago described the nyau as a 'primitive masonic brotherhood' with its special vocabulary, rigid restrictions to initiates only and its similarities to the carnivals of the Mediterranean region. Its essential purpose, they argued, was a 'coming-of-age' cere-mony, and no Chewa man was deemed to have the full status of an adult male if he had not been through the *nyau* initiation (1946: 25).

At the time, they write, however, given the long influence of the Christian Churches, many Chewa men had not been initiated into the *nyau*, and this is still very much the case. More recently, Isaac Lamba wrote that as a secret society the nyau 'constitutes the pith of the Chewa traditional life' (1985: 68).

The *nyau* is an ancient fraternity of men that is specifically associated with the so-called Maravi peoples (Chewa, Nsenga, Nyanja, Chipeta, Nthumba, Mang'anja, Mbo).

The kind of masked dance associated with the *nyau* usually referred to as *gule wamkulu*, the big dance, or *masewero* (play or dance) is by no means restricted to the Maravi peoples for it has clear affinities to the masked dances found throughout central and eastern Africa known variously as *chinyago* (Yao), *isinyago* (Makua), *midimu* (Makonde) and *makishi* (Ndembu) (cf. Turner, 1967: 239–44; Wembah-Rashid, 1975: 123–37; Binkley, 1987).

The term *nyau* has diverse meanings. It is the name given to the secret male societies as well as to the masked dance itself, while the esoteric masked dancers and theriomorphic structures are also described as *chinyau* (plural *vinyau* or *zinyau*). Both Rita Ferreira (1968) and Mlenga (1982) stress its role as the initiation into adulthood; but the nyau masked dancers also play a crucial role at funeral ceremonies (*maliro*), at commemorative rituals for the dead (*mpalo* or *bona*), and during the initiation of girls (*chinamwali*). In recent years *nyau* dancers have also performed at national celebrations and at cultural performances arranged by the Museums of Malawi. There are variations, however, in the degree to which *nyau* is associated with the funeral and the girls' initiation rites.

Given the secret nature of the *nyau* – something not unique to the *nyau* for secrecy surrounds also the initiation rites and customs associated with women – and the fact that *nyau* dances are predominantly held during the dry season from August to October, early travellers like Livingstone made no mention of the nyau. The earliest Europeans to record their observations of the rites tended to emphasize their religious nature. The French traveller, Edouard Foa, who passed through the lower Shire near Chapananga in the 1890s, interpreted the *nyau* performance as a temporary reconciliation between humans and animals, and their subsequent separation, a ritual that Schoffeleers suggests is a re-enactment of the Chewa creation myth (Foa, 1900; Schoffeleers, 1976: 63). Rattray (1908: 178–9) links the nyau 'representations of animals' at the funeral ceremonies, to the spirits of the dead (*mizimu*), as a form of reincarnation.

The origins of the *nyau* is clouded in mystery, and is clearly of great antiquity. Rangeley, in his pioneering study of the *nyau* of Nkhotakota, suggested, probably correctly, that the Chewa brought the ceremonial dances with them when they migrated from the Congo heartland, for the use of ceremonial masks is widespread throughout west and central Africa (Laude, 1971). He record one myth of origin relating to a member of the Phiri clan, Nyanda. During time of famine, Nyanda began dancing for the pleasure of local people who gave him food in return for his efforts. Other people soon joined in the dancing and Nyanda began to invent many variations. These were practised in the bush. When the famine had ended the young men continued the *nyau* dances. Previously, according to Rangeley's informants, the *nyau* never danced at funerals, but after Nyanda died they started to dance nyau at funerals, as well as at the initiation of girls. The *nyau* dancers were invited by old women initiators (*anamkungwi*) to the latter initiation specifically to instruct and frighten the girl initiates. As with Rattray, Rangeley stresses the association of the *nyau* with the spirits of the dead, but he makes two misleading inferences: one is that the spirits of the dead are primarily the concern of men, which is not the case; the second is that women are regarded by the Chewa as 'fundamentally unclean'. This, too, is an exaggeration, although as we have noted, there are important prohibitions relating to menstruation (Rangeley, 1949: 36–8).

It remains unexplained where people found the food to give the dancers during the famine, but the association of *nyau* origins with the famine situation seems to be widespread. Other traditions suggest that *nyau* was initially started by women, as part of the girls' initiation, and that it was later taken over by the men, to be performed at the funeral ceremonies of important chiefs (Jackson, 1929; Mlenga, 1982: 2). Schoffeleers records quite different oral traditions which suggest that the *nyau* and the rain shrines were initially one institution, the *nyau* being particularly respons-ible for the initiation of girls at the shrine. But according to tradition, an accident occurred at the shrine, several girls losing their lives. At one shrine they were crushed under a falling rock; at another they were drowned in the sacred pool. The outcome was that the *nyau* dancers were instructed to leave the shrine. The traditions thus explicates why it is that at the present time the *nyau* dancers are not allowed near the rain shrines and the shrine officials do not attend *nyau* performances (Schoffeleers, 1976: 62). It is worth noting, however, that nowadays the *nyau* are not directly involved in the initiation of girls – this is the responsibility of older women; that the girls' initiation does not take place in the forest associated with the rain rituals but at a site within the village environs; and that because of their association with sexuality and animals – both associated with the generation of heat – the *nyau* would, in Chewa conceptions, be naturally antithetical to the rain rituals, where the simulation of coldness is conducive to the bringing of rain.

As with the girl's initiation, the right to organize the *nyau* is held by the local chief, who is known as *mwini mzinda*, or *mwini dambwe*, owner/ guardian of the village or the initiation site. In the past, this was a mark of high status and normally conferred by the regional chiefs with the offering of a medicinal bundle or tail. The right to *mzinda*, as with the chiefship itself, was passed on from the maternal uncle (*malume*) to a younger brother or sister's son. But the local chief or village headman is not directly involved in the organization of the initiation ceremonies of the *nyau* or with the *nyau* dances themselves; this is the responsibility of the group of senior men, *anamkungwi*, who are well versed in nyau. Often responsibilities are divided between three functionaries.

The *mkulu wakuthengo* or *wakumadzi* (elder of the woodland or of the water) has responsibility for the initiation site, the meeting place of the *nyau* members in the forest (*nkhalango*). This is situated in thick woodland (*thengo*) usually near a graveyard (*manda*) or at the site of an old one, and is always near water. The site is called *dambwe* as well as being referred to as *dambo* (a marshy valley) or *kumadzi* (at the water). It is always away from the paths and villages, and, like the Yao initiation lodges, it is marked with warning signs. These are generally red flags tied to bamboos. Only *nyau* initiates are allowed to enter the *dambwe*, and any person inadvertently stumbling upon the site would be driven away, often severely manhandled. It is at the *dambwe* that the *chinyau* masks and theriomorphic figures are constructed. The *mkulu wakuthengo* was responsible for coordinating the activities of the *nyau* members at the *dambwe* and for maintaining discipline within a specific *nyau* association.

The second functionary is the *mkulu wakumudzi* (the elder of the village) who is responsible for the *nyau* performance itself at the *bwalo*. He acts as a second-in-command to the *mkulu wakumadzi*, and organizes the food, beer and the various activities of the *nyau* dancers at the liunde, the dressing place near the village where the dancers get ready for their public performances.

The third important figure in the *nyau* rites is a senior woman (*namkungwi*) who is also the 'mistress of ceremonies' in the girls' initiation rite. She is known as *wakunjira* ('of the path') and is the only women allowed to enter the dambwe. She acts as a go-between, co-ordinating the *nyau* dancers with respect to their appearance at the girls' initiation rites. She is often a close relative of the chief. In his study of *gule wamkulu* at Malingunde, near Lilongwe, Timpunza Mvula (1992: 36–7) writes of the *wakunjira* or *chiwinda* as the senior male responsible for the smooth running of the *nyau* performances, and for protecting the dancers from witchcraft. *Chiwinda*, which in the past meant 'leader of a caravan', is derived from the verb *ku-winda*, to protect with medicines. He also wrote of the *tsabwalo*, the person specifically responsible for preparing the *bwalo* for dancing, and the *tsangoma* who was responsible for the drummers.

Active membership in a local *nyau* association required that a person, if not a leader, would be a drummer, dancer or an assistant. Initiates might spend a long time as assistants before rising to seniority within the association, and those with most expertise played the more important drums and wore the best masks. Schoffeleers who made a detailed study of the *nyau* societies of the Chikwawa district, estimated that the active membership of a local society averaged about fifty members (1968: 327).

A boy can sometimes be initiated into the *nyau* when quite young, perhaps around nine or ten years of age. Rangeley felt that in the past *nyau* membership was restricted to older men and that the initiation of young boys represented a 'degeneration' of customs – although there is no evidence that this is the case. In the Lower Shire, the average age of initiation into the *nyau* is about 16 with a minimum age of ten years, although Schoffeleers suggests that among the Chewa *nyau* membership was more in the nature of a 'tribal initiation' (1968: 344). Nyau initiates thus tend to be older than these undergoing the jando rite and among neither the Mang'anja nor the Chewa is any form of circumcision practised.

Nyau initiates are described by the same term as that used for girls initiates – *namwali* (pl. *anamwali*). Each initiate has a sponsor or guardian (*phungu*) to give him instruction and guide him though his ordeal. The *phungu* is already a member of the *nyau* and is usually a cross cousin or brother-in-law (*mlamu*), that is an affine (Marwick, 1968: 6). Through the *phungu* a fee is paid to the *nyau* by the parents of the initiate; this can either be a goat or chicken or a cash payment. On the appointed day, after making prior arrangements with the *mkulu wakuthengo*, the young initiate is taken by his *phungu* to the *dambwe*. He is usually taken when the preparations for an *nyau* performance is being made. He is warned that he must observe absolute secrecy with regard to everything he sees and learns at the *dambwe*, and that to divulge anything will have serious and grave consequences. It is for this reason that I never formally joined any *nyau* society although several of my friends were *nyau* members and I have discussed nyau matters with many of them. As fees for initiation and for dances are an important source of income for many *nyau* members, especially the senior men, admittance to *nyau* can usually be obtained by means of a cash payment.

Before reaching the *dambwe* the initiate is blindfolded and stripped. When his eyes are opened, he is confronted with the *zinyau* masked figures. Before this, however, the boy is forced blind to enter one of the theriomorphic structures, usually *kasiyamaliro* and there the *nyau* member already inside the structure beats him. He is thoroughly frightened. Then, as Hodgson writes referring to the Chewa of the Dowa district:

> The figures are pushed against him filling him with terror, and he is told that the *mikhwala* (theriomorphic figures) are the spirits of distant ancestors, and the *visudzo* (masked dancers) those of their children, and that they have emerged from the stream. Then his trials begin.

The boy is then put through a series of ordeals; he is suspended head downwards from a tree over a lighted fire, and swung around so that he does not burn; he is rolled in the grass where gum and itch beans (*chitedze*) have been placed; a string is tied to his testicles and he is dragged about by a string; excrement is smeared over his body. He is beaten, screamed at, mocked and abused – all to test his fortitude and powers of endurance. Central to the initiation is being frightened, like with the girl initiates – and being pushed around by the animal structures (*chinyau*). But unlike the girl initiates, the boy is then himself initiated in the structures and meanings of the *chinyau* figures. All writers of the nyau describe the initiation as an individual induction process and this again is quite distinct from the *jando* initiation and the girls' maturity ritual. Important to this process is his symbolic death and rebirth. Thus the *mkulu wakumadzi* and his associates dig a shallow grave, wrap the boy in a cloth so that he cannot see, and symbolically buries him. He is left to climb out by his own devices (Hodgson, 1933; Rangeley, 1949).

Initiation into *nyau* takes a week or more and concludes with gifts from his mother and kin being presented to his guardian and by the adoption of a new name. During the initiation period, besides the ordeals, three sets of instructions are impressed upon him, namely the secret code of the *nyau*, the customs relating to appropriate adult behaviour, and the close identification they are persuaded to make between themselves and both the animals and the spirits of the dead.

At the *dambwe* the initiate is taught the secret vocabulary associated with the *nyau*, particularly of the names of the various parts of the animals structures. This is done by means of riddles. Thus, for example, castor oil (*nsatsi*) is described a *thamanda* (pool), the mask (*chigoba*) is called *mpeni* (knife), the head ring (*nkhata*) is *mtumbo* (intestines), the leading instructor (*namkungwi wamkulu*) is referred to as *nkwangwa* (axe) or *msompho* (adze). As with the Yao, the various parts of the theriomorphic structures each have an alternative *nyau* term. The branches or bamboos (*nsungwi*) used to make the structures are called *nthiti* (ribs) and the bark string (*luzi*) is called *nkhole* (the hidden, or menstrual blood), the grass (*udzi*) used as a covering is called *ubweya* (fur). (Rangeley, 1949: 41; Schoffeleers, 1968: 257).

There is some variation in the meanings of various objects in different areas but an understanding of the secret *nyau* vocabulary gives a person access to the *nyau* fraternities. Thus strangers are admitted to the *dambwe* if they can prove themselves to be *nyau* members by giving satisfactory answers to all the questions or riddles put to them by senior instructors.

While in the *dambwe* the initiate is also given instruction regarding the appropriate moral and sexual behaviour of an adult role. He is told that he must respect his parents and elders; that he should not enter his parent's rooms without permission or express familiarity with his parents-in-law; that he should never step over a woman's legs or a mortar pestle; that when his wife is pregnant he must not have sexual intercourse with another woman otherwise he could 'cut' (*kudula*) his spouse; that he must never sleep with a menstruating woman and that he must not take food left over in his mother's hut (Schoffeleers, 1968: 344–7; Banda, 1975: 8). Many of these prohibitions are related to the idea that sexual activity increases a condition of 'hotness', and that this, in turn, may give rise to *tsempho* disease, with its various manifestations. During the initiation or a *nyau* performance, it is, therefore, important that both the initiate and the dancers remain 'cool'. There is, therefore, a prohibition on sexual intercourse by all *nyau* members and those closely associated with the initiate.

Also important during the initial period of induction into the *nyau* is what Father Boucher calls 'the process of identification', whereby initiates are compelled to identify themselves with the spirits of the dead and with animals – both of which are associated with the woodland environment. In the *dambwe* they speak a secret language and they are admonished or fined if they inadvertently use a wrong term – the meanings of which often have obscene or sexual connotations. They go about naked and eat raw food and they engage in anti-social behaviour. They even handle such objects as human bones and hair, which in normal circumstances is associated with witchcraft (*ufiti*). When with their *nyau* associates they go into the village domain and behave like wild animals – stealing chickens, aggressively chasing people, using obscene language – the activities of the *nyau* is deemed to be outside the law and the normal jurisdiction of chiefs and headman (Boucher, 1976: 4). Thus there is the general idea that the *nyau* are wild animals, spirits, or even witches. As wild animals they cannot be punished or arrested as their misdemeanours have no moral status.

Throughout the rites of initiation, medicines play an important part. At the beginning of the ritual the boy is given medicated chicken and before he leaves the *dambwe* for the first time he must take a further medicine prepared by the *phungu*. This is made from the root of a Euphorbia tree *kapilapila* (*Flueggea virosa*) which is used in the making of the theriomorphic structures. The root, which is taken in relish or beer, is believed to prevent the boy talking in his sleep and thus divulging *nyau* secrets. (Rangeley, 1949: 42; Rita-Ferreira, 1968: 21). Deborah Kaspin suggest that the purpose of the male initiation is to turn boys into sexual men, and 'predatory' members of the nyau. She describes their entrance into the body of the antelope, 'symbolizing their death as children and their rebirth as beasts', and she notes too the sacrifice of a chicken (*nkhuku*) – without so much as mentioning that these rituals had been described over half a century ago by Hodgson and Rangeley. But her analysis is highly coloured by making one motif in the rites the analogy between hunting (predation) and marriage (sex) into the main axis of the Nyau ritual. Thus the sacrifice of chicken is described as satisfying 'blood lust', and the men are described not just as animals but as carnivores – predators (*chirombo*), while the women are interpreted throughout as being helpless and submissive game animals (meat, *nyama*) (1993: 43). Analogous associations between hunting, sex and eating are common in Malawi, as they are in many cultures including our own, but predation is not the central motif of the nyau rituals. Apart from the *fisi* (hyena), *mkango* (lion), *chigaru* (large dog) and *nkhandwe* (jackal) almost all the theriomorphic figures in the *nyau* rituals are herbivores, and men are most closely identified not with carnivores but with antelopes, particularly the kasiya *maliro* (the eland). In addition, the sacrifice of the chicken is not to satisfy some 'blood lust' but is a form of medicine, which as a *chizimba* or *chirope* (blood) medicine, gives the young boys strength, potential as hunters, and sexuality to perform their role as affinal males, expressed in terms of making them 'warm' (*kufunda*). Hunting in Malawi is ill-understood if interpreted simply as a form of predation. The central motif of the *nyau* rituals – which are enacted as public performances in the village setting – is not an opposition between men as predators (*chirombo*) and women as game animals or meat (*nyama*) as portrayed by Kaspin, but rather between the men as *nyau* figures who represent the male affine as a sexual being, and who are symbolically associated with the woodland, the spirits of the dead, and animals (particularly the powerful *nyama*, like the elephant and eland antelope), and women who are identified with the matrilineal kin group and the village. The terms *mzimu* (spirit of the dead), *chirombo* (wild beast) and *nyama* (game animal) are used almost interchangeably to describe the *nyau*, for the *nyau* 'embody' the spirits (as Yoshida, 1992: 217) accurately portrays the relationship), are associ-ated as *chirombo* with the woodland beyond the village (moral) domain, and have the power of *nyama*, which, as we described elsewhere, is not simply meat, but implies the inherent powers of nature. These terms apply to both the masked dancers like *kasinja* and theriomorphic figures like *nswala*, and it is misleading to see the masked dancers as simply representing 'spirits', and the theriomorphic figures simply as real 'animals' (cf. Probst, 1995: 7). Sembereka (1990) indeed speaks of the *nyau* dancers, both masked figures and theriomorphic structures, as 're-incarnating' the spirits of the dead.

All writers confirm that the *nyau* dancers consist essentially of two types, although both are referred to by participants as *zirombo* – wild animals. In the first category are the masked dancers who imitate human beings and whose enactments are treated as 'exemplary models', as they usually depict certain human traits or characteristics. They are regarded as spirits of dead ancestors who come back in the form of nyau and they are usually associated with the day. Early writers spoke of them generally as *visudzo*.

The second category consists of theriomorphic structures or figures that represent animals. Rangeley suggested that there was no general term for these, but early writers describe them as *mikhwala* derived from the verb *ku-khwala*, to seek or look for. They are usually associated with the night ceremonies. These are only rough categories, some do not belong to either class, and some theriomorphic figures do perform during the daytime (Hodgson, 1933: 146–51; Jackson, 1929; Rangeley, 1949: 42).

Both the masked dancers and the animals structures are manufactured in secrecy and in the *dambwe*. The making of the carved masks usually requires great skill, some are beautifully made and acquire great value, and the masks can be hired out to dancers for a fee. The masks are individually owned, and are mostly coloured black and /or red. Many of the masks have horns, and their hair or beard is made from strips of cloth or hide. The masks are usually head-size and are worn by a single dancer. In the Lower Shire, some theriomorphic figures such as *chikango* (lion) and *tsanchima* (blue monkey) appear as individual masked dancers. Besides the mask, the dancers usually adorn themselves with maize cob leaves (*khoko*), which as Rangeley remarked, is of interest given that maize is a relatively recent introduction to Malawi, but the fibre of banana leaves or stems and strips of bark clothe may also be used as a covering. Some masked dancers cover themselves with red *katondo* clay and in some areas dance naked at night.

In the construction of the theriomorphic figures, a variety of plant materials are used such as bamboo, grass, branches, banana leaves, maize husks as well as skins or cloth. The common *kasiyamaliro* is usually impressively made from woven bamboo much like the traditional maize store (*nkhokwe*) and this constitutes a woven basketwork figure. The theriomorphic figures are sometimes plastered with mud and decorated in different colours, various patterns of red, white and/or black being used. Geometrical designs are often drawn. The black colouring is usually obtained by mixing charcoal with castor oil, the white from flour and the red colouring by mixing oil with the extracts of various plants such as banana or sorghum (*mapira*). The structures on the whole are quite light and they are activated by a single dancer hidden within. But the larger structures, such as *njobvu* (elephant) and *mkango* (lion) – which may be several metres in length – are motivated by several *nyau* members. The *nyau* structures are moved around with tremendous speed and agility, often spinning around in a cloud of dust accompanied by rhythmic drumming. In Eastern Zambia, Yoshida notes that there are three types of *nyau* among the Chewa, those like the *kasinja*, who are 'feathered', or covered with leaves; the masked dancers, and the theriomorphic structures. All are described as *nyama* (animals) and are believed to 'embody' the spirits of the dead, but the theriomorphic figures are called *nyau yolemba*, because while dancing these figures whirl furiously around drawing circles on the ground (*ku-lemba*, to draw) (Yoshinda, 1992: 213–15, 1993: 35).

Significantly, whereas the masks are kept for future use – and are increasingly being sold as tourist items – the theriomorphic structures are ritually burnt at the end of the *nyau* performance, and their ashes scattered in a stream. When the structures are burnt the *nyau* members must not look back at the animal figures, otherwise this is seen as giving rise to the condition chirope.

In an important sense the masks and the theriomorphic structures have a different function relating to the different conceptions of time. The masked dancers encapsulate historical time, often depict historical figures – *kenyoni* for example relates to a past colonial administrator Kenyon Slaney – whereas the theriomorphic figures imply a cosmological conception of time. The latter figures thus return to the woodland, the domain of the spirits.

One could say that the masked dancers represent the spirits of the more recent ancestors as historical personages, while the theriomorphic figures represent the collectivity of the ancestors. The first have a largely moral function; the second being focused on fertility and the regeneration of life. It is significant that Schoffeleers collected essays (1997) are entitled *Religion and the Dramatisation of Life*.

Although in some areas women are beginning to participate as nyau performers, in the past only men were allowed to wear masks and carry the theriomorphic structures. For the simple reason that the *nyau* society is essentially a male organization. Schoffeleers refers to it as a 'kind of men's club' (1976: 60).

Within a given locality there are a limited number of animal structures associated with a specific *nyau* 'club'. Each *nyau* image having its own name, songs and drum beats. But throughout Malawi, the number of masks and structures run into several hundred, even though names of specific masks may vary from district to district. Father Boucher has recorded around 300 different masks form the Mua and Dedza districts alone. I want here to concentrate on the theriomorphic structures, but a brief mention may be made of some of the more common masked figures. As examples, five may be noted.

Chadzunda is derived from the verb *ku-dzunda*, to be thin, poor, diseased. It typically represents a deaf man, and the mask is large and black, with either feathers or animal fur behind the head. It appears at the *bwalo* as an old man or chief, and is very popular, not being fierce or assaulting people.

Makanja (or *titalande*) is a figure on stilts which struts around and dances, rather precariously, only during the day. He wears a costume of banana or jute fibre or has bark cloth, and often has a feathered hat. He carries a medicine tail and a stick to chastize those who misbehave.

Kadyankhadzi means 'to eat the *nkhadzi* tree'. The latter is the milkbush, *Euphorbia tirucalli*, whose latex causes temporary blindness and which is grown around graves. This masked dancer is also known as *chabwerakumanda*, 'one who comes form the graveyard' (dead). The mask is red, surrounded with feathers of guinea fowl or coucal, and the body of the dancer is covered with red earth. Several *kadyankhadzi* dance together and by tradition they are always fierce, charging women and children in the village. Rangeley speaks of this *nyau* as one of the most popular. It is also seen as representing the sister's son (Birch de Aguillar, 1994: 25).

Kang'wing'wi is an extremely fierce *chinyau* with a headdress of leaves and apart from leaves tied around the waist, the dancer is completely naked. He plays the role of an erotic male, and according to Mvula (1922: 43), escorts women to the forest to collect firewood for brewing beer.

Kapori. This masked dancer seems to be equivalent to the Yao *chinyago kasinja*, and it is also known as *kumatewa*. The ones I observed wore a red cloth headband and numerous feathers forming a headdress, and covered the upper part of the body so that the wearer was almost hidden. Around the legs were fastened maize cob leaves. *Kapori* masks are worn mainly by younger members of the *nyau* and they guard the approaches to the *dambwe*. They dance on almost all occasions and two or three usually go together. They engage in banter with the women and sing songs at the *bwalo*. These are often obscene or have sexual connotations, explicitly mentioning a women's genitals (*nyini*).

Both scholars stress the sexual context of the songs of *kapori* and the importance of sexuality and the bearing of children for the Chewa.

Figure 4.6 Kapolo masked figure, Dedza, September 1990

Fecundity, notes Boucher, is a priceless value for this community. Kapori, as said, is equivalent to the *kasinja* figure of the Yao, and to the *nyau* of the same name described by Yoshida among the Chewa of Zambia.

Kasinja is a sexual being, covered in the feathers of the guinea fowl (*nkhanga*) and chickens (*nkhuku*). They represent the male affine – a cross-cousin (*msuwani*) to the women with whom they exchange sexual banter – and are seen as 'embodying' the spirits of the ancestors. They are particularly associated with degenerative woodland, and with the margins of the village, and there is a sense in which while the therio-morphic structures (as affines) are identified with the woodland, the *kasinja* and other masked dancers (which are often therianthropic figures) are what Douglas (1975) described as 'mediators', moving *between* the woodland and the village, which is the domain of living humans, prototypically a group of matrilineally-related women and their 'female' brothers. The conflict expressed in ritual between the 'spirits' (*nyau*) and the 'men' over the control of the women, relates to the inherent duality within matriliny, between men as affines, outsiders, sexual beings, associated with the woodland as hunters of game animals, and men as brothers and guardians of their matrikin. (Yoshida, 1992: 221–3, 237–8; Probst, 1995: 8).

There are many more common masked dancers among the Chipeta, Chewa and Mang'anja; such as *kavinsabwe* (the person with lice), *mbiyazodooka* (broken pot), *nkhalamba* (an old man), *chimbano* (a horned *nyau* who is a guardian of the spirits), *natola* (the thief), and *kachipapa* (whom Boucher links with iron smelting). There are also such masks as Maliya and Simon Petero by means of which the *nyau* mimic, ridicule and mock European culture and Christian religion, and more recently there are masks depicting contemporary political figures, and issues relating to AIDS (Birch de Aguilar, 1994; Probst, 1995).

What is of interest is that not only are these masks referred to as wild animals (*zirombo*) – although they may also be described as *mizimu*, and in their performance they may depict human traits and personality types – but in their construction they often reflect animal characteristics. Thus most of the masks are fringed with feathers or animal skins and such masks as *koweni, gonthi, chimbano, kwakana* and *sakambewa* all have characteristic horns and many large white teeth giving them a very aggressive appearance. Moreover, most of these masks are red and black, colours which signify blood, ashes, fire and sexuality. Thus for many of the masks, it is rather ambiguous whether they represent spirits of the dead (*mizimu*), human archetypes or animals. In essence, they could be said to embody all three.

For further details of masked figures, see Hodgson, 1933: 149; Jackson, 1929; Rangeley, 1950; Makumbi, 1955; Blackmun and Schoffeleers, 1972; and Birch de Aguillar, 1994 who outlines the kinship relationship between the various nyau masked figures.

The theriomorphic structures are perhaps fewer in number than the masked figures but nevertheless, over fifty figures have been noted, representing mammals, birds and reptiles, both large and small. Seven species, are particularly noteworthy, as they are invariably present at almost all important *nyau* ceremonies and throughout a wide area.

Chimkoko (or chiwoko)

This is a huge theriomorphic structure, up to nine metres in length with large ears and humps. It is a mythical creature, often with a cow's head and is said to represent the spirit (*mzimu*) of a respected ancestor. Its body is usually covered with husks of maize cond or grass. It makes its appearance at both funerals and the girls' initiations.

Kalulu (the scrub hare)

As with the previous species, this dancer is, surprisingly, not mentioned by Rangeley (1950), but it is an important figure at most *nyau* performances, invariably opening the ceremony. The hare is also a central figure in many Malawian folk tales. As a structure it is covered with grass and painted dark grey with mud.

Kasiyamaliro

This is perhaps the most important *chinyau*, present at almost all the performances and seems akin to the *chinyago mphalapala* (sable). Its name means 'to leave the funeral'; and it plays an important role at the completion of the funeral ceremony (*maliro*) accompanying the dead to the grave. This theriomorphic figure dances also at *chinamwali* ceremonies, both day and night. Rangeley noted that only one structure dances at any one time (1950: 21) but Laurel Faulkner (1988) suggest that as many as thirty *kasiyamaliro* may dance together. This figure essentially represents an antelope, probably an eland (*ntchefu*) or impala (*nswala*), although its horn structure varies according to district and some distinctly look like a kudu (*ngoma*). Its alternative name is *mkhala* (a general term for theriomorphic figures, of which the antelope seems to be the prototype), and nswala. Rangeley considered the latter to be a generic term for all antelopes, but in everyday use it specifically refers to the impala. The structure may be up to two metres high with a distinctive sag in the middle of its back. Louis Denis referred to it as the 'principle beast' of the nyau. With the elephant it completes the chinamwali ceremony.

Mdondo

This is another mythical animals with several horns and large in size, being carried by up to fourteen men. Fr. Denis (1929) felt it might represent a snake (*njoka*) or millipede (*dzongololo* or *bongolo*) but it is invariably described as a *nyama*, which would suggest a mammal species. As with the Yao chinyago, it is sometimes described as *nyama-mdondo* (*nyama*, wild animals, *dondo*, wilderness, or thick bush), and Hodgson (1933: 147) refers to it as a 'game animal'.

Figure 4.7 The nyau figure Kasiyamaliro, Dedza, September 1991

Mkango (lion)

Blackmun and Schoffeleers (1972) describe this as a masked dancer, made of hide and with tusks of a warthog, but in other areas it may be a large theriomorphic figure several metres in length. It is usually danced only at night, and its appearance is heralded by load roars made on a gourd resonator. It is said to represent the 'bad' spirits (*chiwanda*). Often danced at a chief's funeral, when it is said that the spirit of the chief takes the form of a lion. Among the Shona of Zimbabwe, there is a close association between the spirits of dead chiefs and lions articulated through spirit mediums (*mhondoro*) (Bourdillon, 1976: 253), but the association of lions with chiefs is common in Malawi.

Njobvu (elephant)

Also known by the Yao term *ndembo*, it is the senior and most important theriomorphic structure and its appearance marks the climax of the *nyau*. It appears, however, only in the most important occasions such as the

Figure 4.8 Nyau figures, in mural painting by Father Boucher, Mua, August 1998

funeral of a senior chief. The structure is of enormous size, several metres long, and is made of a strong bamboo framework covered with sacking. In the past bark cloth was used. It is carried around by four men, usually senior members of the *nyau*, who are called its legs (*miyendo*). The *njobvu* is always accompanied by between four and six masked dancers known as *ayere* or *abwenzi*. *Ajere* is a clan name and alludes to past elephant hunters of Chikunda origin – not as Linden (1975: 41) suggested, the original inhabitants of Malawi – who are known as Abatwa. The other term means 'friend'. Each *ajere* carries an axe and during the ceremony they enact the hunting of the elephant; stalking, chasing and then hamstringing the *njobvu*. When following the elephant they call out, 'bwenzi, *bwenzi*' (friend, friend) and when they attack they shout 'ndiyanga, ndiyanga, nyamazo, nyamazo' (it is mine, it is mine, that

Figure 4.9 Nyau figures in mural painting by Father Boucher, Mua, August 1998

animal, that animal) (Rangeley, 1950: 21). Only senior men dance as *ajere* and they only dance with the elephant. As we noted elsewhere in discussing dietary prohibitions, *Jere* is also an Ngoni clan name, whose totemic animal is an elephant. The Ngoni word for elephant is *ndlovu*. Laurel Birch de Aguillar (1994: 41–2) has an interesting discussion on the relationship between the Jere masked dancer and Ngoni culture, but it is worth noting that the Ngoni only came to Malawi at the end of the nineteenth century, and were not specifically involved in the hunting of elephants or in the ivory trade – which was focussed on Chikunda and other groups of specialized hunters. Jere as a clan name is not restricted to the Ngoni, but is also a Maravi clan associated with Phiri (Nurse, 1978: 91). Elephants do not, it seems, figure much in Zulu or Ngoni culture (see Berglund, 1976; D Phiri, 1982).

Nyani (baboon)

Also known as *nkhwere* (*ku-kwera* – to climb), this structure dances only at night. The performers are usually covered in the leaves of maize cobs, support a beard, and several may appear together at the *bwalo*. They imitate the antics and barks of baboons, even climbing trees, and their behaviour is often explicitly sexual in their approaches to the women (see Sembereka, 1995: 12–15).

The above are the main theriomorphic structures that make their appearance at *nyau* performances, but many other chinyago are constructed, their presence varying according to locality. Among those noted are the following: *chigaru* (large dog), *chilembwe* (roan antelope), *chimbwe* or *fisi* (spotted hyena), *gwape* (grey duiker), *kasenye* (Sharpe's grysbok), *mbawala* (bushbuck), *mphalapala* (sable), *ntchefu* (eland), *ngoma* (kudu), *ng'ombe* (cattle), *nguluwe* (bush pig, also known as *kumbadidza* – *ku-kumba*, to dig), *njala* (small pig, the word also means hunger), *njati* (buffalo), *nkhandwe* (jackal) and *tsanchima* (blue monkey). Many of these are game animals hunted mainly for food, but not invariably so, for many are carnivores. In the Lower Shire, the latter seem to be represented by masked dancers, but elsewhere this is not the case. The Museum of Malawi has a magnificent structure of a *mkango* (lion), some five metres long, with a black head and red mouth, ears and eyes, which is carried by several men. It was collected by George Sembereka from the Nankhumba district. Besides these mammals, two species of snake are often represented by the theriomorphic structures, *songo*, the black mamba (*Dendroaspis polylepis*), although the term also refers to the mythical crested cobra, and *nsato*, the python (Python sebae) as well as various bird species. The latter includes birds that are fairly conspicuous and usually associated with water, such as *kakowa* (egret), *nang'omba* (ground hornbill, which often requents graveyards), *ng'ongwe* (saddlebill stork), *tsekwe* (spur-wing goose). It has been suggested to me that *nthiwathiwa* represents an ostrich and *kanswala* a giraffe, but it is worth noting that neither of these species have been recorded from Malawi. It needs little imagination to see many of the masked dancers draped as they often are in feathers or maize cob leaves as ostriches – but this species is not known to local Malawians. Ka – is a prefix meaning small and so would hardly allude to the giraffe. Another animal that is an important character in the folk tales, the tortoise (*kamba* or *fulu*) is also sometimes an *nyau* figure, as is the motor car (*galimoto*).

A final *chinyau* figure worth noting is *kambele wetu*, a theriomorphic figure that sometimes appears at the close of the funeral ceremony. It has affinity in meaning to the Yao *mwanambera* (*bere* – breast milk, kinship; *ku-wetu* – to tend, care for – as domestic animals, *chiweto*).

The masked dancers and theriomorphic figures make their appearance, as earlier noted, on three different occasions: at intervals (both night and day) during the girls' *chinamwali* ceremonies, at funerals (*maliro*) and at commemorative rites for the dead (*mpalo*). Both Hodgson (1933: 132– 3) and Mvula (1992) have given useful accounts of typical *nyau* perform- ances on these occasions. Essentially, the masks and the theriomorphic figures are secretly brought by the *nyau* members from the *dambwe* where they are usually hidden to the *liunde* at the edge of the village. The *bwalo* is cleared and prepared by the *mkulu wakumudzi* (*chiwinda*) and various helpers and the stage set for the performance. The people of the village gather at the *bwalo*, the women and children usually forming a compact group with the senior women (*anamkungwi*) nearest the dancers and facing the drummers across the *bwalo*. The *nyau* members usually feast before commencing the dance. At the appropriate time drumming begins, and the women and various *nyau* begin the singing, usually in the form of the rhythmical chants. The calls of the *nkhandwe* (jackal) and *mkango* (lion) are usually made during the night ceremonies, giving a tense atmosphere to the proceedings. The *bwalo*, as Mvula witnessed, has the form of an open-air theatre, and there is much audience participation. Drumming, singing and hand clapping eventually reaches a crescendo, and responding to the songs, the chinyau make their appearance in turn. At most *nyau* performances it is the *kalulu* who opens the ceremony – and the animal (*chirombo*) is described as *nthenga obwalo*, messenger of the village. The chinyau figures, the *visudzo* (masked dancers) and *mikhwala* (theriomorphic structures) usually alternate with each other. There is continuous interaction between the *chinyau*, usually addressed by the women as *zirombo* (wild beasts), and the women themselves, both in songs and gestures. These invariably have sexual connotations.

At the Chencherere rock shelter there is a charcoal drawing depicting *nyau* figures and the series runs as follows: *kalulu* (hare) *nankhala* (figure on stilts), *njobvu* (elephant), *chilembwe* (roan), *kasiya maliro* (antelope) and *kambele wetu* (to close the ceremony). At many performances the *kapori* dancers continually make their appearance, dancing before the women, accompanying the theriomorphic figures and keeping the path from the liunde to the bwalo clear. In the performance described by Mvula, the following *chinyau* made their appearance; *kalulu* (hare), *chimkoko*, *kapoli, nyolonyo, namalocha*, and *mbiyazodooka*. At important cere- monies the *njobvu* (elephant) usually closes the ceremony. At a night ceremony as part of a commemorative ritual (bona), Yoshinda described

Figure 4.10 Lingyesi Whitlom and the Nyau drawings, Chencherere Rock Shelter, Dedza, November 1990

the appearance of 49 nyau figures, many, like the *kasinja* and *kangwingwi* continually re-appearing. Among the important theriomorphic figures noted were *nyamgomba* (ground hornbill), *nswala* (impala), *fulu* (tortoise), *ng'ombe* (cattle) and *mkango* (lion) (1992: 227–30).

It is worth noting that while many of the masked dancers are gendered figures, the theriomorphic structures tend to represent the animal as type species, whose form 'embodies' the spirits of dead. In an interesting study by Richard Fardon (1990) on the Chamba of the Cameroon, spirits of the dead are conceptualized as masculine. Although during the nyau rituals there is a close identification, as Boucher stressed, between men, wild animals and the spirits, and Rangeley indeed suggested that the spirits were largely the concern of men (1949: 36–8), in fact, the spirits are not explicitly gendered, they are addressed as *ambuye* (grandparent), and conceived as a collectivity of both kin and affines thus that they are referred to as *mizimu ya makolo*, spirits of the ancestors. Because men form the body, the heart of the animal, and the spirits embody its form, it is the women as a collectivity who largely relate to the spirits when they make their appearance in the village setting on specific ritual occasions. It is also important to note that *nyau* dances also sometimes have a therapeutic function, for certain psychosomatic illnesses could only be cured through the staging of a *nyau* ceremony, the need for such a ritual being normally revealed in a dream (Kwapulani, 1982: 11).

I turn now to interpretations of *nyau* ritual that have been made.

The Interpretation of Nyau Rituals

Given their exotic quality, the *nyau* rituals have always fascinated visitors to Malawi, including anthropologists, and there are now restaurants opening up in rural areas that provide *nyau* dancers for the entertainment of tourists. This creates problems within the local community for the essence of the *nyau* has always been its secrecy. Recently there has been an upsurge of research interest in the nyau, with many important studies published (Kubik, 1987; Yoshinda, 1992, 1993; Kaspin, 1993; Birch de Aguilar, 1994; Probst, 1995). It was once quipped that every Navaho family housed an anthropologist, talking to Malawians in the rural areas of Dedza and Lilongwe one gets the distinct impression that almost every village community has, each summer, a visiting student delving into *nyau* ritual secrets. It is important, however, not to exaggerate the social significance of the *nyau* – crucial though they are in the rituals of many Chipeta, Chewa and Mang'anja communities – and thus come to *equate* the *nyau* with cosmological ideas and religious conceptions that are found throughout Malawi, and which are by no means confined to the Nyau or the Chewa (cf. Kaspin, 1993, 1996, and my reflections in the last chapter).

Peter Probst (1995: 4) has described the nyau as a 'total phenomenon', interpreting their rituals as providing a 'zone' (Bakhtin) or 'archive' (Foucault) for moral knowledge and moral discourse. This is indeed true but, as anthropology has long taught us, all major social institutions and ritual complexes, have multiple dimensions, and, as I discussed in relation to Malawian hunting traditions (Morris, 1998: 61–119) even this activity had its economic, gender, religious, symbolic and political aspects and social implications.

Although not proposing to conduct an exhaustive analysis, I want in this section to critically examine the various interpretations of *nyau* rituals that have been suggested by anthropologists, although such interpretations could equally well apply to the *unyago* (*chinambande*) rituals of the Yao. I shall discuss below five interpretative contexts, namely:

1. *Historical*, the suggestion being that the *nyau* represent a 'survival of stone-age hunting rites'.
2. *Mythological*, that they constitute a ritual re-enactment of the Chewa primal myth.

3. *Sociological*, that *nyau* rites have a cathartic function for the solidarity of male affines in a matrilineal society, or alternatively, constitute the formal incorporation of the boy into the matrilineal kin-group.
4. *Cosmological*, that the *nyau* rites are both an expression and are shaped by a cosmological schema, that forms a totalizing 'logic' of the Chewa 'social universe', and finally,
5. An *essentialist* context, namely that the *nyau* reflects an immanent logic characteristic of rituals universally.

Historical Context

The notion that the *nyau* ritual represent a survival of the hunting rituals of earlier foraging societies has been expressed by several scholars. Basing himself on the researches of Matthew Schoffeleers (1968) in the Lower Shire, Ian Linden thus suggests that the *nyau* societies 'were taken by the Bantu from the hunting rituals of the bushmen-type culture in Malawi or the Congo. Similar figures of men wearing animal structures occur in bushman cave paintings in South Africa' (1974: 133). That animals play a fundamental role in *nyau* rituals is evident, that the hunting of animals play an important part in the life of foraging societies is also evident; and animals such as the eland and antelopes were also significant in the religious life of the Khoisan peoples of southern Africa. But there is very little to connect the two social situations. Although hunting mimicry is performed in the *nyau* ceremonies, particularly with respect to the *njobvu* (elephant), and the Ajere hunters, there is very little evidence of any 'hunting magic' being practised by the *nyau*. No medicines are used with regard to hunting in the rites, and none of the rituals are aimed at hunting success. A close identification is, indeed, made between the men as members of the *nyau* society and wild animals, but this identification emphasizes their role as outsiders or affines. It does not effect success in hunting. It is also important to note that theriomorphic structures have little significance in the social and religious life of the foraging peoples of Africa or of foragers elsewhere (cf. Turnbull, 1965; Marshall, 1976; Lee, 1979; Barnard, 1992, with respect to the African hunter-gatherers).

For African foragers, hunting is something that a boy needs to be initiated into, in the sense that it marks the primary identity of an adult male, and the first animal killed is usually ritually celebrated. But among Khoisan foragers like the !Kung and G/wi and forest hunter-gatherers like the Mbuti of Zaire, there is very little evidence of any masked dancers resembling that of the *nyau*. As Laude (1971) indicated, such rituals tend to be developed not among foragers and pastoralists, but among subsistence cultivators. Paradoxically, it is among agriculturists that rituals around hunting are most elaborated (see Douglas, 1954; on the Lele), and theriomorphic structures are most commonly found. The only rituals found among foragers in Africa that resemble the *nyau* ceremonies is the Eland Bull Dance, performed in the occasion of a girls' first menstruation among many Kalahari hunter-gatherers. According to Alan Barnard, it was most elaborate among the Nharo. The girls in the menstrual hut could not be approached by any man, apart from a man who represented the eland bull. Wearing horns and mimicking this animal in his steps, he would chase the women around the fire. They would lift up their skirts provocatively as they danced and according to Barnard, they represent female sexuality in opposition to the powerful 'medicine' of the eland bull. The man, representing the bull, although elderly, is always an affinal category (Barnard, 1992: 60). Earlier, Doke (1936) had described the highly stylized baboon dance among the #Khomani foragers, the man imitating the behaviour of baboons with 'obvious sexual movements' in relation to the women dancers. These obviously have similarities to the *nyau* rituals, the male dancers representing animals in the girl's initiation ceremony – but they are not elaborated among such hunter-gatherers. The wearing of animal skins by dancers, particularly by male dancers, which is evident in the rock paintings in southern Africa and elsewhere, is clearly associated with shamanistic rituals. But taking the outward form of an animal, while also being the medium of a spirit, is by no means restricted to shamans and *nyau* dancers. In Malawi it is also a common practice among herbalist-diviners (*asing'anga*) and circumcisers (*ngaliba*), as well as among spirit mediums. There is, therefore, no strong evidence to suggest that the *nyau* ritual is simply a form of 'hunting magic' derived from the early hunter-gatherers – the Akafula. The rites associated with Chipeta, Chewa and Mang'anja initiations, both boys' and girls' – and with the Chinyau, seems to be more elaborate and more complex than anything found among African foragers.

Mythological Context

A second interpretation of the *nyau* is to suggest that their rituals have a religious function, namely, the reenactment of the Chewa primal myth of creation. This myth suggests that the earth always existed, but that it was waterless and lifeless. God (Chiuta) lived in the sky. Then one day, a storm built up, the skies opened and it poured with rain. Down to earth came Chiuta, the first man and woman and all the animals. They landed on a small, flat-topped hill, Kaphirintiwa, in the mountains of Dzalanyama.

The soft mound where they landed turned to rock and the footprints of the first humans and animals can still be seen there. For a period Chiuta, humans and the animals lived together peacefully and food was plentiful, until one day, quite by accident, man discovered fire. Everyone warned him of the problems that might ensue but the man did not listen. This event caused great commotion among the animals. The goat and the dog ran to the humans for safety, but all the rest of the animals ran away into the woodland. Chiuta, helped by the chameleon and the spider, escaped by ascending into the sky. Thus God was driven from the earth by the 'wickedness' of humans (Werner, 1906: 70–4; Schoffeleers, 1968: 196–8; Schoffeleers and Roscoe, 1985: 19).

Schoffeleers, among others, has seen this creation myth as providing a charter for the nyau brotherhoods, a style of analysis reminiscent of Mircea Eliade. For Eliade essentially saw all rituals as evoking primeval events. As he put it 'Myths serve as models for ceremonies that periodically reactualize the tremendous events that occurred at the beginning of time' (1954: xiv).

But the source of Schoffeleers' thesis was a more immediate one, and seems to have stemmed from a reading of Foa's rather romanticised account of a *nyau* ritual. For Foa, the *nyau* represented the spirits of the dead who periodically returned to the village 'to the sound of drums and to the light of the nocturnal luminary'. He writes of the 'spirit of the forest' sending to the village his 'subjects' and suggests a temporary reconciliation between humans and animals (1900: 40). Schoffeleers suggests that this was a brilliant intuition and that the Chewa creation myths provide a 'script for the *nyau* drama' (1976: 63). With Linden, he spells out the thesis clearly and succinctly. They write that in cosmic terms the *nyau* performances

> may be interpreted as a re-enactment of the primal co-existence of three categories of men, animals and spirits in friendship and their subsequent division by fire. Fundamental to the religious significance of the cult is the belief that underneath his mask the dancer has undergone what might be called a 'spiritual transubstantiation' to become a spirit. The spirits and animals come in from the bush and a temporary reconciliation with man is enacted as they associate with the people in the village around pots of beer. (Schoffeleers and Linden, 1972: 257)

The thesis, as Boucher (1976: 2) suggests, sounds convincing. The animals, symbolized by the theriomorphic structures, and the spirits, represented by the masked dancers, are temporarily reconciled with men (or rather women) around beer of the funeral or of the initiation festivities.

At the end of the rite, the animal structures are burnt. However, the creation myth alludes to Chiuta (God) living with humans and animals in the primeval days, not the spirits, for there were then no spirits as death had not come into the world. Death was to come later, from Chiuta with messages brought by the lizard and chameleon (Werner, 1906: 72).

God and spirits of the dead (*mizimu*), for the Chewa, are distinct beings. But Chiuta seems hardly to play a role at the *nyau* rituals – focused as these are on animals, sexuality and human fertility. A pregnant women is thus not supposed to attend a *nyau* performance. Whereas the spirits of the dead are fundamentally concerned with kinship, with the human life cycle and fertility – Van Breugel (1976; 191) called the nyau dances ritual petitions for fertility – Chiuta is associated with the agricultural cycle and with rain. Water and fire are two creative transformations. Both are associated with important processes – the social and the ecological cyclic processes. Essentially, however, the *nyau* and the spirits are connected with the first process – and thus human fertility – while Chiuta and the primal myth are linked to ecological processes.

Although there are symbolic analogies between these two cyclic processes, this is not to suggest that the *nyau* rites simply enact the primal unity between humans and animals and their subsequent separation.

Both Boucher and Van Breugel indicate that they could find no evidence from the ethnographic material on the *nyau* to support Schoffeleers' interpretation. Boucher, who collated almost 600 *nyau* songs from the Mua area, could not find any songs suggesting the idea of reconciliation or relating to the creation myth – although there were several obscure allusions to fire and hunting (1976: 2). Van Breugel likewise noted that he could find no reference to the symbols of the 'primeval myth' in the 300 *nyau* songs that he analyzed, and he remarked that this religious interpretation seems to disregard the more obvious references to fertility (1976: 199).

As to the ritual performances themselves, what seems clearly evident is that they do not enact a reconciliation or friendship between humans and animals prior to the ritual burning of the theriomorphic structures at the end of the rite. On the contrary, they enact a fundamental but complementary opposition between animals – with respect to which men are identified – and women.

Both Schoffeleers and Boucher make a clear distinction between the masked dancers associated with the day – which are seen as representing the ancestral spirits – and the theriomorphic structures that are associated with the night and are seen as animals. The distinction, as I earlier intimated, is by no means clear cut, as many of the masks clearly have animal features and are universally referred to as *zirombo* (wild animals). Clearly, both the masked figures and the theriomorphic structures represent the spirits of the dead taking the form of animals and – to varying degrees – both are associated with woodland, as they come from outside the village domain. But as the theriomorphic structures are often, in the *nyau* rites, associated with menstrual blood (*nkhole*), and as an analogy is drawn at times between sexual intercourse and hunting, a familiar theme throughout the world, both scholars suggest that whereas the masked dancers are male, the theriomorphic structures are female (Schoffeleers, 1968: 256; Boucher, 1976: 23–9).

Yet there is no identification at all between women and the animal structures: the identification made – which both scholars emphasize – is that between man and the nyau, whether masked dancers or the theriomorphic structures. Moreover, the main feature of the *nyau* that is dominant in the rituals is that they are opposed to the women – and like wild animals they are fierce, aggressive and sexual. The actions of the *nyau* – in chasing women, in being wild and amoral, in deporting themselves in a highly provocative way – suggests, not that they are to be identified with women, but rather with men as affines. Many of the *nyau* carry a penis, sometimes painted a vivid red, and the horns of the theriomorphic structures (and the masked dancers) and the trunk of the elephant are often displayed in a manner that is sexually suggestive. The content of *nyau* songs are explicitly sexual, and Van Breugel remarked that in most of the *nyau* songs he collected there is some mention of the male or female sexual organs. But rather than seeing these as utterly obscene, as did the early missionaries, what they celebrate is the powers of life, the positive aspects of sexuality, and the importance of human fertility (Van Breugel, 1976: 191). The association of menstruation with animal structures has therefore less to do with gender and the supposed 'femininity' of the theriomorphic structures, than with the powers of blood. Both menstrual blood and animal blood have dangers and harmful consequences for men, both can harm by entering the body. The first leads to *kanyera*, a wasting disease, the second to the condition *chirope*. Both these conditions can be fatal to men.

Although not explicitly emphasizing the fertility aspect of the nyau – though he does in terms of Mang'anja culture more generally – Schoffeleers does stress the fact that in nyau rituals men are equated with animals. He also puts a focal emphasis on gender roles and on 'sexual polarity' which he indicates is a preoccupation of the *nyau*. But it seems to me that the crucial distinction expressed in the *nyau* rites and songs is not of gender but of the opposition between women as kin group and men as an affinal category. The meaning of the initiation is very different for boys and girls in Chipeta, Chewa and Mang'anja communities; for the boy it means a cultural identification with the woodland, with the spirits, with wild animals and with their role as affines.

Although animals come into the village during the rituals, embodying the spirits of the dead, there is nothing in the rituals to suggest a 'primal harmony'. But rather an identification is established between the spirits/ animals and the young boys, who from the time of their initiation have their social identity transferred to the woodland – as hunters and affines. Equally, the spirits in animal form (*kasiya maliro*), are responsible for conducting the spirits of the deceased to the woodland. As Schoffeleers puts it: the initiates' 'true identity' is established when the boy is torn from the village and 'goes to share the life of the animals in the forest', which alters his relationship to his kin group, which then also has to be re-established (Schoffeleers and Roscoe, 1985: 238). This leads me to the third form of interpretation of the *nyau*, namely as stated by Rita-Ferreira, that it is a 'reaction of the males against female predominance characteristic of matrilineal and uxorilocal societies' (1968: 20).

Sociological Context

My own immediate response to this interpretation is to suggest that *nyau* is not a 'reaction' to matriliny but rather is intrinsic to it. This interpretation of the *nyau* has been clearly and lucidly expressed by both Schoffeleers (1968: 296–400), Boucher (1976: 9) and Malele (1994). The gist of the thesis is that in a matrilineal society, the bond between brother and sister is emphasized at the expense of the marriage tie, and given that marriage is uxorilocal, the position of the husband is tenuous, his authority within the village and over his children is very limited, and that his loyalties are divided – between his wife (affines) and sister (kin). As Max Marwick put it: among the Chewa there is a 'tendency for the conjugal link frequently to be sacrificed on the altar of the consanguineal matrilineage' (1965: 180). A consequence of this is the loss of authority by the in-marrying spouse. They are frequently alluded to as strangers and outsiders – and their function within the village is simply to be hard working and to provide his wife and her kin group with children.

The *mkamwini* is often described in terms of his purely sexual function – as a male goat (*tonde*), a cock (*tambala*) or hyena (*fisi*). Additionally, as succession to the village headmanship is within the 'sororate group', competition and tension often arises between a man and his sisters's son. The lot of the in-marrying spouse is therefore seen as insecure, full of conflict and tension and, with regard to his wife and her kin, lacking in authority.

Although Marwick (1965: 181) had noted that cross-cousin marriage was seen by the Chewa as a way of alleviating the conflicts – that a man's father-in-law would be his mother's brother – both Schoffeleers and Boucher emphasize that nyau, in a sense, is a way that men solve what Audrey Richards long ago called the 'matrilineal puzzle' (1950: 246). Thus through *nyau* performances men are able to reverse their normal position, which is one of having no control or authority in their wife's village. They are able to assert their superiority over women. Since they are also strangers in the village, the *nyau* provides the men with a way of banding together for mutual support. It provides them with, as Schoffeleers writes (1976: 60) – a kind of 'men's club' which can on occasion also act as a pressure group. Seen as a vehicle for the expression of male frustration within a matrilineal society, *nyau* thus has a cathartic function, acting as a 'safety valve' for the tension and conflicts that are generated within the village. As Kings Phiri wrote, the *nyau* societies may have given married men a 'sense of solidarity' and even considerable influence within the matrilineal context. More recently, Nurse in a review of Kubik's (1987) study has affirmed the role of *nyau* in upholding the dignity of men in a matrilineal society, 'tolerated and encouraged by the women in the interest of social stability' (1988: 39). If *nyau* was simply concerned with asserting male dominance, it is however difficult to understand why *nyau* is tolerated, and obviously much enjoyed by the women. This interpretation has recently been reaffirmed by Schoffeleers (1992: 40) and Probst (1995: 4).

Although there is clearly some validity in this interpretation of the *nyau*, the analysis tends to assume a male perspective, and views the emphasis on masked dancers and affinity as a 'response' by men to the matrilineal situation, rather than as being intrinsic to it. *Nyau*, in a sense, is a means whereby affines are created, rather than being simply a response by them. In the past cross-cousin marriage was the ideal and was probably more widely practised than it is nowadays. In addition, the Chewa/ Mang'anja kinship system implies a 'moiety' system, whereby cross-cousins (*chisuwani*) and affines (*alamu*) are equated. And, as Phiri perceptively notes, a more widespread practice than cross-cousin marriage is that of marrying within one's own neighbourhood. Even today, he remarks, as a Chewa himself, the majority of Chewa men, in rural areas at least, marry within a five kilometre radius of their own matrikin (1983: 262). In other words, the boy to be initiated into *nyau* is not a stranger within the village; he is a member of a matrilineal group, the *mbumba*, of which his mother's brother is a nominal guardian (*mwini*). He has been initiated into his mother's group at birth, through the *kutenga mwana* ceremony. The essence of the *nyau* ceremony, therefore, is to symbolically separate the boy from his kin group, and to make him into an affine – into (symbolically) an outsider. From boyhood he has been on intimate terms with both his kin and 'affines' and will be throughout his life, so he will not – empirically – be an outsider. Moreover in any given neighbourhood, villages or kin groups are closely related to each other through marriage exchanges. These are affirmed on all ritual occasions when 'affines' play an important role. The *nyau* ceremonies, therefore, are not specifically concerned with gender per se, even though, on the surface, there seems to be almost institutional rivalry between men and women. As a brother, a male kin, the initiate is already a member of his own kin group and will be nominally have his own sororate group (*mbumba*), his sisters and their children. What is involved in *nyau* is to make the boy into an affine. This is done by identifying him with the spirits and the animals associated with the woodland (*thengo*). He is symbolically marginalized from the village (kin group), and the emphasis is put on sexuality and on his role as an affine. *Nyau* does not so much make him into a man, as into a male affine.

When Rangeley suggested that the spirits are the concerns of men (1949: 38) it was only partly true – for men do become spirits in the form either of animals or of anthropomorphic figures. But spirits are even more closely associated with women for at the *nyau* performance, women (as a kin group) articulate a relationship with the spirits, especially the theriomorphic figures, whose sexuality is affinal and responded to collectively by the women. The *nyau* dances do not symbolize so much the reconciliation of humans and animals as express a dialectical relationship between women (as a group) and spirits in the form of animals. And it is from the spirits, ultimately, via affinal males, that the kin group derives its fertility and reproduces itself through time. Semen from the male fertilizes the kin group in the same way as water fertilizes the earth. And the continuing reproduction and fertility of both the human group and the earth (agriculture) is derived symbolically from outside the village – from the Brachysteria woodland.

Simply put, the relationship of men to animals is one of kinship (which is why the killing of animals is fraught with danger), the relationship of women to animals is one of affinity.

However, although the dominant motif expressed in the *nyau* rites suggest that the theriomorphic figures (spirits/animals) are outsiders, of the woodlands, fierce, wild and sexual, and thus symbolically affines – and with these figures nyau members identify – the rites do express the complexity of *nyau* relationships with animals. As Boucher has written; the relationship of humans to animals is essentially an ambivalent one; as embodied in the contrasting meanings of the two concepts, *nyama* and *chirombo*. Both terms are frequently used to describe the nyau theriomorphic figures and even outside the ritual context, the terms can be applied interchangeably to the same mammal.

As a hunted species or meat, the *gwape* (grey duiker) and *ngoma* (kudu) are *nyama*; as a wild animal associated with the woodland and potentially harmful to crops they are *chirombo*. But *nyama* is also linked with the 'power of vengeance', which is why hunting is hedged with ritual. Consequently, as Boucher writes, animals have for humans a paradoxical meaning; of edible meat, nourishment, power, wellbeing; and of danger, fear, hostility, vengeance (1976: 3). Both sexuality and the hunting of animals are important for human life; but because they generate 'heat' both have to be kept within bounds, otherwise they lead to madness. Sex, the hunting of animals, and madness are closely linked by Malawians.

This ambivalence towards animals comes out very clearly in the nyau rites, for the theriomorphic figures frighten and punish and may even destroy valued things in the village, but they are called by the women, cheered by the women and as playful characters they also comfort, teach and entertain.

It is, of course, worth noting that male secret fraternities and masked dancers similar to those of the *nyau* are widespread throughout Africa and are by no means restricted to matrilineal/uxorilocal contexts. They are found also among societies with a patrilineal kinship and in matrilineal societies like the Ndembu who practise virilocal marriage.

From the foregoing, it seems evident that the nyau rites are not specifically concerned with the initiation of boys into matrilineal kin groups. This was suggested by Mary Douglas (Tew) who felt that because the father was not allowed to be present at the initiation of his son, and the fact that the boy was presented to his sponsors by his mother, then this signified that the *nyau* rite involved his 'formal incorporation' into the matrilineage (1950: 47). But, as was suggested earlier, the boy is already initiated into the kin group, and the *nyau* rite has the opposite function, namely, to separate the boy form his matrikin. It implies that he becomes a member of the nyau society, a group that is in structural opposition to the *mbumba* group.

Cosmological Context

Another interpretation of the *nyau*, may be described as cosmological, for it situates this phenomenon in the overall cosmology of Chewa culture.

This form of interpretation was signalled by Father Schoffeleers in his pioneering studies of Mang'anja religious culture, for Schoffeleers offered a structuralist analysis that stressed the importance of understanding Mang'anja rites – including the nyau – in terms of an overall cosmological schema, which involved a series of what he described as 'complementary oppositions' (1968: 231). This schema suggested that many primary categories of Mang'anja culture formed part of a cyclic process involving a series of polarities – woodland and village, hunting and agriculture, animals and humans, spirits of the dead and living people, fire and water. This cyclic process had two dimensions, one relating to the seasons – wet and dry – and the climatic cycle, the other to humans and the spirits, involving an on going social process, linking such phenomena as 'nominal re-incarnation', the *kutenga mwana* ceremony, and *nsembe* offerings to the dead. He stressed the analogies between these two cyclic processes.

Deborah Kaspin (1993) has developed this analysis, but focuses specifically on the *nyau*, and on the cyclic process involving the spirits of the dead and living people. She thus suggest an interpretation that links *nyau* to a cosmological schema (or rather one aspect of a cosmo-logical scheme) of which it is the 'expression', the *nyau* rituals being 'shaped' by the logic of the cosmology. Indeed she virtually equates the *nyau* ritual with the cosmology.

Kaspin suggests (1993: 39), that *nyau* ritual was originally a royal ritual of the Maravi chieftainship, and that during the colonial period it was transformed into a 'ritual of resistance' among the Chewa, surviving today only in rural areas as a 'ritual of the underclass'. This interpretation thus runs completely counter to the interpretation that *nyau* rituals have their origin in an earlier hunter-gathering culture or one that connects them with the solidarity of males in a matrilineal context. Although oral traditions affirm that the *nyau*, as well as hunting and the initiation of girls, originally came under the political jurisdiction of territorial chiefs, as Kings Phiri (1975) outlined, there is no evidence at all to suggest that it was a 'royal ritual', in the sense of only being danced at the *mzinda* of the Maravi chiefs – at Mano and Mankhamba. The equation of the Chewa with these Maravi states is misleading, as these states were multi-ethnic, and in any case, as I discuss elsewhere, both the power and the scope of these Maravi chiefdoms was limited, and from the sixteenth to the eighteenth century, much of Malawi, certainly the Chewa heartland around Kasungu and Lilongwe, was probably a decentralized area. Malawi in the nineteenth century was much more politically centralized, but by then the Maravi chiefdoms of Undi and Kalonga had long declined. Contrary to what Kaspin suggest, it is probable that *nyau* were always focused

around the village community, at least those that were politically acknowledged by the local territorial chief, and as Schoffeleers argued, were
always a form of ritual resistance against centralized authority. Indeed
his suggestion that the *nyau* societies were already in existence *before*
the formation of the Maravi state is probably valid (Lindgren and
Schoffeleers, 1985: 41).

With regard to her main argument in terms of Chewa cosmology, she
presents an interpretative approach that has a long tradition in anthropology, namely to interpret rituals in a closed ethnic context, and to see
them as giving expression to a single cosmological system that unites all
aspects of a ritual domain. Thus Kaspin sees the *nyau* as a 'totalizing
ritual system', that expresses a 'subliminal order', a cosmological order
or 'universe of meaning' that forms the implicit framework of the Chewa
'social universe'.

Quite apart from the fact that the *nyau* are only a part of a complex
ritual system, *chinamwali*, which is focussed primarily around women
and that this cyclic regenerative process of exchange between the
woodland and the village, the spirits and living humans is only one aspect
of Malawian cosmology, which as Schoffeleers has cogently described,
involves other cyclic processes; three points may be made regarding her
analysis. Firstly, this cosmology is not specific to the nyau rituals but
also involves other important religious rituals that have little or no
connection with *nyau*; secondly, this cosmology is not specific to the
Chewa but is found among matrilineal people throughout Malawi; and
finally, such a ritual cosmology is not 'totalizing'. The limitations of this
kind of analysis – which Kaspin also applies to the body (1996) – I have
discussed in the last chapter and in my work on the anthropology of
religion (1987: 295–6).

Besides 'nyau cosmology' or 'cosmology of the body' one could
equally well speak of the cosmology of hunting, agriculture, spirits,
healing or the gathering of mushrooms, for the essence of the cultural
representations – in all human societies – is that such 'image schemata'
(Johnston, 1987) or 'cognitive fluidity' (Mithen, 1996) link and unify by
analogical associations diverse aspects of social experience. But this unity
is never 'total'. On the contrary, it is always partial and selective.
Additionally, many of the symbolic equations that are evident in Malawi
culture, and which I have discussed elsewhere in my account of the ritual
aspects of hunting and food (Morris, 1998: 110–13, 206), have very little
connections with the Chewa (or Yao) creation myth. They exemplify,
rather, what Eugenia Herbert (1993) describes as the 'procreative paradigm', found throughout much of sub-Saheran Africa. In any case, the

creation myth is not the basis or 'source' of the 'symbolic order', but rather as aspect or exemplification of it. It is unhelpful to equate myth or religious conceptions with symbolism.

A final interpretation of *nyau* links it with more universal theories of ritual and I focus specifically on the work of Maurice Bloch.

Essentialist Context

The final interpretation of Nyau ritual would situate them in a very different context, namely as an emanation of an immanent logic inherent in all ritual forms. The context here is universalist. This kind of interpretation has recently been suggested by Maurice Bloch. In this study *Prey into Hunter* Bloch (1992), develops a strategy similar to that of Eliade and Turner, in that he postulates that underlying all rituals is a minimal structure or 'core' that constitutes the archetypical essence of this kind of phenomena. Although unlike Turner and Eliade, Bloch offers a more materialist interpretation, his analysis is equally ahistoric and dualistic, with neo-Platonic overtones. It is an elaboration of a theme earlier noted by Eliade, with respect to African initiation ceremonies. Eliade suggested that the masters of the boys' ceremonies, dressed as they were in animal skins, represented the divinities in animal form. By means of circumcision, the initiate is symbolically killed. He is then resuscitated by becoming a full member of the male fraternity and, putting on the skin of the animal, he himself becomes a beast of prey, a hunter. In the end, Eliade concludes, the novice 'becomes both the victim and the murderer' (1958: 24).

This is the essential theme that is elaborated by Bloch in his stimulating but highly speculative study. Like Van Gennep he views all rituals as consisting of three essential phases. In the first, the initiate is symbolically killed by an act of violence such as in the Orokaiva boys' initiation, when the boys are conceived as pigs and ritually hunted and killed. This is seen by Bloch as a process whereby the vital processes of material life are negated, the 'mortal' or 'life' aspects of the initiate being fundamentally eradicated. Thus in the second phase of the ritual, the initiate enters a 'world beyond process'. He becomes, in being identified with the spirits of the dead, an entity that is pure spirit, beyond the material life processes. He becomes something permanent, immortal, part of a transcendental realm that is beyond time and process. The third phase of the ritual Bloch calls a form of 'rebounding violence', which entails the 'conquest' of the here-and-now by the 'transcendental'. As spirits-hunters – the initiates reincorporate vitality from the outside by, usually, the hunting of animals. Thus, simply put, the ritual process – universally consists of: (1) the violent elimination in the initiates of ordinary vitality; (2) a stage when the initiate is pure immaterial spirit; and, (3) the introjection of vitality from external sources into the initiate by the consumption of food. The initiate has now become, at the end of the ritual, a dual being – part vital, living, changing, chaotic, mortal, and part transcendental, superior, spiritual, unchanging and immortal. The latter aspect of the person, Bloch contends, is seen as a constitutive part of a transcendent order, an 'institutional framework' that is unchanging, and which transcends the material processes of life and existence (1992: 1–23).

In its emphasis on violence, in seeing hunting as implying the 'conquest' of the natural world and in the radical antithesis that is postulated between spirit and life processes, Bloch's analysis has a very masculinist and neo-Platonic ring to it. He sometimes writes of death as a reverse 'process' and suggests that 'spirits do not die', without sensing that 'permanence' might be conceived in terms of an ongoing cyclic process rather than in terms of an unchanging spiritual realm.

With a little imagination one could easily fit some of the Malawian ethnographic material into the schema of 're-bounding violence', particularly with respect to the boys' initiation. The novices are conceived of as animals and are placed in the bush. They are ritually 'killed' by the *ngaliba* at the *jando* (Yao) circumcision rite – the circumcisers dressed in the skins of beasts of prey. They symbolically become spirits of the dead when they don the theriomorphic structures. They ritually imbibe medicated meat, usually in the form of a chicken, in order to get strength and vitality.

Yet there is also much in the Malawian ethnography that does not resonate well with Bloch's analysis. Death is not seen as necessarily violent, it represents the end of the natural human cycle. Nor is death seen as the antithesis of life, in fact, almost by definition, death is part of this world, for without death how could humans be mortal. But the *mizimu*, the spirits of the dead ancestors (*makolo*) are not, for the Malawian, in reality 'dead' and they may speak of the *mizimu*, like earth and water, as having *moyo*, life. They do not of course die, but they are reborn – as living human beings. The spirits then do not belong to a 'world beyond process' as Bloch suggests, but are simply an aspect of the cyclic process that includes humans and spirits. Humans (*anthu*) are associated with the villages and with cultivation; the spirits (*mizimu*) are associated with the woodland and with animals. Human life has no beginning or end, it constitutes a cycle, an ongoing process, and birth and death are simply transitions in this cyclic process. Moreover, the Malawian conception of change is one of the transformation. It is essentially metamorphic, for they do not have a dualistic conception of humans, consisting of a body/ mortal frame, and a spiritual essence. And the emphasis on killing and violence in Bloch's account does not invoke an echo in Malawian initiation ceremonies, particularly in the *chiputu* ceremony of the girls.

Malawians make a clear distinction between killing (*ku-pha*) and dying (*ku-mwalira*) and the initiates are spoken of as dying, not being killed. In fact the initiates are referred to as *mwali* (from *ku-mwala*, to be lost or dispersed).

Malawians, as most other peoples, do recognize a 'duality of existence'. *Mzimu* and *munthu* do constitute distinct and contrasting modes of being. However, these do not represent a radical dualism between a static transcendental order and a mundane realm (as in Plato) but rather they are two aspects of a cyclic process. The *mizimu* or spirits of the dead are not beyond process, they are an essential part of it; they do not constitute a negation of life, but rather reflect its essence, as a permanent ongoing process. The kin group, as Bloch, following Durkheim, perceptively suggests, has a kind of mystical permanence, but this 'immortality' in Malawi, is grounded not in some transcendental spiritual realm (as in Platonic idealism) but on the acknowledged permanency of the life processes themselves. Organic life itself, as an ongoing process, has permanence, and is in a sense 'immortal', an idea that would be difficult to directly translate into Chewa as they have a dynamic conception of being. Thus Malawian conceptions are biocentric, rather than theocentric. They acknowledge 'immortal' life, not 'eternal' life. (See Arendt, 1978: 134 on the Greek distinction).

Initiation rites in Malawi are essentially maturity rites that occur between birth and death. They are not, therefore, so much transition rites – despite the symbolism of death and rebirth – as rites of transformation (cf. Heald, 1982).

Bloch, drawing on the authority of Van Gennep (1989: 43), writes that circumcision rites do not make adults out of little boys. Van Gennep was keen to stress that initiation rites were not closely tied to physiological puberty, but it is difficult to find where he expressed the views that Bloch credits him with. On the contrary, he emphasized that initiation rites were focussed on 'social puberty' and were fundamentally concerned with gender identity (1960: 67). This was essentially confirmed by Audrey Richard's classic study (1956) of the girls' initiation ceremony among the Bemba, and has been emphasized by La Fontaine. In both her introduction to Richard's text, and in her more general study of initiation, La Fontaine stressed that maturity rites proclaim the fundamental distinction between men and women. Gender identity and maturity, then, are key aspects of initiation rites (1985: 117–38).

In Malawi, both of these aspects are stressed. The essence of the rituals is to strengthen and aid the growth of the child. For both boys and girls, this is all embodied in the notion of *ku-khwima*, which has a wide fan of meaning. It means to be strong, and firm, to be mature, to be able to understand harmful forces, to grow and to be ripe. The senior women of the *litiwo* rites are called *mtelesi*, which is derived from the verb *ku-teleka*, to put on the fire or brew beer. The elders of the Chewa and Mang'anja ceremonies referred to as *anamkungwi* from the verb *ku-kungwa*, to make firm. The initiation process for both boys and girls is therefore to be conceived in the following images: to 'cook' them, to see that they are properly fermented, like beer or mature like a fruit, or to strengthen them by medicines. All organic metaphors. To die, to become a spirit or an animal, is not therefore seen as a process of devitalization; to the contrary, the vitality of the child is strengthened by the contact with the forces of nature. Vitality, as Bloch suggests, is derived from external forces, from the woodland in the Malawian context. There is however, no prelude or phase of devitalization in the Malawian context. Symbolic death or identification with the animal/spirit world does not imply a devitalized state, it suggests contact with the sources of power and vitality – the woodland.

For boys and girls in Malawi, initiation does not entail the incorporation into the matrilineal kin group. It does, however, imply the separation of the initiate from their parents/immediate kin. The implications of initiation are very different for each gender.

It separates the girl from her mother, and the emphasis is placed upon her fertility and the setting up of her own home – or potential village. At the same time, she is incorporated into the wide kin group of women and the solidarity of women is stressed throughout the rites. For the boy, a fundamental emphasis is placed on symbolically separating him from his mother and kin group and making him not so much a man, as an affinal male. The boy is identified with the spirits and animals, with the woodlands. He is made through the ritual into an affine, an outsider. A crucial emphasis is placed on his sexuality, his potency, his strength and his courage.

The relationship between humans and animals, expressed in the rituals, is also quite different with respect to gender. A fundamental opposition is expressed between women and animals, for while women are associated, indeed identified, with the village, agriculture and the kin group – animals are associated with the woodland, hunting and the male affine, as well as with the spirits of the dead. Women entice the animals from the woodland but the relationship between them is always one of dia-lectical opposition. For women, animals represent fierceness, aggression, sexuality and the male affine – her husband, her father and her brother's son. For men, on the other hand, an essential identity – kinship – is expressed between them and animals. The young initiates become animals and as both Schoffeleers and Boucher suggest with respect to the *nyau*, there is a strong sense of identification between animals and men established during the initiation ceremony. This means that hunting does not imply an opposition or hostility between men and the animal world; on the contrary, it evokes kinship. Killing of an animal is likened to killing a kin-person and may have serious consequences if proper ritual precau-tions are not taken. In her study of the girls' initiation among the Bemba, Audrey Richards suggested that while empirically in the village a man as an outsider must be submissive, quiet, and respect his in-laws, in the ritual he is depicted as an animal; a lion, crocodile or hyena or as a hunter and that his virility is emphasized throughout the *chisungu* rites. Many of the songs sung during the ceremony, and the pottery figurines made of clay, relate to or depict animals – lion, bat, crocodile, hyena, porcupine, monkey, tortoise – all of which also have salience in the Malawian context (1956: 158, 187–212; cf. also Turner, 1968: 225, on the role of the hyena in the Mkang'a ceremony of the Ndembu).

It is important to recognize that in the Malawian context a fundamental distinction is made between the territorial chief, *mwini dziko* – the guardian of the land, and the affinal male, who are both conceptualized as outsiders, sexual, aggressive hunters, and the village headman, *mwini mbumba*, guardian of the matrikin who, as a brother, is identified with the collect-ivity of women who constitute the matrilineal core of the village community. Ideally he should be a male mother.

It is beyond the scope of the present study to discuss the complex relationship of the *nyau* to the pre-colonial chiefdoms, the colonial state and the Christian missionaries, and the present political order – much of this is bound up with what Mvula described as 'Chewa cultural identity', (1992: 41). On these issues the reader is referred to the pioneering studies by Schoffeleers and Linden, 1972; Linden, 1974; Kaspin, 1993; Probst, 1995, as well as archival material MNA NC1/21/12, NCK 6/1/1).

Funerals and Nominal Reincarnation

Malawians make an ontological distinction between four kinds of beings: god, the creator-spirit (Chiuta, Mulungu), the spirits of the dead (*mizimu*), people (*anthu*) and animals (*chirombo/nyama*). Between the spirits of the dead and humans there is a close and intimate relationship, and together they constitute a kin community. We shall explore the beliefs and rituals relating to the spirits of the dead in Chapter 6, suffice to indicate here that the living (humans) and the dead (ancestral spirits) are involved in an ongoing cyclic process, which, as Father Schoffeleers long ago (1968) outlined with respect to the Mang'anja of the Lower Shire, entails an exchange of substances between humans and spirits. This exchange is closely identified with the two cosmological domains, the woodland and the village, which we have discussed elsewhere (1995, 1998: 124–32). From the woodland humans derive meat, medicinal plants, and the fertility of humans, via the spirits who are associated with this domain. Indeed, in an important sense, human infants are symbolically conceived as coming from the woodland (spirits). In return, the spirits make incidental visits to the village and their living kin, to receive food in the form of *nsembe* offering – millet flour, meat, and beer. During rituals, the spirits of the dead return to the village in animal form, or may possess a person, but it would be misleading to suggest that the bodies of the dead on returning to the woodland at burial provide meat for the spirits (cf. Kaspin, 1993). Malawians recognize that the body rots and disintegrates, and this, naturally, is how it should be, but for Malawians only animals like the hyena, or witches in their various forms, whether as an animal or spirit (*chiwanda*) eat the flesh of humans. They never speak of ancestral spirits eating (*ku-dya*) the body (*mtembo*) of the dead. Thus after a burial the graveside is always checked to ascertain whether witches have been in evidence, or for signs that the deceased person has become transformed into a malevolent wild animal. As Soka expressed it with regard to Lomwe burial rites, the *adzukulu* (burial 'friends') go to the burial ground to see if the person has been transformed into something (*kupita kumanda kukayang'ana ngati munthu uja adasanduka kanthu*) (1953: 53).

The essence of the funerary rites is thus to dispose of the body and to ensure that it naturally decomposes, to remember the personality of the dead person, and to witness the transformation (*ku-sanduka*) of the living person into an ancestral spirit (*mzimu*), to become incorporated into the collectivity of ancestral beings (*mizimu ya makolo*). The crucial role of the kasiya maliro ('to leave the funeral'), in the *nyau* ritual, is to accompany the dead spirit to the woodland. At the same time, an aspect of the spiritual essence of the deceased, expressed in his or her name, is incorporated into the personality of a living descendent, usually a grandchild, or a sister's son if a man. It has been described as 'nominal re-incarnation' (Stefaniszyn, 1954). In Chewa the rite is described as *manyumba* (*nyumba*, house).

Funeral rituals in Malawi are complex, and extremely variable, given the important influence of Christianity and Islam over the past hundred or more years. There is a sense in which while the rituals of childbirth are focused essentially around women – men are hardly involved in the birth and *litiwo* ceremonies – death is the primary concern of men. Indeed among some Yao Moslems women are not allowed to go to the graveyard (Mtila, 1980: 8).

Death in old age is very much looked upon as a natural event. But the death of a young child, or a person in the prime of life is deemed to be, in a sense, unnatural, and human machinations are usually suspected – death being put down to malevolent sorcery or witchcraft. Death from a wild animal is serious, and burial, I am told, is usually done without delay. There are many portents of death; hearing the cry of a jackal (*nkhandwe*) near the house, seeing a snake, especially the file snake or burrowing snake, on the path, or perhaps a chameleon – these indicate that death is close, or you will meet it where you are going. Father Boucher (1991) noted that the barn owl (*kadzidzi*) and blue-headed agama lizard (*nampopo*) are seen as 'messengers of death'. As people associate the spirits of the dead with the woodland where people are usually buried, few people ever enter these sacred groves. As these patches of woodland must remain 'cool', no mammal is molested in the graveyard, nor is fire ever lit there.

Funeral rituals in Malawi consist essentially of three phases, the burial ritual (*ku-taya* – to throw away, bury; or *ku-ika* – to put); a ceremony after about a month to end the mourning period (*matapata, chisamba manja* – to wash hands), and a commemorative ritual at the end of the harvest season, which marks the incorporation of the person's spirit into the collectivity of ancestral spirits.

When a person dies, this event is soon announced to all close kin and neighbours, and close relatives of the deceased gather at the homestead. Bereavement is openly expressed, and there is much weeping (*ku-lira*), especially by women. The body is washed, the hair shaved, and the limbs are straightened by close relatives, usually of the same sex. The body of the deceased is then wrapped in a new white cloth – which can be expensive to buy – for white is the colour of death, as it signifies coolness. Death is usually expressed by the words *ku-tsiriza*, (life) is finished. Burial is undertaken without delay, often on the same day, but usually the following day. It is a moral imperative for relatives and close neighbours to attend a funeral, not only to express their respect to the deceased, but to express their moral obligations to others, and thus avoid the aspersion that they are witches.

Burial is made in the wooded graveyard (*manda*), and the pit must be at least two metres deep, to prevent the body being taken by wild animals or witches – who hunger for human flesh. The grave is usually aligned in an east–west direction, although people seem unclear as to which way the head should point. As the *chinambande* (*nyau*) animals/spirits are often described as if they came from the east, from the direction of the rising sun, and *mbwani* (coast), placing the head in the direction of the west would suggest a cyclic process through the day (life) to sunset (death). Boucher indeed suggests (1991) that the head of the deceased among the Chewa always points towards the west. The analogies are worth noting:

birth	death
sunrise	sunset
morning	evening
east	west
(*ku m'mawa*)	(*kumadzulo*)

Heat is associated with the village, people and the day; coolness with the woodland, death, spirits of the dead, and night.

The digging of the grave and the carrying of the body is undertaken by three or four younger people from a neighbouring locality. They are described as 'funeral friends' (*mdzukulu*, or *mbilo*). The term *mdzukulu* refers also to grandchildren or sisters' sons, and a person who is involved in a burial, thereafter has an affinal (i.e. joking) relationship to the deceased's kin group. Flour of millet or maize is poured around the graveside or on the path leading to the *manda*, as offerings to the spirits and to 'cool' the surroundings.

On returning from the grave, the *adzukulu* leading the way, people usually wash themselves with medicines. Those who have attended the funeral usually stay overnight at the household of the deceased, and at some point some of the male relatives, along with herbalist (*sing'anga*) will visit the grave, to put medicines there to protect (*ku-tsirika*) it, and to check if there have been any malefactory happenings there. Boucher (1991) writes that the mourners refrain from eating meat, but my own observations suggest that meat is often given to relatives during the burial ritual. I asked one of my close friends what had happened to the five goats that she had: she replied that she had lost many of her close relatives recently and had to provide meat for the funeral guests. Crucially important is that, from the time of the burial until the end of the mourning period – lasting about a month – all close relatives of the deceased, especially the awilo, must remain 'cool' (*ozizira*), and must therefore refrain from taking salt in food, hunting or sexual intercourse. At the end of the burial rites the close kin have their heads ritually shaved (*ku-meta*) and the village or hamlet is ritually swept (*ku-sesa*). Rubbish (*zinyalala*) is swept either to the edge of the bush (*tchire*) or to the ashheap (*dzala*), or in some areas the sweepings are deposited at the crossroads, the juncture of two paths (*mphambano*). Here, baskets, tools, and pots belonging to the deceased, may be ritually broken and placed there. In the past the hut of the deceased was ritually burned down. At the time of the burial no one visits the graveyard, for fear of being accused of being a witch. It is important to abstain from sex during the mourning period, and there are special medicines known as *mankhwala wa maliro*, from the possible ill-effects of mdulo (*tsempho, ndaka*) caused by a breach of customary rules. (See Morris, 1996: 55–8, on the plants used for such medicine.)

After three or four weeks – 'forty days' one of my friends suggested – rituals are held to bring to an end the mourning period, the period of sexual abstinence and 'coolness'. This involves the brewing of the beer of *matapata*, signifying the decomposition, the breaking down of the body of the deceased (*ku-tapata*, to crumble, break down). At the same time ritual intercourse is undertaken, by a couple who have lost a child or relative or by a widow, who has sex with a man of her own choosing, an affine. He is known as *mbilo*, or more often *fisi* (hyena), as is the husband. Alternatively, instead of sex, people may take medicines to 'warm' (*ku-funda*) themselves, bringing to an end the 'cool' period. These medicines are often described as *pfundabwi* and often consist of strong aromatic herbs. In the past after drinking the *matapata* beer, all fires in the village were extinguished, and a new fire kindled (*ku-pekesa*) by means of fire sticks. The actions involved were seen as analogous to sex (Stannus, 1922: 245). Various trees were used to make fire by friction, but two favourites were *ntonongoli* (*Vitex mombassae*), which represents the female and into which a small hole was made, and the bamboo *nsungwi* (*Oxytenanthera abyssinica*). The bamboo stick was held upright, and seen as the male, being rapidly revolved by means of the hands or a small bow to produce the fire. The ritual sweeping of the village may also be done at this time.

In the past, people accused of being witches, or of dying of leprosy (*khate*), were not buried in the graveyard. Witches were thrown into the bush, while those in the advanced stage of leprosy were placed in specific caves at the top of hills, of which a number, still containing the skulls and bones, can be visited – although local people avoid them.

The final phase of the funerary rites (*maliro*), is the commemorative ceremony, held during the dry season after the harvest, usually in July and August. Thus it may be almost a year after the burial of the deceased. This may involve a short 'thanksgiving' ceremony of close kin and neighbours lasting only a day, in which there is feasting and beer drinking, or it may involve complex rituals and dancing lasting a week. The rites are known as *bona* (*ku-bona* – to look at with admiration, or to witness), or *chikumbutso* (*ku-kumbukira* – to remember), or where Islam has influence, *sadaka*, although the rite is not specifically Islamic. Indeed the beer drinking and dancing that may take place at a *sadaka* is often declaimed by orthodox Muslims. These rites bring together all relatives and neighbours associated with the deceased in a spirit of harmony, goodwill and reconciliation, and serve, for the last time, as an occasion when the life and personality of the deceased is remembered with affection and esteem, especially if the deceased person(s) was someone who was liked and admired in the community. But thereafter, he or she will be forgotten (*ku-iwala*) as a *person*, but remembered as an ancestral *spirit*, who must not be forgotten. From the time of the burial, when the initial transformation took place, to the time of the commemorative rite, the spirit of the deceased is believed to be unsettled, and potentially capricious, its presence being shown either as a visible ghost (*mzukwa*) or as malevolent spirit (*chiwanda*), the latter frequently taking an animal form – leopard, hyena, and jackal especially. Thus the essence of the *bona* rite, as both Schoffeleers and Boucher detail, is to signify the final transformation of the deceased from a person to an ancestral spirit, and his or her incorporation into the collectivity of spirits. As we earlier noted, the *nyau* often play a fundamental role in both the burial and commemorative rites, particularly the eland antelope and the elephant.

(For early accounts of funerary rituals see Stannus, 1910: 313–16, 1922: 240–5; Young, 1931: 164–77; Hodgson, 1913: 155–60; on the relation between funerals and *nyau* see Schoffeleers, 1968: 365–86; Yoshinda, 1992: 217–40).

An important ritual that is often conducted during the mortuary rites, although it may be held at other times, is that of *manyumba*. This involves a form of 'nominal re-incarnation', whereby the name of the deceased is taken by one of his or her living descendants, of the same sex and usually of the second ascending generation. It has been suggested that name inheritance for men is 'patrilineal', but usually a man takes the name of his maternal uncle or his father's father (both referred to as *ambuye*), and it is important to note that the later kin category belongs in fact to his matrikin.

The ceremony is usually conducted after the death of the elder person, but if that person is old and frail it may be held before his or her death.

The *manyumba* (*nyumba*, house, household) rite, may involve either gender, but it is usually focused around a person who is well liked in the community, and who will assume the duties of either the local village head (*mfumu*) or the head of the sororate group (*mwini wa mbumba*). The person involved in the nominal reincarnation is always of the same sex as the deceased – who was held to be a respected person – and is thought by the local or kin group to be someone who has the potential to care for and look after people – *wosunga anthu*. The ceremony involves singing, dancing and feasting, and often simulated possession by the deceased. The ceremony is found throughout Malawi, and people may even name their young children after some elderly person they respect, and in areas where there are nyau fraternities, *nyau* dancers are intrinsically involved in the *manyumba* ceremonies (Marwick, 1968: 11–14; Sembereka, 1990: 7–12).

How important the ancestral spirits are in Malawian culture is reflected in the fact that one of the most 'controversial' religious sects in Malawi is the 'Mpingo wa Makolo Achikuda', (Church of the Black Ancestors). Often known simply as Makolo, it repudiates the mediation of Jesus, emphasizing the importance of the ancestral spirits and traditional dances and medicines. As one preacher put it, one enters the kingdom of god only through the ancestral spirits (Schoffeleers, 1985: 210–15, *Malawi News* 27 May 1995).

It is evident, from the above discussion of both the *nyau* and mortuary rites, that Malawians see an essential continuity between life and death. These two aspects of existence are not seen as a radical dualism, but as an interdependent, complementary opposition. Thus life (*moyo*) and death (*imfa*), village and woodland, living humans and spirits of the dead, form two *aspects* of a regenerative process, as both Schoffeleers (1968) and Kaspin (1993) have described. This kind of cosmology seems to be very different from that described among many societies, such as the Lugbara, Merina and Bara, where a radical dualism is expressed between life and death. (see Huntington and Metcalfe, 1979: 98–101; Bloch and Parry, 1982: 22–7; Bloch, 1982).

As we have discussed earlier, Bloch has generalized this kind of dualism to all ritual processes, and interpreted such beliefs in ancestral spirits as an ideological system that essentially upheld traditional (male) authority (Bloch 1989; 1992). Such a cosmological schema implies a radical dualism (Platonic?) between life and spirit, sees ancestral spirits not as 'immanent' but as 'eternal' beings beyond both time and process, and identifies order, spirits and fertility with men. Although such a schema is no doubt consonant with patrilineal societies, and those with state systems, particularly Asian and Indonesian cultures, it fits uneasily the Malawian ethnography for a number of reasons.

Firstly, the spirits of the ancestors are not identified with males, nor are they seen as 'lifeless', or beyond time and process – for they are essentially a *part* of an ongoing generative process. The spirits have seniority as *makolo*, and more power than humans, and they are seen as a source of fertility, but they do not stand in radical opposition to humans. There is no gnostic opposition between the village and the woodland, women and men, humans and spirits – for they are reciprocally related, inter-dependent, and form a *complementary* not a dualistic opposition. Thus the matrilineal kin group is neither located in the woodland, nor in the village, but in both: although it has a quasi-mystical quality (as do all social collectivities), it is not conceived by Malawians as a static spiritual order beyond time and space, but as concretely consisting of both living humans (in the village) and ancestral spirits (in the woodland), between which there must be constant exchange – as Kaspin alludes – for the mutual wellbeing of both, and together they constitute the kin group. Secondly, the notion of a spiritual realm beyond time, space and process is a mystical notion that is foreign for Malawians for even god as creator (Mulenga, Chiuta) has a presence *in* the world, and is embodied in atmospheric phenomena, in the python, as well as in created beings, *chilengedwa* – trees, plants, animals *and* ancestral spirits. Although horns, bones, and skins are often identified, in Malawi, with spirits and with males, they represent, as we earlier noted, the *essence* of life as an ongoing process (embracing life *and* death, creative processes involving sex and fire, as well as processes of decomposition and dissolution, involving water) rather than the radical antithesis of life. The radical dualism between spirit (social) and life (organism), reflected in a dualistic conception of the person, is a characteristic of patriarchal ideology, and this, as I have tried to suggest, is *not* a predominant theme in how Malawian people conceptualize the ancestral spirits.

What I have emphasized in this chapter, and in my earlier studies (1995, 1998), is the crucial importance in Malawian social life of an ideational system that prioritizes cyclic and transformative processes, and posits analogical associations between various modalities of social existence (hunting, the cycle of the seasons, agricultural production, eating, human reproduction – both sexual and social, iron-smelting and beer-brewing).

—5—

God and the Rain Deities

Prologue

In his seminal discussion of African religions and philosophy John Mbiti (1969) suggested that African theories of existence – ontology – consist essentially of five categories of being. These are, respectively: *God*, as the ultimate source of existence, and the provider of sustenance for both humans and the world; *spiritual beings*, including various deities, nature spirits and the spirits of dead ancestors; *living humans*; animals, plants and *organic life* more generally; and *things* and phenomenon that have no biological life (1969: 16). In addition to these beings or categories, Mbiti suggests that for Africans the whole universe is permeated with a power, force or energy. In African culture he sees such power as ultimately derived from god. This power, he writes, approximates to the Melanesian concept of *mana*, but significantly he distances himself from Placide Tempels, who had argued in his '*Bantu Philosophy*' (1959) that the central concept of African ontology was the notion of 'vital force' as the essence of being. The 'force', which permeates the universe, and which is manipulated and used by herbalists, priests, diviners and rainmakers – as well as by witches – has, Mbiti notes, 'nothing to do with Tempels' "vital force"' – though he never tells us why (1969: 16). Given his theological background, Mbiti emphasizes that this power emanates from god, and thus implies that the natural world itself – the physical and organic realms – have no intrinsic powers or potency. But Mbiti does suggest in his discussion of magic, that while this 'mystical power in the universe' *ultimately* derives from god, 'in practice it is inherent in, or comes from or through physical objects and spiritual beings. That means that the universe is not static or "dead"; it is a dynamic "living" and powerful universe' (1969: 203).

Such an account does not seem to be very different from that of Tempels, but it is of interest that in neither Tempels nor Mbiti is there a clear analysis of the indigenous conceptions of this 'mystical' (Mbiti) or 'vital' (Tempels) force, though the latter writer mentions both *bwanga* (the power of medicine) and *munthu* (person) as manifestations of this 'vital energy'.

What is also important about Mbiti's account is that although he emphasizes that African ontology is essentially a *religious* ontology – even suggesting that an African person throughout his or her life in 'immersed in a religious participation' – he also, and with equal emphasis, writes that African ontology is anthropocentric, as well as being a concrete metaphysic. No formal distinctions are made, he writes, between the spiritual and material aspects of life, and that the human relationship with god is 'pragmatic and utilitarian rather than spiritual and mystical'. African religion lacks both a mystical and apocalyptic vision, and there is a focus on a long past (zamani) and the present time, rather than on the future (1969: 5–28).

In acknowledging the existence of a divine being who is the origin and sustenance of all things, including humans, as well as in the existence of various other spiritual or superhuman agencies, African religious culture, Mbiti contends, cannot be adequately described as either 'animism' or 'pantheism'. For in the African context, he suggests, god is conceived as being transcendental – beyond the earthy domain, and in the long 'past' – and immanent, in being manifested in natural phenomena and in the powers of other spiritual beings – who are, Mbiti suggests, conceived as intermediaries between humans and the divinity.

In postulating an African religious ontology that consists of a hierarchy of beings or existences, Mbiti's writings, like those of both Tempels and Kagame (1956), reflect the implicit influence of Aristotle's philosophy, although god in the African context is conceived concretely as the origin and sustenance of a world centred on humans, rather than as unrealized potentiality, or a rather abstract 'unmoved mover'. But given Aristotle's 'earthbound' philosophical approach, and the primacy he gives to material substance, there are undoubted affinities between his metaphysics and African ontology, for, as Karen Armstrong suggests, Aristotle essentially developed a philosophical version of the pre-socratic emanation accounts of the relationship between the deity and the world (1993: 47–8).

Malawian religious ontology exemplifies that characteristic of Africa more generally, in postulating a hierarchy of existences. I want in this chapter and the next to focus on four categories of being, which, although closely related – they may all be referred to a *mzimu* ('spirit' is the gloss I give) – are nevertheless usually spoken about as four distinct categories – god, the various rain spirits (or spirit mediums) associated (usually) with specific hills, mountains or shrines (in the anthropological literature they are usually described as 'territorial spirits'), the spirits of the ancestors, and the various spirits associated with possession rites. Although, as I shall suggest, these do not form a distinct category, I stress throughout the close relationship that pertains between these religious categories and the animal domain.

The Creation, Myth, Chameleons and Fire

In the creation myths of the people of Malawi, which relate to the beginning of human society, wild animals play a crucial and central role, and god is situated on earth. As in the myths of many people throughout the world, the material world itself is not usually seen as being created by god *ex nihilo* (out of nothing), but, as one early missionary alluded, god and the world simply co-exist, the earth usually being 'taken for granted, as having existed before all things' (Werner, 1968: 21). There is no thought of the world as ever having a beginning. The creation of something from nothing is not a part of human experience; but nevertheless the dominant image of creation in Malawi associated with divinity is embodied not in the term 'to make' (*ku-panga*) but in the verb *ku-lenga*. This implies the power to create, and to do wonders beyond the scope and powers of ordinary mortals. Yet is it worth noting that within the Eurasian context, as Armstrong suggests, the notion that the world was created out of nothing (*ex nihilo*) was a late development even within Christianity and was associated with such theologians as Arius and Athanasius. It was a new doctrine, quite different from the creation myths of the early Hebrews, which implied that god had created – formed – the world out of a primordial chaos (1993: 127). Mbiti, however, has argued that the belief in creation *ex nihilo* is common in many African societies, but it is also worth mentioning that all the metaphors associated with the original act of creation – potter, carver, mother, architect – all presuppose the existence of a material world (1969: 39). Yet although the creation of the world (*dziko*) is not explicitly expressed in Malawi; people do frequently speak of the natural world, such as the woodland, or wild mammals as being created (*cholengedwa*).

Two Malawian creation myths are worth relating: both indicate an original unity between god, humans and animal life. Among the Yao, there is a myth, first recorded by Duff MacDonald (1882: 295–7), but which has since been variously rendered. Briefly, it is as follows:

In the beginning there were no people, only god (Mulungu) and animals (nyama). There was peace and contentment in the world, and god lived on earth. One day the horned chameleon (kalilombe) went fishing in the river with a basket trap (mono) made of bamboo. The next morning he collected the fish, and took them back to the village to eat. The next day, when he inspected the trap, he found nothing. To his chagrin an otter (katumbwi) had entered the trap, and taken his fish. The following morning however, much to his surprise, he found that he had trapped two small unknown creatures. The chameleon did not know what to do, so he took them to god (Mulungu). He asked Mulungu what he should I do with them. Mulungu replied that he should put them on land, so that they would grow. And this he did, and in time they became two full-grown human beings, male and female. All the animals and birds came to observe these two curious beings, and to watch what they did.

One day, quite by accident the humans made fire by rubbing two sticks together. They soon set the woodlands ablaze, and the animals had to run to escape the flames. The humans caught a buffalo (njati) by means of fire, and they roasted it on the fire for meat. Every day they set fires, and killed some animal and ate it. Mulungu complained to the chameleon about this state of affairs, for humans were burning the woodland, and killing all the animals. All the animals, in fact, had retreated into the woodlands to get as far away from the humans as they could. The chameleon had climbed into the trees, but Mulungu was old and unable to get away from the earth. He called the spider (tandaubwe) to help. The spider spun a web ladder, and Mulungu went with the spider on high. Thus Mulungu left the earth because of cruelty of humans towards the animals, proclaiming that when humans die they would also go on high. (Sproul, 1979: 37; Schoffeleers and Roscoe, 1985: 13–19)

The second myth is associated with the Chewa and Mang'anja and is as follows:

In the beginning there was the earth and Chiuta (god). The earth was then lifeless and without water, and Chiuta lived in the sky. One day the clouds built up, there was lightning, and it poured with rain. Chiuta came down to earth with the rain, together with the first man and woman, and all the animals. They alighted on a hill called Kaphirintiwa, (literally, a small, flat-topped hill, which tradition suggests is in the Dzalanyama Mountains). Afterwards the ground on the rock where they landed, which was originally of soft mud, hardened, and the footprints of the humans, and the tracks of animals like elephant and eland can still be seen there. For a while, with the earth yielding an abundance of food, Chiuta, humans and the animals lived together in peace and harmony. Then one day the humans by accident discovered fire. They set light to the woodland and this created both destruction and confusion. Fear entered the hearts of the animals, and, now hunted, they retreated into the woodlands. Domestic animals ran to the humans for safety and the chameleon climbed into the trees, calling the aged Chiuta to follow him. Chiuta disturbed by the conflict between humans and animals, thus went back to the sky, climbing up the web of the spider. Henceforth, Chiuta proclaimed humans must die, and after death return to god on high. (Werner, 1906: 80–1; Schoffeleers and Roscoe, 1985: 19; for a synopsis of the myth drawn from several sources see Schoffeleers 1968: 196–8.)

Similar myths are found throughout southern and central Africa, a common theme being that humans and animals emerged originally from the primal waters, or from some subterranean cave, and that the surrounding rocks bear indentations that are believed to be the footprints of the first humans and animals (Werner, 1968: 22; cf. Vyas, 1974: 1; Hodgson, 1982: 19). Equally important, such primal myths depict a time when humans and animals lived together in peace and harmony, along with god, and death was unknown. Yet there is another mythical tale recorded from Malawi that links the mortality of humans to a message sent by Chiuta (god).

It runs like this:

Chiuta deputed the horned chameleon (*kalilombe*) and the lizard (*nampopo*) to take the human beings a message, the one of life and the other of death. The chameleon was to inform humans that when they died they would return to life again, while the lizard was to tell them that when they died it would be for good. The chameleon started first but his pace was very slow and hesitant, so he was soon overtaken by the lizard, who reached the humans ahead of the chameleon and gave them Chiuta's message that death was final. A little while later the chameleon arrived, and announced that though humans would die they would return to life again. But the humans were very angry with the chameleon for bringing the message so late, as they had already accepted the earlier message from Chiuta. (Werner, 1906: 72; see Schoffeleers and Roscoe, 1985: 23 for a Sena variation on this).

This mythical tale is found widely throughout Africa, and essentially depicts two contrasting ontologies, one empirical, the other religious. There are two points of interest in these accounts. The first is that the chameleon plays a crucial symbolic role in all three accounts: in the discovery of humans, in encouraging the aged Chiuta to leave the earth, and in failing to bring humans the message of life after death. In another Chewa myth the chameleon is credited with the origin of both animals and humans, which emerge from its own body. Long ago, the story goes, the chameleon was the only living creature on earth. One day the chameleon climbed high into a tree, searching for a companion. There, he fell asleep, after eating fruit. But a mighty wind came up, shook the tree violently, and the chameleon fell into the ground. His stomach burst open, and out came all earthly creatures, including humans (Schoffeleers and Roscoe, 1985: 17). Schoffeleers suggests that the chameleon is not only 'the world's first martyr', but is clearly intended to be a symbolic manifestation of the divine (Schoffeleers and Roscoe, 1985: 27), or at least his emissary. This he links to the spectacular way in which the reptile is able to change colour. Yet the overwhelming connotations of the chameleon in Malawi is a negative one, and it is the focus of numerous folk beliefs. There are seven species of chameleon to be found in Malawi, but the two larger species, the horned chameleon [*Chameleon melleri*, *Kalilombe* (C,Y) and the flap-necked chameleon (*Chamaeleo dilepsis*, *nazikambe* (C), *birimankhwe* (N,C), *nalwi* (Y) *nalwi* (Y)] are those with which people are most familiar. Besides the ability to change colour, three other characteristics of chameleons are noteworthy: the way in which their turret-like eyes are able to move independently, their long sticky tongue that captures insects of all kinds, and their divided feet, which are adapted to grasping branches. Throughout Malawi chameleons are held in fear and awe, and when at Zoa I picked up some horned chameleons, everybody ran away in fear, and kept their distance. Indeed, chameleons seem to be more feared than snakes and the fact that the chameleon is able to inflate its body and hiss quite loudly adds to its fierce reputation. Many people think that the chameleon is highly poisonous, and Schoffeleers records the widespread belief that the bite of the chameleon turns the victim into a snake (Schoffeleers and Roscoe, 1985: 28), though I never heard this myself. Coudenhove noted that its bite was supposed to cause an incurable disease (1925: 242) and has a photograph in his book of a local young man holding a stick with the 'dreaded chameleon'. There is also a widespread belief that the chameleon gives birth to its young by an act of self-sacrifice, falling from a tree, and dying in the process of giving. Normally people will keep out of the way of the chameleon, but if one enters the household, the chameleon will be dispatched by the placing of a wad of tobacco in its gaping mouth by means of a long forced stick. Within minutes it normally dies. (On the biology of chameleons see Sweeney, 1970: 2/34–38; Hargreaves, 1979).

The second important feature of the myths is that they indicate the crucial role that fire plays in the cultural life of Malawi, both materially and symbolically. The discovery of fire, as in the Greek myth of Prometheus – the legendary hero who stole fire from the gods and gave it to humans – is portrayed as the crucial event in the transformation of human life. The myths outline an earlier period when, as noted, there was a 'primal unity' between humans and animals who lived together, along with the

Figure 5.1 The horned chameleon

deity, in a state of quiet tranquillity and close harmony. The accidental discovery of fire destroyed this unity: Schoffeleers describes the event as the 'cataclysm' (1968: 198). The outcome was in essence an ambivalent one. On the one hand it gave humans powers over nature, and over the animal world – and was clearly linked to the advent of hunting and cooking. On the other hand, it created a series of oppositions: between humans and the divinity (who had retreated into the sky), between life and death (for death came into the world with the discovery of fire), and between humans and the animal world. The myths also reflect, the crucial parameters of Malawian socio-economic life, namely the contrast between the wet and dry seasons, and between agriculture and hunting, as well as the crucial role that animals play in the cultural life of Malawi, although significantly neither the chameleon, agama lizard or spider have socio-economic salience. Also important, in contrast with the Genesis myth (which makes no mention of fire) is the fact that gender is not highlighted in the creation of myths, and the discovery of fire is not a sinful act in need of atonement, but something that happened by chance.

Fire, as Johan Goudsblom observes (1992: 3) has, as a subject for study, been totally neglected in the social sciences, as well as by anthropology. A recent encyclopedia (Ingold, 1994), which has an emphasis on evolutionary theory, has no discussion of fire at all, either in terms of its evolutionary significance or of its symbolism. Darwin described the discovery of fire as probably the greatest ever made by humans, and as Goudsblom writes, the ability to handle fire is more exclusively a human attribute than either tool-making and language, which have long engaged the attention of anthropologists. Humans are the only mammals to cook their food, and the use of fire to control the environment goes back into antiquity. The importance of the 'hearth', and of fire as an agent to create savannah or grassland prairies conducive to the spread of larger game mammals, was long ago emphasized by the American geographer Carl Sauer (cf. Sauer, 1981: 129–56). It is of significance that there is evidence of the human use of fire from an early period, circa 1,400,000 million years ago, long before the full development of human culture, and the use of the bow and arrow (Goudeblom, 1992: 17).

In the Malawian context fire has long played an important role in economic life – in the smelting of iron, in the firing of the cleared woodland prior to the planting of millet or sorghum – for slash-and-burn agriculture (*visoso*) was important in the past – and in the communal hunt (*uzimba*). Fires and hunting are closely associated in the Malawian context, and fire has positive not negative connotations. Sauer noted that early human communities probably held fire to be essentially beneficial – providing warmth, facilitating the cooking of meat and vegetables, as aids in the active transformation of the environment, and in the hunting of mammals (1981: 143–4). Malawians have a similar attitude to fire, for as Schoffeleers notes 'it is nothing less than the most fundamental aspect of culture', for it is the control of fire which allows humans 'to escape the realm of nature and begin a mode of life superior to that of the rest of creation' (Schoffeleers and Roscoe, 1985: 29). Humans are not able to escape from nature – except in religious ideology – but Schoffeleers' reflections are nonetheless valid and salient.

The importance of the annual bush fires in Malawi was often remarked upon by early European observers. 'One of the best sights in Africa', wrote Duff MacDonald (1882: 34), 'is a large grass fire'. Another early missionary, Alice Werner, wrote graphically about bushfires in Nyasaland, citing the Periplus to suggest that such fires formed one of the characteristic features of African travel since earliest times. 'On a moonless night in September', she wrote, 'perhaps, you will see the black hills seamed with curved and zigzag lines of fire, as the blaze advances' (1906: 11), and it is significant, at a personal level, to reflect on the fact that the first article I ever published began with a discussion of bushfires at Zoa.

The emphasis on fire (*moto*) in the creation myths is thus a reflection of the crucial importance of fire in people's daily economic life – cooking, hunting, iron smelting, agriculture, beer brewing and in the firing of pots – but as Father Schoffeleers has explored in a number of perceptive essays, bushfires, and the use of fire more generally, has also a religious significance in Malawi. While the firing of the woodland, as we shall explore, plays a crucial role in the communal hunt, the woodland in certain areas is also burnt ceremonially by local headman. An example is Bunda Hill, some 29 km south of Lilongwe where, in August each year, the hill is ritually fired. The bush is burned both as an act of respect towards the ancestral spirits, and because it is believed to be necessary for the regular provision of rain, for it is commonly held in Malawi that the smoke from bushfires form the rain clouds that eventually bring rain. Drawing on the Kaphirintiwa myth, Schoffeleers suggest that the myth embodies an implicit cosmology, with several important symbolic contrasts: between earth and sky, between water and fire, and between downward and upward movements. Linked to climatic cycle of alternating wet and dry seasons, and the occupational cycle, with a contrast between agriculture and hunting and bush clearance, this cosmological schema suggests an annual cyclic movement involving both material transformations and the movement of the spirits. It may be expressed in Figure 5.2.

In this cosmology there is a close identification between god and the spirit world, with the provision of rain, and thus the regeneration of the woodland and the cultivation of crops.

Yet fire also plays a significant role in transition rites, and Schoffeleers suggests that there is a symbolic analogy between the seasonal (ecological) cycle, and rites of social transition (puberty and death) – the female puberty rites (*chinamwali*) being 'the archetype of all transition' (1971: 277), for fire serves as a symbolic ritual marker between two domains – and is manifested in the ritual burning of the huts of the initiates, of (in the past) the dead person's house, and of the theriomorphic structures in the *nyau* rituals. This leads Schoffeleers to suggest that the *nyau* rituals are simply a re-enactment of the primal myth – a primal theory that we have discussed earlier. Importantly, both blood and ritual sexual intercourse have a symbolic function analogous to that of fire, and in the use of heat (*ku-funda/itsa* – to warm a person or place) to engender a social transformation. Yet the wild animals' role in these cyclic transformations, both human and ecological, is very much earth bound. Although initially

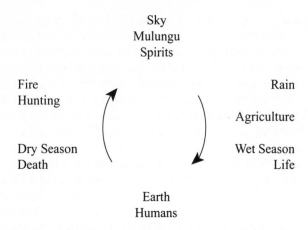

Sky
Mulungu
Spirits

Fire
Hunting

Rain

Agriculture

Dry Season
Death

Wet Season
Life

Earth
Humans

Figure 5.2 Schoffeleers' cosmological schema (Schoffeleers 1971: 274–77)

coming to earth with humans, or even existing prior to humans, wild animals in Malawi, are not conceptualized as in many hunter-gathering countries as having a spiritual essence or soul, and thus implicated in the spiritual re-cycling of essences, but mammals are closely identified with the woodland, and with the domain of the ancestral spirits, and such spirits may often, as we shall see, assume the form of animals.

It is important to note that in burning the bush for the communal hunt or ritual purposes, and for rekindling the household fire after a period of mourning, the fire is always, or at least ideally, made by the use of fire sticks and hand-induced friction (*ku peka moto*).

The long standing association of fire with the culture of Malawi is reflected in the name of the country, for according to Scott (1929: 263), the name Malawi means 'fire flames' and its meaning and origins have been discussed by several writers. The term is closely identified with the early Maravi chiefdoms, especially that of Kalonga on the Lake Shore, and with the prevalence of iron-smelting in the region. The ruling Phiri clan, are said to have brought fire with them when they moved into the region around the fourteenth century, and Schoffeleers highlights the importance of fire in dynastic and chiefly rituals, for chiefs are often portrayed as the 'custodians of fire', and deceased chiefs as providers of both rain and fertility, as well as of political stability (1972: 99).

Given the widespread hostility towards bushfires expressed by Europeans, as well as by the Forestry Department and the Department of National Parks and Wildlife – who equate hunting with bushfires – many

Malawians now express ambivalent attitudes towards the burning of the woodland. This prompted a member of a wildlife club to write to the newsletter *Kamba* (June 1985) enquiring whether it was 'bad to hunt with the aid of bush fires'. The reply given was that it *was* bad – wrong, illegal according to Malawi law and ecologically destructive.

The Supreme Being

In a useful essay on Chewa concepts of god – although the concepts discussed are by no means specific to the Chewa but are widespread throughout Malawi and the Northern Zambezi region – Joseph Chakanza (1987) spoke of a dearth of written materials on these concepts. Yet the memoirs and writings of all the early missionaries offer reflections on local conceptions of god – even if these reflections are somewhat hazy and misleading – and as long ago as 1930 Levi Mumba, whose mother was a Senga, and who worked in his youth at the Livingstonia Mission, wrote an interesting article entitled 'The Religion of My Fathers'. One of the problems, however, in writing on this topic, is that local conceptions of deity have long been influenced by both the teaching of Christian Missionaries and by Islamic Mwalimu – and this influence has been both intensive and strident. Thus it is problematic to assume that there is some authentic Malawian conception of deity, for all contemporary accounts, as with Chakanza, have a theistic and androcentric bias. In examining local conceptions of the supreme being I shall divide the discussion into three parts, and will examine, respectively, early accounts of deity as expressed by various missionaries and administrators, the names and meanings of the various names/concepts that are used by local people to describe the supreme deity, and, finally, the associations that are made between this deity and the animal domain.

All the early accounts of the deity in Malawi, stress that in contrast with the ancestral spirits, the supreme being was a rather remote figure, and indeed, even more recently, Father Patrick Kalilombe has suggested that the Chewa conception of religion leaned more towards deism than towards theism (1980: 41). Antonio Gamitto, for example, who journeyed from Tete to King Kazembe in 1831, wrote of the Marave (Chipeta, Nyanja), that

> No religion is known to these people apart from a crude idolatry. Their dominant belief is metempsychosis: the existence of a supreme and invisible power; and the existence of Muzimos (mizimu) or ancestral spirits. (Gamitto, 1960: 73).

Similarly, Lovell Proctor, who journeyed up the Shire in 1862, wrote that the Mang'anja and Yao believe that there is a 'great being' (*njasi, mpambe*) who 'lives above in the clouds and sends rain, but they do not know anything about him' (Bennett and Ylvisaker, 1971: 316).

At the turn of the twentieth century Rattray wrote that the people of Nyasaland

> believe in one all-powerful Being who has his abode in, or above the sky. He is the creator of all things, and rules the great forces of nature – rain, thunder and lightning, earthquakes, winds. He has many names, Chiuta or Chauta, Mpambe, Leza, Chanjiri, but all these names refer to one power. He is not a spirit (mzimu), for mzimu is the soul of a person who once lived on earth. He is rather a supreme power. (1907: 198)

The conception of the supreme deity as an 'otiose' being was perhaps a little overdrawn by the early writers, but it seems evident that in the past – as now – a clear distinction was made between the supreme deity (Chiuta) and the ancestral spirits (*mizimu*), and that, as John Buchanan (1982: 146) records, the deity was largely forgotten during times of prosperity. Only in 'calamitous circumstances' was assistance sought from the deity – yet dependent as people are on agriculture, and on rainfall in appropriate amounts and at appropriate times – the relationship between humans and the supreme being has never been too distant. But in the past, as at the present time, people are never very forthcoming as to the nature of the supreme being: it is thus difficult to ascertain a coherent theology as religious conceptions are largely expressed in symbolic action and concrete rituals. Nevertheless although Chiuta many be described a somewhat remote from everyday life, it is misleading I think to describe the supreme being as a 'vague idea' (Stigand, 1907: 130), or the spiritual macrocosm as 'dull and lifeless' (Stuart, 1974: 60). The somewhat ambivalent attitude towards such beliefs on the part of early Europeans, is expressed by the well-known game hunter R.C.F. Maugham, who wrote that the Sena 'believe firmly in the existence of a supreme being called Mlungu', yet also suggested that this being was 'wholly neglected' by them (1910: 363–4).

The supreme deity in Malawi is described under a variety of names: no one term has universal recognition, and although the names are widely known, different ethnic communities tend to utilize or be more familiar with different names. Thus the Yao in everyday conversation use Mulungu, the Tumbuka and Chewa Chiuta, the Lomwe Namalenga, while the Nyanja use the term Mphambe. We may discuss each of these names in turn; for they indicate the various attributes associated with the deity.

Mulungu

This is the commonest term for the supreme spirit. It is widely used throughout Malawi, and cognate forms are found also throughout East Africa. It has been suggested to me that the term was introduced in Malawi by nineteenth-century missionaries from Mozambique, but early Portuguese records mention this term as having been commonly used on the Zambezi in the sixteenth century, and Livingstone noted it also on his Zambezi expedition – as 'Morungo' (Livingstone, 1887: 88). Cullen Young suggested that the term was derived from the verb ku-lunga, which refers to active agency, whereas Werner links Mulungu to the Yao word *kulungwa*, which means to be great, large, or senior, a synomym of the Chewa – *ukulu* (1906: 55). Meredith Sanderson in his Yao dictionary, writes that Mulungu properly means 'omnipotent . . . but formless force' – which is approached through the spirits of dead chiefs (1954: 188), but both MacDonald and Hetherwick suggest that Mulungu may refer not only to the supreme deity, the creator, but also to spirits of the dead (MacDonald, 1882: 59; Hetherwick, 1902: 91–4).

Namalenga

Among the Lomwe Namalenga denotes, according to Bob Boeder (1984: 47), a rather shadowy, all-powerful deity, which transcends the ancestral spirits (*mizimu*) and is associated with communal concerns relating to an epidemic or drought. The verb *ku-lenga*, as earlier noted, refers to the act of creation, and to wonders, as well as to the soaring flight of a bird, such as the yellow-billed kite (*nankabai*). The heavens or firmament is described as *mlengalenga*, thus *namalenga* essentially alludes to the supreme being as a creator spirit, even though this may not entail creation *ex nihilo*. Many Lomwe use the term *mulengi* (creator).

Mphambe

This name for the supreme being has strong connotations with atmospheric conditions, and in Chewa the term also means thunder or the rains, as in the expression cited by Scott, *tsopano tikabzala mbeu, mphambe alikufupi*, 'now we plant the seeds, the rains are close' (1929: 320). There is indeed a close association in Malawian culture between the deity and thunder (as in early Indo-European culture), and thunder may be referred to as *mau a mulungu*, the words of god. A person struck by lighting is believed to be a victim of god's displeasure. The correlate *mbamba* means lightning, as does the term *njazi* (*Yao* – *njasi*), which is also a term used to refer to the deity. The usual term for lightning however is *mphenzi*.

Leza, Mlezi, Lezi

These terms carry the same meaning, and variants are to be found throughout central and south-east Africa. In the Malawian context the terms are derived from the verb *ku-lera*, which has a wide spectrum of meaning focused on the main idea of nurture or nourishment. *Ku-leza* is the causative form of the verb. But the verb also has connotations of being gentle, kind, helpful and supportive – in the sense of helping a sick person, or a mother caring for her child . . . *Nkhuku yolera anache* 'the chicken nourishes her own (brood)' (Scott, 1929: 236). As James Amanze suggests the connotations here is not of 'god the father' but of the deity as a 'mother', in tune with the matrilineal principle. In this the supreme deity is conceived as a power that is concerned with the nurture of creation (Amanze, 1986: 262; Cullen Young, 1950: 53). Significantly the rainbow in Malawi is described as *uta-wa-leza*, the bow of the deity *leza*, and in certain Chewa and Tonga dialects *kaleza* means lightning (Chakanza, 1987: 4).

Chiuta

The term *chiuta* means 'great bow' – *uta*, the hunting bow, *chi* – a prefix for large size or greatness. Scott interprets this as meaning that the deity stretches the rainbow across the sky, and thus extends in space, and whose active power is manifested in thunder, lightning and the rain (1929: 91). For a hunter, Cullen Young adds, such a metaphor is an appropriate way to illustrate the power and concern of the deity (1950: 51). Ian Linden even suggests that the reference to the bow might suggest that the name applied to the deity as the 'lord of the bush and of hunting' (1979: 203), but the focus of the supreme deity is primarily on the ecological cycle, and the provision of rain, while the spirits of the dead (*mizimu*) are mainly appealed to for the success in the hunt.

Chisumphi

This term seems to have a wide range of meaning, but one of its key meanings, especially in the Mchinji area, is that of the supreme spirit, which is associated with the provision of rain.

I have detailed above the meanings and association, relating to the six key names that are used in Malawi to refer to the supreme spirit. Essentially Chiuta (god) is conceived as an active power, and is associated with the sky and the atmosphere, and as being the main provider of rain. Although often addressed in anthromorphic terms and in prayer the supreme being is not the focus of any cult and is usually not embodied in any form apart from spirit mediums associated with the rain shrines and the python. The deity, unlike the spirits of ancestors and witches, never assumes animal form, and is essentially a transcendental being. As there is no pantheon of gods to be found in Malawi, comparable to that found among many other African cultures, Chakanza (1987: 7) affirms that the Chewa concept of god is 'monotheistic'. Yet the deity, though in essence spirit, is also viewed in personal terms as a mother, and as giving nourishment and nurturance, and as having an immanent presence in the material world. Social and individual wellbeing in rural Malawi is fundamentally focused on agricultural prosperity – and this is dependent on the fertility of the land and a controlled supply of rain – at the right time and in the right amount. The supreme being manifested itself in nature largely through the provision of rain – and when this fails, people turn to god, but the deity is also the focus of other communal calamities, such as epidemics of disease or the presence of 'man-eating' lions.

In his essay on 'The Religion of My Fathers' – which reflects to an important degree his Ngoni background – Levi Mumba stressed the importance of mediation in Malawian social life. As the 'social fabric', as he put it (in very Durkheimian fashion), provides the 'model of the spirit world' (1930: 363), it is necessary, he felt, to emphasize the important role that the spirits (*mizimu*) of the ancestors (*makolo*), particularly deceased chiefs, play as mediators between humans and the 'rain' deity. An important distinction is always maintained between the supreme deity (*chiuta, mulungu*) and the spirits of the ancestors, but as spiritual beings (both are sometimes addressed as *mizimu* or *mulungu*) they are often closely identified. As one person said to me: 'There are two kinds of spirits' (*mizimuyi iripo mitundu iwiri*) – Mulengi, the creator, who protects people and shows mercy (*chifundo*) towards them, and the *mizimu yu anthu wokufa*, the spirits of people who have died. Christians will also speak of the holy spirit (*mzimu woyera*). The essence of the spirits is that they are immaterial; they are thus not seen with the eyes (*simaoneka ndi maso*), but only manifest themselves in phenomena through their powers (*mphamvu*), but because of the close association between the deity and the ancestral spirits, the latter are described as living, or being with god: *aku-mulungu*. Amanze cites the Chewa riddle.

Nidiri ndi nsengwa ziwiri,
Imodzi ndimaseweretsa koma ina se.

'I have two small baskets, one I play with, one I don't.' The answer is 'the earth and the sky', suggesting a contrast between the earthly abode (*dziko la pansi*) of humans, and the sky (*thambo*), the abode of spirits (Amanze, 1986: 263).

Although Mumba stressed that Malawians believe that the supreme spirit is prevalent in every created being – material and immaterial, air, water, trees, animals, mountains, and ancestral spirits, he was also adamant that local people 'never for a moment think of animals, mountains and trees as having a soul or spirit' (Mumba, 1930: 368). Talking to many Malawians on the subject this too has been my experience, and so it would be quite misleading to describe Malawian religious culture as 'animistic' (but cf. Price, 1964: 122–3). Because of this, and because only humans become spiritual beings – wild mammals are very closely associated with the earthly domain, with the human lifecycle rather than with the supreme deity. Besides the python, which I shall discuss below, there are two animals that are closely associated with divinity – the warthog and the monitor lizard. This association tends to be found mainly in the Lower Shire.

Warthogs are common in Malawi wherever there are protected areas, and among European naturalists it is often described in unflattering terms – as quaint, repulsive, hideous. Harry Johnston, who kept one as a pet in Zomba, described it as 'beast of another epoch' (1897: 298) From the Malawian point of view what is significant is that it holds its tail erect when running, that its tusks (*mano*) are important as protective medicine (*kachilisi*), and that it has a habit of suddenly falling sideways when it wants to rest. Thus the warthog (*njiri*), is an animal that is closely associated with epilepsy (*nkhunyu*, which is often described as *manjirinjiri*). This ailment in turn is associated with spirit possession. Thus the deity is described among the Nyungwi of Mozambique, as chanjiri, alluding to the power and endurance exhibited by the warthog.

Two species of monitor lizard are found in Malawi, the Rock Monitor (*Varanus exanthematicus*), which is locally common in Savanna woodland, and the Nile Monitor (*V. niloticus*), which is common in Malawi wherever there are large rivers.

The Nile monitor (*gondwa* C, *sakata*, Y, *mnganzi*, N), which as Scott (1929: 313) puts it, has a 'standing quarrel with the crocodile', is associated with the supreme deity, and often shares its name, *chiuta*, *mphambe*. According to Schoffeleers this lizard – the largest in Africa –

Figure 5.3 The monitor lizard with two young Yao girls. Domasi, April 1991

is thought of living above the clouds, and is linked to such phenomena as lightning and thunder. The Monitor is highly sought after for medicine, and its skin is the only one used for the sacred drums of the Mbona rain cult (Schoffeleers, 1968: 184; cf. Stannus, 1910: 301). It is of interest that the white lizard paintings found on such rock shelters as Namzeze, Mphunzi, and Chigwenembe in the Dedza district, which are distinct in age and type from both the older red schematic paintings and the more recent nyau sketches, were identified to me as that of the monitor lizard. This may suggest an early association with rain cults, although the shelters do not seem to be used for that purpose at the present time.

The Rain Shrines and the Serpent Spirit

In his pioneering studies of Mang'anja religion, and particularly of the Mbona cult at Nsanje, Father Schoffeleers (1966, 1968, 1992) made an important distinction between what he describes as the 'territorial cults', and the various rites associated with the ancestral spirits – focused as these are on the local matrilineage and the household. The territorial cults form part of a network of rain shrines dedicated to the high god – the supreme being – and are characterized by a permanent structure of ritual ceremonials. Theologically he writes, 'they emphasize the creative and directive power of god rather than of the family and nature spirits which are the focus of village and matrilineage veneration' (1975: 16).

There is however some ambiguity as to whether these shrines were dedicated to the supreme spirit (*chisumphi, chiuta, mulungu*), or whether such territorial spirits are, as Cullen Young put it 'god locally conceived', or whether the spirits associated with the various shrines or mountains were ancestral spirits – specifically those of deceased chiefs, and thus act simply as mediators. Although there is a wealth of literature on those territorial cults associated with the Maravi chiefdoms – Undi, Lundu and Kalonga – it is evident that in the pre-colonial period almost every mountain and larger hill in Malawi had an associated rain shrine. And even at the present time, my own enquiries suggest, whenever there is a severe drought, recourse is made to the spirits of deceased chiefs, or to spirits associated with specific mountains, and supplications are made for rain. At the turn of the century Alfred Swann, who was a lay missionary and an administrator at Nkhotakota, wrote that

> The lofty mountain peak is not looked on with a sense of awe because its summit is lost in cloud, but rather because it is the watchtower of some departed chief's spirit. (1910: 348)

Many mountains in Malawi are closely associated with the spirit world – as well as with the early inhabitants of the country, the Akafula, and evoke feelings of awe and fear (*-mantha*) among many Malawians. I have personal testament to this when camping or climbing on such mountains as Soche, Mulanje, Malawi Hills, Michesi (discussed below in relation to the Napolo spirit), Thyolo, Dedza and Mchinji, accompanied only by a local Malawian herbalist or guide. My companion when camping on the top of Mt. Chiperoni in Mozambique in September 1960 also conveyed a sense that the spirits of the ancestors (*mizimu*) were present in the evergreen forest that clothed the high south-eastern slopes. All the early observers and missionaries in Malawi mention the ancestral spirits associated with specific mountains, and before discussing the more important territorial cults, or rain shrines, these may be briefly noted – as these pertain particularly to the Shire Highlands.

In his ethnological notes on beliefs about god in the Blantyre district at the end of the nineteenth century, Duff MacDonald wrote of the association of the spirit of an 'old chief(s)' with the mountains, and gave several examples. The 'god of Mountain Soche', he noted, was Kankhomba, a deceased Nyanja chief, whose spirit, as a 'local deity' received the supplications of the Yao chief Kapeni. Offerings of floor (*ufa*) and beer (*mowa*) were made to the spirit as gifts (*mutulo*), and prayers made for rain (1882: 70; Werner, 1906: 51). The chief always makes offerings on behalf of the whole community, and thus both the chief and the territorial spirit mediate between people and the supreme spirit. Mtanga, described by Sanderson as the 'spirit of famine' (1954: 184), was specifically associated with Mangochi Mountain, MacDonald noting that it was both equated with Mulungu – as the supreme spirit – and was also 'distinctly localized'. He suggests that these associations were akin to Greek beliefs about Mt. Olympus (1882: 71). In her valuable study Alice Werner indicates that rain 'deities' and rain shrines were associated with many other hills of the Shire Highlands – near Mloza crater on Mulanje (Chief Chipoka), as well as on Malabvi, Michiru, Mpingwe, Thyolo, and Ndirande Mountains during the 1890s (1906: 46–61).

The early observations by Werner have been confirmed by recently collected oral traditions from the southern region. Although related in the past tense, and referring always to the ancestors (*makolo*), in fact, at times of drought, rain rituals are still widely practised. For example, on Zobwe hill near Mwanza, elderly women who were not co-habiting with men (*sanalkugundana ndi amuna*) would brew beer and this would be offered (kutsira), together with a black goat (*mbuzi zakuda*) to the ancestral spirits (*mizimu ya makolo*). The goat would be roasted, its smoke (*utsi wache*) going to the ancestors (Department of Antiquities, 1971: Mnz 4/1). Rain rituals were also noted on Michiru and Soche Mountains in the Blantyre district – the latter shrine being referred to as the 'rock of Kankhomba' – a deceased chief who had the ability to make rain (*analikupanga mvula*) mvula. Even now, Michiru is described as a hill of spirits (*ndi phiri la mizimu*), where offerings were made (*kutsira nsembe*) at a shrine (*kachisi*) on the summit.

Equally important; the shrines where *nsembe* (offerings) were made was not only associated with the mountains, but also a place where snakes (*njoka*) had their abode (Department of Antiquities, 1971: CO 3/1, BT 15/2).

Although Mulanje Mountain is often mentioned by early writers as lacking a rain shrine, in fact, the mountain is always described as a place of spirits, and is held in much awe. The summit is described as *sapitwa* 'don't go', and offerings of beer are made to the spirits at times of drought (Kaddy Silungwe in Boeder, 1982: 64–5).

Although Schoffeleers (1979) suggests that all these southern shrines were simply manifestations of two territorial cults – the 'great well-organized cults' of Chisumphi and Mbona – it is evident that rain shrines in the past were ubiquitous in the country, and though associated with specific mountains or the larger hills, were focused more on the ancestors of local chiefs, rather than on either the supreme spirit, or the various dynasties – Kalonga, Undi, Lundu, Kaphwiti – who claimed political hegenomy during a particular historical period. I will discuss in turn the six territorial 'cults' or rain shrines which were of crucial importance during the early years of this century, focusing on the symbolism of *thunga*, or *nsato*, the serpent-spirit that was associated with the rains.

Chikang'ombe

In his memoirs of his missionary endeavours, Donald Fraser wrote that throughout the region there were 'local sub-gods who dwell on mist crowned hills', and that the deity that was important to the Tumbuka was called Chikang'ombe, whose abode was on a high hill above Njakwa gorge, near Rumphi. He was conceived as a male god, and 'his body was like that of a great snake, but he had a mane like a lion'. When strong winds blew, the course of his journey could be traced by the maize stalks that had been broken during his progress across the landscape. A young girl was dedicated to the deity, and was considered to be his wife. She lived apart and never married, and 'in her the god was incarnated' (1914: 121–2). Fraser alludes to a close association between Chikang'ombe and *mangadzi*, a female deity to the South. Samuel Ntara suggests that *mangadzi* was the name given by the Mang'anja to their god (1973: 39). Cullen Young also suggests an association between these two deities – although, as we shall see, it is misleading to interpret *mangadzi* as a 'god' or 'goddess' – but he affirms that it was chiuta who was entreated for rain at the *chikang'ombe* shrine. Not very long ago, he wrote, the summit of Chinkang'ombe Hill was well covered with votive offerings (1931: 130–1).

According to a contemporary writer the Njakwa Gorge was a 'holy shrine' of the Tumbuka people, a dwelling place for the spirits, and was associated with 'miracles' and mysterious events. The place where the road from Bwengu to Rumphi crosses the South Rukuru River, Chipokawawoli, is still a place associated with mystery, and with the spirits. In the past it was a subsidiary shrine to that of Chikang'ombe (Boeder 1982). The term Chikang'ombe is derived from the general term for cattle, *ng'ombe*, and alludes to the fact that cattle were used as sacrificial offering (*nsembe*) at the shrine: its literal meaning is 'the great one associated with cattle' (Vail, 1979: 230).

More recent research by Leroy Vail into the oral traditions of the southern Tumbuka has confirmed the somewhat meagre observations of

Fraser and Cullen Young. Chikang'ombe is said to be a spirit that is associated with hills over a wide area along the Zambia/Malawi watershed, with shrines at Nthembwe, Pelekezi and Manda hills in the Mzimba district, in the Muchinga Mountains of eastern Zambia, as well as on Njakwa Hill near Rumphi. The spirit is conceived as taking the form of a very large snake, which has its abode on earth, and it is closely identified with the rains. When thunder occurs, the Tumbuka will say 'Chikang'ombe speaks' (Young, 1930: 13) The Chikang'ombe spirit was seen as controlling the rain: when rains were plentiful he was content, when he was angry, there was drought or adverse thunderstorms. Conceived as a masculine force, strong winds signify his movements over the land. A certain woman was consecrated to his service, and considered to function as a spirit wife to the rain deity, and the spirit would visit her hut in the form of a snake. She was thus often called Chikan'gombe, and at the Pelekezi shrine was a woman of the Phiri clan. Often she was a sister of the chief whose clan was responsible for the shrine. As these shrines function only during times of drought or adversity, and as the Mzimba district lacked political unity on the pre-colonial era, Vail suggests that there was no centralization of the shrine organization (Vail, 1979: 214–15, for an account on another rain cult associated with Mwanda Hill in the Rumphi district see Luhanga, 1983).

Emphasizing the 'cultural unity' of the peoples of Malawi in the pre-colonial period – they are he wrote 'mixed peoples with mixed cultures having mixed histories' – Leroy Vail noted the important similarities between the Chikang'ombe cult among the Tumbuka, and the various territorial cults associated with the central region of Malawi. It is to these cults that we may turn next.

Makewana

The territorial cults found in the central regions of Malawi, among the Chipeta, Chewa and Nyanja peoples, have been described under various designations – *chauta, makewana, chisumphi, mangadzi, matsakamula* – and this has inevitably led to some confusion. In his history of the Chewa, Ntara, in his discussion of the Msinja Shrine, made a list of the names of the priests, who, he suggested, were always women, as in the past 'our ancestors did not have chiefs'. Unfortunately his history includes local names of the supreme being (Leza, Mulungu, Chisumphi, Mphambe), as well as of the various spirit mediums (*makewana, mangadzi*), who he misleading describes as gods or goddesses (1973: 38–9). It is important then to make a distinction between: the supreme spirit (*Chiuta, Chisumphi,*

Leza), the various manifestations of divinity which, as a masculine force, took the form of a snake (*thunga*), the spirit mediums who were considered to be the spirit wives of these manifestations (*chauta, mangadzi, makewana*), and, finally, the various religious functionaries who maintained and serviced the rain shrines.

The rain shrines of central Malawi have been the subject of numerous studies, which have generated a wealth of literature. As elsewhere it is evident that rain shrines exist throughout the central region, and those of Matsakamula near Ntchisi, and Cherenje near Nkhoma (Chauwa) were important shrines in the past, and still function as rain shrines in times of drought (Hodgson, 1933: 154; Makombe, 1983), but the most important rain shrine among the Chewa was that located at Msinja, to the south of Diampwe river in the Dedza district. It owed its importance to its close association with the Undi chiefdom, located at Maano in Northern Mozambique, some 160 km to the west of the shrine. The history of the rain shrine was the subject of a classic article by W.H.J. Rangeley (1952), who incorporated into his account information derived from Samuel Ntara.

The central figure at the Msinja rain shrine was always a woman, known as *mangadzi* or *chauta*. The term *chauta* means 'of the hunting (rain) bow', and is a correlate of *Chiuta*, one of the recognized names of the supreme being. She was a member of the Phiri clan, and mangadzi, in tradition, was sister of the Undi chief. Some accounts suggest *mangadzi* was a Banda, being the daughter of *chauwa*, the rain-maker associated with Chirenje mountain. The important point, however, was that *chauta's* position was not hereditary; as after the death of a *mangadzi* a new spirit medium was installed when a woman appeared at Msinja, and uttered strange prophesies (*kubwebweta*). Her behaviour indicated that the spirit had taken hold of her (*am'gwira*), and her selection was confirmed by the shrine officials after she had successfully answered the ritual questions put to her (1952: 35). She was also known as Makewana 'mother of children', which symbolized her position and role as the one responsible for the wellbeing, prosperity and sustenance of the people (Kalilombe, 1980: 40). She was also chosen as the wife of god, and thus was unmarried, or broke her marriage ties when she assumed the role of *mangadzi*. She was tended by a group of unmarried girls (*matsano*) who were also known as *akazi a chauta* (wives of god). Neither the *makewana* nor the *matsano* had sexual relations with human males. Only *thunga* (sacred serpent) or *nsato* (python), considered to be a epiphany or manifestation of the supreme spirit (*chiuta*) in the form of a snake, would visit the *makewana* on specified ritual occasions. *Thunga* (or *nthunga*) is the cultural equivalent of the spirit *chikan'gombe*, and was believed by the Chewa to be a kind of spirit entity that manifested itself as a huge snake. Father Boucher (1991) suggested that *thunga* was the mystical counterpart of the python (*nsato*). It habitually lived in the mountains, or in some deep sacred pool, and it was seen as moving from place to place, and as controlling the rains. *Thunga* was associated with mountains and hills throughout the central region. At Msinja, the serpent spirit *thunga* was symbolized by one of the shrine officials Kamundi, who was of the Mbewe clan. It was Kamundi who made offerings to the spirit house, and was responsible for the ritual making of fire by means of fire sticks (*wopeka moto*). And he was also importantly *thunga*. As Ntara writes:

> Kamundi analinso thunga. Mudziwa kuti chauta sakakwatiwa ndi munthu koma njoka dzina lache thunga. Koma chinali chinsinsi cha akulu kusankha munthu wine wolowa m'nyumba ya chauta. Ndipo kamundi anamusankha ndi undi kuti akhale thunga.

> Kamundi is also Thunga. You know that chauta is not married to a person but to a snake whose name is Thunga. But it is a secret of the elders to choose another man (person) to enter the hut of the Chauta. Then Kamundi is chosen by Undi to be Thunga. (Ntara, 1945: 36, my translation, cf. Ntara, 1973: 40 for a different translation)

Kamundi was the most important ritual official at the shrine – the most 'powerful' figure (*anali ndi mphamvu yaikulu*), as Ntara describes him. He was the male consort of Makewana, who was essentially a prophetess or spirit-medium, not a goddess. She lived alone, unmarried, and largely hidden from ordinary people. She neither cultivated the ground, nor partook of meat or beer. According to Rangeley, she lay on a bed of ivory tusks, covered with a black cloth, which symbolized dark clouds. She never cut her hair, for she controlled the rains, and if she cut her hair this was believed, by analogy, to 'cut' (*-dula*) the rains. Only Kamundi, representing the snake, Thunga, entered her hut, to perform ritual intercourse (*kutha misinda* – to finish sexual abstinence; *kubweza* – to bring together). This act has been interpreted as symbolizing the union of the sky (*chiuta*) and the earth, *mangadzi* representing the earth (*dziko la pansi*) as a mother.

The relationship between the spirit-snake Thunga, as a manifestation of Chiuta, and the mangadzi, the prophetess of the shrine, was seen as explicitly sexual, with the snake being associated with the male principle, and the prophetess with the female (Vail, 1979: 217; Kalilombe, 1980: 41).

Other ritual functionaries at Msinja included the *tsangoma* (person of the drum) who was the keeper of the sacred drum (the skin of which was taken from the monitor lizard), and who was of the Mwale clan; the Tsakabambe who kept the shrine clean and interpreted the words of the Mangadzi when she was in a trance state (*kubwebweta*); and the Masanda and Kanthungo who were responsible for the offerings made to the spirits. All these officials were members of the Nkhoma clan. Only black/dark (*wokuda*) cloth and animals were accepted as offerings at the shrine, and the animals were killed using a short stabbing spear (*kathungo*). Goats and sheep were the usual sacrificial animals. According to tradition, offerings were reduced to ashes, which were then cast in the sacred pool of Malawi. There were many other ritual officials associated with the shrine, which functioned critically at times of drought. Importantly, no *nyau* dancers were allowed to go near the rain shrines.

A few hundred yards from Msinja, was the sacred pool, named Malawi. As with other sites associated with the spirits, this was a protected area, and no bird or mammal could be molested in the vicinity of the pool. According to Ntara the priests at Msinja were responsible for installing the Kalonga to the throne (Ntara, 1973: 38–41; Rangeley, 1952).

In an interesting account of a rain cult among the Chewa, recorded by Bruwer (1952), Chauta was conceived as representing the supreme spirit (*mulungu wakumwamba* – god on high), her husband was deemed to be a python (*nsato*), and her ritual officials were described as asumphi. These officials were said to carefully watch the activities of the trap-door spider (species of *Mygalomorphae*), which close their moveable door when rain is forthcoming. Important in the rain ritual was the decoration of the prophetess Chauta with black and white spots (using flour and charcoal), interpreted by the Chewa as analogous to a balanced rainfall pattern of alternating wet and dry days, and the sacrifice of a black goat. The goat was roasted on a fire, and its blood was gathered in an earthenware pot was together with some scorched hair deposited in a nearby whirlpool. After sharing the meat, the participants returned from the shrine to the village singing songs

Besides the sacrificial offerings, also important at the shrine was the rain dance *mgwetsa*, which literally means the one who 'causes to fall' (*ku-gwa* – to fall) and alludes both to the falling of the rain, and to the possession of *chauta* by *thunga* or *nsato*, the python spirit, which is conceived as a manifestation of the supreme spirit (*chiuta, mulungu*), or as a messenger (*nthenga*, from *ku-tenga* – to bring). It is, however, misleading to conceive this possession rite (dance), as involving the incarnation by *mangadzi* of the 'spirit' of the python, but rather the python-snake (*thunga*) is the form which the spirit takes (whether 'spirit' is expressed as *chiuta, mulungu, mzimu,* or *chiwanda*).

The python in Chewa thought is closely identified mythologically (as well as empirically) with water, with rivers and deep pools, and thus with rainfall; it is therefore a key symbolic mediation between the supreme being and humans, for Chiuta is a being also closely identified with rainfall. But the people of Malawi are not animists and do not conceive of mountains, plants, or animals being 'animate' in a spiritual sense, for neither mammals nor snakes are believed to possess 'spirit' or 'souls'. But the spirit world (*mizimu*) is the associated with the woodland, and with the earth or underground (*pansi*) – because the dead are buried in the ground, usually in wooded groves. It is commonly believed that the spirits of the dead, particularly those of chiefs, often return to the village in the form of snakes (*njoka*), and the most celebrated of these is the python (*nsato*). In such contexts no harm is done to the snake, as they are looked upon as the concrete form of the spirits (*mizimu*) of the departed. Besides the python (*nsato, Python sebae*), the other snake associated with the spirit world and with the rains, is the file snake, *njokandala* (*Mehelya capensis*). As with the chameleon, a good deal of awe surrounds this snake, whose name essentially means 'white snake'. It is a large snake, to 130 cm long, with a triangular body, greyish-brown in colour, with a white vertebral stripe. It is considered extremely dangerous to kill this snake, and it is usually left well alone. Hodgson (1933: 154) records its association with the rainmaker (spirit medium) Matsakamula, while it is also believed to be utilized by sorcerers to accomplish the magical theft of maize and other goods (Sweeney, 1971: 27). People also do not kill the python. If one is killed and left unburied, it is believed that god (Mphambe, *Chiuta*) may withhold the rains, given the close association of the snake with the spirits. In such a case, the python must be ritually buried on the banks of a river, and the feathers of a black chicken and pieces of black cloth placed on its burial mound (Makombe, 1983: 15).

Although not specifically associated with the rains, two other snakes have salience in the folklore of Malawi, and are worth noting here. The first is a 'fabulous snake with a red head' – as Fraser (1914: 128) described it. It is usually known as kasongo or songo. Just as thunga is a larger, more mystical version of the ordinary nsato, so kasongo, is a larger version of the black mamba (*Dendroaspis polylepis*, also known as songo, or songwe). The 'mythical' snake is described as a large poisonous snake, dark in colour, with a red crest, like that of cocks' comb (*chimodzi tambala*). It is said to crow like a cock, and to be extremely fierce (*ukali kwambiri*), and is reputed to lie in wait for an unsuspecting victim. Not only Ntara, but all early European observers made of note of this common belief (cf. Ntara, 1973: 52; Duff, 1903: 138–9; Sanderson, 1954: 245). The snake in the literature is usually referred to as the 'crowing crested cobras' and its call is said to derive from the eerie wailing call of the buff-spotted crake (*Sarothrura elegans*), which lives in the rain forests of many mountains throughout the southern and central region. As this bird is also called songo in both Nyanja and Yao, an association between the snake and the crake is clearly made by local people.

It is misleading, I think, to equate the water-serpent thunga, with the 'crowing snake' *songo*, for the thunga (or *nsato*) is viewed in positive terms, and killing it is believed to have dire consequences; a person might go insane, or a serious drought might result (Kwapulani, 1982: 8). On the other hand, the latter 'mythical' snake is seen as highly malevolent and dangerous (cf. Linden, 1979: 207). Local people always make a clear distinction between the two types of snake.

The other snake which is important in local custom is the blind snake (*Typhlops schlegelii*). *Nthonga, chirere, biritsi, and mbituy* are among its common names. It is a blind burrowing snake, bluish grey, and some 50 cm long. It feeds mainly on termites, and is seen above ground only rarely during the rains, and is harmless. People, however, describe it as having two heads, as being poisonous, and if seen, as a harbinger of misfortune.

From the published record and oral tradition it is evident that there was no rain 'deity' specifically associated with the Msinja shrine, but that Thunga was a serpent-spirit who was a manifestation of the supreme spirit Chiuta. The Mangadzi, which is said to have been the name of the first Makewana, was essentially a spirit medium, not a goddess. Associated with the earth, she symbolically mated with her husband Thunga, who represented the divinity as the provider of rain. In the Mgwetsa rain dance she embodies the serpent spirit, hence her familiar name Chauta. But as both Cullen Young and Rangeley insisted, Mangadzi, like Mbona, and like also the spirits (mizimu) of the ancestors, was an earthly being, and distinct from the supreme spirit (cf. Rangeley to Cullen Young, 30 April 1952. Rangeley Papers).

The Msinji shrine is still functioning, through its influence is limited and local, and it was given a new lease of life during the severe drought years 1992–4 when there were serious food shortages in Malawi. In her recent important studies of the shrine, which is now situated in Kachikoti village in the Dedza district – its traditional name is Msinja – Isabel Phiri (1996) notes that this 'Chisumphi cult' is still focused around women. The current keeper of the shrine, Nandinesi Nabanda, is a widow, for there is still a strong belief that women must be celibate in order to serve god effectively. She does not consider herself *makewana*, but as the perpetual sister of the prophetess. As 'wife' of the supreme spirit Chisumphi the shrine keeper conducts two ceremonies within the village – the annual rain-calling ceremony and a thanksgiving ceremony for 'first fruits' which acknowledge that god is the source of food. The village chief serves also as an official at the shrine, and the shrine keeper is supported by a small group of older women who have reached menopause. The term *matsano* seems to have been forgotten, and the black cloth, *biliwita*, which was said to symbolize and attract dark clouds, is no longer worn. The young girls who sing songs and make libations of maize porridge at the rain-calling ceremony, have not yet reached puberty, and their faces are covered in powdered charcoal spotted with maize flour. The area around the shrine and at the sacred pool is still considered sacred, and no sexually active person, menstruating woman, or even *nyau* dancers are allowed near these sites, Phiri (1996: 166) writes:

> There is still a belief that there is a python that stays at that place (*pakabvumbwa*) and comes to eat the food offered at the shrine which is about a kilometre away. No one has seen the python, but they see its tracks the following morning after the ritual has been performed.

The ritual significance of the python is not explored, but *Pakabvumbwa cave* is considered the 'male side' of the sacred place, and in tradition is associated with *kamundi mbewe*, a functionary who was ritual husband to the *makewana*.

Although the *Chisumphi* shrine is 'female led' Phiri interprets the traditions surrounding the cult – re the negative attitude towards menstruation and sexuality – as adversely affecting women, but what was crucial about the *makewana* is that it emphasizes that women were the principal mediators between god and the community with respect to ecological problems such as the lack of rain. (On the history of the Chewa rain shrines see also I.A Phiri, 1997: 23–31.)

Mwali

The Msinja rain shrine lay midway between the capitals of two early Maravi states, the Kalonga chiefdom centred on Mankhamba on the lakeshore near Mtakataka, and the Undi chiefdom in northern Mozambique. Whereas the *sister* of Undi seems to have been associated with the spirit-medium Chauta at Msinja, (according to Rangeley) and conceptualized as the 'wife' of the supreme spirit (Chiuta, chisumphi), it was the *wife* of Kalonga who is important at the Mankhamba shrine. She was known by the title 'Mwali', and was considered to have kinship links – either as sister or daughter – to the spirit – mediums Chauwa of Chirenje Mountain, and the Makewana at Msinja. Like these other mediums the Mwali's 'real' husband was said to be the snake Thunga. But the shrine itself, in a thicket on the north bank of the Nadzipulu River, is associated also with the spirits of the dead Kalonga chiefs, who were of the Phiri clan. Oral traditions insist that the Mwali is the real Mwini *dziko*, guardian of the land, and as Rangeley wrote, Mankhamba 'is and always was Banda country' (letter to Cullen Young, 30 April 1952, in Rangeley Archives, Linden, 1972: 11–12).

Linden has given a good account of the shrine officials and rituals at the Mankhamba shrine, which is seen as part of a widespread Chisumphi cult – Chisumphi being one of the names of the supreme being. It is seen as an 'expression' of a proto-Chewa religious culture, although it is misleading, I think, to conflate the Maravi chiefdoms with the Chewa, and both with the religious culture of the region. The senior ritual official at the shrine was Mbuzimaere ('goat with breasts') who like Kamundi at the Msinja shrine, belonged to the Mbewe clan. He was the main celebrant during the Mfunde rain ritual, which involved the smearing of young children with charcoal (*mikala*), and the offering of beer to the ancestral spirits at a specially constructed spirit hut (*kachisi*). Sand was spread on the floor of the shrine to keep it cool. After the ritual the thunga snake appeared to the Mbuzimaere, looking 'very beautiful', with 'pink markings on a black body' (Linden, 1979: 191–2). Linden notes that while near Mchinji thunga is a 'water spirit' that possesses mainly women, at the Mankhamba shrine Thunga was seen as the 'husband' of Mwali, who accompanied her into the shrine and was said to be 'tame like a chicken' and that Mwali 'understood its wishes' (Linden, 1979: 194). The snake thunga, and its earthly embodiment in the persons of Kamundi and Mbuzimaere, thus symbolizes a spirit intermediary between the 'high god' (Chisumphi, Chiuta) and a local community, represented by spirit mediums who are women. Linden describes the thunga – spirit as a 'phallic messenger' (1979: 201). Thus we have a contrast, and a dialectic or complementary opposition, between different facets of social existence, expressed through the affinal relationship between two inter-marrying clans, one of which – the Phiri (or Mbewe) – are conceptualized as outsiders or invaders, or with respect to the Maravi states, as politically dominant. Thus a symbolic equation is made between the snake thunga, water, masculinity, outsider status and the ancestral spirits of the chiefs. This may be expressed schematically as follows:

Phiri	Banda
(Mbewe)	
Water	land
(Thunga)	(Spirit-medium)
masculinity	motherhood
hunting	agriculture
forests, deep	village
pools, mountains	environs
affines	matrilineal kin group
semen	blood

Many scholars have drawn attention to the dual traditions in Chewa history and culture, between the various dynastic states (Kalonga, Undi, Changamire, Kaphwiti), who as political rulers all belonged to the Phiri clan, and were conceptualized as 'invaders', and members as the Banda clan, who were associated with the land, and with ritual powers related to rain calling. The various spirit mediums associated with the rain shrines (*mangadzi, mwali, chauwa, salima*) all belonged, according to Ntara, to the Banda clan. The two intermarrying clans are thus seen as representing secular and religious authority respectively (Ntara, 1973: 11–12; Schoffeleers, 1979: 149–150).

A number of features common to both the Msinja and Mankhamba shrines are worth noting.

The first is that the spirit mediums (mangadzi, mwali), in being symbolically 'married' to the supreme being, as represented by the Thunga serpent spirit, are also symbolically separated themselves from ordinary everyday life. They become celibate, lived alone, and did not consume either beer or meat, or cut their hair. They thus remained permanently in a 'cool' condition.

Secondly, the main priests at the shrine, who acted as mediators between the supreme being (Thunga) and the spirit mediums, were invariably men belonging to the Mbewe clan, which in tradition is associated with the Mchinji district and the Mkanda chiefdom (Ntara, 1973: 74–6).

Finally, the 'central cult object' of these rain shrines, as Schoffeleers emphasizes, was conceived of as a snake, called thunga, who was associated with sacred pools, and with deep forest thickets (nsitu).

In identifying these traditions with a period prior to the arrival of the Phiri clan, and the establishment of the Maravi states (circa sixteenth century onwards), Schoffeleers suggests that Maravi religious culture was different from that outlined above; for this culture focused on the spirits of the Phiri chiefs, and their associated shrines, and a member of the local chiefly lineage acted as both a medium and rain caller. He writes:

> Deceased chiefs were (and are) thought to manifest themselves in the form of a lion and to possess their mediums in that form. Spirit wives did not feature in their cults, nor did python manifestations or python rituals, and shrine complexes consequently have no sacred pools.

These chiefly cults thus involved the veneration of deceased rulers, culminating in the ancestral spirit Nyangu, the mother of both Kalonga and Undi (Schoffeleers, 1979: 155) Schoffeleers discusses at some length the complex interrelationship between the various chiefdoms, and their attempts to control and utilize the rain shrines (Schoffeleers, 1979: 154–61). Importantly, the rain shrines were an expression of the fact that the Chewa, like other communities of the region, had a highly ritualized attachment to the land. For the local chief was responsible for the rain rituals at the end of the dry season, as well as being considered the guardian of the land (*Mwini ya dziko*). In this respect, as Rau (1979) has explained, the matrilineal peoples of Central Africa, the Chewa specifically, contrasted significantly with that of the pastoral Ngoni, whose religious system centred on the chiefly ancestors and cattle kraal.

Among the Ngoni there was thus an absence of any developed ritual attachment to the land. It is important I think to note that although thunga may manifest itself as a male spirit – a 'phallic messenger' in the words of Linden – neither thunga, nor the supreme spirit is conceived of as entirely masculine. Both essentially are androgynous beings, and may also manifest themselves in feminine form. Thus Makewana was, in a sense, a manifestation of the supreme spirit, which is why writers like Kwapulani describe the spirit-medium as a goddess (1982: 134), but as Chewa thought does not imply a radical dualism between spirit and matter it is misleading I think to conceive of the Makewana's religious role as involving the 'in dwelling' or 'incarnation' of Chiuta. It is rather best expressed by suggesting that the spirit takes human form, in the same way as ancestral spirits, especially those of chiefs, may taken an animal form.

In writing of the *makewana* (*mangadzi*) and the Chewa rain shrines, Isabel Phiri emphasizes the important and crucial role that women had as spirit mediums in relation to the divinity, for when possessed the *makewana* 'could speak as if it were god speaking to the people'. She stresses, too, the feminine nature of god, and writes that among the Chewa 'God was without sex' (Phiri, 1997: 25–8). Malawians I knew well all addressed the deity not as 'father' (bambo), but as *ambuye*, which although it may refer to the mother's brother, essentially means grandparent of either sex.

Bimbi

In January 1907, H.S. Stannus records, there was a severe drought in the Mangochi district. The Yao chief Mponda, therefore, with a group of headmen, went to visit a local rainmaker, called Bimbi. They appealed to this spirit medium for rain and he entered into a hut in the Ulongwe forest, and went through 'certain incantantions', conferring with the spirits. These were 'said to be a male and female snake. God is said to speak to these, these to Bimbi, and Bimbi to the people'. Rain came soon afterwards. (Stannus, 1910: 307). In a later paper Stannus wrote of an Anyanja woman called Bimbi Chikasowa, who was well known in the Zomba district, and who was consulted about rain, and about the prevention of disease. She was, he wrote, a woman of quiet ways, and of no fixed abode, and was greatly respected in the district (1922: 317).

Such were the scant records of the Bimbi cult during the colonial period, although there is every reason to suspect that it is one of the oldest cults in Malawi. It has recently been the subject of some important researches by James Amanze (1980, 1986), and I shall here merely draw on some of his observations relating to its main rituals. The term *bimbi* means spirit medium, prophet or diviner, and in the past the role of the 'rain caller' could be filled by either a man or woman. The present incumbent is an Nyanja man, a devout Moslem who has had no formal education. On his assumption of this role, he is believed to have been possessed by the spirits of former Bimbi. The main Bimbi shrine is located some 5 km from Bimbi village, in the Makanga forest along the banks of the Shire River. It is a small thatched hut with a fence around it, and anyone entering the shrine must be in a 'cool' condition, having refrained from sexual intercourse. Amanze describes the shrine as a 'meeting place' between this world and the spiritual world, between the living and the ancestral spirits (1980: 6). There is a strong association between these spirits, spirits like Mkulukutwa and Namanje, and Lake Malombe, where the spirits are believed to live, as well as with snakes. The Bimbi wears a black cloth, Mtambo (cloud), which symbolizes the dark clouds of rain. Oral traditions suggest links between the Bimbi and the shrines of Central Malawi, as well as with Nyangu, the ancestors of the Phiri clan, and Amanze notes that there are indications that the Bimbi originally belonged to the Mbewe clan. The Ulongwe Forest is commonly known as *Kachisi wa nyangu*, Shrine of Nyangu. The Yao chiefs, Liwonde and Kawinga, it is worth noting, both belonged to the Mbewe clan and had rain-making ritual functions (see Kumwembe, 1978).

Importantly the Bimbi plays an important ritual role in the Upper Shire during all times of crisis – such as drought, famine and epidemics. At the end of the dry season – in October or November – the Bimbi shrine becomes a focus of spiritual activities. A special dance is performed, Chilewe, in which hundreds of local villagers participate, and which is focused around Bimbi's sorority group. There is singing and dancing, as maize is collected for making the sacrificial beer. The climax of the festivities is the Milawe ritual, undertaken at the shrine, during which the Bimbi goes into a trance, and becomes possessed by the spirits. The seance takes place at night, in the presence of the chiefs and village elders. The shrine itself is seen as an abode of the spirits (and snakes, whose form they take). After the Milawe rite, chiefs will then make offerings at their own local shrines for rain. Supplications and entreaties are made to the supreme spirit (Chauta, *Namalenga*), who like the ancestral spirit is often addressed as Ambuye (grandparent), and offerings (*kutsira nsembe*) of beer (*mowa*) are made to the spirits. The brewing of beer is undertaken by young girls and elderly women, for they are held to be 'cool' (*ozizila*) and calm (*kuyera mtima*). Coolness is essential for the success of the ritual. Sexually-active women, who would be in a 'hot' (*wotentha*) condition would be the antithesis of this. As said, no person in a 'hot' condition is allowed to enter the ancestral shrines. Equally important, Amanze emphasizes that the rain rituals (*nsembe ya mvula*) will only be a success if peace (*mtendere*) and a spirit of harmony and reconciliation are actively present in the community, for peace is seen as conducive to prosperity and the fecundity of the land and of the people (1986: 208). Also important, the graveyards of the local chiefs, which are in a forested locales, will be ritually swept (*kutsetsa kumanda kwa mfumu*) prior to the rain offerings, and the floor of the spirit huts themselves (*kachisi*) will be spread (*kumwalamwaza*) with sand (*nchenga*). This again symbolically creates a cool condition – conducive to rain. The beer itself, which is poured into a pot in the ground, as an offering to the spirits, is believed to be a symbol of rain, and to make the earth cool and wet.

Although Amanze stresses that the Bimbi cult was an important 'unifying' factor in the area, and that there was a close, even if complex, relationship between the Bimbi and local chiefs, particularly the Yao chiefs, it is important to note that Bimbi was a ritual personage, and that there were several Bimbi evident in the Upper Shire and Zomba area. Moreover, each local chief was to a large degree autonomous, and also had a ritual function, and thus performed offerings to the ancestral spirits with regard to rain, although often acknowledging the ritual paramouncy of the local Bimbi. But in the context of the present study, what is important is the fact that snakes were a 'dominant symbol' in the Bimbi cult. As Amanze wrote: 'Territorial ancestral spirits in the form of snakes play an extraordinary role in the Bimbi cult', in a sense 'representing' the deity itself (1986: 269). The ancestral spirits, particularly the spirits of dead chiefs, become, in the form of snakes, spiritual intermediaries between people and the supreme spirit, who is ultimately responsible for the provision of rain.

The rain shrines, usually located in forests or thickets, and often near a large *boabab* or *njale* (*Sterculia appendiculata*) tree, are always seen as being inhabited by 'snake-spirits' (Amanze, 1980: 20) – that is, ancestral spirits in the form of snakes, the python being the main hierophony.

What is particularly important is that the Bimbi and the local chiefs are seen as having an important function in countering, through rituals, the malevolent activities of witches (*afiti*), for throughout Southern Malawi it is believed that people through the use of powerful medicines (*mankhwala yomanga mvula*) is able to stop the coming of the rains. Nothing could be more detrimental to community wellbeing. This act is described as *kumanga mvula* – to bind or tie the rains.

The role of the Bimbi, however, was not confined to rain-calling. He was consulted as a spirit medium on all occasions of communal distress – such as epidemics of disease, widespread crop destruction either by wild pigs (*nguluwe*), or by insect pests (*kapuche*), or to counter the rampages of 'man-eating' lions.

Napolo

Most of the hills and mountains of the Shire Highlands have rain shrines associated with them, and local chiefs at the end of the dry season often conduct rituals or make offerings to the spirits of the ancestors. Some of the mountains, particularly Michesi, Mulanje and Zomba Mountains, are also associated with a mythical being called Napolo who is described as a huge serpent spirit. This serpent spirit is associated with the rains but particularly with thunderstorms and floods. I found no evidence of any shrines specifically dedicated to Napolo, but in the eyes of local people both Mulanje and Michesi have a legendary quality, and are specifically associated with Napolo, the serpent spirit, and with the spirits of the ancestors.

In a small booklet on the history of the Lomwe people of Malawi – written in Chewa – L.D. Soka describes Michesi Mountain as the 'Mountain of Spirits'. (*Malo otchuka a mizimu yotereye ndi pa phiri a michese* – 'the famous place of spirits (we say) is Michesi mountain'.) The spirits (*mizimu*) according to Soka are feared by people (*kuchititsa mantha*), and are to be found in such places as graveyards, shrines (*kachisi*) and evergreen thickets (*nsitu*). When a person dies, he explains, they change (*amasanduka*) into something else, into an invisible thing, and it is this that people fear. People therefore do not wander far from the village. If they do venture into the forest on Michesi they may be beaten, or see lighted torches (*miyuni*) but not the people carrying them, or they may encounter signs of evil import (*olaulidwa*). Lomwe people, Soka contends, fear the spirits much more than they do wild animals (*chirombo*) or those people who steal humans (*chifwamba*). One can easily run away from animals and humans; not from the spirits. If you are troubled with spirits you thus need the help of the diviner (*sing'anga*), who, with the aid of medicines, makes the spirits return to the uninhabited places – like the forests on Michesi Mountain. There are many places where spirits are found; Michesi, however, is the place where they are particularly associated – so writes Soka (1953: 28–9).

The sentiments expressed by Soka are of interest. Nineteenth century scholars often spoke of preliterate people as 'fearing' the spirit world: contemporary anthropologists, on the other hand, like Mary Douglas (1966), have tended to repudiate such ideas – stressing the matter-of-fact attitudes that most people have towards the spirits. Yet here Soka is writing of Lomwe peasants fearing the *mizimu*, and certainly the emotions of dread and fear (*kuchita mantha, ku-opsya*) are widely expressed by Malawians to indicate their feelings towards the spirits of the dead, as well as towards wild animals.

This association of Michesi – as well as the nearby mountains of Mulanje and Mausi – with the spirit world, is confirmed by oral traditions. All these traditions refer to Michesi as the 'Mountain of the Spirits' (*phiri la mizimu*). People would say they often heard the *mizimu*, making shrill calls or yodelling (*nthungululu*) or beating drums (Department of Antiquities 1971: MJ 6/2).

Mulanje mountain, too, has strong associations with the spirits, and most people living around the mountain, Stephen Msiska records, think of it as 'a holy place evoking awe and foreboding' (1997: 30). Although the Malawian attitude to mountains is one of awe and reverence, and they are closely identified with the spirits, Malawians do not, like the Daur Monguls, actually 'worship' mountains (Humphrey, 1996: 86).

Michesi mountain, however, is not only associated with the spirits of the dead (*mizimu*), but also with the Batwa people. These people are also referred to as *amwandionerapati*, which literally means 'where did you see me?'. Throughout Malawi, there are oral traditions relating to these people. Known also as Akafula, the diggers, they are said to be the original inhabitants of the country. To people living on the vicinity of Mulanje and Michesi mountains, these Batwa people still have a living presence – although it is often difficult in conversation to distinguish whether people are referring to the spirits of the Batwa or to the Batwa themselves. Some even suggested that the *mizimu* became *batwa*.

There is one particular spirit that is also associated with the mountains of southern Malawi – especially Michesi – and that is the serpent spirit Napolo. Unlike the *mizimu*, the spirits of the dead, which are invoked in initiation rites (*chinamwali*) and during divination and healing rites, Napolo, like the deity Chauta, is rarely invoked by people. There is no mention of Napolo in Soka's or Boeder's (1984) history of the Lomwe and the pioneering studies of the Mang'anja and Yao culture by Schoffeleers (1968) and Stannus (1922) respectively also make no reference to this spirit. But significantly Napolo features prominently in contemporary Malawian literature, which draws extensively on local religious beliefs and proverbs. The hero of Legson Kayira's novel 'The Detainee' (1974) is called Napolo, and poet and critic Steve Chimombo (1987) has written a long poem focused entirely on Napolo, alluding not only to many themes drawn from Chewa religious culture, but to the devastation that occurred at Zomba in December 1946 when several bridges were washed away and many villages destroyed by a huge deluge of water that came down the mountain after torrential rain on the plateau (cf. Edwards, 1948).

In March 1991, Napolo it seems struck again – or rather, to be faithful to the cultural tradition, it moved again from the mountains to Lake Chilwa. This time, its impact was felt by the people living at Phalombe, at the foot of the Michesi mountain. During the weekend 9–10 March 1991 there was torrential rain throughout southern Malawi, but especially in the Mulanje district. The incessant heavy rains seems to have been particularly intense on the higher slopes of Michesi, although exactly how much rain fell in those critical hours may never be known. On the morning of Sunday 10 March it seemed to the people of Phalombe and neighbouring villages that the whole mountain was coming down up on them. An immense flash flood occurred, bringing down with it huge rock boulders, floating tree trunks and a deluge of mud, that completely swept away all the bridges on the Phalombe–Mulanje road, and completely obliterated Phalombe. The flood affected an area of around 500 square km, with a population of around 21 thousand people, and constituted one of the worst natural disasters ever to occur in Malawi. Around 470 people were reported dead or missing, buried by the debris, or swept away by the flood, and damage to property and gardens was extensive.

Having friends in Migowi I knew the area well. Over the years I had often climbed Michesi and the neighbouring Machemba hill (which is where John Chilembwe took refuge in 1915), usually accompanied by a local hunter or herbalist. A month after the Michesi disaster, I again went exploring on Michesi Mountain. I was accompanied by my friend Davison Potani and a local hunter. We traversed the woodland high on the northern slopes, and I was struck by the devastation – all the streams and gulleys on the mountain had been completely scoured, and there was not a scrap of vegetation anywhere near the main water courses. But I was equally struck by the conversation (in Chewa) of my two companions – for every time we came to cross a stream or river, or a gulley where rock boulders had been piled-up, the conversation turned spontaneously to Napolo. And Napolo was described as a spirit (*ziwanda*), as a fierce wild animal (*nyama chopsya, chirombo*) or as a snake (*njoka*) and these terms were used interchangeably. It was described as having left the mountain (*amchoka mphiri*) and as having moved to Lake Chilwa, coming down with the water (*amabwera ndi madzi*). Napolo was further described as having pulled up trees (*kudzula mitenga*) and as having separated or detached (*kugumula*) the earth or soil from the mountain. It was said to live in the mountain, at the place of spirits (*malo wa mizimu*). Like the other spirits and the Batwa, I was assured that Napolo could never be seen. If it was observed, then the person would certainly die (*aona amafa*).

As people in the area do not make a categorical distinction between spirit and matter, Napolo tends to be seen as a huge subterranean serpent-spirit, associated with water. It is invisible, but it has the form of a huge snake (*njoka*), and it is active like a wild animal (*chirombo*) destroying people and property as it makes it way, at intervals, to the lake. And, to the agricultural people of southern Malawi, water (*madzi*) is the ultimate source of power and sustenance.

Napolo seems to represent the snake spirit in its most destructive guise, and many people identify it with the inyago figure *namungumi* (*namukumi*), which is important in Yao initiation rites. Sanderson hints that it may depict or represent a 'primaeval water-mother' (1954: 195). As with the *chikang'ombe* serpent-spirit, Napolo is associated with mountains, (*pamakhala malo ena kuphiri*), as making strong winds (*pamachita mphepo yambiri*) and as moving across the country – often from the

Figure 5.4 The late Davison Potani, at the path of Napolo, Michesi Mountain, April 1991

mountain to the lake. All people speak of Napolo as a snake (*njoka*), that comes together with water (*imabuka pa modzi ndi madzi*), and as expressing the powers of the divinity (*idali mphamuu ya mulungu*). Equally, people speak of Napolo as being a spirit (*Napolo ndi mizimu*), but they usually make offerings to the spirits of the ancestors, not to the serpent spirit directly. In the Phalombe and Mulanje districts people make a distinction between Napolo, and such snakes (*njoka*) as *kasongo* (mamba), *nsato* (python) and *mbona*, a spirit associated with Thyolo Mountain and the Malawi Hills near Nsanje which also takes the form of a snake. It is to the Mbona cult, that we may finally turn.

Mbona

When Lomwe people in the Mulanje district are asked about Mbona they invariably describe it as a snake (*njoka*), or as a spiritual being that takes the form of a snake. Or they may say that Mbona was a person who lived at Nsanje, and was a famous rain maker, and that when he died he became a snake (*iye adamwalira ndasanduka njoka*).

The spirit/snake Mbona was often mentioned by early missionaries and travellers, and was specifically associated with two shrines, one on Thyolo Mountain, the other at Khulubvi forest, at the foot of the Malawi Hills near Nsanje. In July 1862 Lovell Proctor climbed Thyolo Mountain and described it as a mountain that is 'full of spirits' (*mizimu*), and that the place never wants for rain. The local chief Mankhokwe often prayed to the spirit of Thyolo Mountain for rain. A month later he noted in his journal that mboma (Mbona), the 'ghost of a chief' has a village of seven huts where he lives, and that he is 'consulted by a sort of priestess who is called is wife'. His wife, under the name Zarima (*Salima*), is thus a kind of 'oracle', and she lives, he notes, in seclusion (Bennett and Ylvisaker, 1971: 303–5).

Other early missionaries speak of Mbona of Thyolo Mountain as a 'local deity', and note that in the seclusion of her hut his 'wife' acts as a spirit medium, giving advice to the Mang'anja paramount chief Rundo (Lundu) (Werner, 1906: 60; Young, 1868: 91). James Stewart described Mbona as the 'spirit of some departed chief', and that his wife, 'a sort of pythoness', was confined to a sacred hut, and acted as an oracle (Wallis, 1952: 93–4).

The story of Mbona has been related many times, and was first recorded in the *District Book of the Lower Shire* (Vol. 1, 1907: 49), to be later inscribed in Murray's *Handbook of Nyasaland* (1932: 197–8). Murray describes Mbona as the 'patron saint' of the Lower Shire, with control over the rainfall, who intercedes with Mulungu, on behalf of the Mang'anja people. Father Schoffeleers has outlined in detail, both in Mang'anja and English, the various 'biographies' of Mbona (Schoffeleers, 1992: 175–255).

In these accounts Mbona is viewed as a spiritual manifestation of a man who clearly belonged to the ruling Phiri clan, a nephew of Undi and Kaphwiti. In other traditions he is linked with Lundu, said to be the son of the chief's sister, Chembe, although his father was unknown. In one account Mbona is described as the god of the Mang'anja (*ndiye anali mulungu wa amang'anja*) (Schoffeleers, 1992: 198), but he is invariable treated a male person (*munthu wamwamuna*) and the village head Rambiki was emphatic in suggesting to me that Mbona was not the supreme spirit.

However many in the Nsanje district stress that they offer religious worship – in the sense of making entreaties – to the Mbona spirit *(ndi mapembedza Mbona)*. Like his uncle Mlauli – whose name suggests being a diviner *(maula* – divination) Mbona was considered to be a person who knew much about medicine (or 'magic') *(wodziwa matsenga kwambiri)*, and was said to possess the power of God *(mphamuu za mulungu)*, and merely had to point his finger to the sky and rain would come. He had the ability to fly, transforming himself into a guinea fowl *(anasandulitsa nkhanga)*. (Department of Antiquities, 1971: NS 1/1), and he left impressions of his body on many rocky outcrops in the Lower Shire Valley.

The Khulubvi shrine is situated some 4 km south of Nsanje, and lies within a small evergreen thicket. Both the shrine and the forest are considered sacred, and no one is allowed to cut trees or kill animals within the forest – not even young boys on hunting expeditions. The dominant trees in the forest are *mlambe*, baobab *(Adansonia digitata)*, *mkundi* *(Parkia filicoidea)*, and *njale* or *msetanyani* 'the tree the baboon slips down' *(Sterculia appendiculata)*. Fire is kept out of the forest, and there is no cultivation, and only Mang'anja people are allowed into its preserve, and then only with permission of the shrine officials. There are many rumours about Europeans entering the shrine illicitly, only later to succumb to madness or to die from a mysterious gun accident or fever shortly afterwards. (Rangeley Papers, correspondence, letter M. Metcalfe to WHJR, 9 August 1952).

It is significant that Father Schoffleers who spent almost twenty years studying the Mbona cult, and was for many years a Catholic missionary in the Lower Shire, only had the opportunity of inspecting the shrine on one occasion, and never witnessed a seance of the spirit-medium (1992: 49, 85). People entering the shrine must go barefoot, and wear dark clothing – never red clothes, and no huts must be built close to the shrine. The shrine itself consists of a group of huts, all of which are of a temporary nature. Two are of particular importance; the main shrine of Mbona *(kachisi)* and the hut of the spirit medium, Salima. Both are enclosed in a bango reed fence, and in the past a tusk of ivory served as a door stopper. Mbona's hut is circular structure, some 3 m across, beneath which is said to be buried Mbona's head close to an *njale* tree. Salima's hut is some 15 m away to the east of the structure, and is of similar construction to the shrine. It is known as *nyumba ya Mbona*, the house of Mbona, and contains Mbona's bed covered in a black cloth, at the top of which are placed his spears. On this bed, the spirit-medium Salima is reputed to sleep. Offerings for rain – in the form of beer, black calico, baskets of fish, millet flour or a black goat – are made – or should be made – at

Mbona's shrine each year, especially when the rains are late, and prayers and supplications are made (*mapembero*). It is believed that the spirit of Mbona is very much alive at such times (*mzimu wache uli wamoya*) (Rangeley, 1953: 20–1; Department of Antiquities, 1971: NS 1/1; Schoffeleers, 1992: 49–53).

Some 5 km east from the Khulubvi shrine is the Ndione pool, which is a moon-shaped enlargement of Mulanga stream, on the edge of the Ndindi Marsh. It is the place where Mbona is reputed to have been killed, and the reddish colour of the pool is probably due to iron oxide. Sacrifices are also made at the pool – usually at night. It is forbidden to fish in the pool, and the surrounding plants are said to have great medicinal value.

Ndione, which literally means 'I see' or 'see', is a place where unusual things are said to happen, as well as being the abode of the python. Human sacrifices are reputed to have been made there in the past (Schoffeleers 1992: 54), young girls being thrown to the crocodiles. Evidence for this is not strong although it is recalled in oral traditions. That human sacrifice took place was strongly denied by local people when one administrator visited Ndione pool in 1952 (Rangeley Papers, 1/1/3). The pool, said to have been formed of Mbona's blood, is strongly associated both with the python (*nsato*) and with the spirits (*mizimu*).

As on other ritual occasions, whether with respect to hunting or initiations, people must be in a 'cool' condition before entering the shrine at Khulubvi or the area around Ndione pool. Even in the brewing of the ceremonial beer for the offering to Mbona, the women brewing the beer must be 'cool', that is abstain from sexual activity. The chiefs mainly responsible for making the sacrificial offerings (*akutsira msembe*) to Mbona are Ngabu, Tengani and Malemia. Although the Khulubvi Forest and shrine is part of the country of Chief Tengani, who is *mwini dziko*, the main ritual officials at the shrine are the following: Malemia who is the main custodian of the shrine, and to whom persons wishing to enter the forest must first go; Ngabu the chief ritualist whose function is always to see that the sacrificial pots are filled with beer; Mbukwa, who is the actual guardian of the shrine; Mphamba who is responsible for looking after Mbona's spear and bow (hence the association between Mbona and hunting), and Kambalame, 'small bird' who is a messenger for the Mbona spirit. The most important personage at the shrine is Salima, who is reputed to be the wife of Mbona (*mkazi wa Mbona*) and whose name literally means 'don't hoe'. As with the Mangadzi at the Msinja shrine, she is a spirit-medium, and lives in seclusion. She does not draw water, cook food or gather firewood – all these tasks are undertaken by her assistant called Chamanga, who sleeps in a kitchen close to Salima's hut – the hut of

Mbona. Salima, as spirit-wife to Mbona, was celibate, and was, according to Rangeley, either a girl who had not yet reached puberty, or a woman who was past childbearing, or alternatively she may be divorced or a widow.

When Mbona communicated his wish to have a wife, tradition has it that she was always drawn from the family of the paramount chief Lundu, who was located at Mbewe-wa-Mitengo, south of Chikwawa. She was escorted by Kambalame, who acted as *nkhoswe*, the marriage advocate, and during the journey of some 150 km from the Lundu capital to the Khulubvi shrine Kambalame and the escort team, often seized chickens and goats from the local villages (Department of Antiquities, 1971: CK 3/2).

As Mbona's ritual wife Salima is seen as belonging to the family of Lundu (*ku banja la mfumu yaikuru*), it follows that the spirit medium, belonging to the clan of her mother, was a Banda. As Mbona, like Lundu, is a Phiri, this ritual marriage is thus a symbolic reflection of the complementary dualism that underlies much of Mang'anja (and Malawian) culture.

It is of interest that although Rambiki, Chief Mphamba, in his discussions with me, and Rangeley in his seminal article on Mbona (1953), make no mention of the python – in fact there is a close identification between Mbona, as a spirit being, and the python (Nsato) whose form the spirit often takes. This snake (*njoka yaikuru*) often comes to Mbona's hut, where Salima sleeps, as the embodied form of Mbona – her husband – and is described as playing with her body, without biting her or causing harm. Not only people in the Thyolo and Mulanje districts identify Mbona with the python (or a large snake), but it is emphasized in all the oral traditions relating to Salima as the 'wife' of Mbona. Mbona is seen as having powers to 'turn into a snake' (as Chakanza describes it – in Schoffeleers, 1992: 254) coming to his wife at night in order to proclaim messages, relating to famine conditions or to the oncoming rains.

Schoffeleers expresses the relationship well when he suggests that the spirit medium Salima is visited (*ku-cheza*) by Mbona 'in the *form* of a python', and that she thus performs the role of an oracle transmitting matters relating to communal well-being (Schoffeleers, 1992: 69). It is important to realize that people in Malawi do not make a radical division between spirit and matter, and the relationship between Mbona and the snake is one of transformation, a metamorphosis (*ku-sanduka*), of spirit into the form of a snake, rather than a form of incarnation, metapsychosis, the snake incarnating Mbona's spirit. Mbona was a person who after death became a spirit, which now takes the form of a python. Equally it may take the form of lightning, a rainbow or a thunder squall. In the same way, when the spirit medium, Salima, who is Mbona's wife, becomes an oracle for the spirit, it is described not as incarnation, but more in terms of the woman being seized or held (*ku-gwira, -gwidwa*) by the spirit, (*mzimu*), and while in that state to rave and babble (*ku-bwebweta*) – words that are interpreted as oracles (Scott, 1929: 29).

There are striking similarities, as both Rangeley and Schoffeleers noted, between the cult shrines of Msinja and Khulubvi. At both places there was a distinction between the main shrine and the sacred pool, which lay to the east of the shrine and was associated with the python. Schoffeleers sees this having symbolic significance, with respect to a number of contrasts:

West	*East*
Shrine	Sacred pool
Spirit-medium	Python-spirit
Female	Male
Land	Waters (rains)

(Schoffeleers, 1992: 49, 295)

There is however no consistent structural correspondence, for though the spirit Mbona is associated with the python and masculinity, it is also strongly identified with the rains and the pool (in the east). At both shrines, too, the spirit medium was a woman, a recluse and celibate, whose husband was a spirit (i.e. conceived as a male) and identified with the python. Importantly, at the Msinja shrine, and also at the Mankhamba shrine, the python was represented by a ritual official, a member of the Mbewe clan. Schoffeleers describes him as a 'python priest', who though not viewed as the husband of Mangadzi (or Mwali), nevertheless performed ritual intercourse, as a snake, with the spirit medium. However, there is no ritual equivalent of the 'python priest', Kamundi, at the Khulubvi shrine (Schoffeleers, 1968: 239–47). Even more significant, as Schoffeleers has explained, the serpent/spirit Mbona, in the context of the Lower Shrine, was symbolically transformed into a martyr figure, the Khulubvi shrine becoming the locus of a martyr cult. Schoffeleers has also discussed in great detail the political role of the Mbona cult among the Mang'anja, and its complex relationship with the Lundu state, and with various 'foreign' invaders – the Portugese slave raiders like Matakenya, European missionaries and colonial administrators, and the Kololo petty chiefdoms that destroyed the Thyolo shrine (Schoffeleers, 1972, 1975, 1992: 92–139; cf. also Wrigley, 1988).

I have outlined above the sociology of the more well-known rain shrines in Malawi, and the important role that the serpent spirit (*nsato, thunga*) plays in the rain rituals, for the serpent is both identified with the territorial (ancestral) spirit, and seen as a manifestation of the powers of the divinity as a provider of rain. As Thomas Price suggested there are no 'hill deities' or 'rain deities' as such in Malawi, for the deity, Mulungu, is one, though manifested in various phenomena associated with the rains – thunder, rainbow, lightning, rain clouds. The basic fact about rain, Price wrote, is that it is 'at once recurrent and uncontrollable, essential to life but unprocurable by work'. It depends on something beyond human grasp, and this something is what Malawians conceive of as deity – as the source of life and activity (Price 1964: 115). The local spirits, like Kangomba, Bimbi and Mbona are thus simply spiritual intermediaries (*mizimu*), identified with the snake, which both symbolizes the rains and associated phenomena and is a manifestation of the divinity. In regions where state systems developed under Phiri hegemony – Kalonga (*mwali*), Undi (*makewana*) and Lundu (*Salima*), women belonging to the Banda clan were important as spirit mediums. They were linked to the divinity both directly as mediums, and indirectly as the wife of the serpent spirit. This implied that they were rain callers of more than local importance, for the shrines associated with them were secured by permanent ritual officials, and it involved, as Price put it, 'a special intermediary with Mulungu' (Price, 1964: 117). Outside these regions, however, rain shrines may simply involve spirits of deceased chiefs, who, although also linked or identified with the python-spirit, acted as more direct intermediaries with the deity. Figure 5.5 schematically outlines the essential relationships:

Schoffeleers' writings suggest that two contrasting social dimensions were evident at the rain shrines. On the one hand, there was an emphasis on hierarchy, both through the ritual hierarchy of the shrine officials themselves, and through the symbiotic link between the rain shrines and the local chiefdoms. The rain shrines thus tended to 'underscore' the political legitimacy of the local rulers. On the other hand, it was through the medium of the shrines, particularly through the spirit mediums, that popular interests and concerns were expressed. This implied a more egalitarian conception, the rain shrines reflecting the needs of the local community. At times of crisis, popular needs took precedence over those of the political establishment (Schoffeleers, 1974: 77; 1992: 72).

It is of interest that animals do not play a significant role in the rain rituals, apart from the sacrificial offerings of domestic livestock, chickens, goats, or sheep – which ideally should be of a dark colouration. With both the Mang'anja and Chewa, the *nyau* dancers are not allowed within

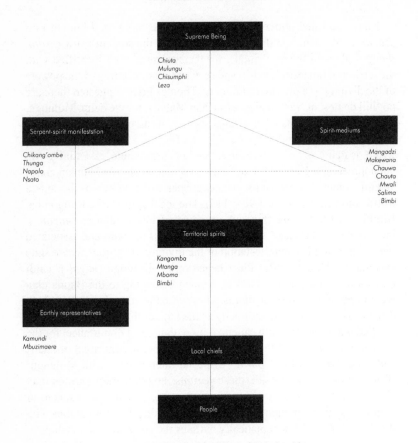

Figure 5.5 Schematic Outline of Relationships

the rain shrines, and this may reflect the fact that they are focused around human fertility and sexuality, with the associations of blood, fire, heat, redness – associations contrary to those of the rain rituals, which emphasize water, coolness, blackness and the fertility of the land. But the key symbol in all the rain rituals, whose focus is ultimately on the supreme deity, *chiuta, or mzimu waukulu*, the 'great spirit', as Rattray (1907: 128) records, is, as we have outlined above, the serpent spirit (*chikang'ombe, nsato, thunga*). Throughout Malawi, the serpent spirit, usually identified as a large variety of python (nsato), is seen as a manifestation of the power of the supreme deity, and is closely associated with rainfall. It is thus closely identified with the evergreen (cloud) forests that clothe the larger mountains, especially evergreen thickets (*nsitu*), with deep pools and river gorges, with rivers – Wrigley writes (1988) of the 'river god' – and with the winds, thunder, and rainbow that accompany the rain storms. It is a concrete manifestation – whether as a snake or as an atmospheric phenomenon, which are closely identified in Malawian thought – with the powers of the divinity. Although its meaning and social significance may vary in different cultural contexts, the symbolic association of the snake (especially the python) with rainfall and water, and with ecological cycles, with fertility and ritual power, and with images of death and resurrection, is found, of course, not only throughout Africa, but worldwide. The fact that it sheds its skin, and its structure has an androgynous quality, that it coils around itself, and that, like the monitor lizard, it moves between land and water, no doubt explains why, according to many scholars, the snake (python) is an apt cultural symbol, or in Jungian terms, an almost universal 'archetypal image' (see Henderson and Oakes, 1963; Mundkur, 1983; Willis, 1990; Knight, 1991: 455–79).

–6–

The Ancestral Spirits

The Spirits (Mizimu) of the Ancestors

Thomas Price was certainly correct when he argued that there is a good deal more to the religion of the Malawian people than to assert that it is simply a 'form of ancestor cult' (1964: 114), but when Malawians are themselves asked about their religion (*chipembedzo*) they invariably suggest that the religion of their ancestors (*makolo*) consists of entreaties (*ku-pembedza*) and offerings (*ku-tsira nsembe*) to the spirits (*mizimu*). *Mzimu*, essentially means 'spirit' or 'invisible powers'.

I have thus translated *mzimu* as 'spirit' rather than use such terms as 'supernatural', 'personage' or 'superperson'. I do this for two reasons. The first is that the term 'spirit' still retains the connotations of its original Latin meaning – despite the dualisitic emphasis of Christian neoplatonism and Cartesian philosophy – namely, that of breath, life, wind, awe, mystery and invisibility, and this accords with Malawian conceptions. Secondly, Malawian scholars themselves have tended to utilize the term 'spirit' in translating the indigenous concept *mzimu* (S.K Msiska, 1997).

Although, as Price alludes, every person in the flesh embodies a *mzimu*, and that it is often recognized that people re-embody a *mzimu* which animated a remembered ancestor (1964:115), it is, I think, misleading in the Malawian context to speak of different *kinds* of spirits (*mizimu*). According to Kenji Yoshida, the Chewa people of Zambia recognize the existence of various spiritual beings. 'These include the souls of the living (*chiwanda*), the spirits of the deceased (*chiwanda cha munthu wakufa*), the spirits of the ancestors (*mzimu*) and the spirits of animals (*chiwanda cha nyama*)' (1992: 240). Just as the deity is in essence a unity, but manifests itself, and is experienced, in different forms – as python, weather, thunder, nurturer, rain clouds – so the spirits of the dead or ancestors in Malawi (*mizimu*) manifest themselves in different *forms*.

The key religious idea in Malawi is not that of 'reincarnation' or metempsychosis, which implies a dualistic metaphysic, a radical demarcation between the material and spiritual worlds, but that of 'transformation', or metamorphosis. This implies a change of *form* expressed by the verb *ku-sanduka* – to change, or turn into something else, the image invoked being the transformation, the metamorphosis, of a caterpillar into a butterfly, or a tadpole into a frog (*mbululu isanduka chule*). Nor does this underlying ontology of metamorphosis imply that Malawians lack a sense of personal identity or psychological integrity (as Yoshida, 1992; 204 implies) or that Malawians believe in the simple 'transformation of humans into animals'. Ordinary humans are not able to change themselves into animals, only spirits have this capacity; so do humans in special circumstances, in rituals, and by the possession and knowledge of powerful medicines – medicines associated with diviners (*sing'anga*), chiefs, witches and some hunters.

People in Malawi believe that when a person dies he or she becomes, or is ritually transformed into, a spiritual being, *mzimu*. As L.D. Soka expressed it, 'when a person dies s/he is transformed into something else. . . spirits one cannot see, though feared' (*kuti anthu akafa amasanduka kanthu kena . . . mizimu yosaoneka, ndipo yoopsya*)' (1953: 28). Such a 'spirit' (*mzimu*) is seen as retaining the life of the person who has died (*mzimu utsala wamoyo munthu akafa*). People speak of the spirits of the ancestors not so much as 'dead', in the ordinary sense of the word, but as having life (*wamoyo*), and as having the essential attributes of a living person – other than they are immaterial, have more power, and ideally live (*kukhala*) outside the village environs. One informant suggested to James Amanze that the ancestors 'are alive and live a life much like our earthly life. We believe that their contacts with us are very close' (1980: 25).

A spirit *mzimu* is not a 'soul', or some aspect or part of the deity – as in gnostic theology – for although, as earlier indicated, a close association is perceived between the deity (*mulungu*) and the spirits, there is no identity, and people speak of the spirits (*mizimu*) as being a part of this world, as *created* beings, along with humans and animals. The spirits are seen as 'immortal', not subject to death, the spiritual expression of the ongoing continuity of life, rather than as 'eternal' – beyond time and space, and thus having an identity with the deity – as in the mystical traditions. Malawians make a clear ontological distinction between humans (including the *mizimu*), and the deity (*mulungu*), as well as between humans and animals (cf. Arendt, 1978: 134 on the Greek distinction between 'immortal' and 'eternal').

There has been a growing tendency among postmodern, or rather 'new age', anthropologists to emphasize the existential reality of the 'spirits' and to imply that only ethnographers who themselves believe (or who have actually seen) the existence of spirits are able to write authentic accounts of African cultures. This seems to me to be both unnecessary and somewhat patronizing. I do not myself believe in the ancestral spirits or in the Christian transcendental deity, but I have no doubt that these beings have a reality for Malawians and Christians (like my own mother). Edith Turner, for example (1992), castigates anthropologists for denying – through the use of metaphor – the reality of indigenous spiritual experience thereby maintaing an 'intellectual imperialism' (1992: 30). She herself records of 'seeing' an Ndembu spirit 'a large grey blob of something like plasma', emerging from a woman's back during a *ihamba* rite of affliction. Then she writes, 'there *is* spirit stuff. There *is* spirit affiliation' (1992: 28, see also Turner, 1992b: 165–77). Her vision and description of spirit as a 'grey blob like plasma' seems to be more akin to Blavatsky's visions than to African reality. For Malawians, as for the Ndembu, spirits manifest themselves not only in rituals, but in dreams and in everyday experiences of the world – a world of diverse beings. And, rather like Eckhart, the supreme being (*mulungu*) is likewise manifested in the world – for people, trees, animals, fungi, herbs, insects, are all created beings and manifestations of divinity for those who have eyes to see or 'god consciousness' as Eckhart describes it (Blakney, 1941).

No anthropologist, as far as I am aware, has ever doubted that spirits and the deity have a reality for the people they study. It is, however, of interest, that postmodern anthropologists do not emphasize themselves that witches are also real – which they are for the Ndembu and Malawians. They thus do not advocate the harassment of the accused person, still less the burning of witches (see Noel, 1997 for a critique of this new-age anthropology, which largely reflects one of the preoccupations of Western culture, namely, the search for new forms of spirituality to replace moribund Christianity). Many people, of course, throughout history, have argued that you can never know or see God (or the spirits) except by means of hierophanies (symbolism). Many Malawians thus stress that spirits are by definiton beings that are invisible, that you cannot see (*saona*) them apart from their manifestations. The Ihamba tooth, or the 'grey blob' that Turner experienced was not of course the spirit, only a manifestation of the spirit of the dead hunter, which could take many other forms.

Essentially then, Malawians recognize that when a person dies he or she becomes a spiritual being (*msimu*), who is immortal, and they therefore firmly maintain that there are no ancestral spirits that were not at one time or another existing in a living bodily personality (Amanze, 1986: 267). This recognition may be based on memories of an individual person or relative, or of a named chiefly ancestor (such as Kankhomba or Mbona), or the *mizimu* may essentially refer to a collectivity of ancestors (*makolo*) associated with one's own matrikin. For Malawians the burial rites are of supreme importance in that they crucially involve the ritual transformation of a living person (*munthu*) into a spiritual being (*mzimu*). It is the final rite of transition in the life of an individual person, the *mzimu* that he or she has embodied (not incarnated) during a lifetime in the village community, returning to the spirit domain (not world). Malawians do not normally speak of a person as having a spirit (*mzimu* or *chiwanda*), and to ask someone if they have a spirit (*muli ndi mzimu*) invariably involves a puzzled response, for it is felt that a person *becomes* – is transformed into – a spirit (*mzimu*) after death. But people will speak of elderly people as if they were already in the process of becoming a spirit (*mzimu*).

People describe the *mizimu* as taking various forms or manifestations. Because of their associations with forested graveyards they may be referred to as '*amanda*' those of the grave (*sing m'manda*). Because of their association with dreams, through which they communicate their needs and concerns to their living kin, they may also be described as *atulo* (those who speak in dreams – *tulo*, sleep or dream). But essentially the *mizimu* take two distinct forms, and people frequently speak of there being two kinds (*mitundu iwiri*) of *mizimu*, the good spirits (*mizimu yabwino*) and the bad spirit (*mizimu yoipa*). The good spirits, the prototypical spirits of the matrilineal kin group, are conceived as beings created by God (*ndi chinthu cholengedwa ndi Mulungu*), as being immaterial (*sitimazione*) or like the wind (*ngati mphepo*), as having life (*wamoyo*) and as being essentially supportive and protective of their kin folk or the community. They are closely *identified* with the ancestors, and so are normally referred to as spirits of the ancestors (*mizimua makolo*), the term 'kolo' in Malawian context having strong associations with the maternal ancestors and matrikin. Some people may speak of *msimu*, as being a part of a person (*gawo la munthu*) but essentially *mzimu* is seen as a spiritual being which a person on death becomes, re-uniting with a collectivity of ancestral beings.

Mizimu yoipa has very different connotations. It essentially takes two forms, as *mzukwa*, a ghost or apparition, in which the spirits take a quasi-human form, and as a *chiwanda*, in which the spirits take a visible form (either through possession or as an animal). These forms are often closely identified with witchcraft (*ufiti*) and with sorcerers (*anthu achita matsenga*). Mzukwa relates to people who have died (*wakufa*), but who have in a sense risen from the grave, for the spirits are associated initially with the earth (*wapansi*). The meaning of the verb *ku-dzuka* is to get or rise up, or to become awake, and *mzukwa* essentially refers to the apparition of a dead person. It is described as the transformation (*chosanduka*) of a person who died long ago (*zinafa kale*) into a ghost (*mzukwa*), and it is invariably seen as due to sorcery (*matsenga*).

Chiwanda, (plural *ziwanda*), on the other hand, is not seen as the 'soul of the living person' (cf. Yoshida, 1992: 240); it is rather a 'visible' malevolent spirit (*mzima woipa*) – usually conceived of as the spirit of a deceased person who was once a witch. It is also associated with possession by spirits who are non kin (foreign), with madness, and with spirits who take the form of animals such as the jackal, leopard, bushpig, or other animals (*nyama/chirombo*), or as bats (*chiputiputi*) or owls (*kadzidzi*). People usually identify chiwanda as a malevolent spirit (*chiwanda ndi mzimu woipa*) who takes the form of an animal, who may then possess i.e. take hold (*-gwira*) of a person, and make them (*imapangitsa*) enter a trance state (*ku-bwebweta* – to rave or become delirious).

In the rain rituals it is, I think, misleading to interpret the possession rites as involving the incarnation by Kamundi or Salima of the 'spirit' of the python, but rather it is the deity or spirit (*chiuta, mzimu*) which takes hold of the person in the *form* of the snake (*thunga, nsato*). Likewise, it is not the 'spirit' of the owl, or the leopard or jackal that takes possession of a person as '*chiwanda*', but rather '*chiwanda*' is a spiritual being, that takes the *form* of an animal or bird – into which it transforms (*wosanduka*) – and may in certain circumstances take possession of a person. Like the Greeks (apart from Plato), Malawians are neither mystics – believing in an eternal soul which is an inherent part of the divinity or deity – nor animists, in believing that animals, birds, reptiles and inanimate objects have 'souls'. Yet the 'spirits' (*mizimu*) of the ancestors or other humans (which may or may not be malevolent) do in a sense embody themselves in (or are closely associated with) certain natural phenomena. They thus may become the python, certain trees, certain animals, certain places, and in an important sense are embodied (not incarnated) in their living kin. Just as the witch (*mfiti*) is a malevolent human, so *chiwanda* is a malevolent spirit – of human not of animal origin. *Chiwanda cha nkhandwe* does not mean the 'spirit of the jackal' but rather implies that the spirit – here in a malevolent sense – has taken the form of the jackal, which may be experienced simply by hearing the cry of a jackal. In the *nyau* (and *chinyago* rituals of the Yao) the spirits of the dead take two *forms*, as masked dancers simulating *human* personalities, and as theriomorphic figures. The latter *nyau* figures represent not animals, even less the 'spirits' of animals, but rather the spirits of the dead in animal form. As again with the Greeks (see Ovid), the concept of 'metamorphosis' is a key idea among Malawians, as Gamitto (1960: 73) long ago recognized, but such transformations are possible only through the active powers of the spirits, or through the powers of activating medicines – known only to chiefs, diviners (sing'anga) and certain hunters – and in a malevolent sense, by witches (*afiti*). Ultimately both these forms of power derive from the deity (*mulungu*). One might conclude by saying that the spirits, whether or not malevolent, often manifest themselves in the form of animals – and this manifestation is expressed in various ways, as a human person (diviner, circumcisor (*ngaliba*) or spirit medium), as the therio-morphic figure in rituals (*nyau, chinyago*), or as the animal itself in the woodland. The distinction between the two forms of spirit often expressed by distinction between msimu and chiwanda and in Yao between *mzimu* and *lisoka* (plural *masoka*) or in Tumbuka between *viwanda vipovu* – gentle spirits and *viwanda vikali* – hostile spirits (Young 1931: 131)), is in essence a moral, not an ontological, distinction.

Importantly of course, as in many other cultures, there is a liminal period between when a person dies, and when the *mizimu* becomes incorporated into the collectivity of ancestral spirits – which occurs about a year after burial. During this period the spirit is very prone to take the form of a ghost *mzukwa*, or a malevolent spirit *chiwanda* (Boucher, 1991).

Except on certain ritual occasions, the *mizimu* spirits, in their proto-typical form, are seen as residing outside the village community. They are associated with the earth (*pansi*), with the graveyard, with the wooded hillsides and evergreen forests that clothe the mountains, with deep pools of rivers, and with the sky. Yao, in particular, speak of the spirits as being *aku Mulungu*, with God. This leads Stannus to suggest that Mulungu means 'the place where the spirits dwell', a 'semi-materialistic heaven' (1922: 312–13). But as we have seen, the attributes of the deity are many and diverse, and often personal. Amanze has suggested that the relation-ship between humans and the spirits and deity has both a horizontal (time) and vertical (space) dimension (1986: 272). This is true, but the two dimensions are homologous, and may be expressed schematically as in Table 6.1.

But it must be noted that the spirits of the dead are both associated with the immediate past and historical time in relation to named ancestors, or people, and to the long past in relation to the collectivity of ancestral spirits. It is noteworthy that *mulungu* (deity), *mzimu* (spirit) and *ambuye* (grandparent) are terms that may be used to refer or address both the divinity and the ancestral spirits.

The Ancestral Spirits

Table 6.1 Relationship between humans, spirits and deity

Beings	Deity	Territorial	Spirits of	Living
-Nthu	Mulungu	Spirits	Ancestral	People
	Chiuta	(Of chiefs)	Kin	
	Mphambe	Mbona	Mzimu	Munthu
		Mtanga	Animals (Nyama)	
		Kankhomba		
Time	Long Past	Historical	Immediate	Present
Nthawi	(Zamani)	Time	Past	
	Kale Kale	Kale	Nthawi Ya Pita	Tsopano
Space	Sky	Mountains	Woodland	Village
Dziko	Atmosphere	Evergreen	Graveyard	(Mudzi)
	Heavens	Forest	(Thengo)	
	(Mlengalenga)	(Nkhalango)	(Manda)	
	Kumwamba		La Pansi	

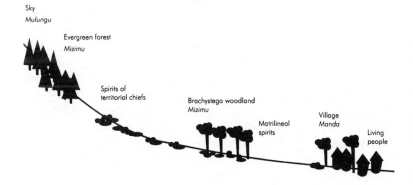

Figure 6.1 The ecology of spiritual beings

Among the Yao there is a close association between the spirit (*msimu, lisoka*), and the shadow of a person, and Hetherwick recorded around the turn of the century the hostility of one Yao chief at Zomba to having his photograph taken – fearing that the picture (*chiwilili* or shadow) might lead to bewitchment (Hetherwick, 1902: 90; Stannus, 1922: 311). This association, nowadays, is not widely recognized, but it is of interest that *mwalathunzi*, 'rock of the shade', near Thyolo (*mthunzi* – shade, or shadow) is thought by local people to be associated with the spirits and may well, in the past, have been used as a rain shrine, overlooking, as it does, Thyolo Mountain.

– 227 –

Animals and Ancestors

Although living outside of the village community, which is the abode of living humans, the spirits of the ancestors have close and intimate links with their descendants. The spirits are said to be at rest (*ipumula*) and have peace (*iri ndi mtendere*), and to be protective and supportive towards their living kin, who in relation to the spirits describe themselves as their children (*ana*). The spirits and their living descendants, in essence, form complementary parts of a single moral community, with shared obliga-tions, and to express this intimacy, many Malawian scholars, following Mbiti (1969), describe the *mizimu* as the 'living dead'. And, as Father Kalilombe remarks, peaceful, ordinary life in the community is 'pre-dicated on harmonious relations between the living and the spirits' (1980: 42). People must not forget or neglect the spirits, and must show them proper respect (*ulemu*). This is done by seeking their guidance, and by observing the customary rules, rituals and moral edicts that constitutes the local culture. The spirits are concerned to uphold the local tradition (*mwambo*). Indeed, to an important degree they are seen as its custodians, particularly as this relates to the kin community, there being a particular emphasis on kinship amity, on co-operation (*thandizana*), on peace and harmony within the village community. Hatred (*chidano*) and strife (*ndewu*) within the community, a neglect of sacrificial offerings (*nsembe*), a disregard of customary rules – such as passing the name of the deceased person on to a descendent . . . or the failure to conduct specific rituals – all these may anger the spirits, and they may show their dissatisfaction by withdrawing support, or by sending misfortunes, such as accidents, illnesses or discord. Importantly, however, the spirits of the ancestors are seen mainly in terms of positive support, and Van Breughel records (1976: 76) that among the Chewa in only nine cases out of 451 were spirits believed to cause the *death* of a person. Crucially important, the spirits of the ancestors act as intermediaries between humans and the deity, and in many rituals prayers are addressed to *chauta* or *mulungu*, while offerings of material substances – beer, flour – are made to the spirits.

People in Malawi do not articulate a 'two world theory', but conceive of spirits (and the deity) as being a part of this world. They do not make a radical division, as in the metaphysics of Plato (and many world religions), between an empirical world of appearances, and a spiritual realm, or a world of (true) Being (cf. Arendt, 1978, 23–5). The powers and hidden force of nature, which are particularly manifested in animals, though ultimately derived from the deity, are within this world. So, too, are the spirits of the ancestors. They are created beings within the world, though like the wind, they are unseen, and have powers and capacities beyond that of living humans. The ongoing relationship of human beings

– 228 –

Figure 6.2 Women kneeling beside an ancestral shrine Migowi, April 1991

to these spirits is expressed in four main ways. These are: through libations and offerings (*nsembe*), through the medium of dreams (*tulo*), through rituals associated with the human life cycle, and through divination and spirit-mediums. We discuss in this section the first two items.

Nsembe (*Yao, Mbepesi*) denotes the making of an offering to the ancestral spirits. The offerings are made at a specially constructed shrine (*kachisi*), usually in the forested thicket (*mzitu*) at the edge of the village, sometimes in the wooded graveyard or in a wooded ravine associated with the spirits, as well as with snakes (python), sometimes even within the village itself. Rain rituals are more likely to be conducted in evergreen forests associated with the mountains – places only infrequently visited, and not normally associated with offerings made by a local matrilineal group. The shrines often have a small grass fence around them; normally, however, they consist only of one or two clay pots buried at the foot of an *mpoza*, custard apple (*Annona senegalensis*) or a *msolo* tree (*Pseudolachnostylis maprouneifolia*). Both these trees have edible fruits and are widely used as medicines and both are associated with the *mizimu* who are said to be fond of their fruit. People do not conceive of the trees as either having 'spirits' or 'souls', or as incarnating the spirits of the dead ancestors. But the trees are never cut and they may be described as 'trees of the spirits' (*mitenga ya mizimu*). In the past *kachisi* was a term that also applied to the hut of the deceased person, which was abandoned on their death or sometimes fired. As with the rain shrines, all woodland areas and evergreen thickets associated with the spirits of the dead, are considered in a sense sacred, and this includes graveyards and local village shrines. Within these areas animals are not hunted, and trees are not cut for firewood – although thatching grass may be utilized from some *amanda*.

The offerings made at the shrines – chickens (meat), the flour of millet and sorghum and beer (especially) – are said to be either put (*ku-ika*), or poured (*ku-tsira*), or given (*ku-pereka*) to the ancestral spirits, who are seen as taking the 'essence' of the offerings. If the beer has gone, or if mice (*mbewa*) have eaten the flour, or a carnivore the meat this is interpreted as an indication that the *mizimu* have accepted the offering. From the evidence of the early missionaries (such as Hetherwick, 1902: 93) it is clear that in the past every village had a communal shrine or 'prayer tree' associated with the village headman, and the local spirits were the focus of communal rites.

As with other rituals, and all important economic activities involving material transformations – beer brewing, pot making, hunting – people must refrain from sexual relations prior to making the *nsembe*. As with the woodland itself, the ancestral spirits are looked upon as 'cool' (*ozizira*), and any person in a 'hot' condition through sexual activity, is believed to spoil the effect of the ritual offering, as well as showing disrespect towards the spirits.

Offerings and entreaties to the spirits of the ancestors may be made at any time of the year – and are undertaken especially at times of crisis (illness, poverty, drought) or when someone is about to undertake an important activity, such as pot-making, a long journey, or hunting.

Offerings to the spirits will also be made at the time of the first maize, but many affirm that the crucial time to make offerings (*nsembe*) to the ancestral spirits is in the dry season (*nthawi ya chilimwe*), when the bush has been burnt, and food is still plentiful, and that the right time of day is in the hours shortly before daybreak (*dangakucha*). Then the spirits are said to be close (*pafupi*), still around the village environs prior to returning to the woodland domain at dawn. While the village headman is an important figure in conducting communal rituals on behalf of the village community, especially for rain, it is the household head who makes offerings on behalf of a kin group. Dancing, especially the *likwata*, feasting and beer drinking are the usual activities in the day (or days) following an *nsembe*. Beer plays an important role in Malawian social life. It is the crucial offering poured for the spirits, who are said to like beer (*ku-konda mowa*) and such beer is brewed by women of the kin group collectively. They always refrain from sexual relations during this brewing. Besides being an important component at all rituals, beer is also simply drunk for pleasure, at times when there is a need to iron out difficulties and problems within a community, as well as when there is a need, as one person put it, for people to 'forget their troubles' (*amaiwala zobvuta zao*). It is of interest that I once asked a person why they made offerings of beer to the spirits, and he replied that it was because the *mizimu* ask for it! (For details of the brewing of beer see Hodgson, 1933; 162–3; Williamson, 1975: 261–5).

Almost all people in rural Malawi emphasize that the *mizimu* act as intermediaries between people and the deity, and that the powers of the spirits ultimately derive from Mulungu, the supreme spirit. But the crucial aspect the nsembe rituals, and the reason the ancestors – those who have died long ago (*anamwalira kale*) – play such a central role in Malawian culture, is that there is an ongoing system of symbolic exchange between the living and the dead. People show fear and respect for the *mizimu*, and by their moral actions and *nsembe* offerings provide both spiritual and material sustenance for the spirits of the dead. In return, the spirits provide their living descendants with the basic necessities of life, and in Malawi three are given prominence in relation to the spirits. One is the provision of game animals for meat, the success of hunting being invariably associated with a correct and viable relationship with the spirits. There is indeed a close identification of animals with the spirits of the ancestors. Secondly, the spirits are often invoked to provide knowledge of special medicines. And finally, and most importantly, it is widely believed that it is the ancestral spirits who are responsible for human fertility – that they are, as Father Boucher (1991) writes, the 'channel' through which fertility comes to humans. Thus the *mizimu* are not only closely associated with wind, but with life (*moyo*) as an ongoing process. One could well translate *mzimu* not as 'spirit' but as 'immaterial life', or the 'life essence', as the spirits are the medium whereby human life has cyclic continuity. The relationship between the living and the 'living' dead could well be viewed as involving an exchange of material essences, and the Malawian scholar John Kandawire has written perceptively on African religion, emphasizing that it should be interpreted not in 'functionalist' terms, but rather as involving a 'structure of exchange', an ongoing reciprocal exchange between living people and the spirits of the ancestors. He even suggests that Malawians conceive of themselves as living in a society which is 'co-extensive' with the 'society of the dead', the living providing for the needs of the spirits, while the dead – the *mizimu* – provide the living with the means of livelihood (1976: 57–65). The important point is that the spirits of the dead are seen as having a living presence, and to have active powers over the living, and as Cullen Young long ago intimated, the 'two societies' (Kandawire) form a single continuing unit or community. Thus, there is no *radical* distinction between members living on earth – in the village – and those members that are now spiritual ancestors and are living elsewhere – afar in the wooded hills, many suggest, when asked where the spirits reside (Young, 1950: 39).

A second form of communication between the living kin and the spirits of the ancestors is through the medium of dreams (*atulo, tulo* – sleep; *ku-lota* – to dream), and even the undertaking of *nsembe* may be prompted by a dream. For the *mizimu* may communicate to a person their need for beer or meat. There is, in Malawi, a very close association between dreaming and the spirits, and just as the latter may be of two 'kinds' in terms of their moral propensities, so people speak of two kinds of dreams, good dreams (*maloto abwino*) and bad dreams (*maloto oipa*). As with people in all cultures, Malawians make a distinction between everyday working life and dreaming, but dreams are believed to carry messages from the spirits, or to convey meanings. These have to be interpreted, either by the individual concerned, or by a *sing'anga*. Interpretation is usually signified by the verb *ku-tanthauza*, to explain or expound. Too much dreaming is regarded negatively, as a sign that there is definitely something that is out of kilter in a person's life. Good dreams essentially indicate a positive state. To dream of climbing a mountain, of catching fish or being successful in hunting, and of flying through the sky, are all considered positive signs, of good health or of good luck (*mwayi*). On the other hand, to dream of a burning fire, of wild animals such as jackals or hyenas, of crossing a river, of the illness of a relative, or sexual relations with close kin, or the digging of a pit – dreams such as these may signify a misfortune, or potential witchcraft. In making interpretations symbolic analogies are made based on cultural associations. Thus a person may dream of being chased by a lion. As lions are associated with chieftainship, and the spirits of chiefs may often take the form of a lion (*mkango*), if a person escapes a lion this may signify that he will become a chief, while if he is seized by the lion, this may indicate the chief is plotting against him (Hodgson, 1926: 67).

The spirits of the ancestors communicate many things through dreams. A person may dream the whereabouts of specific medicines, or, among the Lomwe, dreaming of a specific mammal such as a gerbil (*phanya*) or a creek rat (*mende*) will indicate the need to undertake a *nantongwe* ceremony. Through dreams the spirits may also indicate a particular course of action, the reasons for a particular illness (*nthenda*) that may be inflicting a person, or as with *nantongwe*, the need of their kin to undertake specific rituals. Animals play an important role in dream interpretations, for animals are seen as the concrete expression – in dreams – either of spirits of the ancestors or of witches (*afiti*). To dream of the python (*nsato*) or *mphiri* (the puff-adder, *Bitis arietans*), or of domestic animals, or of a lion, may be viewed positively as these may be interpreted as hierophanies of the spirits; to dream, on the other hand, of hyenas, bushpig, baboons, or such snakes as the mamba (spitting cobra, *Naja mossambica*) or mbubvi (or chirumi, the water snake *Lycodonomorphus rufulus*), or of the owl (*kadzidzi*) may be viewed negatively, for these are associated with witchcraft (*ufiti*) and are thus seen as evil dreams (*maloto oipa*). It is of interest that to dream of drinking beer (*alota kumwa mowa*) is not seen as a good sign but rather as a evil omen (*mpingu*) being associated with the medicine of witches, that is of the *mwabvi* poison ordeal. In dreams, as in life, whiteness is associated positively with the spirits, blackness with death, while redness may have various connotations – conflict, childbirth, hunting.

Unlike ghosts (*mzukwa*), it is suggested that *mizimu* are never seen outside dreams, and many affirm that it is through dreams that the spirits instruct (*ku-uza*, to tell) their kin (for short discussions of dreams in Malawi see Hodgson, 1926; Peltzer, 1987: 125–32).

The spirits of the dead are often thought to frequent the village during the night hours. Watching over their kinfolk, they are also believed to return to the village during the dry season, to participate in the rituals associated with the human life cycle, particularly the initiations (*chinamwali*) and the comemorative rites for the dead. In these rituals the *mizimu* are not only present but often take the form of animals, as theriomorphic figures. We have discussed these in an earlier chapter.

Finally, the powers of the ancestral spirits are invoked by diviners and spirit mediums. With respect to divination this is discussed more fully in my study *Chewa Medical Botany* (Morris, 1996: 143–62). The role of the spirit mediums was discussed earlier with reference to the rain rituals, and in the next section we discuss the spirit rituals that are associated with various spirit-possession cults that have arisen in Malawi, in various regions, and at various times.

What is clearly evident from the Malawian ethnography is the very close association perceived between the ancestral spirits and various wild animals. This was remarked upon by all the early ethnographers and their observations still have reasonance in the present context. Duff McDonald, for example, though he misleadingly refers to the spirits (*lisoka, msimu*) as 'gods', significantly notes that it is usual to distinguish between the spirit and the *form* it takes, and that the spirits of the departed may take the form of animals. He writes:

> A spirit often appears as a serpent . . . A great hunter generally takes the form of a lion or a leopard; and all witches (asawi) seem to like the form of a hyena. (1882: 62–3)

Donald Fraser noted the 'special affinity' that the spirits of departed chiefs had for lions, and their association with the *msoro* tree, but remarked, significantly, that he found no belief that animals have 'souls' (1914: 127–28). In similar fashion Walter Elmslie remarked that disembodied spirits among the Tumbuka 'are thought to enter certain snakes, which consequently are never killed. When seen in the vicinity of houses, they are left unmolested; and if they enter huts, sometimes food and beer are laid down for them' (1901: 71, cf. also Ngara district book. 1907; NCG 1/6/2 on a tame snake being seen as the spirit of a former chief).

The general belief that the 'souls of men', particularly the souls of departed chiefs, enter into lions or the 'bodies' of other wild animals, was widely reported by earlier travellers and missionaries in Malawi (cf. Livingstone, 1997: 111; Johnson, 1922: 119). According to Stannus, this belief was less prevalent among the Yao, but he noted that 'spirits of the departed may enter into animals or may take the form of animals', commonly lions and sometimes large snakes (python). An animal which is so possessed is called lisyuka, from ku-syuka, 'to be transformed' (1922: 316). Apart from this idea, Stannus remarked, there were no animistic beliefs among the Yao.

Two points are worth noting. The first is that the relationship between the spirit (*mzimu* or *chiwanda*) and the animal is described essentially in terms of a change or transformation (*ku-syuka* (Y), *ku-sanduka* (C)) not as an 'incarnation'.

Secondly, such transformations relate to three different contexts namely, when *mizimu* take the form of a lion or snake in a positive sense; when malevolent spirits (*mizimu waipa*, or as *chiwanda*) take the form of harmful animals; and when through the use of medicines living humans, usually with some evil intent, are able to transform themselves into animals. These three facets were clearly delineated by Levi Mumba, who wrote:

> The Bantu believe that the spirit of the departed returns to the world in the form of a serpent, and visits the grave or the house of the dead; when this happens, the snake is not usually molested. The spirits of bad people of the magician class, and sometimes of hunters and witches, return in the form of either a lion, a leopard or a hyena to take revenge on the living of the locality

who may have done them wrong. Magicians and witches are believed to take the form of lions and hyenas even before death (1930: 360)

They do this by the use of powerful medicines.

Such beliefs are still widespread among people in the rural areas of Malawi. People hold (*khulupirira* – to believe) that the ancestral spirits, particularly those of local chiefs, may become transformed (*amasanduka*) into an animal (*nyama*), and thus reveal themselves to their living kin in the form of a lion, leopard, hyena, or a cat (*mphaka*), or as a bird such as the ground hornbill (*nang'omba*) or as a snake (*njoka*). In the form of leopard or a lion, the *mzimu* is not necessarily harmful, but may have a protective role, clearing a locality of those animals such as bushpigs or baboons that cause depredations to local crops. When the spirits take the form of a snake, three species are usually implied, the python (*nsato*), the file snake (*njokandala*) and the puff adder (*mphiri*, *Bitis arietans*). Although people recognize that the latter species is deadly poisonous, nevertheless, when a spirit (*mzimu*) takes the form of this snake it is said to be gentle and non-aggressive. People will not kill it, as it is believed not to bite (*wosaluma*). Offerings of flour may be put out for the spirit.

Although the majority of Malawians now consider themselves Muslims or Christians, at least in the nominal sense, belief in the reality and importance of the ancestral spirits is still prevalent, although, as Van Breugel remarked (1976: 90) there are not so many *kachisi* shrines in villages, as there was in the past. This salience is reflected in the fact that one independent Church, which has flourished in recent years, is focussed specifically on the ancestral spirits. Allegedly founded by Peter Nyambo, an Ngoni from Ntcheu, in 1942, it is known as Mpingo wa Makolo Achikuda, the Church of the Black Ancestors. It stresses the importance of local shrines for the ancestral spirits, approves of polygamy, and supports the use of local medicines, and, in Nsanje, the Mbona cult. However, as it is vehemently anti-Christian, describing the Bible as *kaunjika* (to heap up, i.e. rubbish), many of the shrine leaders at Nsanje are opposed to the activities of the Church. The Ancestors Church appears to appeal mainly to poor and non-literate members of the community (Wishlade, 1965: 47–8; Chakanza, 1980: 11; Schoffeleers, 1985: 21–31).

Spirit Rituals

Spirit possession cults are found throughout Malawi, even though their social significance varies a good deal, according to the locality and with respect to historical circumstances. All these cults, which essentially involve curing rites, are focused around the spirits of the dead. They diverge however along three dimensions. Thus a 'spirit illness' (as Peltzer, 1987:165 describes them) may refer to three distinct spiritual agents; spirits that are related to a person, usually one of their close matrilineal ancestors, spirits that are non-kin, or of foreign derivation, and the spirits of dead witches. With regard to a specific ailment, these are not, however, exclusive categories, for they are inter-related in complex ways. The spirit disease *vimbuza*, for example, which is associated with Bisa and Bemba spirits, and whose curing ritual may be specifically described as 'driving away evil spirits', may also perhaps involve possession by the spirit of a close relative and the curing rite entail placating this spirit through offerings of flour and beer. One healer, recorded by Peltzer as treating Vimbuza, suggested that 'the possession spirits are usually those who loved the patient most during their life time' (1987: 181). Equally important, the healer, who is a spirit medium, draws on support from their own ancestral spirits.

The distinctions therefore – which are essentially ethical rather an ontological – between *mizimu* and such subcategories as *chiwanda*, *matsoka* and *mashawe* are highly contextual. The latter terms may or may not refer to related ancestors, but they usually imply some malevolent implications.

In Malawi, to become possessed is usually expressed by the term *ku-gwira*, to hold or catch, and the person is usually said to have been seized by the spirit (*munthu agwidwa ndi mzimu*), and in this state may act as a medium for the spirit (*kuti auze anthu onse amve* (Scott, 1929: 359). Becoming 'possessed' is also expressed by the verb *ku-gwa*, to fall, and *kugwa mizimu* means essentially 'to fall into spirits'. In the southern areas, however, the spirits are often described as entering the head or body of the person (*imalowammutu, imakhala m'thupi*). Although drumming and dancing are important in inducing a trance state, plant medicines are also used to induce possession. In the Lower Shire, Matthew Schoffeleers noted that during possession rituals, the *sing'anga*, usually a woman who is both a herbalist and a medium, scrapes the roots of the *nsangomwa* tree – which is almost certainly *Afzelia quanzensis* – and collects these scrapings on a plate. These are slightly threaded and held to the patient's nose. Her mouth is held shut (1968: 436–44). At a *matzoka* ceremony in the Thyolo district which I observed, I noted three plants that were used to induce a trance state: *chalima, Elephantorrhiza goetzei* (roots), *ncheule*, *heteropyxis natalensis* (a tree with aromatic leaves), and the common herb, chanzi or *mpungabwe, Ocimum canum*. They were referred to as *mankhwala kununkha* (medicine to smell) or as *mithengo wa madzoka* (spirit trees). At Nsanje, Bruce Hargreaves has described, in a pioneering article, four plants used to induce matzoka spirit possession. These are the roots of *mtsitsi la manda* ('roots of the graveyard', also known as *katsitsi mzukwa*, 'spirit root'), *Asparagus africana*, *mpoza*, *Annona senegalensis*, and *bwazi*, *Securidaca longepedunculata* and the leaves of *njoka*, *Chenopodium ambrosioides* (so named as its powerful smell is believed to drive away snakes) (Hargreaves, 1986). We have noted earlier the close association of *mpoza* with the spirits.

The possessed state is manifested in various ways, and its 'symptoms' include becoming unconscious or faint (*-komoka*), trembling (*-njenjemera*), raving (*-bwebweta*), shaking (*-gwedeza*), giddiness (*mutu zungulira*), rigidity of the body (*-uma*) and the contraction of the limbs (*-pindika*). When possessed a person may go into a trance state, and become completely dissociated from the immediate environment, and express amnesia at the end of the ritual. But such a 'psychogenic seizure' as Peltzer describes it (1987: 167) is not necessarily an expression of a pathogenic state – a 'convulsion disorder' or 'depressive neurosis' – for possession by the spirit medium is viewed positively and has a 'prophetic' or divinatory function. A possessed person is not normally described as mad (*misala*), although, as I have described elsewhere (1985: 23–5), there is a close association between spirit illness (*matsoka*) and madness. A distinction is also made between spirit possession and epilepsy (*chifufu*).

As with the rain rituals, I shall describe each of the more well-known spirit cults in turn, beginning with *vimbuza* rites among the Tumbuka, and moving south to the spirit rituals in Nsanje, and will focus on the role that animals play in these rituals.

Vimbuza

Vimbuza is a complex dance ritual, found mainly among the Tumbuka in the Rumphi and Mzimba districts. Oral tradition suggests that the cult was introduced to the patrilineal Tumbuka by the Bisa of Zambia, but Boston Soko suggests that the term *vimbuza* is a broad category which covers three distinct types of possession – disease. Indeed, *vimbuza* refers both to the disease and to the dance-ritual, which in essence is a curing rite. Soko writes:

> It is generally believed that the vimbuza is a result of the presence of spirits in the body of a human being. These are supposed to be wandering spirits whose origin is usually unknown. (1981: 3)

The spirits associated with *vimbuza* do not normally have a direct ancestral relationship with the patient, yet their identity is often expressed during possession, and Soko suggests that such possession refers to essentially three types of spirits. These are:

Vimbuza spirits, which relates to the spirits of Bemba or Bisa chiefs, such as Kazembe or Chitimukulu.

Virombo spirits, which are associated with spirits of either Nsenga or Chewa origin and which are linked to the Nyau and Malombo rituals of central Malawi.

Vyanusi spirits, which are of Ngoni origin, and which are of two types, *mngoma* and *mthwasi*.

These three types of spirits are distinguished in the possession rites by the songs that are sung, by the language that the possessed person involuntarily speaks, by the dancing style, and by the nature of the disease symptoms and their treatment. While possessed by *virombo* (wild animal) spirits, a person is prone to aggressive behaviour, and when 'highly possessed' a person may dramatize animal forms. Soko mentions that the animal form the possessing spirits take include guinea-fowl, snake, warthog (munjiri), lion, leopard and the red locust (*dzombe*) (1981: 43–4; 1988: 12). It is significant that Soko writes of the vimbuza spirits appearing to the patient in different 'forms', not that the person is possessed by the 'spirit' of the locust or lion. They are essentially spirits that have no kin relationship with the possessed person, and they often take an aggressive or animal form. Moreover, a person may be possessed by either an ancestral spirit – often a person's mother's spirit – or an alien spirit, and Soko writes that the two types of spirit often came together either in the ritual, or at the Msoro shrine associated with the ancestors (1988: 14).

The onset of the disease *vimbuza* is manifested in many ways – through dizzy spells, loss of memory, coughing, headaches, many life problems (*mabvuto*) or being troubled in dreams by ancestral spirits (*mizimu ya makolo imandibvuto kutulo*) (Peltzer, 1987: 165–8). In fact, a wide spectrum of ailments may come to be diagnosed under the rubric *vimbuza*, if, that is, they do not respond to herbal or hospital treatment. Chronic ailments are particularly prone to be seen as caused by the vimbuza spirits. As Boston Soko writes:

The disease has no symptoms to distinguish it, but instead, any kind of ailment might present sufficient grounds for suspicion. The patient might be suffering from paralysis of the body, pneumonia, headache, fever, failure of hands and legs as a result of sickness, mild forms of mental sickness and many other symptoms. (1981: 6)

Vimbuza affects both men and women, but evidence suggests that *vimbuza* patients are mainly women and young girls. The *vimbuza* healer (*nchimi* or *sing'anga*) is usually a person who was a former patient or sufferer, and although the *sing'anga* may be of either sex, the more famous spirit healers in the north are all men. Some have a reputation that extends over a wide area.

The term *vimbuza* is said to derive from the Bemba term for the pottery models (*mbusa*) used in the initiation of girls (Soko, 1987: 10; cf. Richards, 1956: 101); and Chilivumbo (1972) who sees it as a synonym of *mashawe*, which is a name given to spirit possession cults that are widespread in Zambia and Zimbabwe (cf. Gelfand, 1959: 121–52; Colson, 1969).

A form of therapy, *vimbusa* spirit rituals take place at night. It is a public dance ceremony, usually held at the home of the *sing'anga*. Singing, drumming and dancing, are performed in an atmosphere that is often festive and they may draw large crowds. Both the healer, as a spirit medium, and the patient usually become possessed when dancing, as do many of the participants. Although *vimbuza* dances may take place at any time, they are, like *nsembe* rituals, more frequently held in the dry season, when the maize has been harvested.

The *nchimi* (or *ng'anga*) usually acts as master of ceremonies, and begins the dancing. Thus the ritual initially has the appearance, as Soko puts it, of a 'one man show' (1981: 9). He wears a special costume consisting of headgear made of guinea-fowl (*nkhanga*) feathers, and is often covered with various animal skins, serval, monkey or grey duiker, or may wear a skirt consisting of strips of animal skins, including those of a goat or monkey. At a *vimbuza* dance I attended near Bwengu, the *nchimi* also wore a red tunic, a string of beads with an amulet (medicine bundle), bells on ankles and wrists, and he carried a medicine tail and a small hand axe. In being a medium for the spirits, the *nchimi*, like other diviners and the circumcisors (*ngaliba*) of Yao boys initiation – who are similarly dressed – assumes an outward animal form. Patients may also don such ritual paraphernalia during the possession ritual.

The *vimbuza* ritual goes on through the night, with much dancing, and heightened emotion as many participants fall into a trance (possessed)

Figure 6.3 Vimbuza spirit medium, Chikanji Msuya, Bwengu, March 1991

state. Herbs may be used to induce a trance, and shaking, glossolalia, and shrieking are taken as signs of a possession. Women attendants (*musamu*) associated with the healer, often uniformly dressed, assist in the possession rites, and in the administering of the medicines – a first possession being in the nature of an initiation into a specific cult group.

The culmination of the ritual, is the *chilopa* ceremony, undertaken just after daybreak. The term *chilopa* is derived from the widespread term *mlopa*, which signifies blood as a life energy. The patient is covered with a black cloth, and seated on a goat skin in the house of the *sing'anga*. A goat sheep or chicken is sacrificed – the chicken ideally being white in colour (signifying coolness) – and the blood of the animal is collected in a pot, and together with herbal medicines, is drunk by the patient. Only the patient drinks the blood, not the other participants. This action is said to reflect the 'transfer of life' from the animal to the human being, and to assist in exorcising the bad spirits (*mizimu yoipa*) or countering the forces of witchcraft (*ufiti*). (Soko, 1981: 22–3; Peltzer, 1987: 182–9).

The *vimbuza* rituals have usually been interpreted, by Malawian scholars as offering a socially sanctioned means of expressing social tensions, and of resolving conflicts or disturbed social relationships within the rural setting, particularly as these relate to gender relations (Chilivumbo, 1972: 6; Soko, 1981: 23; cf. Lewis, 1971). In the past there was much opposition to the *vimbuza* rites by the Christian missionaries, as well as by Christian converts like Revd Charles Chinula, but nowadays, although it is still a flourishing therapy, it has also taken on the guise of a cultural entertainment. One *vimbuza* dancer, Siyayo Mkandawire has won wide renown, often performing at national celebrations, although the dance is essentially for public entertainment, not therapy (Ndiwula, 1990: 3/21).

In a more recent study Steven Friedson (1996) has provided a pioneering account of the *vimbuza* phenomenon – a seminal, well-written work that shows that music – drumming-dancing – is intrinsic to *vimbuza* as a phenomonological experience. Largely following Heidegger's obscurantist metaphysics – and bypassing entirely Malawian ethnography (Boston Soko, who has published some pioneering studies of Vimbaza, is mentioned only in a footnote) – Friedson's text, however, indicates some rather misleading emphases.

One of the problems with Friedson's analysis is that he treats the *virombo* as a distinct category or kind of *vimbuza* (or *mizimu*). In some contexts this well may be the case, as when *virombo*, as Soko indicates, refers to the spirits of the neighbouring Chewa. However, rather misleadingly, Friedson suggests that the Tumbuka are animists, and he describes the *virombo* as a distinct category of 'animal spirits', which in turn consists of different 'kinds' of *vimbuza* spirits. He notes only the *munkwele* (monkey), *munjiri* (warthog), *nkharamu* (lion) and *kalulu* (hare). He writes of these as the 'spirits of wild animals' (p. 178) and suggests that these 'incarnate' people just like the *vimbuza* spirits of neighbouring people. All this seems to me quite misleading. Munkwele, to begin with, does not refer to the monkey, let alone to the 'spirit' of the monkey, but to the baboon. The monkey in Tumbuka is *mbwengu*, and for the Tumbuka they are quite different species. Nor is the duiker a 'small deer': it is an antelope. The Tumbuka, like other people in Malawi (with whom they share a common culture, long ago stressed by Cullen Young) are not animists, and they to not make a categorical distinction between *mizimu* (*vimbuza*) and the *virombo* spirits. They do not believe (if I may use this now contentious term) that animals – lion, hare, locust, duiker, puff adder, guinea fowl, eland – have spirits, and that these spirits 'incarnate' people, but they rather sense a close identity between the *mizimu* and wild animals. It is a transformation or metamorphosis (*ku-saduka*), not an incarnation, for the Tumbuka do not express a dualistic metaphysic.

Chisumphi

The term *chisumphi*, as we earlier noted, is one of the words used to describe the deity, especially in relation to rain, the supreme spirit often manifesting itself as a snake (*thunga*). In the form of the snake – not the spirit of the snake – the supreme spirit often possessed spirit mediums (*chauta, mwali*) at the important rain shrines such as Msinja, the 'Mecca of the Maravis', as Carl Wiese (1983: 272) described the shrine. There is evidence, however, at least from the turn of the century, that possession rites that were initially focussed on the shrines, and on rain calling, became spirit-possession cults – cults of affiliation – particularly in the central region. This was most certainly related to the social disruptions that arose from the invasion of the Ngoni into Malawi at the end of the nineteenth century. Wandering groups of dancers, described as *avirombo-a-chisumphi* (the wild animals of the deity) are said to have moved freely in the area of the Ngoni invasions, inducing possession by *chisumphi*, which mani-fested itself as a snake. Thus, as Rau put it 'The concept of chisumphi was altered under the influence of Chewa-Ngoni intermarriage and social interaction to assume the form of malevolent spirit possession' (1979: 138–9). Although such *chisumphi* possession may have pre-dated the Ngoni conquest (cf. Gamitto, 1960: 76–7 on Chisumphi), its frequency, and the diversity of its associations – which come to include many afflictions besides that of drought – certainly increased. As with the rain rituals, the *chisumphi* cult is focused on the deity – rather than on the ancestral spirits – which manifests itself in the form of the snake (*nsato, thunga*), which in turn has strong associations with water, especially deep pools.

The possessed person is thus not possessed by the python, or even by the 'spirit' of the python (as Yoshida, 1991: 203, 241, suggests), but by the *chisumphi* spirit which is identified with the python, with the wind, and with the power of rain.

Many scholars have suggested that with the demise of the *Msinja* rain shrine during the colonial period, and its fragmentation into constituent units, the *chisumphi* prophetic cult, focused essentially on rain-calling, developed into what Ioan Lewis (1971) called a 'peripheral' spirit possession cult. Though affecting both men and women, it was focused mainly around women who became possessed by the python spirit. Ian Linden has written a perceptive essay on the transformation of the *chisumphi* religions complex from the controlled mediumship of the Msinja rain shrine, to a more popular conception of *chisumphi*, though still focused around possession by divinity in the form of *thunga* (or nsato). A village headman confirmed that thunga possession mainly involved women, and that a distinction was made been possession by water-spirits (*ziwanda za mimadzi*) and lion-spirits (*ziwanda za mikango*) – the latter being seen as of Bisa origin (Linden 1979; 197). Although Linden suggests that Lewis's distinction between central and peripheral possession cults is a 'static categorization', and has little explanatory value, Lewis, of course, like Linden himself, explores many examples in the historical transformation of possession cults. Although Schoffeleers writes that 'prophetism and ecstasy have completely vanished, even in their peripheral forms' (1979: 175), in central Malawi, especially in the Mchinji district, spirit-mediums (*asumphi*) associated with rain rituals are still in evidence, especially during times of acute drought, although oral traditions often refer to these rituals in the past tense. An important distinction however was often made, Aleck Kwapulani (1982) suggests, between possession by the ancestral spirits – called *mizimu* or *ziwanda* – for which a dance was held, and offerings made to the spirits (a dance ritual described as *malombo*), and the possession associated with the thunga spirit. Thunga was always described as a large snake that lived in deep pools (*kumayiwe*), and was considered sacred in that killing the snake could lead to drought or possible madness. Possession in the Mchinji district was described as *achiuta* (*chiuta*, the deity), men being possessed by female thunga, *women* by male *thunga*, which were thought to have been sent (*kutumizidwa*) by the deity. The therapy essentially involved the taking of medicines, and a dance ritual at the place where the thunga was thought to reside. Kwapulani noted the sexual connotations implied between the patient who became possessed, and the thunga spirit (1982: 8–10). Since the colonial period, it seems, new forms of spirit possession have become prominent in the Mchinji district, particularly *vimbuza* and *malombo*, which are associated with spirits that originate among the Tumbuka and Nsenga respectively.

Mambo Spirits

We have noted above that spirits of the ancestors (*mizimu, chiwanda*) frequently take the form of animals, and these may range from that of a red locust or mouse, to that of the large carnivores such as the leopard or lion. Certain animals, however, such as the jackal and hyena, are considered malevolent, and are normally associated with the spirits of witches (*afiti*, i.e. malevolent kin), or involve, through the use of medicines, the transformation of the witch or some malevolent person, into this animal form, but the two animals that are most commonly associated with the ancestral spirits (*mizimu*) are the snake, especially the python, and the lion. Throughout the Zambezi region the spirits of the ancestors, particularly those of chiefs, are associated with lions. Among the Shona, for example, the spirits of departed chiefs are known as *mhondoro*, and these spirits take the form, or enter into, lions – thus that both the spirit medium, and the wild lion are also referred to as *mhondoro* (Bourdillon, 1976: 253–9); Lan, 1985: 32–3).

In Malawi it is widely recognized that the spirits of chiefly ancestors often take the form of a lion, but there are no cult fraternaries associated with these spirits such as are found in Zimbabwe. However, at Chapananga, west of Chikwawa, there are spirit-cults in which animals are given prominence, especially the lion, due to the fact that many Nyungwe and Chikunda people moved into the area from the Zambezi in the early part of the century. These cults are described as *mambo* cults, the term *mambo* referring, in its original sense, to a territorial chief. It has also come to mean both the spirit medium – who may be either a man or woman – and the possessing spirit, the latter being a chiefly ancestor who takes an animal form. David Faiti (1987) writes that people become spirit mediums in two ways. Either they become in a sense 'mad', wandering aimlessly in in the bush for several days, or they contract an illness, and this is interpreted as possession by a spirit. In both cases, they undertake a special ceremony (*kutoya*), which involves the sacrifice of a goat, its blood, mixed with beer, being given to the initiate to drink. There are special shrines dedicated to the ancestral (*mambo*) spirits, where offerings of beer and flour are made.

Importantly, the mambo spirits are identified with and take the form of animals, and each kind has a particular association. Thus the lion spirit is responsible for protecting people and crops from wild animals like the bushpig; the leopard spirit is associated with hunting; the python spirit – as elsewhere – with rain calling; the baboon spirit also with crop protection and the crocodile spirit protects fishermen from the river crocodiles. It is clear from Faiti's interesting account that the lion and the python are the most prominent and important manifestations of the ancestral chiefs (*mambo*) spirit, both being involved in rain rituals. He notes, too, that some people have been killed by a wild lion, mistakingly thinking that it was an ancestral spirit (1987: 6–15).

Matzoka

Among the Yao of the Zomba district, communication with the ancestral spirits is made not only through sacrificial offerings and in dreams but also through possession rites. These Stannus described as 'revelation seances' (1922: 316), but the three modes of communicating with the spirits, or rather, the spirits communicating with the living kin, are, however, intrinsically connected. It is, then, believed widely, that the ancestral spirits reveal their wishes to their kin through possession. The ancestral spirit may feel aggrieved at being neglected, or at the flaunting of the kinship norms by their descendants. They therefore make their wishes known by taking hold (-*gwira*) of a person, or by 'breaking' them down (-*kuwa, ku-wanda* has a similar meaning), or by entering the head of the living relative (*imalowa m'mutu mwache*).

Although both men and women may become possessed, it is usually women who act as mediums, and it is often the spirit of a grandmother who had been offended by neglect. The spirits which possess people are generally spoken of as *masoka* (singular: *lisoka* – ancestral spirit), but they may also be described as *majini*, and the possession rites themselves as *matsoka* (singular: *tsoka* – problems, misfortunes). Among Yao speakers although a distinction is made between epilepsy (*khunyu, chifufu, manjirinjiri*), madness (*misala*) and spirit possession (*matzoka, majini*), nevertheless, the possessed state is often described in terms of frothing at the mouth (*amaturuka thofu*), and a close relationship is always emphasized between madness and spirit-possession. Many people confirm the suggestions of early writers that *masoka* refers both to the ancestral spirits, in their more active guise, and to madness (Stannus, 1922: 316; Sanderson, 1954: 151). One person said to me that the spirit-illness *majini*, was simply a head ailment (*nthenda yamajini ndi mutu basi*). It is of interest that the term *majini* – which, of course, derives from the Islamic concept of jinn (cf. Quran 55:15), and is often interpreted as a 'nature spirit' – essentially refers in the Malawian context to the ancestral spirits. It is thus a synonym of *misoka*, or in Chewa, *chiwanda*, the *mizimu* in their potentially malevolent form.

In the Zomba district there is no clear link between the *majini* and animals, and the rites associated with them often have less of a collective orientation, the ailments associated with them being simply treated by medicines. But, in being focused around lineage spirits there are clear affinites between the Yao rites and the Matzoko rituals found throughout southern Malawi, and the Malombo rites of the Central region.

In his studies of spirit possession in the Lower Shire Valley, Father Schoffeleers noted that the Matzoka-type spirit possession occurred among both the Sena and Mang'anja people. Possession affected both men and women, but that the majority of those suffering from spirit-related ailments were women (84 per cent). The spirit causing the affliction, which was usually of a somatic nature, is normally of the same sex as the patient; a real or classificatory grandparent. The motivation behind the affliction, for which the possession rites are held, is that the deceased relative feels neglected or that some norm of behaviour has not been adhered to. The motivation of the spirit, therefore, as Schoffeleers writes, is always 'normative and corrective'. Many of the men afflicted are migrant workers who have neglected their kin obligations, and thus the beliefs tend to emphasize 'traditional' values, and to strengthen lineage cohesion. Having through divination ascertained that the cause of a disease is a disgruntled grandparent, a possession rite is held, the needs of the spirit discovered, and a 'spirit' basket installed in the hut. Such possession rites, which are known as matzoka or malombo, are always held in the homestead of the afflicted. The spirits once placated are often inherited by the daughter. Henceforth libations of flour must be made to the spirit. (Schoffeleers, 1969: 10–12).

At a *matzoka* ceremony I attended in the Thyolo district, all the participants, apart from the drummers and a few young men hanging about, were women. The woman *sing'anga*, who acted as the spirit medium, wore a red scarf, and carried a headdress of feathers and a belt of snake-skin, which represented the spirits. As with the *vimbuza* healer, she also carried a medicine tail, and a small axe (made of *Dalbergia melanoxylon* wood). Held at the house of the afflicted person – a diviner having already ascertained that it was a spirit-induced ailment – the essence of the ceremony, which involved dancing and singing and much unlulating (*ntungululu*), was to exorcise the offending spirit (*mizimu imachoka*). The patient collapsed in a trance state at a nearby stream, and with liberal libations of flour (*ufawa chimanga*), the spirit was induced to leave the patient and enter the water. The whole ceremony was a kind of dance drama, and the leader of the ritual, the sing'anga, was a woman who combined the roles of both spirit-medium and herbalist.

Nantongwe

The Nantongwe rituals of the Lomwe people follow a similar pattern to the Matzoka rites outlined above, the offending spirit being a spirit of a deceased relative. Again, cult members are mostly women. Nantongwe is a term that has several meanings: it refers to the night-long ceremony that involves possession; it refers to the spirit-illness itself, which essentially focuses around splitting headaches, often described as *mpwesa* or *mutu waukulu*, 'large head(ache)': as well to the medicines that are used in its treatment. Unlike the 'matzoka' rites, however, *nantongwe* is intrinsically connected with wild animals.

Whenever people are asked about *nantongwe*, it is invariably described as an ailment of the head (*ndi matenda amene mutu amakhala ukuwawa*), and as being of different kinds, according to the animal associated with it, *nantongwe wa phanya* (gerbil), *nantongwe wa nangwale* (grey duiker), *nantongwe wa nsato* (python) and so forth. It is thus initially indicated by a severe and painful headache, described as *mutu waukulu*. Normally this ailment is considered to be a severe headache for which no etiology is sought, and it is linked to dizziness, to temporary loss of vision (*chidima*), to bad dreams, nose bleed, and to a throbbing or splitting headache (*pweteka* – pain; *wawa* – ache). But it may also be linked to stomach pains, loss of appetite, or weak limbs – and to describe this ailment as a 'pure psycho-neurotic disorder' seems to me highly limiting (cf. Peltzer, 1987: 171). It may initially simply be treated by medicinal herbs.

This ailment, however, is closely associated with *nantongwe*, and should it prove chronic, then the patient, with his or her close kin, will seek the help of a diviner (*sing'anga kukawombeza*). The diviner will then indicate whether the ailment is simply a headache, a disease due to sorcery or witchcraft, or whether the person is suffering because she has been possessed by an ancestral spirit (*mzimu*). If the latter, the patient will need to consult a *sing'anga* who conducts *nantongwe* rituals. Such a person is usually a woman and is called *namkungwi* a term also used to describe ritual leaders in the initiation rites. Such *sing'anga* are usually elderly women who were possessed in the past, and having suffered, been cured of the *nantongwe* disease.

Preparations are then made for the ritual: beer is brewed, flour prepared for offerings to the spirit; chicken and food collected for the participants, and a new clay pot to hold the chirope medicines is made. The rites are complex, and involve night-long festivities, involving drumming, dancing, the singing of *nantongwe* songs, the sacrifice of flour to the ancestral spirits, which are induced to possess the patient and so articulate their concerns and needs. The crucial part of the ceremony is the identification of the animal that is associated with the *nantongwe* possession, and the taking of the *chirope* medicine, *chirope*, as we noted elsewhere, being associated with the powers of animals that are killed during the hunt.

Initially, the sing'anga gives the patient special herbal medicines. These induce dreams, through which the ancestral spirits – described as relatives who died long ago (*abale andamwalira kale*) – indicate to the patient the animal that is associated with the possessing spirit, and which will form the essential ingredient of the chirope medicine. People will dream, or the *sing'anga* may indicate, a variety of animals that will constitute the healing medicine: these include *phanya* (bushveld gerbil), *mende* (creek rat), *zumba* (rock hyrax), *gwapi* (grey duicker, the Lomwe terms are *nangwale* and *nahe*), *nsato* (python), *sakhwi* (elephant shrew), *jugu* (pouched rat), *likongwe* (bush squirrel), *nkunda* (dove), *nsomba* (fish) and the *dzombe* (locust). The patient may go into the woodland in a possessed state to seek out the animal, or the animal will simply be revealed in a dream, and then it will be hunted or captured prior to the *nantongwe* ritual. Ideally the animal will be taken alive, and killed during the ritual. If no animal is available, then a domestic chicken (*nkhuku*) may be used.

The crucial parts of the *nantongwe* ritual are twofold: that the ancestral spirit that is afflicting the patient be revealed during the possession rite; and that the blood of the animal, taken with herbs, is drunk by the patient in the *chirope* rite. Both these rites are important. The offending spirit will be placated and a viable relationship will be established between the ancestral spirit and a member of her matrikin (who in their supplications describe themselves as the 'children' (*ana*) of the spirit); and the *chirope* medicine, which includes the blood of the animal, most frequently a species of mouse (*mbewa*), is seen as having therapeutic qualities, neutralizing the severe headaches. Throughout the ritual, the patient and the participants must be in a 'cool' condition and thus refrain from sexual activity. People suggest that animals for the *nantongwe* ceremony are usually easily caught, as the ancestral spirits binds (-*mange*) them, and they are thus not able to make their escape (*amalephera kuthawa* – fail to run away). Important in the rituals is that the *sing'anga*', and at times the patient – who in essence is an initiate to the cult – put on the skin of a bushbaby (*chikopa cha changa*). The skin embodies the ancestral spirits, and while wearing the skin they dance around the hut.

The *nantongwe* rite is an important social event, and it is usually held at night, and at the hut of the sick person. After feasting and further sacrificial offerings – often at the Mpoza shrine – the final rites are called *kutola matsoka* – 'to carry away the misfortunes'. This involves the digging of a pit, towards which the patient has to crawl (*amakwawa pansi*), the throwing away of the remainder of the *chirope* medicine or the mixture of the meat of the animal with maize porridge (*nsima*) – which the participants had earlier eaten. This is described as *kutaya mankhwala* – to throw away the medicine – and it symbolizes the return of the animal (and the disease) to the woodland. The rite concludes with the planting of a banana sapling, ritual intercourse between the patient and a selected partner, and the ritual washing of the patient with herbs, and with castor oil (nsatsi), thought to be protective medicines (*kutsirika mankhwala*). (The above outline is based on my own notes and observations, but for further details see the important essays by Maganga, 1983; Boeder, 1984: 47–51; Nazombe, 1988).

Most writers on *nantongwe* have suggested that it was a means of resolving village conflicts and that through the rites tensions, fears, and interpersonal disputes, between spouses, between matrilineally related women, and between the matrikin and the in-marrying male affine (*nkamwene*), were expressed. In his study of Magomera village, Landeg White relates this form of spirit-possession to the colonial *thangata* system, and to the erosion of the women's autonomy (White, 1987: 182–6; Nazombe, 1990).

Chikwangali

In his study of spirit possession cults in the Lower Shire Valley, Father Schoffeleers described not only spirit rituals focussed around related spirits – and which were linked to somatic ailments of a diverse nature – but also possession cults that were linked to alien or witch spirits.

The first of these occurred mainly among Sena people, who have a patrilineal kinship system. Possession was almost exclusively confined to married women, and was spontaneous and uncontrolled. The possessing spirits are known as 'mazinda'. They are the spirits of some deceased hunter or warrior, and are not related to the afflicted. The spirit is motivated by the need to 'marry' the woman. The symbolism of the possession and its curative ritual are derived from that of marriage, the *mazinda* spirits being symbolized by a red shoulder cloth. Sexual potency and hunting are central motifs of the rite, which consists of the consecration of an animal (usually a goat or sheep), the initiation of the women as the spirit's medium (wife), and the permanent accommodation of the spirit in her hut. This is done by means of a basket shrine. The woman is usually given new clothes, and the women who become possessed tend to be those who are neglected by their husbands either in their maternal or socially accepted affectional needs. The men who become possessed are often impotent. (Schoffeleers, 1969: 8–9).

Spirit possession cults focussed around the witch spirits were quite different. These spirits were considered the 'most terrifying spirits of all'. The existence of these spirits indicates that there is no hard and fast line between spirits and witches. In the past victims of the *mwabvi* poison ordeal were not considered human but almost beasts (*zirombo*), and they were either burned or left to the hyenas. Witches (*afiti*), alive or dead, are always killers and hunters after human flesh; but they not only kill: they also cause diseases. In theory, as Schoffeleers notes, diseases caused by *afiti* may be of any kind. An analysis of a number of cases, however, revealed that, in practice, the witch-spirits show a marked preference for diseases and abnormalities related to the system of human reproduction. These include male and female sterility, sexual frigidity, abortions, and infant mortality. This does not mean, he suggests, that spirit activity is the only explanation for such misfortunes. Again the great majority of patients are women, and this kind of possession is again more frequent among the patrilineal Sena.

The *chikwangwali* ritual associated with these witch-spirits (*afiti*) is essentially a curing rite designed to 'trap' and exorcise the offending spirit. This is done under the direction of a *sing'anga* (herbalist-medium) who identifies the spirit by inducing it to enter the patient. The ceremony is always held in the bush (*thengo*), often at a road junction or near an anthill (*chulu*) and the spirit is usually offered an animal that it desires – a dog, rat, or black chicken perhaps. During the possession-trance the creature is often torn open by the patient, and its blood smeared over the body.

The *chikwangwali* ceremony is essentially a rite of exorcism, and is viewed quite differently from the *malombo/matzoka* rites. The possessing spirits, those of people who were witches (*mfiti*) in the past, are seen as wholly malevolent. They are described as *mzimu woipa*, bad spirits. These spirits are identified with wild animals (*zirombo*), the hyena (*fisi*) being prototypical. The symbolism of the rite is to induce the spirit to return to the woodland, and objects used in the rite are ritually buried in a pit that is described as *dzimba*, the antbear, Orycteropus afer. This animal, Schoffeleers suggests, may be regarded as the 'destroyer of witches' (1967: 17), although the antbear's deep burrows only imply an earthly abode, which is associated with the spirits. Schoffeleers also notes that whereas the 'malombo' spirits desire and are offered domestic animals, such as goat, sheep or a white chicken, the *chikwangwali* spirits express the desire for, and are given, dog, rat, cat, frog or a black chicken – and may even ask for human flesh – *nyama yopanda ubweya* (meat without hair). This reflects the moral distinction between the two 'kinds" of spirits, the latter, witch spirits, being seen as wholly malevolent, even though such witch spirits may in fact be related to the victim (patient) (Schoffeleers, 1967: 10–14; 1968, 1969: 12).

Conclusions

In her study of spirit possession among the Tonga of the Zambezi Valley, Zambia, Elizabeth Colson wrote that these people

> identify the various types of spirits by the circumstances in which they manifest themselves. Indeed perhaps there is but one class of spirits and the various names refer only to the different ways in which this impinges upon men'. (1969: 72)

This very much reflects the situation in Malawi where the *mizimu*, the spirits of the dead, manifest themselves in many ways, and in various forms, and thus have varied names. The *mizimu* reveal themselves in supportive and positive ways, in the dreams of their living kin, in empowering diviners and spirit-mediums (who frequently assume the outward form of an animal), and in taking the form of animals, as pythons, lions, leopards, or even as such humble creatures as the locust, guinea fowl or gerbil. On the other hand, the *mizimu* may manifest themselves in a malevolent form, as *masoka, ziwanda, mashawe* or *afiti* (witch-spirit), and inflict harm and misfortunes on people, irrespective of whether or not they are kin relatives. Again, they may take animal form – as a hyena, jackal, or as a generic wild beast (*chirombo*).

Although the *mizimu* are associated with the wind (*mphepo*) and are seen as having life *moyo* (which extends to other living creatures), Malawians do not hold, as Colson suggests for the Tonga, that all phenomena are endowed with soul or spirit (*muuya*), not only human beings and animals, but bicycles, cars, aeroplanes, trains, and disembodied creatures of the bush (1969: 72). As Stannus and Levi Mumba long ago suggested, and Malawian scholars have more recently affirmed, it is misleading to interpret Malawian religious beliefs as 'animistic'. Alexander Hetherwick's early article entitled *Some Animistic Beliefs among the Yaos* (1902), is significant in that he gave no evidence of all of animism in its usual sense, either in the belief of an animate universe, or the notion that plants, animals and natural phenomena are endowed with 'souls' or 'spirit'. He noted that for the Yaos 'the human being is believed to be the sole possessor of a lisoka', and defined animism in terms of three conceptions (none of which imply animism): namely, the belief that *lisoka* (spirit) is an agent in dreams and possession, that they are an object of reverence and important in the fortunes of living people, and that *Mulungu* 'the great spirit agency' (as he describes the deity), is the creator and source of all things animate and in animate (Hetherwick, 1902: 95). He recognized, however, that by special medicines powerful sing'angas were able to transform themselves into lions, crocodiles or leopards, but suggested that this implied transmutations of the body, not the 'trans-migration of souls' (Hetherwick, 1902: 91).

Yet although Malawians do not believe that animals, plants and other material objects have 'souls', there is a sense in which the world is believed to be filled with mystery, and with powers, both spiritual, in relation to the *mizimu*, and material, in relation to the powers of nature, embodied in medicines. Many things, but particularly animals, therefore, become the 'vehicles' of this 'dynamism' as Musopole (1984: 36) describes it.

Many Malawian scholars have noted the affinities between the various spirit-rituals found throughout Malawi – *vimbuza, mashawe, malombo, mambo, matzoka, chikwangwali, nantongwe* – and have explored some of their differences, with regard to the spirit agency involved, and with respect to their therapeutic content (for example, Nazombe, 1981). *Matzoka* and *vimbuza* for example, seem to focus on a wide range of ailments, many somantic, while *nantongwe* (and *majini* among the Yao) seem to be closely associated with head (*mutu*) or mental disorders. And as we have noted, the spirit involved in the possession rite may be diverse – the spirit of a close relative, spirits of foreign origin, or witch spirits. But what is common to all these spirit rituals are the following: (1) all tend to be public ceremonials under the direction of a spirit healer, and involve drumming, dancing, singing, and possession by the spirit; (2) the use of medicines is intrinsic to the rituals, to induce a trance-state, as protective (*ku-sirika*) substances against witchcraft, and as therapeutic agents to strengthen (*-limbitsa*) and heal the patient. The *sing'anga* thus combines the roles of herbalist and spirit-medium; (3) animals play an important role in the rituals, for the *sing'anga* in embodying the spirits often takes the outward form of an animal (symbolized by skins of the duiker or serval, or the feathers of the guinea fowl); the spirits of the dead in possessing individuals may often manifest themselves as an animal – in varying forms (ranging from a red locust and gerbil to a lion, python or crocodile); animals are given as sacrificial offering to the spirits of the dead; and, finally, animals in the form of medicines are given to the patient, their blood (*chirope*) being an essential ingredient; and (4) although spirit-illness effects both men and women, and the *sing'anga* dealing with spirit ailments may be of either sex, evidence suggests that in Malawi, both patients and the main participants in the spirit-possession cults, tend to be women.

In his important study of the cults or rites of affliction – spirit rituals involving therapy – in central and southern Africa, John Janzen (1992) suggests that these exemplify an 'ancient institution', the *ngoma* (drum), which is the 'core feature' of the classical healing system of the region. Janzen bewails the preoccupation that Western scholars have for 'trance' and 'possession' with the implication that the therapeutic orientation of these spirit rituals (*ngoma*) is psychological only (Peltzer, 1987 tends this way), and he emphasizes the 'centrality of discourse' in these rituals [1992: 176–77)]. As language is central to human life, 'discourse' is important in *all* social contexts, not only in rituals, and, of course, such spirit rituals, that is, the therapeutic rites involving spirits, usually of the dead, is not only widespread in Africa, but is a pan-human phenomenon, found throughout the world. The limitations of Janzen's study is that in putting a focal emphasis on the 'spirit' hypothesis, and on spirit healing, Janzen completely oblates, or marginalizes, the central importance of medicines in African society and culture. The use of medicines permeates African culture, whether it is used for positive (therapeutic) or malevolent purposes – by witches – which gives rise to what Janzen describes as 'man-caused misfortunes' (1992: 65). As I have described elsewhere, herbalism forms a therapeutic tradition, which is distinct from spirit healing, and there is often antagonism between the two traditions – especially with the rise of Churches involving spirit healing (Van Dijk 1995). Moreover, neither spirit healing nor herbalism focus on healing simply in terms of individual therapy, but relate to all aspects of social life. Yet what is lacking in Janzen's study is that although he notes the importance of domestic animals as sacrificial offerings, and of snake-handling rituals in Tanzania (1992: 104, 150), he nowhere discussed the intrinsic relationship that exists throughout African between animals and spirits of the dead. This is no doubt due to the fact that his study focuses on prominent spirit healers in urban contexts, but as we have explored in the present chapter, it is through animals that the spirits of the dead – and with respect to the python, even the deity – manifest themselves, that is make themselves visible. Animals, particularly the larger mammals and reptiles, are the form that the spirits of the dead take, and what kind is involved depends on the nature and motivations of the spirit. *Chiwanda, masoka, mashawe*, usually refer to the spirits *mizimu*, in this visible, and often malevolent form.

In this study I explored the crucial sacramental role that animals still play in the ritual and religious life of the matrilineal peoples of Malawi. In their lifecycle rituals animals form, along with the spirits of the dead, a critical element in their ceremonials, and the spirits of the ancestors, taking the form of animals (as masked or theriomorphic figures) temporarily reveal their presence in the village domain. There is, I suggested, a close identification of male affines with the spirits of the dead and with animal life (hunting), both of which are associated with the woodland. This constitutes a symbolic domain that forms a complimentary opposition to that of the village, which is associated with agriculture, women, and the matrilineal kin group.

In the various cults of affliction (*vimbuza, matsoka, nantongwe*) animals likewise play a prominent part in the rituals, the possessing spirits often taking the form of animals, and the ritual ingestion of animal meat and blood (*chirope*) is an important part of the rites, especially among the Tumbuka and Lomwe. Throughout the text I have therefore emphasized the close association that pertains in Malawi between the spirits (*mizimu*) in their many forms, and animal life.

Equally important, I explored the role that animals played in the creation myths of Malawian people, and the fundamental importance of the serpent spirit (often identified with the python, *thunga*) in many rites. For this animal, associated with rivers and pools, plays a crucial role in rainmaking rituals, being interpreted as a manifestation of the supreme being, the deity Chiuta.

In recent years with the emergence of radical forms of Islam, and of various fundamentalist Christian sects in Malawi, there has been a sustained opposition to those cultural traditions associated with the rural context – herbalism, initiations, spirit rituals, dancing and beer drinking. It thus remains to be seen to what degree animals continue to play an important part in the rituals and in the religious imagination of Malawian people.

Glossary

Ambuye	Grandparents
Banja	Family, home, household
Bwalo	Cleared space in centre of village
Bwenzi	Friend, lover
Chibale	Kinship, friendship
Chinamwali	General term for initiation rites
Chiputu	Girls' maturity rite among Yao
Chirombo	Wild animal, useless or obnoxious organism
Chirope	Blood, ailment associated with hunting, ritual eating of meat
Chisamba	Dance and rituals associated with a woman's first pregnancy
Chizimba	Activating medicine
Dambo	Marsh, valley glades/grassland
Dziko	Country, land
Jando	Boys' circumcision ritual among the Yao
Kachisi	Small hut or shrine where sacrificial offerings made to the spirits
Litiwo	Ceremony relating to a woman's first pregnancy among Yao
Lupanda	Boys' initiation rite among Yao
Makhalidwe	Disposition, nature, character
Maliro	Funerary rites
Malume	Maternal uncle
Manda	Forested graveyard
Mankhwala	Medicinal substances
Matsenga	Sorcery, trick, mysterious happenings
Matsoka	Ill-luck, misfortunes
Maula	Divination
Mbumba	Matrilineal, or sorority group
Mdulo	Disease complex related to sexual norms and hot/cold Symbolism (also *Tsempho*)
Mfiti	Witch

Mfumu	Chief or village headman
Mkamwini	In-marrying male affine, son-in-law
Mlamu	Affine of own generation (plural *Alamu*)
M'michira	Ritual specialist or healer (who possesses medicine tail, *Mchira*)
Mowa	Beer
Mudzi	Village
Mulungu	Common name for the divinity
Munthu	Person
Mwali	Initiate
Mwambo	Tradition, custom, wisdom
Mwayi	Good fortune, luck

Bibliography

1. Archival Material

National Archives of Malawi (MNA), Zomba.
Malawi Section, University Library, Chancellor College, University of Malawi, Zomba.
Society of Malawi Library, Limbe.
Wildlife Research Unit, Kasungu National Park, Department of National Parks and Wildlife.
Library/Archives, Wildlife Society of Malawi, Environmental Educational Centre, Lilongwe Wildlife Sanctuary, Lilongwe.

2. Malawi

Abdallah, Y.B. (1973), *The Yaos* (Chiikala cha Wayao) Orig. 1919. London: Cass.

Amanze, J. (1980), *The Bimbi Cult and its impact among the Chewa, Yao and Lomwe of the Upper Shire Valley.* Chancellor College, Zomba: History Seminar Paper.

—— (1986), *The Bimbi Cult of Malawi*, PhD thesis, University of London.

Baker, C.A. (1971), Malawi's exports, in B Pachai *Malawi Past and Present.* Blantyre: Claim, pp. 88–113.

Balestra, F.A. (1962), The man-eating Hyenas of Mlanje. *African Wildlife*, 16: 25–27.

Banda, N.I. (1975), Nyau in Mchinji District. Chancellor College, Zomba: Dept. Human Behaviour Dissertation.

Bennett, N.R. and M. Ylvisaker (1971), *The Central African Journal of Lovell J Proctor 1860–64.* African Studies Centre, Boston University.

Berry, V. and C. Petty (1992), (ed) *The Nyasaland Survey Papers 1938–1943*, London: Academy Books.

Birch de Aquillar, L. (1994), Nyau masks of the Chewa. *Society Malawi Journal,* 47/2: 1–53.

Blackman, B. and J.M. Schoffeleers (1972), Masks of Malawi. *African Arts*, 5/4: 36–41.

Bibliography

Boeder, B. (1982), Malawi: Land and Legend. *Society Malawi Journal,* 35/2: 52–65.

—— (1984), *Silent Majority.* Pretoria: African Institute. South Africa.

Boucher, C. (1976), *Some interpretations of Nyau Societies.* MA Dissertation. SOAS University of London.

—— (1976), *The Nyau Secret Society.* Mua Catholic Mission. Unpublished paper.

—— (1991), *Explanation of a mission banner.* Mua Catholic Mission. Unpublished paper.

Bruwer, J.P. (1948), Kinship terminology among the Chewa of E Province of North Rhodesia. *African Studies, 7: 185–7.*

—— (1949), Composition of a Chewa Village. *African Studies, 8: 191–8.*

—— (1950), Notes on Maravi Origins and Migration. *African Studies,* 9: 32–4.

—— (1952), Remnants of a rain cult among the Acewa. *African Studies,* 11: 179–81.

Buchanan, J. (1982), *The Shire Highlands.* Blantyre Printing and Publishers.

Chakanza, J.C. (1980), Annotated list of independent churches in Malawi 1900–1981. Chancellor College, Zomba: Religious Studies Department.

—— (1985), Provisional list of witch-finding movements in Malawi 1850–1980. *Religion in Africa,* 15/3: 227–43.

—— (1987), Some Chewa Concepts of God. *Religion in Malawi,* 1: 4–8.

—— (1998), On Matriliny. *The Lamp,* p. 28.

Chilivumbo, A.B. (1972), Vimbuza or Mashawe: a mystic therapy. *African Music,* 5: 6–9.

Chisiza, D.K. (1964), The Outlook for contemporary Africa, in *Africa's Freedom,* London: Allen & Unwin, pp. 38–54.

Chimombo, S. (1987), *Napolo Poems.* Zomba: Manchichi Publishers.

Clark, J.D. (1959), Rock art in Nyasaland, in R Summers (ed.) *The Rock Art of Federation of Rhodesia and Nyasaland.* Salisbury National Publishers Trust, pp. 163–221.

—— (1973), Archaeological investigations of painted rock shelter at Mwana wa Chencherere, Dedza. *Society Malawi Journal,* 26/1: 28–46.

Cole-King, P.A. (1968), Mwala Wolemba on Mikolongwe Hill. Zomba Government Press, Dept. Antiquities Publ. No 1.

Coudenhove, H. (1925), *My African Neighbours.* London: J Cape.

Debenham, F. (1955), *Nyasaland: the Land of the Lake.* London: HMSO.

Denis, L. (1929), Maladie et mort d'un Mchewa. Mua Catholic Mission. Unpublished paper.

Dudley, C.O. (1919), History of the Decline of Larger Mammals of the Lake Chilwa Basin. *Society Malawi Journal,* 32/2: 27–41.

Bibliography

Duff, H. (1903), *Nyasaland under the Foreign, Office.* London: Bell.

Edwards, A.C.T. (1948), Zomba Flood: December 1945. *Nyasaland Journal,* 1/2: 53–59.

Elmslie, W.A. (1899), *Among the Wild Angoni,* Edinburgh: Oliphant Anderson.

England, H. (1996), Witchcraft, Modernity and the Person. *Critique of Anthropology,* 16/3: 257–79.

Faiti, D. (1987), The Mambo Spirits of Chapananga. Chancellor College, Zomba: History Seminar Paper.

Faulkner, L. (1988), Basketry masks of the Chewa. *African Arts,* 21/3: 28–31.

Fields, K.E. (1985), *Revival and Rebellion in Colonial Central Africa.* Princeton: Princeton University Press.

Foa, E. (1900), *La Traversee de L'Afrique du Zambiese au Congo Francais.* Paris: P. Cie.

Franzen, H. (1977), Rock paintings of the Dedza area. Unpublished manuscript.

Fraser, D. (1914), *Winning a Primitive People.* London: Seeley.

—— (1915), *Livingstonia: The Story of Our Mission.* Edinburgh: United Free Church of Scotland.

—— (1923), *African Idylls.* London: Seeley.

Friedson, S.M. (1996), *Dancing Prophets.* Chicago: University Chicago Press.

Gamitto, A.C.P. (1960), *King Kasembe and the Marave, Cheva, Bisa, Bemba, Lunda and other Peoples of Southern Africa,* (Expedition 1831–32), 2 vols. (Ed. 1 Cunnison). Lisboa: Estodios de Ciencias Politicas e Sociais.

Garland, A.V. (1989), The Red Rock Art of Malawi. University Durham BA dissertation.

Gwengwe, J.W. (1965), *Kukula Ndi Mwambo.* Blantyre: Dzuka.

Hargreaves, B.J. (1979), Cautious carnivorous clowns: chameleons of Malawi. *Nyala,* 5: 32–39.

—— (1981), Parallels in plant use in Africa and North America. *Society Malawi Journal,* 34: 56–71.

—— (1986), Plant induced 'spirit possession' in Malawi. *Society Malawi Journal,* 39/1: 26–35.

Heckel, B. (1935), The Yao tribe, their culture and education. University London Institute Education Report No.4.

Hetherwick, A. (1902), Some animistic beliefs among the Yaos of British Central Africa. *Journal Royal Anthropological Institute,* 32: 89–95.

Hodgson, A.G.O. (1926), Dreams in Central Africa. *Man,* 39: 66–8.

—— (1931), Rainmaking, witchcraft and medicine among the Anyanja. *Man*, 31: 266–70.

—— (1933), Notes on the Achewa and Angoni of the Dowa District. *Journal Royal Anthropological Institute*, 63: 123–65.

Jackson, J. (1929), Description of the Chinyao dance, Central Province, Nyasa-land, Mss Africa 556, Rhodes House Library, Oxford.

Johnson, W.P. (1922), *Chinyanja Proverbs*. Cardiff: Smith Bros.

Johnston, H.H. (1897), *British Central Africa*, (1969 edn). New York: Negro University Press.

Juwayeyi, Y.M. (1993), Problems of rock art documentation and preservation in Malawi. Intern. Council of Archives, Conference Paper: Mangochi.

Kalilombe, P.A. (1980), An outline of Chewa traditional religion. *African Theological Journal,* 9/2: 39–51.

Kalinga, O.J.M. (1984), The Balowoka and the established states west of Lake Malawi, *in* A.I Salim (ed). *State Formation in Eastern Africa.* Nairobi: Heinemann, pp. 36–52.

Kandawire, J.A.K. (1976), Reality and symbolic exchange in African religion. *Journal Social Science,* 5: 57–64.

Kaphagawani, D.W. (1998), African Conceptions of personhood and Intellectual Identities, *and* Themes in Chewa Epistemology *in* P.H. Coetzee and A.P.J. Roux (eds) *The African Philosophy Reader.* London: Routledge pp. 169–76, 240–44.

—— and HF Chidammodzi (1983), Chewa Cultural ideas and systems of thought as determined by proverbs. *Botswana J African Studies,* 3/2: 29–37.

Kaspin, D. (1993), Chewa visions and revisions of power: transformations of Nyau dance in Central Malawi, *in* J & J Comaroff (ed.) *Modernity and its Malcontents*, University Chicago Press pp. 34–57.

—— (1996), A Chewa cosmology of the Body. *American Ethnologist,* 23/3: 561–78.

Khaila, S. (1995), Cultural causes of violence against women. *The Nation,* September 21/28.

Kishondo, M.F. (1970), Development and change: Changes in initiation ceremonies among the Yao. Chancellor College, Zomba: Department: Human Behaviour dissertation.

Kubik, G. (1978), Boys circumcision school of the Yao. *Rev. Ethnology*, 6: 1–56.

—— (1985), African graphic systems – a re-assesment. *Mitteliungen der Anthrologischen Gesellschaft in Wein,* 115: 77–101.

—— (1987) *Nyau*. Vienna: Osterreichischen Akademie der Wisserschaften.

Kumakanga, S.L. (1975), *Nzeru za kale*. Blantyre: Dzuka.

Kumwembe, N.H. (1978), The development of the Mbewe Chiefdoms 1840–1915. Chancellor College, Zomba: History Seminar Paper.

Kwapulani, A.M. (1982), Spirit possession in the religious history of Mchinji District. Chancellor College, Zomba: History Seminar Paper.

Laws, R. (1934), *Reminiscences of Livinstonia*. Edinburgh: Oliver & Boyd.

Linden, I. (1972), 'Mwali' and the Luba origins of the Chewa. *Society Malawi Journal*, 25/1: 11–19.

—— (1974), *Catholics, Peasants and Chewa Resistance in Nyasaland, 1889–1939*. London: Heinemann.

—— (1975), Chewa initiation rites and Nyau societies, *in* TO Ranger and J Weller (eds) *Themes in Christian History of Central Africa*. London: Heinemann pp. 30–44.

—— (1979), Chisumphi theology in the religion of Central Malawi, *in* JM Schoffeleers (ed.) *Guardians of the Land*. Gwero: Mambo pp. 187–207.

Lindgren, N.E. and J.M. Schoffeleers (1978), *Rock Art and Nyau Symbolism in Malawi*. Government Press, Zomba: Dept Antiquities Publ No.18.

Livingstone, D. and C. (1887), *Expedition to the Zambezi and its Tributaries*. London: J Murray.

Luhanga, T. (1983), The Mwanda Cult. Chancellor College, Zomba: Papers on Regional Cults, pp. 1–7.

Lumeta, M.F. (1975), Yao first born child ceremonies in the context of social change. Chancellor College, Zomba: Department of Sociology dissertation.

McAuliffe, E. (1994), Aids – the barriers to behaviour change. Zomba: Centre for Social Research.

MacDonald, D. (1882), *Africana: or the Heart of Heathern Africa,* 2 vols. Edinburgh: J Menzies.

MacMillan, H. (1975), The African Lakes Company and the Makolo 1878–1884, *in* R.J. MacDonald (ed.) *From Nyasaland to Malawi*, Nairobi: E. Africa Publishing House pp. 65–85.

Maganga, J.L. (1983), Nantongwe: a spirit possession ritual among the Lomwe. Chancellor College, Zomba: Papers on Regional Cults pp. 8–14.

Mair, L. (1951), A Yao girl's initiation. *Man,* 51: 60–63.

Bibliography

Makombe, J.D. (1983), Rainmaking among the people of Nkhoma and Mwera. Chancellor College, Zomba: Papers on Regional Cults pp. 15–25.

Makumbi, A.J. (1955), *Maliro Ndi Miyambo Ya Achewa*. Blantyre: Dzuka.

Malcolm, D.W. (1936), The Story of Amini Bin Saidi of the Yao Tribe of Nyasaland, *in* M Perham (ed) *Ten Africans*. London: Faber, pp. 139–157.

Malele, P.B. (1994), The social and religious impact of the Nyau among the Chewa of Mitundu in Lilongwe. Chancellor College, Zomba: Dept Religious Studies, unpublished paper.

Malipa, F. (1971), Christianity in Relation in Chewa Customs and Family Life. Salisbury: Gaba.

Marwick, M.G. (1950), Another Modern anti-witchcraft movement in East-Central Africa. *Africa*, 20: 100–12.

—— (1965), *Sorcery in its Social Context*. Manchester: Manchester University Press.

—— (1968), Notes on Chewa Rituals. *African Studies,* 27/1: 3–14.

Maugham, R.C.F. (1910), *Zambezia*. London: Murray.

Metcalfe, M. (1956), Some rock paintings in Nyasaland. *Nyasaland J.* 9/1: 58–70.

Mills, D.S. (1911), *What we do in Nyasaland*. London: UMCA.

Mitchell, C. (1956), *The Yao Village*. Manchester: Manchester University Press.

Mlenga, D.K.C. (1982), Nyawu initiation rites in Dowa District. Chancellor College, Zomba: Seminar Papers, African Traditional Religion.

Morris, B. (1962), A denizen of the evergreen forest. *African Wildlife,* 16: 117–121.

—— (1984), The Pragmatics of Folk Classifications. *J Ethnobiology,* 41/1: 45–60.

—— (1985), Chewa conceptions of disease – symptoms and etiologies. *Society Malawi Journal,* 38/1: 14–43.

—— (1987), *Common Mushrooms of Malawi*. Oslo: Fungi Flora.

—— (1991B), Mwanawamphepi: Children of the wind. *Nyala,* 15/1: 1–17.

—— (1994B), Animals as meat and meat as food: Reflections on meat-eating in Southern Malawi. *Food and Foodways,* 6/1: 19–41.

—— (1995), Wildlife Depredations in Malawi: The historical dimension. *Nyala,* 18: 17–24.

—— (1996), *Chewa Medical Botany*. Intern. African Institute Hamburg: Lit.

——(1996B), Hunting and the Gnostic Vision. *J Human & Environment Society,* 1/2: 13–39.

——(1996C), A Short History of Wildife Conservation in Malawi. Centre African Studies Occ. Papers No 64 Edinburgh University.

——(1998), *The Power of Animals: An Ethnography.* Oxford: Berg.

——(1998B), The Powers of Nature. *Anthropology and Medicine,* 5/1: 81–101.

Msiska, A.W.C. (1995), The spread of Islam in Malawi and its impact on Yao rites of passage 1870–1960. *Society Malawi Journal,* 48/1: 49–86.

Msiska, S.K. (1997), *Golden Buttons: Christianity and Traditional Religion among the Tumbuka.* Blantye: Claim.

Mtila, A. (1980), In what ways have Muslim Ayao of Malawi been affected by adherence to Islam. Chancellor College, Zomba: History Seminar Paper.

Mumba, L. (1930), The Religion of my fathers. *Intern. Rev. Missions,* 19: 362–76.

Murray, S.S. (1922/1932), *A Handbook of Nyasaland.* London: Crown Agents.

Musapole, A.C. (1984), The Chewa concept of God and its implications for Christian faith. Zomba University Malawi: MA thesis.

Mvula, E.S.T. (1992), The performance of Gule Wamkulu, *in* C Kamlongera (ed.) *Kubvina: Dance and Theatre in Malawi.* Zomba: University Malawi pp. 34–57.

Nazombe, A. (1981), Spirit possession songs and social tensions: a comparative study of Vimbuzza and Nantongwe. University York: Conference Paper, Literature and Society in Africa.

——(1988), Nantongwe: a Lomwe spirit possession ritual. *Religion in Malawi,* 2/1: 15–18.

——(1990), The theme of marriage in Nantongwe spirit possession songs. *Tizame* (UNESCO), 2: 11–14.

Nkondiwa, G. et al. (1977), Yao traditions III Dept. History. Chancellor College, Zomba: University Malawi.

Ntara, S.J. (1973), *The History of the Chewa* (*Mbiri Ya Achewa*). Weisbaden: F Steiner. (Originally published 1950.)

Nurse, G.D. (1978), *Clanship in Central Malawi.* Wein: Acta Ethn. et Linguist. Series Africana 12.

——(1988), Review of G Kubik. *Nyau Man,* 23/2: 391.

Pachai, B. (1973), *Malawi: The History of the Nation.* London: Longman.

Paliani, S.A. (1971), *1930 Kunadza Mchape.* Lilongwe: Likumi Press.

Bibliography

Peltzer, P.E. (1987), *Some Contributions of Traditional Healing Practices towards psychological health care in Malawi.* Eschborn: Fachbuchhandling for Psychologia.

Peters, P.E. (1997), Against the odds: Matriliny, Land and Gender in the Shire Highlands of Malawi. *Critique of Anthropology*, 17/2: 189–210.

Phiri, D.D. (1982), *From Nguni to Ngoni.* Limbe: Popular Publ.

Phiri, I.A. (1996), The Chisumphi Cult: The Role of Women in preserving the environment, *in* RR Ruether (ed.) *Women Healing Earth*, London: SCM Press pp. 161–71.

—— (1997), *Women, Presbyterianism and Patriarchy.* Blantyre: Claim.

Phiri, K.M. (1975), Chewa history in Central Malawi and the us of oral tradition 1600–1920. Madison Univeristy, Wisonsin, PhD thesis.

—— (1983), Some changes in the matrilineal Family System among the Chewa of Malawi. *J. African History,* 24: 257–74.

—— (1988), Pre-Colonial States in Central Malawi. *Society Malawi J*, 41/1: 1–29.

Phiri, K.M. et al. (1977), Amachinga Yao traditions II. Zomba, Chancellor College: Dept. History.

Price, T. (1964), Malawi rain cults. University Edinburgh, Seminar Proceedings: Religion in Africa, pp. 114–24.

Probst, P. (1995), Dancing aids, moral discourses and ritual authority in Central Malawi. Berlin: Institute fur Ethnologie Arbeitspapiere No 66.

Rangeley, W.H.J. (1948), Notes on Chewa Tribal Law. *Nyasaland J*, 1/3: 5–68.

—— (1949–1950) Nyau in Kota Kota District. *Nyasaland J*, 2/2: 35–49, 3/2: 19–33.

—— (1952), Makewana, mother of all people. *Nyasaland: J*, 5/2: 31–50.

—— (1953), Mbona – the Rainmaker. *Nyasaland J*, 6/1: 8–27.

Rattray, R.S. (with A Hetherwick) (1907), *Some Folklore Stories and Songs in Chinyanja.* London: SPCK.

Rau, W.E. (1979), Chewa religion and the Ngoni conquest, *in* J.M Schoffeleers (ed.) *Guardians of the Land,* Gwero: Mambo pp. 131–46.

Rita-Ferreira, A. (1968), The Nyau Brotherhood among Mozambique Chewa. *S. African Journal Science,* 64: 20–24.

Rogers, B. (1980), *The Domestication of Women.* London: Tavistock.

Ross, A.C. (1969), The Political Role of the Witchfinder in Southern Malawi 1964–65, *in* R Willis (ed.) *Witchcraft and Healing.* Edinburgh: Centre African Studies pp. 55–64.

Sanderson, G.M. (1954), *A Dictionary of the Yao Language,* Zomba: Govn. Press.

—— (1955), Inyago – the picture models of Yao initiation ceremonies. *Nyasaland Journal*, 8/2: 36–57.

Schoffeleers, J.M. (1966), Mbona, the Guardian Spirit of the Mang'anja. Oxford University B Litt. thesis.

—— (1967), Evil spirits (afiti) and rites of exorcism in the Lower Shire. Valley, Malawi, Limbe: Montford Press.

—— (1968), Symbolic and social aspects of spirit worship among the Mang'anja, PhD thesis, Oxford University.

—— (1968), Evil spirits and problems of human reproduction in the Lower Shire Valley, *Malawi Medical Bulletin,* 2: 12–27.

—— (1969), Social functional aspects of spirits possession in the Lower Shire Valley. University East Africa, Religious Studies Papers, pp. 51–63.

—— (1971), The Religious significance of bush fires in Malawi. *Cahiers des Religions Africaines,* 10: 271–87.

—— (1972), The meaning and use of the name Malawi in oral traditions and pre-colonial documents, *in* B Pachai (ed.) *The early history of Malawi*. London: Longman, pp. 91–103.

—— (1972), The history and political role of the M'bona cult among the Mang'anja, *in* T.O. Ranger and I.N. Kimamabo (ed.) *The Historical study of African Religion*. London: Heinemann, pp. 73–94.

—— (1975), The interaction of the M'bona cult and Christianity 1859–1963, *in* T.O. Ranger and J. Weller (ed.) (1975) *op. cit.,* pp. 14–29.

—— (1976), The Nyau Societies: our present understanding. *Society Malawi J*, 29/1: 59–68.

—— (1979), *Guardians of the Land*. Gwero: Mambo.

—— (1985), *Pentecostalism and Neo-Traditionalism*. Amsterdam: Free University Press.

—— (1992), *River of Blood*. Madison: University Wisconsin Press.

—— (1997), *Religion and the Dramatisation of Life*. Blantyre: Claim.

Schoffeleers, J.M. and I. Linden (1972), The resistance of the Nyau Societies to the Roman Catholic Missions in Colonial Malawi, *in* T.O. Ranger and I.N. Kamambo (ed.) *op. cit.,* pp. 252–76.

Schoffelleers, J.M. and A.A. Roscoe (1985), *Land of fire: Oral literature from Malawi*. Limbe: Popular Publ.

Scott, D.C. (1929), *Dictionary of the Nyanja Language*. London: Lutterworth.

Sembereka, G. (1990), The place of Gulu Wamkulu in dreams attributed to spirits. Blantyre, Museum of Malawi: unpublished paper.

—— (1995), Women and sex in Gulu Wamkulu. Blantyre, Museum of Malawi: Unpublished Paper.

Shepperson, G. (1966), The Jumbo of Kota Kota and Some aspects of Islam in British Central Africa, *in* I.M Lewis (ed.) *Islam in Tropical Africa*. London: Hutchinson, pp. 253–65.

Soka, L.D. (1953), *Mbiri Ya Alomwe*. Limbe: Malawi Publ.

Soko, B.J. (1985), The Vimbuza phenomenon : disease or art? Zomba: Chancellor College, unpublished paper.

—— (1987), An Introduction to the Vimbuza phenomenon. *Religion in Malawi*, 1: 9–13.

—— (1988), The Vimbuza possession cult: the onset of the disease. *Religion in Malawi*, 2: 11–15.

Stannus, H.S. (1910), Notes on some tribes of British Central Africa. *J. Royal Anthr. Institute*, 40: 285–335.

—— (1922), The Wayao of Nyasaland. *Harvard African Studies III*, pp. 229–372.

Stannus, H.S. and J.B. Davey (1913), The initiation ceremony for boys among the Yao of Nyasaland. *J. Royal Anthr. Institute*, 42: 119–23.

Stigland, C. (1907), Notes on the natives of Nyasaland NE Rhodesia and Portugese Zambezia, their arts, customs and modes of subsistence. *J. Royal Anthr. Institute*, 37: 119–32.

Swann, A.J. (1910), *Fighting the Slave Hunters in Central Africa*. London: Seeley.

Sweeney, R.C.H. (1970), *Animal Life in Malawi*. 2 Vols. Beograd: Yugoslavia.

Tembo, K.C. and T.B. Phiri (1993), Sexually based cultural practices implicated in the transmission of HIV/Aids. *Society Malawi J*, 456/1: 44–49.

Tew, M. (1950), *Peoples of the Lake Nyasa Region*. Oxford: Oxford University Press.

Vail, H.L. (1979), Religion, Language and the Tribal Myth: the Tumbuka and Chewa of Malawi, *in* M. Schoffeleers (1979) (ed.) *op. cit.*, Gwero: Mambo, pp. 209–233.

—— (1983), The Political Economy of East-Central Africa, *in* D. Birmingham and P.M. Martin (eds) *History of Central Africa*. Vol 2 London: Longman.

Vail, H.L. and L. White (1989), Tribalism in the Political History of Malawi, *in* L. Vail (ed.) *The Creation of Tribalism in Southern Africa*. London: J Currey, pp. 151–92.

Van Breugel, J. (1976), Some traditional Chewa religious beliefs and practices. Lilongwe, White Fathers, unpublished manuscript.

Van Dijk, R.A. (1992), Young Puritan Preachers in Post-Independence Malawi, *Africa,* 62/2: 159–89.

—— (1995), Fundamentalism and its moral geography in Malawi. *Critique of Anthropology,* 15/2: 171–91.

Wallis, J.P.R. (1952), (ed.) *The Zambezi Journal of James Stewart 1862–63.* London: Chatto & Windus.

Werner, A. (1906), *The Natives of British Central Africa.* London: Constable.

—— (1968), *Myths and Legends of the Bantu.* London: Cass. (Originally published 1933.)

White, L. (1987), *Magomero: Portrait of an African Village.* Cambridge: Cambridge University Press.

Wiese, C. (1983), *Expedition to East Central Africa 1888–91.* Ed. HW Langworthy. London: Collings.

Williamson, J. (1940), The growth and development of Africans in Nyasaland from birth upwards. Unpublished manuscript.

—— (1956), Salt and potatoes in the life of the Chewa. *Nyasaland J,* 9: 82–7.

—— (1975), *Useful Plants of Malawi.* Zomba: University Malawi.

Wishlade, R.L. (1965), *Sectarianism in Southern Nyasaland.* IAI Oxford University Press.

Wrigley, C. (1988), The River God and the historians: myth in the Shire Valley and elsewhere. *J. Afr. Hist.,* 29/3: 367–83.

Yoshida, K. (1992), Masks and Transformation among the Chewa of Eastern Zambia, *Senri Ethnol. Studies,* 31: 203–73.

—— (1993), Masks and secrecy among the Chewa. *African Arts,* 26/2: 34–45.

Young, E.D. (1868), *The Search after Livingstone.* London: Simpkin.

Young, T.C. (1931), *Notes on Customs and folklore of the Tumbuka-Kamanga Peoples.* Livingstonia: The Mission Press.

—— (1950), Kinship among the Chewa of Rhodesia and Nyasaland. *African studies,* 9: 29–31.

—— (1950), The idea of God in Northern Nyasaland, *in* E.W Smith (ed.) *African Ideas of God.* London: Edinburgh House Press, pp. 36–60.

Young, T.C. and H. Banda (1946), (eds) *Our African Way of Life.* London: University Society Christian Literature.

3. General

Abraham, W.E. (1962), *The Mind of Africa.* London: Weidenfield & Nicolson.

Bibliography

Abu-Lughod, L. (1991), Writing against Culture, *in* R.G. Fox (ed.) *Recapturing Anthropology.* Santa Fe: School of American Research Publishers, pp. 137–62.

Adam, B. (1994), Perceptions of Time, *in* T. Ingold (ed.) *Companion Encyclopedia of Anthropology.* London: Routledge, pp. 503–26.

Adams, C.J. (1990), *The Sexual Politics of Meat.* Cambridge: Polity Press.

Allen, M. (1967), *Male Cults and Secret Initiations in* Melanesia, Melbourne University Press.

Alpers, C.A. (1975), *Ivory and Slaves in East Central Africa.* London: Heinemann.

Anati, E. (1985), The rock art of Tanzania and the East African sequence. *Bull. del Centro Camuno di Stud. Preistorici,* 23: 15–68.

—— (1994), *World Rock Art: the Primordial Language.* Valacamonica, Italy: Edizoni del Centro.

Anderson, P. (1983), *In the Tracks of Historical Materialism.* London: Verso.

Appadurai, A. (1996), *Modernity at Large: Cultural Dimensions of globalisation.* Minneapolis: University Minnesota Press.

Archer, M.S. (1998), *Culture and Agency.* Cambridge: Cambridge University Press.

—— (1995), *Realist Social Theory.* Cambridge: Cambridge University Press.

Arendt, H. (1978), *The Life of the Mind.* New York: Harcourt Brace.

Aristotle (1925), *The Nicomacheon Ethics.* Trans. D Ross. Oxford: Oxford University Press.

Armour, R.A. (1986), *Gods and Myths of Ancient Egyptians.* Cairo: American University Press.

Armstrong, K. (1993), *A History of God.* London: Heinemann.

Assister, A. (1996), *Enlightened Women.* London: Routledge.

Atran, S. (1990), *Cognitive Foundations of Natural History.* Cambridge: Cambridge University Press.

Barrett, W. (1986), *Death of the Soul.* Oxford: Oxford University Press.

Barnard, A. (1992), *Hunters and Herders of Southern Africa.* Cambridge: Cambridge University Press.

Barth, F. (1975), *Ritual and Knowledge among the Baktaman of New Guinea,* New Haven: Yale University Press.

—— (1992), Towards greater Naturalism in Conceptualising Societies, *in* A. Kuper (ed.) *Conceptualising Society.* London: Routledge, pp. 17–33.

—— (1994), A Personal View, *in* R. Borofsky (ed.) *Assessing Cultural Anthropology.* New York: McGraw Hill, pp. 349–61.

Bibliography

Beattie, J. (1980), *Representations of the Self in Traditional Africa*. Africa, 50/3: 313–20.

Beidelman, T.O. (1986), *Moral Imagination in Kaguru Modes of Thought*. Bloomington: Indiana University Press.

—— (1997), *The Cool Knife*. Washington: Smithsonian Institute Press.

Bell, C. (1992), *Ritual Theory: Ritual Practice*. Oxford: Oxford University Press.

Benton, T. (1993), *Natural Relations*. London: Versa.

Berglund, A. (1976), *Zulu Thought-Patterns and Symbolism*. London: Hurst.

Berlin, B. (1992), *Ethnobiological Classification*. New Jersey: Princeton University Press.

Bhaskar, R. (1975), *A Realist Theory of Science*. Brighton, Sussex: Harvester Press.

—— (1979), *The Possibility of Naturalism*. Brighton, Sussex: Harvester Press.

Biesele, M. (1993), *Women Like Meat*. Bloomington: Indiana University Press.

Binkley, D.A. (1987), *Avatar of Power: Southern Kuba masquerade figures*. Africa, 57/1: 75–97.

Bird-David, N. (1990), The Giving Environment, *Current Anthropology*, 31: 189–96.

Blakely, T.D. (1994), *Religion in Africa*. London: J Currey.

Blakney, R.B. (1941), *Meister Eckhart*. New York: Harper & Row.

Bloch, M. (1974), Symbols, song, dance and features of articulation. *European Journal Sociology*, 15: 55–81.

—— (1977), The Past and the Present in the Present. *Man*, 12: 278–92.

—— (1982), Death, women and power *in* M. Bloch and J. Parry (ed.) *Death and the Regeneration of life*. Cambridge: Cambridge University Press, pp. 211–230.

—— (1986), *From Blessing to Violence*. Cambridge: Cambridge University Press.

—— (1989), *Ritual, History and Power*. L.S.E Mongr. 58. London: Athlone Press.

—— (1992), *Prey into Hunter*. Cambridge: Cambridge University Press.

Bloch, M. and J. Parry (1982), *Death and the Regeneration of Life*. Cambridge: Cambridge University Press.

Bockie, S. (1993), *Death and the Invisible Powers*. Bloomington: Indiana University Press.

Bookchin, M. (1990), *The Philosophy of Social Ecology*. Montreal: Black Rose Books.

——(1995), *Re-Enchanting Humanity*. London: Cassell.
Boudet, J. (1964), *Man and the Beast, Translation A Carter*. London: Bodley Head.
Bourdieu, P. (1990), *The Logic of Practice*. Cambridge: Polity Press.
Bourdillon, M.F.C. (1976), *The Shona Peoples*. Gweru: Mambo Press.
Brown, D.E. (1991), *Animals of the Soul*. Rockport, Mass: Element.
Brumann, C. (1999), Writing for culture: why a successful concept should not be discarded. *Current Anthropology*, 40: 1–27.
Bruno, G. (1964), *The Expulsion of the Triumphant Beast*. (ed. introduction AD Im erti). Lincoln: University Nebraska Press.
Burofsky, R. (1994), (ed.) *Assessing Cultural Anthropology*. New York: McGraw Hill.
Busby, C. (1997), Permeable and partible persons. *J. Royal Anthropology Institute*, 3: 261: 78.
Campbell, J. (1959) *The Masks of God: primitive mythology*. Harmondsworth : Penguin.
Caplan, P. (1987), *The Cultural Construction of Sexuality*. London: Tavistock.
Clark, S.R.C. (1988), Is Humanity a Natural Kind, *in* T. Ingold (ed.) *What is an Animal?* London: Routledge, pp. 17–34.
——(1993) *How to think about the Earth*. London: Cassell.
Classen, C. (1993), *Worlds of Sense*. London: Routledge.
Collard, A. (1988), *Rape of the Wild*. London: Women's Press.
Collier, A. (1994), *Critical Realism*. London: Verso.
Collins, R. (1981), On the Microfoundations of Macrosociology. *American Journal Sociology*, 86: 984–1014.
Colson, E. (1962), *The Plateau Tonga of Northern Rhodesia*. Manchester: Manchester University Press.
Corin, E. (1998), Refiguring the person, *in* M Lambek & A Strathern (eds) *Bodies and Persons*. Cambridge: Cambridge University Press.
Crader, D.C. (1984), *Hunters in Iron Age Malawi*. Lilongwe: Department Antiquities Publication No: 21.
Das, V. (1994), The Anthropological Discourse in India, *in* R. Borofsky (ed.) *op. cit.*, pp. 133–44.
De Certeau, M. (1984), *The Practice of Everyday Life*. Translation S Rendall. Berkeley: University California Press.
De Heusch, L. (1985), *Sacrifice in Africa*. Manchester: Manchester University Press.
Delluc, B. & G. (1990), *Discovering Lascaux*. Bourdeaux: Sud Ouest.
Descartes, R. (1970), *Philosophical Letters*. Ed. A Kenny. Oxford: Clarendon Press.

Descola, P. (1996), Constructing Natures: Symbolic ecology and Social practice, *in* P Descola and G Palsson (ed) *Nature and Society.* London: Routledge, pp. 82–102.

Devisch, R. (1993), *Weaving the Threads of Life.* Chicago: University Chicago Press.

Devitt, M. (1984), *Realism and Truth.* Oxford: Blackwell.

Doke, C.M. (1936), Games, plays and dances of the !Khomani Bushmen. *Bantu Studies*, 10: 461–71.

Douglas, M. (1954), The Lele of Kasai, *in* D. Forde (ed.) *African Worlds.* IAI Oxford: Oxford University Press, pp. 1–26.

—— (1966), *Purity and Danger.* Harmondsworth: Penguin.

—— (1970), *Natural Symbols.* Harmondsworth: Penguin.

—— (1975), *Implicit Meanings.* London: Routledge & Kegan Paul.

Droogers, A. (1980), *The Dangerous Journey.* The Hague: Mouton.

Eliade, M. (1958), *Rites and Myths of Initiation.* New York: Harper & Row.

Elias, N. (1978), *Time – An Essay.* Oxford: Blackwell.

Ellen, R.F. (1993), *The Cultural Relations of Classification.* Cambridge: Cambridge University Press.

—— (1996), The Cognitive Geometry of Nature, *in* P. Descola and G. Palsson (eds) *Nature and Society.* London: Routledge, pp 103–123.

Epictetus (1995), *The Discourses.* Trans R Hard. London: Dent.

Eriksen, T.H. (1993), *Ethnicity and Nationalism.* London: Pluto Press.

Evans-Pritchard, E.E. (1956), *Nuer Religion.* Oxford: Oxford University Press.

Fabian, J. (1983), *Time and the other.* New York: Colombia University Press.

Fardon, R. (1990), *Between God, the Dead and the Wild.* Edinburgh: Edinburgh University Press.

Fernandez, J. (1982), *Bwiti.* Princeton University Press.

Fiddes, N. (1991), *Meat: A Natural Symbol.* London: Routledge.

Flader, S.L. (1974), *Thinking Like a Mountain.* Madison: Unversity Wisconsin Press.

Foltz, B.V. (1995), *Inhabiting the Earth.* New Jersey: Humanities Press.

Fortes, M. (1987), The Concept of the Person, *in* J Goody (ed) *Religion, Morality and the Person.* Cambridge: Cambridge University Press.

Foucault, M. (1979), T*he History of Sexuality.* Volume 1 Harmondsworth: Penguin.

—— (1980), *Power/Knowledge.* Brighton: Harvester Press.

Frazer, J.G. (1992), *The Golden Bough.* London: Macmillan.

Fromm, E. (1949), *Man for Himself.* London: Routledge & Kegan Paul.

Bibliography

—— (1984), *On Disobedience and other Essays*. London: Routledge & Kegan Paul.

Garlake, P. (1987), *The Painted Caves. Harare*: Modus Publishers.

Geertz, C. (1973), *The Interpretation of Culture*. New York: Basic Books.

Gelfand, M. (1959), *Shona Ritual*. Cape Town: Juta.

Gell, A. (1992), *The Anthropology of Time*. Oxford: Berg.

Gellner, E. (1995), *Anthropology and Politics*. Oxford: Blackwell.

Giddens, A. (1984), *The Constitution of Society*. Cambridge: Polity Press.

Ginzburg, C. (1991), *Ecstasies*. London: Hutchinson.

Goodman, F.D. (1992), *Ecstacy, Ritual and Alternative Realities*. Bloomington: Indiana University Press.

Goudsblom, J. (1992), *Fire and Civilisation*. London: Penguin.

Gould, S.J. (1987), *Time's Arrow, Time's Cycle*. London: Penguin.

Graham, A.D. (1973), *The Gardener's of Eden*. London: Allen & Unwin.

Greenwood, J.D. (1997), (ed) *The Mark of the Social*. Lanham MA: Rowman & Littlefield.

Griaule, M. (1965), *Conversations with Ogotemmeli*. Oxford: Oxford University Press.

Guenther, M. (1988), Animals in Bushmen Thought, Myth and Art, *in* T Ingold et al. (ed.) *Hunters and Gatherers*, Vol 2. Oxford: Berg, pp. 192–202.

Guthrie, S. (1993), *Faces in the Clouds*. Oxford: Oxford University Press.

Gyeke, K. (1987), *An Essay in African Philosophical Thought*. Cambridge: Cambridge University Press.

Hallowell, A.I. (1958), Ojibway Metaphysics of being and the perceptions of persons, *in* R. Taguire & L Petrullo (ed.) *Person Perception and Interpersonal behaviour*. Stamford University Press, pp. 63–85.

Harris, M. (1980), *Cultural Materialism*. New York: Random House.

Hauser-Schaublin, B. (1993), Blood: cultural effectiveness of biological conditions, *in* B.D. Miller (ed.) *Sex and Gender Hierachies*. Cambridge: Cambridge University Press, pp. 83–107.

Heald, S. (1982), *The Making of Men. Africa*, 52/1: 15–35.

Heelas, P. & A. Lock (1981), (ed) *Indigenous Psychologies*. London: Academic Press.

Hegel, G.W.F. (1995), *Lectures in the History of Philosophy*, Vol. 3. Lincoln: University Nebraska Press.

Heidegger, M. (1959), *An Introduction to Metaphysics*. Trans. R Manheim. New Haven: Yale University Press.

——. (1962), *Being and Time*. Oxford: Blackwell.

Henderson, J.L. and H. Oakes (1963), *The Wisdom and the Serpent*. New Jersey: Princeton University Press.

Herbert, E.W. (1993), *Iron, Gender and Power*. Bloomington: Indiana University Press.

Herdt, G.H. (1982), (ed.) *Rituals of Manhood*. Berkeley: California University Press.

Hicks, D. (1976), *Tetum Ghosts and Kin*. Palo Alto, Mayfield.

Hill, K. (1982), *Hunting and Human Evolution. J Human Evolution*, 11: 527–44.

Hinde, R.A. (1987), *Individuals, Relationships and Culture*. Cambridge: Cambridge University Press.

Hodgson, J. (1982), *The God of the Xhosa*. Cape Town: Oxford University Press.

Hollinger, R. (1994), *Postmodernism and the Social Sciences*. London: Sage.

Hollis, M. (1994), *The Philosophy of Social Science*. Cambridge: Cambridge University Press.

Holy, L. (1986), *Strategies and Norms in a Changing Matrilineal Society*. Cambridge: Cambridge University Press.

Horton, R. (1983), Social Psychologies: African and Western, *in* M. Fortes *Oedipus and Job in West African Religion*. Cambridge: Cambridge University Press.

Howell, S. (1984), *Society and Cosmos*. Oxford: Oxford University Press.

—— (1996), Nature in culture and culture in nature? Chewong ideas of 'humans' and other species, *in* P. Descola and G. Palsson (eds) *Nature and Society*. London: Routledge, pp. 127–44.

Howell, S. and M. Melhuus (1993), The Study of Kinship. The Study of Person: The study of Gender, *in* T. Der Valle (ed.) *Gendered Anthropology*. London: Routledge, pp. 38–53.

Hultrantz, A. (1979), *The Religions of the American Indians*. Berkeley: University California Press.

Humphrey, C. (1996), *Shamans and Elders*. Oxford: Clarendon Press.

Huntington, R. and P. Metcalf (1979), *Celebrations of Death*. Cambridge: Cambridge University Press.

Ingold, T. (1988), (ed.) *What is an Animal?* London: Routledge. (1994 edition).

—— (1986), *The Appropriation of Nature*. Manchester: Manchester University Press.

—— (1991), From Trust to Domination: An Alternative History of Human-Animal Relations. Paper Conference: Animals and Society. Edinburgh Royal Society.

—— (1993), The Art of Translation in a Continous World, *in* Gisli Palsson (ed.) *Beyond Boundaries*. Oxford: Berg.

—— (1994), (ed.) *Companion Encyclopedia of Anthropology*. London: Routledge.

Jackson, M. (1989), *Paths Towards a Clearing*. Bloomington: Indiana University Press.

Jackson, M. and I. Karp (1990), (ed.) *Personhood and Agency*. Stockholm: Almquist & Wiksells.

Jacobson-Widding, A. (1979), *Red-White-Black as a Mode of Thought*. Stockholm: Almquist & Wiksells.

Janzen, J.M. (1992), *Ngoma*. Berkeley: University California Press.

Johnson, M. (1987), *The Body in the Mind*. Chicago: University of Chicago Press.

Katz, R. (1982), *Boiling Energy*. Harvard University Press.

Kent, S. (1989), (ed.) *Farmers as Hunters*. Cambridge: Cambridge University Press.

Kenyatta, J. (1938), *Facing Mount Kenya*. London: Secker & Warburg.

Knight, C. (1991), *Blood Relations*. New Haven: Yale University Press.

Krell, D.F. (1978), (ed.) *Martin Heidegger: Basic Writings*. London: Routledge.

Krige, E.J. and J.D. (1943), *The Realm of a Rain-Queen*. Oxford: Oxford University Press.

Kroeber, A. and C. Kluckhohn (1963), *Culture: A Critical Review of concepts and Definitions*. New York: Random House.

Kuhn, H. (1956), *The Rock Pictures of Europe*. London: Sidgwick & Jackson.

Kuper, A. (1982), *Wives for Cattle*. London: Routledge & Kegan Paul.

La Fontaine, J.S. (1985), *Initiation*. Harmondsworth: Penguin.

Lambek, M. (1998), Body and Mind in Mind, Body and Mind in Body, *in* M. Lambek and A. Strathern (eds) *Bodies and Persons*. Cambridge: Cambridge University Press, pp. 103–26.

Lambek, M. and A. Strathern (1998), (ed.) *Bodies and Persons*. Cambridge: Cambridge University Press.

Lan, D. (1985), *Guns and Rain*. London: J. Currey.

Laude, J. (1971), *The Arts of Black Africa*. Berkeley: University California Press.

Lawson, A.J. (1991), *Cave Art*. Princes Risborough: Shire.

Layder, D. (1994), *Understanding Social Theory*. London: Sage.

Leakey, M. (1983), *Africa's Vanishing Art: Rock Paintings of Tanzania*. London: Hamish Hamilton.

Leclerc, I. (1958), *Whiteheads Metaphysics*. Bloomington: Indiana University Press.

Lee, R.B. (1979), *The Kung San*. Cambridge: Cambridge University Press.

Leroi-Gourhan, A. (1982), *The Dawn of European Art*. Cambridge: Cambridge University Press.

Levine, R.A. (1982), The Self and its Development in an African Society, *in* R. Lee (ed.) *Psychological Theories of the Self*. New York: Plenum Press, pp. 43–65.

Levi-Strauss, C. (1966), *The Savage Mind*. London: Widenfield & Nicolson.

Lewis, H.S. (1998), The Misrepresentation of Anthropology and its Consequences, *American Anthropologist*.

Lewis, I.M. (1971), *Ecstatic Religion*. Harmondsworth: Penguin.

Lewis-Williams, J.D. (1983), *The Rock Art of Southern Africa*. Cambridge: Cambridge University Press.

——(1990), *Discovering Southern African Rock Art*. Cape Town: Philip.

Lewis-Williams, J.D. and T.A. Dowson (1988), The signs of the times: Entopic Phenomena in Upper Paleolithic Art. *Current Anthropology*, 29: 201–45.

Liebenberg, L. (1990), *The Art of Tracking*. Claremont: D. Philip.

Lipuma, E.1998 Modernity and Forms of Personhood in Melanesia, *in* M. Lambek and A. Strathern (eds) *Bodies and Persons*. Cambridge: Cambridge University Press, pp. 53–79.

Lonsdale, S. (1981), *Animals and the Origins of Dance*. London: Thomas & Hudson.

MacCormack, C.P. and A. Draper (1987), Social and cognitive aspects of female sexuality in Jamaica, *in* P. Caplan (ed.) 1987 *op. cit.,* pp. 143–65.

McFadden, P. (1992), Sex, Sexuality and the Problem of aids in Africa, *in* R. Mena (ed.) *Gender in Southern Africa*. Harare: Sapes, pp. 157–95.

MacMurray, J. (1957), *The Self as Agent*. London: Faber.

Manicas, P.T. (1987), *A History and Philosophy of the Social Sciences*. New York: Blackwell.

Marcus, G. (1994), After the Critique of Ethnography, *in* R. Borofsky (1994) *op. cit.,* pp. 40–54.

Marsella, A.J. (1985), Culture, Self and Mental Disorder, *in* AJ Marsella et al. *Culture and Self*. New York: Tavistock, pp. 281–308.

Marshall, L. (1976), *The !Kung of Nyaenyae*. Cambridge Mass: Harvard University Press.

Martin, M.L. (1975) *Kimbangu*. Oxford: Blackwell.

Marx, K. (1973), *Grundrisse*. Trans. M Nicolaus. Harmondsworth: Penguin.

Mayr, E. (1982), *The Growth of Biological Thought*. Cambridge: Harvard University Press.

Bibliography

Mbiti, J.S. (1969), *African Religions and Philosophy*. London: Heinemann.

Merton, R.K. (1957), *Social Theory and Social Structure*. Glencoe, Illinois: Free Press.

Miller, D. (1983), *The Pocket Popper*. London: Fontana.

Mithen, S. (1993), Pictures in the mind. *Times Higher*, July 9: 17.

—— (1996), *The Prehistory of the Mind*. London: Thames & Hudson.

Moore, H. (1994), *A Passion for Difference*. Cambridge: Polity Press.

Morris, B. (1975), Jesus the Shaman. *New Humanist*, 92: 64–65.

—— (1985), The rise and fall of the human subject. *Man*, 20: 722–42.

—— (1985B), Gandhi, sex and power. *Freedom*, 46.

—— (1987), *Anthropological Studies of Religion*. Cambridge: Cambridge University Press.

—— (1989), Thoughts on Chinese Medicine. *Eastern Anthropology*, 42: 1–33.

—— (1991), *Western Conceptions of the Individual*. Oxford: Berg.

—— (1994), *Anthropology of the Self*. London: Pluto.

—— (1997), In Defence of Realism and Truth. *Critique of Anthropology*, 17/3: 313–40.

Mudimbe, V.Y. (1988), *The Invention of Africa*. Bloomington: Indiana University Press.

Mundkur, B. (1983), *The Cult of the Serpent*. Albany: State University New York Press.

Murdoch, I. (1992), *Metaphysics as a Guide to Morals*. Harmondsworth: Penguin.

Murphy, R.F. (1990), The dialectics of deeds and words. *in* R. Burofsky (1994) (ed.) *op. cit.,* pp. 55–61.

Murray, M. (1931), *The God of the Witches*. Oxford: Oxford University Press.

Nelson, R.K. (1983), *Make Prayers to the Raven*. Chicago: Chicago University Press.

Noel, D.C. (1997), *The Soul of Shamanism*. New York: Continuum.

Noske, B. (1997), *Beyond Boundaries: Humans and Animals*. Montreal: Black Rose Books.

Oakley, A. (1972), *Sex, Gender and Society*. New York: Harper & Row.

O'Neill, J. (1993), *Ecology, Polity and Politics*. London: Routledge.

Pfeiffer, J.E. (1982), *The Creative Explosion*. New York: Harper & Row.

Phillipson, D.W. (1976), *The Prehistory of Eastern Zambia*. Nairobi: British Institute Memoir No. 6.

Poole, F.J.P. (1994), Socialisation, enculturation and the development of personal identity, *in* T Ingold (1994) *op. cit.,* (ed.) pp. 831–60.

Popper, K. (1992), *In Search of a Better World*. London: Routledge.

Bibliography

Porpora, D.V. (1989), Four Concepts of Social Structure. *J. Theory Society Behaviour*, 19/2: 195–211.

Radcliffe-Brown, A.R. (1952), *Structure and Function in Primitive Society*. London: Cohen & West.

Ranger, T. (1983), The Invention of Tradition in Colonial Africa. *in* E. Hobsbawm and T. Ranger (ed.) *The Invention of Tradition*. Cambridge: Cambridge University Press.

Reichard, G.A. (1950), *Navaho Religion: A Study of Symbolism*. New Jersey: Princeton University Press.

Richards, A.I. (1950), Some types of family structure amongst the Central Bantu, *in* A.R Radcliffe-Brown and C.D Forde (eds) *African Systems of Kinship and Marriage*. London: Oxford University Press, pp. 207–51.

—— (1956), *Chisungu*. London: Tavistock.

Riesman, P. (1986), The person and life-cycle in African social life and thought. *African Studies Rev.*, 29/2: 71–138.

Ritvo, H. (1987), *The Animal Estate*. Harmondsworth: Penguin.

Robinson, M.H. and Tiger, L. (1991), (eds) *Man and Beast Revisited*. Washington: Smithsonian Institute Press.

Rowan, A.N. (1988), (ed.) *Animals and People Sharing the World*. Hanover: Tufts University.

Rubin, G. (1984), Thinking Sex: notes for a radical theory in the politics of sexuality, *in* C.S Vance (ed.) *Pleasure and Danger*. London: Harper Collins, pp. 267–319.

Samuel, G. (1990), *Mind, Body and Culture*. Cambridge: Cambridge University Press.

Sandelands, L.E. (1997), The Body and the Social, *in* J.D. Greenwood (1997) (ed.) *op. cit.*, pp. 133–152.

Sarup, M. (1996), *Identity, Culture and the Postmodern World*. Edinburgh: Edinburgh University Press.

Saunders, N.J. (1995), *Animal Spirits*. London: Macmillan.

Sauer, C.O. (1981), *Selected Essays 1963–1975*. Berkeley: Turtle Island Publishers.

Schapera, I. (1940), *Married Life in an African Tribe*. (1971 ed.) Harmondsworth: Penguin.

Schwartz, T. G.M. White and C. Lutz (1992), (ed.) *New Directions in Psychological Anthropology*. Cambridge: Cambridge University Press.

Scruton, R. (1986), *Sexual Desire*. London: Weidenfield & Nicolson.

Secord, P.F. (1997), The Mark of the Social in the Social Sciences, *in* J.D.Greenwood (1997) (ed.) *op. cit.*, pp. 59–80.

Senghor, L. (1965), *Prose and Poetry*. London: Heinemann.

Serpell, J. (1986), *In the Company of Animals*. Oxford: Blackwell.

Seton, E.T. (1898), *Wild Animals I Have Known*. New York: Scribners.

Shweder, R.A. and E.J. Bourne (1984), Does the concept of the person vary cross-culturally, *in* R.A. Shweder and R.A. Levine (eds) *Culture Theory*. Cambridge: Cambridge University Press, pp. 158–99.

Smith, A. (1991), *National Identity*. Harmondsworth: Penguin.

Soloman, R.C. (1988), *Continental Philosophy since 1750*. Oxford: Oxford University Press.

Speck, F. (1938), Aboriginal conservators, *in* R. Nash (ed.) *Environment and Americans*. New York: Holt, Rinehard, pp. 74–8.

Sperber, D. (1975), *Rethinking Symbolism*. Cambridge: Cambridge University Press.

—— (1996), *Explaining Culture – A Naturalistic Approach*. Oxford: Blackwell.

Sproul, B.C. (1979), *Primal Myths*. New York: Harper Collins.

Stefaniszyn, B. (1954), African reincarnation re-examined. *African Studies*, 13: 131–146.

Steffens, L. (1931), *Autobiography*. New York: Harcourt Brace.

Steward, J.H. (1977), *Evolution and Ecology*. Urbana: University Illinois Press.

Strathern, M. (1988), *The Gender of the Gift*. Berkeley: University California Press.

—— (1992), Parts and Wholes: Refiguring Relationships in a post-plural world, *in* A. Kuper (1992) (ed.) *Reconceptualising Society*. London: Routledge, pp. 75–104.

Strauss, C. and N. Quinn (1997), *A Cognitive Theory of Cultural Meaning*. Cambridge: Cambridge University Press.

Sundkler, B.G.M. (1948), *Bantu Prophets in South Africa*. Oxford: Oxford University Press.

Swantz, M.L. (1970), *Ritual and Symbol in Transitional Zaramo Society*. Uppsala: Almquist & Wiksells.

Taylor, J.V. (1963), *The Primal Vision*. London: S.C.M. Press.

Tembo, M.S. (1985), The Concept of African Personality, *in* M.K. and K.W. Asante (eds) *African Culture*, Trenton NJ: African World Press, pp. 193–206.

Tempels, P. (1959), *Bantu Philosophy*. Paris: Presence Africaine.

Turnbull, C. (1965), *Wayward Servants*. New York: Natural History Press.

Turner, E. (1992), The Reality of Spirits. *Revision*, 15/1: 28–32.

—— (1992B), *Experiencing Ritual*. Philadelphia: University Pennsylvania Press.

Turner, J.H. (1997), The nature and dynamics of 'the social' among humans, *in* J.D. Greenwood (1997) (ed.) *op. cit.*, pp 105–31.

Turner, V.W. (1967), *The Forest of Symbols*. Ithaca: Cornell University Press.

—— (1968), *The Drums of Affliction*. Oxford: Clarendon Press.

—— (1974), *The Ritual Process*. Hamondsworth: Penguin.

—— (1975), *Revelation and Divination in Ndembu Ritual*. Ithaca: Cornell University Press.

Tyler, S. (1986), Post-modern ethnography, *in* J. Clifford and G. Marcus (eds) *Writing Culture*. Berkeley: University California Press, pp. 122–40.

Van Gennep, A. (1960), *The Rites of Passage*, (orig. 1908), London: Routledge & Kegan Paul.

Vansina, J. (1966), *Kingdoms of the Savanna*. Madison: University Wisconsin Press.

Vinnicombe, P. (1976), *People of the Eland*. Pietermaritzberg: University Natal Press.

Vyas, C. (1974), *Folk Tales of Zambia*. Pietermaritzberg Lusaka: Neczam.

Wallace, W.L. (1997), A Definition of Social Phenomena for the Social Sciences, *in* J.D. Greenwood (1997) (ed.) *op. cit.*, pp. 37–57.

Wembah-Rashid, J.A.R. (1975), The Ethnography of the Matrilineal Peoples of Southeast Tanzania, *Acta. Ethnol. et Linguistica Ser Africana* 9: 32.

White, G. (1998), Review B Morris, *Anthropology of the Self*, (1994) *American Ethnologist*, 24/1: 215–6.

Whitehead, A.N. (1920), *The Concept of Nature*. Cambridge: Cambridge University Press.

—— (1929), *Process and Reality*. New York: Free Press.

—— (1938), *Modes of Thought*. Cambridge: Cambridge University Press.

Willis, R. (1990), The meaning of the snake, *in* R. Willis (1990) (ed.) *Signifying Animals*. London: Unwin Hyman, pp. 246–52.

Wilson, E.O. (1997), *In Search of Nature*. London: Penguin.

Wolf, E.R. (1982), *Europe and the People without History*. Berkeley: University Press.

Yates, R.J. Parkinson and T. Manhire (1990), *Pictures from the Past*. Pietersmaritzberg: Centaur.

Index

Abraham, W.E., 48
adultery, 71
affinal male, 99, 112, 138, 157, 159, 166–7, 254
affinal relations, 101
African conceptions of personhood, 48–50
agama lizard, 122, 169
Aids, 83
Akafula, *see* Batwa
Alpers, E., 17
Amanze, J., 189, 205–7, 223
anamkhungwi, 74, 92, 95, 98, 105–6, 110, 116, 133
ancestral shrines, 229–30
ancestral spirits, 30, 62, 121, 150, 164, 174, 189, 221–35
Anderson, P., 8
animals and initiations, 87–90
animal-human relationships, 19–24, 29, 31–41, 55
animal medicines, 105
animal structures, 101–3, 123–6, 138–50
animism, 38, 176, 241
anthropology, 2–3
anthropomorphism, 38–9
Appadurai, A., 11
Arendt, H., 222
Aristotle, 12, 36–7, 57
Armstrong, K., 176–77
Assister, A., 4, 69
attitudes to animals, 34–41

Banda clan, 203
Barnard, A., 87, 153
Barth, F., 27
Batwa, 31, 146, 153, 192, 209
beer brewing, 92, 230–1
Bemba, 238–9
bereavement, 169

Bhaskar, R., 9–10
Biesele, M., 80–82
Bimbi, 205–7
Bisa, 23, 237, 243
blind snake, 200
Bloch, M., 97–8, 163–6
blood, 53–4, 84, 138, 156
blood sports, 20
Boeder, R., 187, 209
Bockie, S., 25
Boucher, C., 137, 141–2, 150, 154–5, 160, 172, 231
bourgeois ideology, 12, 47
boy's initiation, 113–30
Brachystegia woodland, 15
Brown, D.E., 44–5
Bruno, G., 23
Bruwer, J., 77, 198
Buchanan, J., 186
Bunda hill, 183
bushfires, 182
Bwiti, 24

Cartesian philosophy, 5–6, 8, 12, 34, 44–5, 47, 49
castor oil, 75
categories of being, 175
Catholicism, 97
Chakanza, J., 15, 185, 189
chameleon, 179–80
chattel slaves, 32
Chauta, 196–7
Chencherere rock shelter, 149–50
Chewa, 18–9, 31, 78, 91, 97–8, 101, 107, 154, 158, 221
chicken, 100, 137–8
Chikang'ombe, 194–5
chikwangwali ritual, 249–50
childbirth, 73–7, 81
Chilembwe, J., 210

– 281 –

Index

naturalism, 3
nchimi, see spirit medium
ndakula, see menstrual rituals
Ndembu, 23, 93, 96, 223
Ndiona pools, 214
neoplatonism, 12, 163–4
Netall, S., 64
Newton, I., 6
ngaliba, see circumciser
Ngoni, 15, 147, 204, 238, 242
Nharo, 87
nicknames, 64
Njobvu (elephant) animal structure, 145–6
nominal re-incarnation, 168, 172–3
Northern Zambezia, 17, 31, 48, 112
Noske, B., 38
Ntara, S., 71, 194, 196–7, 203
Nuer, 87–8
Nyangu, 204
nyani (baboon) animal structure, 148
nyau,
    cosmology, 160–2
    fraternities, 131, 134–5, 140, 158
    interpretation of, 151–67
    myths of origin, 132–3
    ritual, 131–8, 149–50
    ritual functionaries, 133
    theriomorphic structures, 139–40,
      143–50, 155–6
nsembe, see offerings to spirits

Oakley, A., 69
observation, 58, 62
offerings to spirits, 229–30
Ojibwa, 50
Orokaiva, 163

pantheism, 176
partible person, 54–5
Peltzer, K., 52
Pentacostalist churches, 25
personhood, 43, 46, 48, 61–7
person-centred anthropology, 42, 49
phenomenology, 35, 49
Phalombe, 34, 113
Phiri clan, 196, 203
Phiri, I., 200–1, 204
Phiri, K.M., 158, 161
Poole, F.J.P., 43

Popper, K., 5
postmodernism, 3–4, 8, 10–12, 36, 46,
   49, 99
Potani, D., 210
potency medicines, 122
pragmatism, 40
predation, 138
pregnancy, 73
Price, T., 221
primal unity, 154
Probst, P., 96
Proctor, L., 186
Prometheus, 180
proverbs, 98
psychological anthropology, 41, 46
puff adder, 233, 235
purification, 100, 108–9
python, 50, 70, 197–9, 217–19, 233, 254

Radcliffe-Brown, A.R., 46
radical alterity, 11
rain deities, 191–216
rain shrines, 191–216
Rangeley, W.H.J., 100, 132–3, 135,
   138–9, 150, 158, 196
Ranger, T., 48
Rau, W.E., 204, 242
Read, M., 76
realism, 36
reductive materialism, 5
reification, 9
respect for elders, 65, 96
Richards, A., 158, 165, 167
Riesmann, D., 49, 52
Rita-Ferreira, A., 132
ritual intercourse, 76, 99–100, 106
ritual sponsor, 111
rituals of childbirth, 73–7
rock art, 21–2, 87
Rowan, A., 20

sable antelope, 102
sacred trees, 233
sacrifices, 138
Salima, 215
Samuel, G., 12, 97
Sandelands, L., 7
Sanderson, M., 96, 102, 122, 130, 187,
   193, 210

Sauer, C., 182
Schoffeleers, J.M., 97, 106, 109, 132–3, 140, 152–4, 158, 160, 183–4, 213, 216, 236, 246, 249
Schopenhauer, A., 63
self, 45, 48
self-identity, 45–6
Sembereka, G., 138, 148
semen, 54, 74, 79
Senghor, L., 48
senses, 57–61
sensory models, 58
Serpell, J., 22
Seton, E.T., 37–8, 40
sexual,
    abstinence, 85, 96, 137
    imagery, 54–5
    intercourse, 70–2, 156
    instruction, 94–5
sexuality, 69–73
shame, 65
sharing, 63–4
shifting cultivation, 13, 73
Shona, 244
Shweder, R., 47
Skaife, S.H., 28
smell, 60
Smith, A., 16
sociocentrism, 64
socialization, 43
social praxis, 8, 42–3, 49–50
social structure, 10
society, 8–11
sociological tradition, 2
Soka, L.D., 107, 208–9, 222
Soko, B., 237–9, 241
songo snake, 199–200
sorcery, 56
sorority group, 112, 159
Southern Bantu, 78–9
species-being, 35–6
Speck, F., 20
Sperber, D., 13, 97
spider, 198
spirit,
    illness, 56
    mediums, 70, 239, 245–6
    possession, 56, 236–7
    rituals, 237–50

spirits of the dead, *see* ancestral spirits
Stannus, H.S., 12, 75–6, 99, 111–12, 120, 131, 205, 226, 245
Stefaniszyn, B., 168
stomach ailments, 56
Strathern, M., 47
subsistence agriculture, 13–14, 33
supreme being, 35, 50, 185–90, 206
Swahili, 15, 120
Swann, A.J., 192
Swantz, M.L., 25

taste, 61
Tempels, P., 36, 175
territorial cukts, 191
territorial spirits, *see* rain deities
textualism, 3
theriomorphism, 39
thunga, *see* python
Thyolo Mt., 212, 216, 227
totemism, 39
tradition, *see* custom
trance-dance, 80
Trois-Freres sorcerer, 22, 87
tsempho, *see* mdulo
Tumbuka, 18, 91, 113, 226, 237
Turner, E., 223
Turner, V.W., 88, 96, 163

understanding, 3
Undi, 16, 31, 161, 203

Vail, L., 14, 19, 194–5
Van Breugel, H., 155–6, 228
Van Gennep, A., 163, 165
Van Rijk, R., 26, 47
village community, 15, 125, 151, 226
village headman, 92, 106, 114–15, 133
vimbuza ritual, 237–41
visualism, 58–60
vital force, *see* life-force
voluntarism, 9

warthog, 190
Wembah-Rashid, J.A.R., 114
Werner, A., 177, 187, 193
White, L., 19
Whitehead, A.N., 4, 36–7
Williamson, J., 64, 72, 100, 106, 108

Index